Java EE 8 Development with Eclipse

Third Edition

Develop, test, and troubleshoot Java Enterprise applications rapidly with Eclipse

Ram Kulkarni

BIRMINGHAM - MUMBAI

Java EE 8 Development with Eclipse
Third Edition

Commissioning Editor: Richa Tripathi
Acquisition Editor: Sandeep Mishra
Content Development Editor: Anugraha Arunagiri
Technical Editor: Madhunikita Sunil Chindarkar
Copy Editor: Safis Editing
Project Coordinator: Ulhas Kambali
Proofreader: Safis Editing
Indexer: Mariammal Chettiyar
Graphics: Tania Dutta
Production Coordinator: Nilesh Mohite

First published: December 2012
Second edition: September 2015
Third edition: June 2018

Production reference: 1260618

Published by Packt Publishing Ltd.
Livery Place
35 Livery Street
Birmingham
B3 2PB, UK.

ISBN 978-1-78883-377-6

www.packtpub.com

To my wife Vandana and son Akash for their love and support

`mapt.io`

Mapt is an online digital library that gives you full access to over 5,000 books and videos, as well as industry leading tools to help you plan your personal development and advance your career. For more information, please visit our website.

Why subscribe?

- Spend less time learning and more time coding with practical eBooks and Videos from over 4,000 industry professionals

- Improve your learning with Skill Plans built especially for you

- Get a free eBook or video every month

- Mapt is fully searchable

- Copy and paste, print, and bookmark content

PacktPub.com

Did you know that Packt offers eBook versions of every book published, with PDF and ePub files available? You can upgrade to the eBook version at `www.PacktPub.com` and as a print book customer, you are entitled to a discount on the eBook copy. Get in touch with us at `service@packtpub.com` for more details.

At `www.PacktPub.com`, you can also read a collection of free technical articles, sign up for a range of free newsletters, and receive exclusive discounts and offers on Packt books and eBooks.

Contributors

About the author

Ram Kulkarni has more than two decades of experience in developing software. He has architected and developed many enterprise web applications, client-server and desktop applications, application servers, and IDE and mobile applications. He is also the author of *Eclipse 4 RCP Development How-To*, published by Packt Publishing. You can find him at *RamKulkarni.com*.

Writing this book has been a long process and it would not have been possible without the support and patience of my family. I would like to thank my parents, my wife, Vandana, and son, Akash, for their continued love and support.

About the reviewer

Borja Pérez Dopazo is a software architect with around 10 years of experience. He strongly believes in reuse and standardization. He is involved in architecture, design, implementation of microservices architectures, service-oriented architectures, and development of his own frameworks.

Packt is searching for authors like you

If you're interested in becoming an author for Packt, please visit authors.packtpub.com and apply today. We have worked with thousands of developers and tech professionals, just like you, to help them share their insight with the global tech community. You can make a general application, apply for a specific hot topic that we are recruiting an author for, or submit your own idea.

Table of Contents

Preface

Java Enterprise Edition (JEE) has been used for developing enterprise applications for many years. It provides a standard way of implementing many aspects of enterprise applications, such as handling web requests, accessing databases, connecting to other enterprise systems, and implementing web services. Over the years, it has evolved and made enterprise application development easier than before. It has also changed its name from J2EE to JEE after J2EE version 1.4, and, more recently, from Java Enterprise Edition to Jakarta Enterprise Edition in February 2018. Currently, JEE is in version 8.

Eclipse is a popular Integrated Development Environment (IDE) for developing Java applications. It also has a version specific to JEE development, which makes writing code faster and deploying JEE applications to the server easier. It provides excellent debugging and unit testing support. Eclipse has a modular architecture and many plugins are available today in order to extend its functionality to perform many different tasks.

This book provides you with all the information you need to use Eclipse in order to develop, deploy, debug, and test JEE applications. The focus of the book is to provide you with practical examples of how to develop applications using JEE and Eclipse. The scope of this book is not limited to JEE technologies, but also covers other technologies used in different phases of application development, such as source control, unit testing, and profiling. This book also covers deployment to cloud platforms, microservices, and JEE security features.

JEE is a collection of many technologies and specifications. Some of the technologies are so vast that separate books could be written on them, and some already have been. This book takes the approach of providing a brief introduction to each technology in JEE and provides links for detailed information. It then jumps to developing sample applications using specific technologies under discussion, and explains finer aspects of the technologies in the context of the sample applications.

Who this book is for

This book could be useful to you if you are new to JEE and want to get started with developing JEE applications quickly. You will also find this book useful if you are familiar with JEE and are looking for a hands-on approach to using some of the technologies in JEE.

What this book covers

Chapter 1, *Introducing JEE and Eclipse*, explains in brief different technologies in JEE and where they fit in a typical multitiered JEE application. The chapter also describes installing Eclipse JEE, Tomcat, GlassFish, and MySQL, which are used to develop sample applications in later chapters.

Chapter 2, *Creating a Simple JEE Web Application*, describes the development of web applications using JSP, servlet, JSTL, and JSF. It also explains how to use Maven for project management.

Chapter 3, *Source Control Management in Eclipse*, shows how to use SVN and Git plugins of Eclipse for source code management.

Chapter 4, *Creating JEE Database Applications*, explains the creation of database applications using JDBC and JPA. You will learn how to execute SQL statements directly using JDBC, map Java classes to database tables, set relationships between classes using JPA, and use database connection pools.

Chapter 5, *Unit Testing*, describes how to write and run unit tests for Java applications, mock external dependencies in unit tests, and calculate the code coverage.

Chapter 6, *Debugging the JEE Application*, shows techniques for debugging JEE applications and debugging support in Eclipse.

Chapter 7, *Creating JEE Applications with EJB*, describes using EJBs to code business logic in the JEE applications. It also explains connecting to remote EJBs using JNDI and injecting EJBs in container-managed beans.

Chapter 8, *Creating Web Applications with Spring MVC*, describes the creation of web applications using Spring MVC and how some of the JEE technologies could be used in a Spring MVC application.

Chapter 9, *Creating Web Services*, explains the creation of SOAP-based and RESTful web services in JEE applications. You will also learn how to consume these web services from JEE applications.

Chapter 10, *Asynchronous Programming with JMS*, shows you how to write applications to process messages asynchronously. It describes how to program queues and topics of messaging systems using JMS and MDBs.

Chapter 11, *Java CPU Profiling and Memory Tracking*, describes techniques for profiling CPU and memory in the Java applications to find performance bottlenecks.

Chapter 12, *Microservices*, describes how to develop and deploy microservices. It also covers the deployment of microservices in Docker container.

Chapter 13, *Deploying JEE Applications in the Cloud*, describes how to deploy JEE applications in Amazon and Google Cloud platforms. Specifically, it describes the deployment of applications in AWS EC2, Beanstalk, Google Compute Engine, and Google App Engine. It also describes Eclipse tools that can be used for deployment to the Cloud.

Chapter 14, *Securing JEE Applications*, describes how to secure JEE applications using authentication and authorization features of JEE containers. It also covers some of the JEE 8 security enhancements.

To get the most out of this book

You will need JDK 1.7 or later, Eclipse Oxygen or later, Tomcat 7 or later, GlassFish Server 4 or later, and MySQL Community Server 5.6 or later.

Download the example code files

You can download the example code files for this book from your account at www.packtpub.com. If you purchased this book elsewhere, you can visit www.packtpub.com/support and register to have the files emailed directly to you.

You can download the code files by following these steps:

1. Log in or register at www.packtpub.com.
2. Select the **SUPPORT** tab.
3. Click on **Code Downloads & Errata**.
4. Enter the name of the book in the **Search** box and follow the onscreen instructions.

Once the file is downloaded, please make sure that you unzip or extract the folder using the latest version of:

- WinRAR/7-Zip for Windows
- Zipeg/iZip/UnRarX for Mac
- 7-Zip/PeaZip for Linux

The code bundle for the book is also hosted on GitHub
at `https://github.com/PacktPublishing/Java-EE-8-Development-with-Eclipse-Third-Edition`. In case there's an update to the code, it will be updated on the existing GitHub
repository.

We also have other code bundles from our rich catalog of books and videos available
at `https://github.com/PacktPublishing/`. Check them out!

Download the color images

We also provide a PDF file that has color images of the screenshots/diagrams used in this
book. You can download it here: `https://www.packtpub.com/sites/default/files/downloads/JavaEE8DevelopmentwithEclipseThirdEdition_ColorImages.pdf`.

Conventions used

There are a number of text conventions used throughout this book.

`CodeInText`: Indicates code words in text, database table names, folder names, filenames,
file extensions, pathnames, dummy URLs, user input, and Twitter handles. Here is an
example: "To stop the GlassFish Server, run the `stopserv` script in
the `glassfish/bin` folder."

A block of code is set as follows:

```
public class LoginBean {
  private String userName;
  private String password;
}
```

Any command-line input or output is written as follows:

```
mysql>use mysql;
Database changed
mysql>create user 'user1'@'%' identified by 'user1_pass';
mysql>grant all privileges on *.* to 'user1'@'%' with grant option
```

Bold: Indicates a new term, an important word, or words that you see on screen. For example, words in menus or dialog boxes appear in the text like this. Here is an example: "Select **Dynamic Web Project** and click **Next** to open the **Dynamic Web Project** wizard."

 Warnings or important notes appear like this.

 Tips and tricks appear like this.

Get in touch

Feedback from our readers is always welcome.

General feedback: Email `feedback@packtpub.com` and mention the book title in the subject of your message. If you have questions about any aspect of this book, please email us at `questions@packtpub.com`.

Errata: Although we have taken every care to ensure the accuracy of our content, mistakes do happen. If you have found a mistake in this book, we would be grateful if you would report this to us. Please visit `www.packtpub.com/submit-errata`, selecting your book, clicking on the Errata Submission Form link, and entering the details.

Piracy: If you come across any illegal copies of our works in any form on the Internet, we would be grateful if you would provide us with the location address or website name. Please contact us at `copyright@packtpub.com` with a link to the material.

If you are interested in becoming an author: If there is a topic that you have expertise in and you are interested in either writing or contributing to a book, please visit `authors.packtpub.com`.

Reviews

Please leave a review. Once you have read and used this book, why not leave a review on the site that you purchased it from? Potential readers can then see and use your unbiased opinion to make purchase decisions, we at Packt can understand what you think about our products, and our authors can see your feedback on their book. Thank you!

For more information about Packt, please visit `packtpub.com`.

Introducing JEE and Eclipse 1

Java Enterprise Edition (JEE, which was earlier called J2EE) has been around for many years now. It is a very robust platform for developing enterprise applications. J2EE was first released in 1999, but underwent major changes with the release of version 5 in 2006. Since version 5, it has been renamed **Java Enterprise Edition (JEE)**. Recent versions of JEE have made developing a multi-tier distributed application a lot easier. J2EE had focused on core services and had left the tasks that made application development easier to external frameworks, for example, MVC and persistent frameworks. But JEE has brought many of these frameworks into the core services. Along with the support for annotations, these services simplify application development to a large extent.

Any runtime technology is not good without good development tools. The **Integrated Development Environment (IDE)** plays a major part in developing applications faster, and Eclipse provides just that for JEE. Not only do you get good code editing support in Eclipse, but you also get support for build, unit testing, version control, and many other tasks important in different phases of software application development.

In this chapter, we are going to cover the following topics:

- Introduction to different technologies in JEE
- Introduction to the Eclipse development environment
- Installation and configuration of some of the frequently used software in this book, for example, JEE servers, Eclipse IDE, and MySQL Database Server

The goal of this book is to show how you can efficiently develop JEE applications using Eclipse by using many of its features during different phases of the application development. But first, here is a brief introduction to JEE and Eclipse.

In 2017, Oracle agreed to hand over control of Java EE to Eclipse Foundation. In April 2018, Eclipse Foundation renamed Java EE as Jakarta EE. You can find more information about Jakarta EE at `https://jakarta.ee/`. At the time of writing, the latest Java EE version is 8. But all future versions of Java EE will be called Jakarta EE.

JEE

JEE is a collection of many of the Java Community Process (https://www.jcp.org) programs. Currently, JEE is in Version 8. However, different specifications of JEE are at their own different versions.

JEE specifications can be broadly classified into the following groups:

- Presentation layer
- Business layer
- Enterprise integration layer

Note that JEE specification does not necessarily classify APIs in the preceding broad groups, but such classification could help in better understanding the purpose of the different specifications and APIs in JEE.

Before we see APIs in each of these categories, let's understand a typical JEE web application flow, as shown in the following diagram, and where each of the preceding layers fits in:

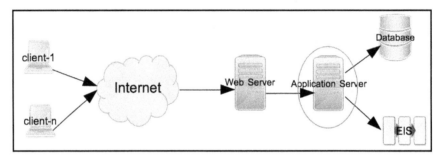

Figure 1.1: A typical JEE web application flow

Requests start from the clients. A client can be any application requesting services from a remote application—for example, it could be the browser or a desktop application. The request is first received by the web server at the destination. Examples of web servers include Apache web server, IIS, and nginx. If it is a request for static content, then it is served by the web server(s). However, a dynamic request typically requires an application server to process. JEE servers are such application servers that handle dynamic requests. Most JEE specification APIs execute in the application server. Examples of JEE application servers are WebSphere, GlassFish, and WildFly.

Most non-trivial JEE applications access external systems, such as a database or **Enterprise Integration Server** (**EIS**), for accessing data and process it. A response is returned from the application server to the web server and then to the clients.

The following sections provide a brief description of each of the JEE specifications in different layers. We will see how to use these specifications and their APIs in more detail in subsequent chapters. However, note that the following is not the exhaustive list of all the specifications in JEE. We will see the most commonly used specifications here. For the exhaustive list, please visit
http://www.oracle.com/technetwork/java/javaee/tech/index.html.

The presentation layer

JEE specifications or technologies in this layer receive requests from the web server and send back the response, typically in HTML format. However, it is also possible to return only data from the presentation layer, for example in **JavaScript Object Notation** (**JSON**) or **eXtensible Markup Language** (**XML**) format, which could be consumed by **Asynchronous JavaScript and XML** (**AJAX**) calls to update only part of the page, instead of rendering the entire HTML page. Classes in the presentation layer are mostly executed in the web container—it is a part of the application server that handles web requests. Tomcat is an example of a popular web container.

Now let's take a look at some of the specifications in this layer.

Java Servlets

Java Servlets are server-side modules, typically used to process requests and send back responses in web applications. Servlets are useful for handling requests that do not generate large HTML markup responses. They are typically used as controllers in **Model View Controller** (**MVC**) frameworks, for forwarding/redirecting requests, or for generating non-HTML responses, such as PDFs. To generate HTML response from the servlet, you need to embed HTML code (as a Java String) in Java code. Therefore, it is not the most convenient option for generating large HTML responses. JEE 8 contains servlet API 4.0.

JavaServer Pages

Like servlets, **JavaServer Pages** (**JSPs**) are also server-side modules used for processing web requests. JSPs are great for handling requests that generate large HTML markup responses. In JSP pages, Java code or JSP tags can be mixed with other HTML code, such as HTML tags, JavaScript, and CSS. Since Java code is embedded in the larger HTML code, it is easier (than servlets) to generate an HTML response from the JSP pages. JSP specification 2.3 is included in JEE 8.

JavaServer Faces

JavaServer Faces (**JSFs**) make creating a user interface on the server side modular by incorporating the MVC design pattern in its implementation. It also provides easy-to-use tags for common user interface controls that can save states across multiple request-response exchanges between client and server. For example, if you have a page that posts form data from a browser, you can have a JSF save that data in a Java bean so that it can be used subsequently in the response to the same or different request. JSFs also make it easier to handle UI events on the server side and specify page navigation in an application.

You write the JSF code in JSP, using custom JSP tags created for JSF. JavaServer Faces API 2.3 is part of JEE 8.

The business layer

The business layer is where you typically write code to handle the business logic of your application. Requests to this layer could come from the presentation layer, directly from the client application, or from the middle layer consisting of, but not limited to, web services. Classes in this layer are executed in the application container part of JEE server. GlassFish and WebSphere are examples of web container plus application container.

Let us take a tour of some of the specifications in this group.

Enterprise JavaBeans

Enterprise JavaBeans (**EJBs**) are the Java classes where you can write your business logic. Though it is not a strict requirement to use EJBs to write business logic, they do provide many of the services that are essential in enterprise applications. These services are security, transaction management, component lookup, object pooling, and so on.

You can have EJBs distributed across multiple servers and let the application container (also called the EJB container) take care of component lookup (searching component) and component pooling (useful for scalability). This can improve the scalability of the application.

EJBs are of two types:

- **Session beans**: Session beans are called directly by clients or middle-tier objects
- **Message-driven beans**: Message-driven beans are called in response to **Java Messaging Service (JMS)** events

JMS and message-driven beans can be used for handling asynchronous requests. In a typical asynchronous request processing scenario, the client puts a request in a messaging queue or a topic and does not wait for immediate response. An application on the server side gets the request message, either directly using JMS APIs or by using MDBs. It processes the request and may put the response in a different queue or topic, to which the client would listen and get the response.

Java EE 8 contains EJB specification 3.2 and JMS specification 2.0.

The enterprise integration layer

APIs in this layer are used for interacting with external (to the JEE application) systems in the enterprise. Most applications would need to access a database, and APIs to access that fall in this group.

Java Database Connectivity

Java Database Connectivity (JDBC) is a specification to access a relational database in a common and consistent way. Using JDBC, you can execute SQL statements and get results on different databases using common APIs. A database-specific driver sits between the JDBC call and the database, and it translates JDBC calls to database-vendor-specific API calls. JDBC can be used in both the presentation and business layers directly, but it is recommended to separate the database calls from both the UI and the business code. Typically, this is done by creating **Data Access Objects (DAOs)** that encapsulate the logic to access the database. JDBC is actually a part of Java Standard Edition. Java SE 8 contains JDBC 4.2.

The Java Persistence API

One of the problems of using JDBC APIs directly is that you have to constantly map the data between Java objects and the data in columns or rows in the relational database. Frameworks such as Hibernate and Spring have made this process simpler by using a concept known as **Object Relational Mapping (ORM)**. ORM is incorporated in JEE in the form of the **Java Persistence API (JPA)**.

JPA gives you the flexibility to map objects to tables in the relational database and execute queries with or without using **Structured Query Language (SQL)**. When used in the content of JPA, the query language is called **Java Persistence Query Language**. JPA specification 2.2 is a part of JEE8.

Java Connector Architecture

Java Connector Architecture (JCA) APIs can be used in JEE applications for communicating with **enterprise integration systems (EISes)**, such as SAP, and Salesforce. Just like you have database drivers to broker communication between JDBC APIs and relational databases, you have JCA adapters between JCA calls and EISes. Most EIS applications now provide REST APIs, which are lightweight and easy to use, so REST could replace JCA in some cases. However, if you use JCA, you get transaction and pooling support from the JEE application server.

Web services

Web services are remote application components and expose self-contained APIs. Web services can be broadly classified based on following two standards:

- **Simple Object Access Protocol (SOAP)**
- **Representational State Transfer (REST)**

Web services can play a major role in integrating disparate applications, because they are standard-based and platform-independent.

JEE provides many specifications to simplify development and consumption of both types of web services, for example, JAX-WS (Java API for XML—web services) and JAX-RS (Java API for RESTful web services).

The preceding are just some of the specifications that are part of JEE. There are many other independent specifications and many enabling specifications, such as dependency injection and concurrency utilities, which we will see in subsequent chapters.

Eclipse IDE

A good IDE is essential for better productivity while coding. Eclipse is one such IDE, which has great editor features and many integration points with JEE technologies. The primary purpose of this book is to show you how to develop JEE applications using Eclipse. So the following is a quick introduction to Eclipse, if you are not already familiar with it.

Eclipse is an open source IDE for developing applications in many different programming languages. It is quite popular for developing many different types of Java applications. Its architecture is pluggable—there is a core IDE component and many different plugins can be added to it. In fact, support for many languages is added as Eclipse plugins, including support for Java.

Along with editor support, Eclipse has plugins to interact with many of the external systems used during development. Examples include source control systems such as SVN and Git, build tools such as Apache Ant and Maven, file explorers for remote systems using FTP, managing servers such as Tomcat and GlassFish, database explorers, memory and CPU profilers. We will see many of these features in the subsequent chapters. The following screenshot shows the default view of Eclipse for JEE application development:

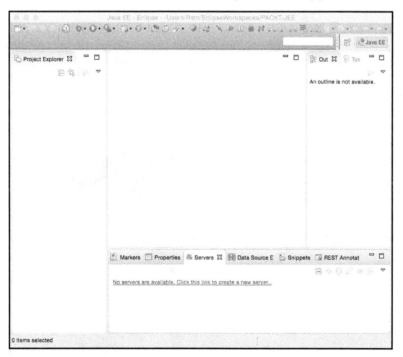

Figure 1.2: Default Eclipse view

When working with Eclipse, it is good to understand the following terms.

Workspace

The Eclipse workspace is a collection of projects, settings, and preferences. It is a folder where Eclipse stores this information. You must create a workspace to start using Eclipse. You can create multiple workspaces, but only one can be opened at a time by one running instance of Eclipse. However, you can launch multiple instances of Eclipse with different workspaces.

Plugin

Eclipse has pluggable architecture. Many of the features of Eclipse are implemented as plugins, for example, editor plugins for Java and many other languages, plugins for SVN and Git, and many more. The default installation of Eclipse comes with many built-in plugins and you can add more plugins for the features you want later.

Editors and views

Most windows in Eclipse can be classified either as an editor or a view. An editor is something where you can change the information displayed in it. A view just displays the information and does not allow you to change it. An example of an editor is the Java editor where you write code. An example of a view is the outline view that displays the hierarchical structure of the code you are editing (in the case of a Java editor, it shows classes and methods in the file being edited).

To see all views in a given Eclipse installation, open the **Window** | **Show View** | **Other** menu:

Figure 1.3: Show all Eclipse views

Perspective

Perspective is a collection of editors and views, and how they are laid out or arranged in the main Eclipse window. At different stages of development, you need different views to be displayed. For example, when you are editing the code, you need to see **Project Explorer** and **Task** views, but when you are debugging an application, you don't need those views, but instead want to see variable and breakpoint views. So, the editing perspective displays, among other views and editors, **Project Explorer** and **Task** views, and the **Debug** perspective displays views and editors relevant to the debugging activities. You can change the default perspectives to suit your purposes.

Eclipse preferences

The Eclipse **Preferences** window (*Figure 1.4*) is where you customize many plugins/features. Preferences are available from the **Window** menu in the Windows and Linux installations of Eclipse, and from the **Eclipse** menu in Mac:

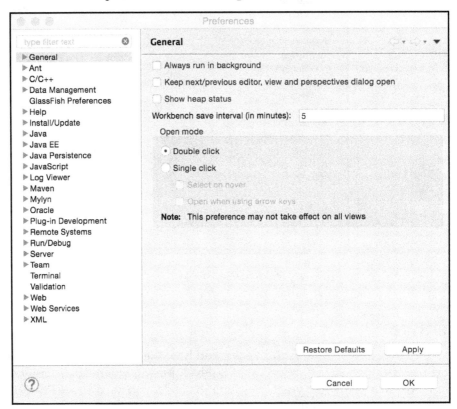

Figure 1.4: Eclipse preferences

Installing products

In the subsequent chapters, we will learn how to develop JEE applications in Eclipse. But the applications are going to need a JEE application server and a database. We are going to use the Tomcat web container in the initial few chapters and then use the GlassFish JEE application server. We are going to use a MySQL database.

We are going to need these products for many of the applications that we are going to develop. So the following sections describe how to install and configure Eclipse, Tomcat, GlassFish, and MySQL.

Installing Eclipse

Download the latest version of Eclipse from `https://eclipse.org/downloads/`. You will see many different packages for Eclipse. Make sure you install the **Eclipse IDE for Java EE Developers** package. Select an appropriate package based on your OS and JVM architecture (32 or 64 bit). You may want to run the command `java -version` to know whether the JVM is 32-bit or 64-bit.

If you plan to use Eclipse for AWS development, then it is recommended to download Eclipse from the Oomph installer. Refer to `https://wiki.eclipse.org/Eclipse_Installer` and `https://docs.aws.amazon.com/toolkit-for-eclipse/v1/user-guide/setup-install.html`.

Unzip the downloaded ZIP file and then run the Eclipse application (you must install JDK before you run Eclipse). The first time you run Eclipse, you will be asked to specify a workspace. Create a new folder in your filesystem and select that as the initial workspace folder. If you intend to use the same folder for the workspace on every launch of Eclipse, then check the **Use this as the default and do not ask again** checkbox:

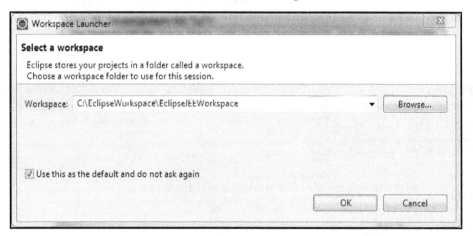

Figure 1.5: Select Eclipse workspace

You will then see the default Java EE perspective of Eclipse as shown in *Figure 1.2*.

Installing the Tomcat server

Tomcat is a web container. It supports APIs in the presentation layer described earlier. In addition, it supports JDBC and JPA. It is easy to configure and could be a good option if you do not want to use EJBs.

Download the latest version of Tomcat from `http://tomcat.apache.org/`. Unzip the downloaded file in a folder. Set the `JAVA_HOME` environment variable to point to the folder where JDK is installed (the folder path should be the JDK folder, which has `bin` as one of the subfolders). To start the server, run `startup.bat` in Command Prompt on Windows and `startup.sh` in a Terminal window on Mac and Linux. If there are no errors, then you should see the message `Server startup in --ms` or `Tomcat started`.

The default Tomcat installation is configured to use port `8080`. If you want to change the port, open `server.xml` under the `conf` folder and look for a connector declaration such as the following:

```
<Connector port="8080" protocol="HTTP/1.1"
            connectionTimeout="20000"
            redirectPort="8443" />
```

Change the port value to any port number you want, though in this book we will be using the default port `8080`. Before we open the default page of Tomcat, we will add a user for administration of the Tomcat server. Open `tomcat-users.xml` under the `conf` folder using any text editor. At the end of the file, you will see commented example of how to add users. Add the following configuration before the closure of `</tomcat-users>` tag:

```
<role rolename="manager-gui"/>
<user username="admin" password="admin" roles="manager-gui"/>
```

Here, we are adding a user `admin`, with password also as `admin,` to a role called `manager-gui`. This role has access to web pages for managing an application in Tomcat. This and other security roles are defined in `web.xml` of the `manager` application. You can find it at `webapps/manager/WEB-INF/web.xml`.

For more information for managing Tomcat server, refer to `http://tomcat.apache.org/tomcat-8.0-doc/manager-howto.html`.

After making the preceding changes, open a web browser and browse to
`http://localhost:8080` (modify the port number if you have changed the default port).
You will see the following default Tomcat page:

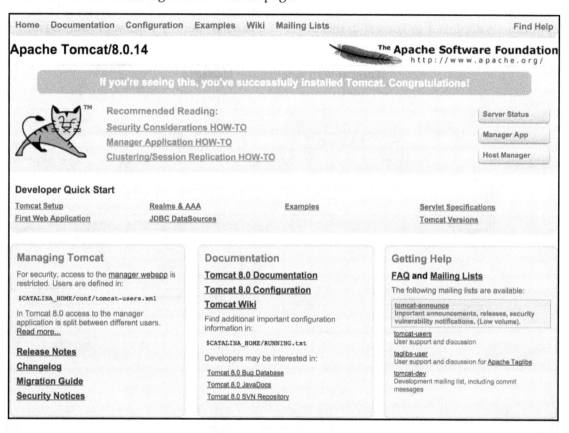

Figure 1.6: The default Tomcat web application

Click on the **Manager App** button on the right. You will be asked for the username and password. Enter the username and password you configured in `tomcat-users.xml` for `manager-gui`, as described earlier. After you are successfully logged in, you will see the **Tomcat Web Application Manager** page, as shown in *Figure 1.7*. You can see all the applications deployed in Tomcat in this page. You can also deploy your applications from this page:

Tomcat Web Application Manager

Message:	OK

Manager

List Applications	HTML Manager Help	Manager Help	Server Status

Applications

Path	Version	Display Name	Running	Sessions	Commands
/	None specified	Welcome to Tomcat	true	0	Start Stop Reload Undeploy Expire sessions with idle ≥ 30 minutes
/docs	None specified	Tomcat Documentation	true	0	Start Stop Reload Undeploy Expire sessions with idle ≥ 30 minutes
/examples	None specified	Servlet and JSP Examples	true	0	Start Stop Reload Undeploy Expire sessions with idle ≥ 30 minutes
/host-manager	None specified	Tomcat Host Manager Application	true	0	Start Stop Reload Undeploy Expire sessions with idle ≥ 30 minutes
/manager	None specified	Tomcat Manager Application	true	2	Start Stop Reload Undeploy Expire sessions with idle ≥ 30 minutes

Deploy

Deploy directory or WAR file located on server

Context Path (required):	
XML Configuration file URL:	
WAR or Directory URL:	
Deploy	

WAR file to deploy

Select WAR file to upload	Choose File No file chosen
Deploy	

Figure 1.7: Tomcat Web Application Manager

To stop the Tomcat server, press *Ctrl/cmd* + C or run the shutdown script in the `bin` folder.

Installing the GlassFish server

Download GlassFish from `https://glassfish.java.net/download.html`. GlassFish comes in two flavors: Web Profile and Full Platform. Web Profile is like Tomcat, which does not include EJB support. So download the Full Platform.

Unzip the downloaded file in a folder. The default port of the GlassFish server is `8080`. If you want to change that, open `glassfish/domains/domain1/config/domain.xml` in a text editor (you could open it in Eclipse too, using the **File | Open File** menu option) and look for `8080`. You should see it in one of the `<network-listener>`. Change the port if you want to (which may be the case if some other application is already using that port).

To start the server, run the `startserv` script (`.bat` or `.sh` depending on the OS you use). Once the server has started, open a web browser and browse to `http://localhost:8080`. You should see a page like the following:

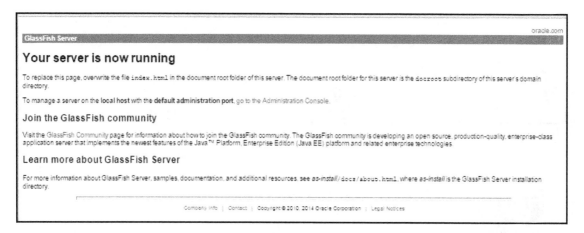

Figure 1.8: The default Glassfish web application

This page is located at `glassfish/domains/domain1/docroot/index.html`. Click on the **go to the Administration Console** link in the page to open the GlassFish administrator (see the following screenshot):

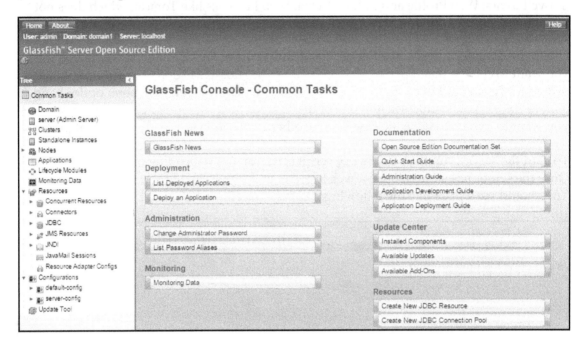

Figure 1.9: The Glassfish administrator

 For details on administrating the GlassFish server, refer to `https://javaee.github.io/glassfish/doc/5.0/administration-guide.pdf`.

To stop the GlassFish Server, run the `stopserv` script in the `glassfish/bin` folder.

Installing MySQL

We will be using a MySQL database for many of the examples in this book. The following sections describe how to install and configure MySQL for different platforms.

We would like to install MySQL Workbench too, which is a client application to manage MySQL Server. Download MySQL Workbench from `https://dev.mysql.com/downloads/workbench/`.

Installing MySQL on Windows

Download MySQL Community Server from `http://dev.mysql.com/downloads/mysql/`. You can either download the web installer or the all-in-one installer. The web installer would download only those components that you have selected. The following instructions show the download options using the web installer.

The web installer first downloads a small application, and it gives you options to select the components that you want to install:

1. Select the **Custom** option and click on **Next**:

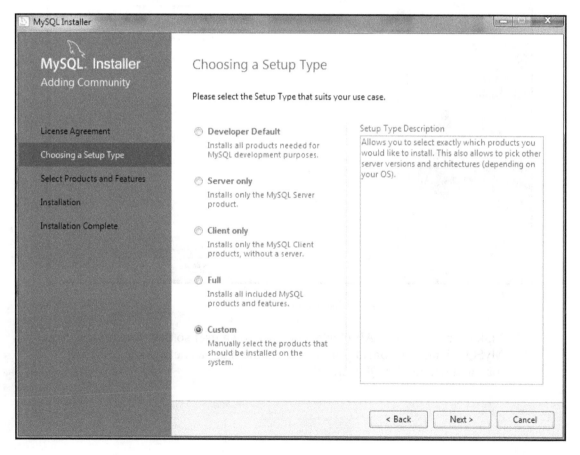

Figure 1.10: MySQL Installer for Windows

2. Select the **MySQL Server** and **MySQL Workbench** products and complete the installation. During the installation of the server, you will be asked to set the root password and given the option to add more users. It is always a good idea to add a user other than root for applications to use:

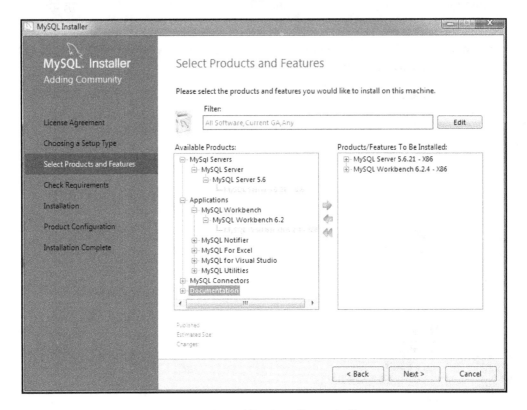

Figure 1.11: Select MySQL products and features to Install

3. Make sure you select **All Hosts** when adding a user so that you are able to access MySQL database from any remote machine that has network access to the machine where MySQL is installed:

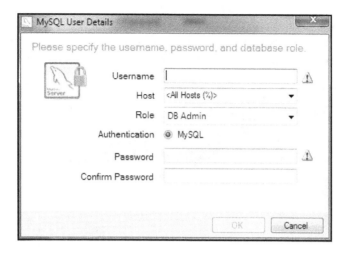

Figure 1.12: Add MySQL user

4. Run MySQL Workbench after installation. You will find that the default connection to the local MySQL instance is already created for you:

Figure 1.13: MySQL Workbench connections

5. Click on the local connection and you will be asked to enter the `root` password. Enter the `root` password that you typed during the installation of MySQL Server. MySQL Workbench opens and displays the default test schema:

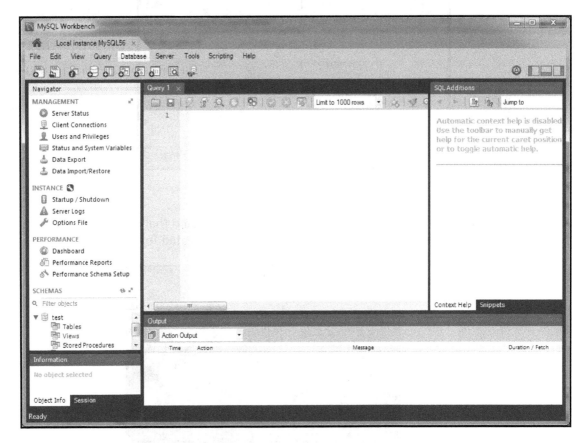

Figure 1.14: My SQL Workbench

Installing MySQL on macOS X

OS X versions before 10.7 had MySQL Server installed by default. If you are using OS X 10.7 or later, then you will need to download and install MySQL Community Server from `http://dev.mysql.com/downloads/mysql/`.

There are many different ways to install MySQL on OS X. See
http://dev.mysql.com/doc/refman/5.7/en/osx-installation.html for installation
instructions for OS X. Note that users on OS X should have administrator privileges to
install MySQL Server.

Once you install the server, you can start it either from Command Prompt or from the
system preferences:

1. To start it from Command Prompt, execute the following command in
   the Terminal:

   sudo /usr/local/mysql/support-files/mysql.server start

2. To start it from **System Preferences**, open the preferences and click the **MySQL**
   icon:

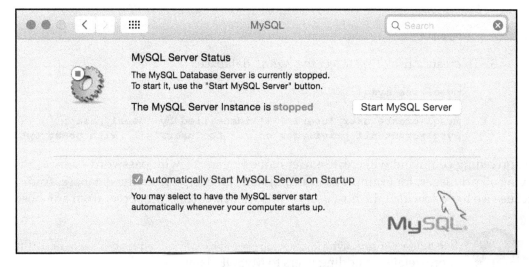

Figure 1.15: MySQL System Preferences - OS X

3. Click the **Start MySQL Server** button.

Installing MySQL on Linux

There are many different ways to install MySQL on Linux. Refer
to `https://dev.mysql.com/doc/refman/5.7/en/linux-installation.html` for details.

Creating MySQL users

You can create MySQL users either from Command Prompt or by using MySQL
Workbench:

1. To execute SQL and other commands from Command Prompt, open
    the Terminal and type the following command:

    ```
    mysql -u root -p<root_password>
    ```

2. Once logged in successfully, you will see the `mysql` Command Prompt:

    ```
    mysql>
    ```

3. To create a user, first select the `mysql` database:

    ```
    mysql>use mysql;
    Database changed
    mysql>create user 'user1'@'%' identified by 'user1_pass';
    mysql>grant all privileges on *.* to 'user1'@'%' with grant option
    ```

The preceding command will create a user named `'user1'` with password `'user1_pass'`
having all privileges, for example to insert, update, and select from the database. And
because we have specified the host as `'%'`, this user can access the server from any host.

See `https://dev.mysql.com/doc/refman/5.7/en/adding-users.html` for
more details on adding users to MySQL database

If you prefer a **graphical user interface** (**GUI**) to manage the users, then run MySQL
Workbench, connect to the local MySQL server (see *Figure 1.13* MySQL Workbench
connections), and then click on **Users and Privileges** under the **Management** section:

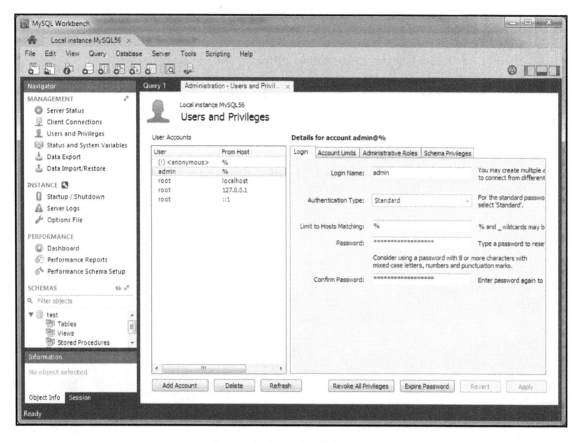

Figure 1.16: Creating a user in MySQL Workbench

Having installed all the preceding products, you should be in a position to start developing JEE applications. We may need some additional software, but we will see how to install and configure it at the appropriate time.

Summary

In this chapter, we had a brief introduction to different JEE specifications for the presentation layer, business layer, and enterprise integration layer. We learned some of the important terminologies in Eclipse IDE. We then learned how to install Eclipse, Tomcat, Glassfish, MySQL, and MySQL Workbench. We are going to use these products in this book to develop JEE applications.

In the next chapter, we will configure the JEE server and create a simple application using servlets, JSPs, and JSFs. We will also learn how to use Maven to build and package the JEE applications.

Creating a Simple JEE Web Application

2

The previous chapter gave you a brief introduction to JEE and Eclipse. We also learned how to install the Eclipse JEE package and also how to install and configure Tomcat. Tomcat is a servlet container and it is easy to use and configure. Therefore, many developers use it to run JEE web applications on local machines.

In this chapter, we will cover the following topics:

- Configuring Tomcat in Eclipse and deploying web applications from within Eclipse
- Using different technologies to create web applications in JEE, for example, JSP, JSTL, JSF, and servlets
- Using the Maven dependency management tool

Configuring Tomcat in Eclipse

We will perform the following steps to configure Tomcat in Eclipse:

1. In the Java EE perspective of Eclipse, you will find the **Servers** tab at the bottom. Since no server is added yet, you will see a link in the tab as shown in the following screenshot—**No servers are available. Click this link to create a new server...**.

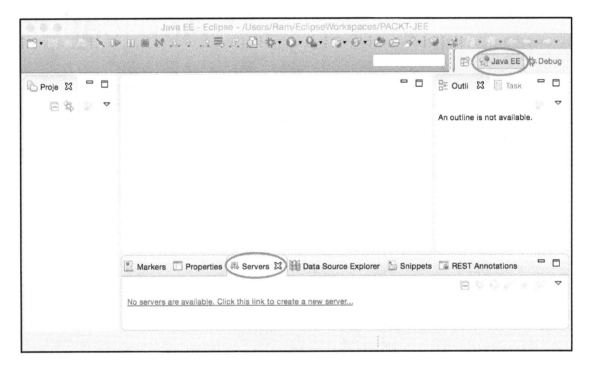

Figure 2.1: The Servers tab in Eclipse JEE

2. Click the link in the **Servers** tab to add a new server.

3. Expand the `Apache` group and select the Tomcat version that you have already installed. If Eclipse and the Tomcat server are on the same machine, then leave **Server's host name** as `localhost`. Otherwise, enter hostname or IP address of the Tomcat server. Click **Next**:

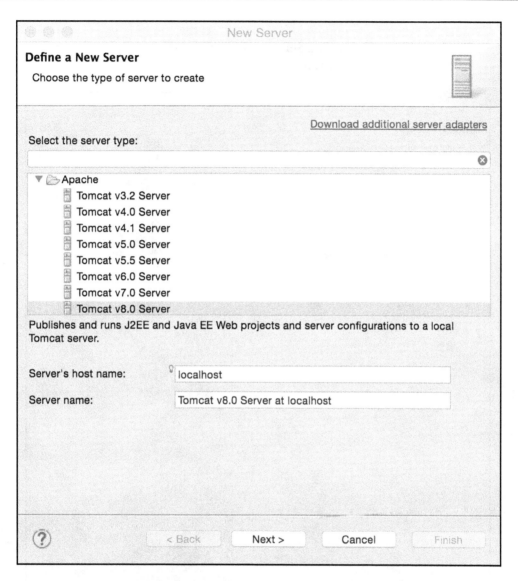

Figure 2.2: Selecting a server in the New Server wizard

4. Click the **Browse...** button and select the folder where Tomcat is installed.

5. Click **Next** until you complete the wizard. At the end of it, you will see the Tomcat server added to the **Servers** view. If Tomcat is not already started, you will see the status as stopped.

Figure 2.3: Configuring Tomcat folder in the New Server wizard

6. To start the server, right-click on the server and select **Start**. You can also start the server by clicking the Start button in the toolbar of the **Server** view.

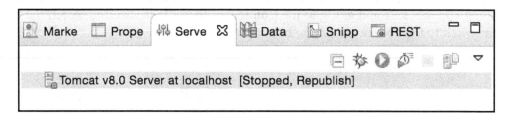

Figure 2.4: The Tomcat server added to the Servers view

Once the server is started successfully, you will see the status changed to Started. If you click on the **Console** tab, you will see console messages that the Tomcat server outputs during startup.

If you expand the **Servers** group in the **Project Explorer** view, you will see the Tomcat server that you just added. Expand the Tomcat server node to view configuration files. This is an easy way to edit the Tomcat configuration so that you don't have to go look for the configuration files in the filesystem.

Double-click `server.xml` to open it in the XML editor. You get the **Design** view as well as the **Source** view (two tabs at the bottom of the editor). We have learned how to change the default port of Tomcat in the last chapter. You can easily change that in the Eclipse editor by opening `server.xml` and going to the **Connector** node. If you need to search the text, you can switch to the **Source** tab (at the bottom of the editor).

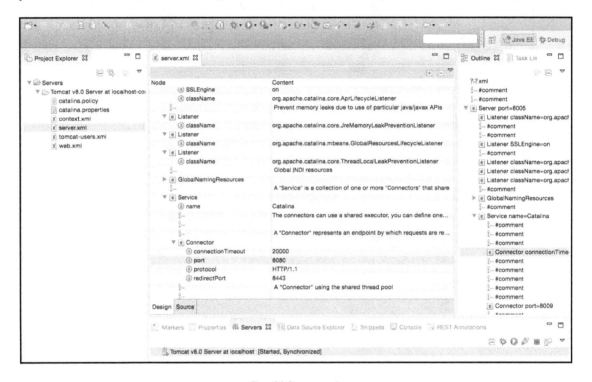

Figure 2.5: Open server.xml

You can also easily edit `tomcat-users.xml` to add/edit Tomcat users. Recall that we added a Tomcat user in `Chapter 1`, *Introducing JEE and Eclipse*, to administer the Tomcat server.

By default, Eclipse does not change anything in the Tomcat installation folder when you add the server in Eclipse. Instead, it creates a folder in the workspace and copies Tomcat configuration files to this folder. Applications that are deployed in Tomcat are also copied and published from this folder. This works well in development, when you do not want to modify Tomcat settings or any application deployed in the server. However, if you want to use the actual Tomcat installation folder, then you need to modify server settings in Eclipse. Double-click the server in the **Servers** view to open it in the editor.

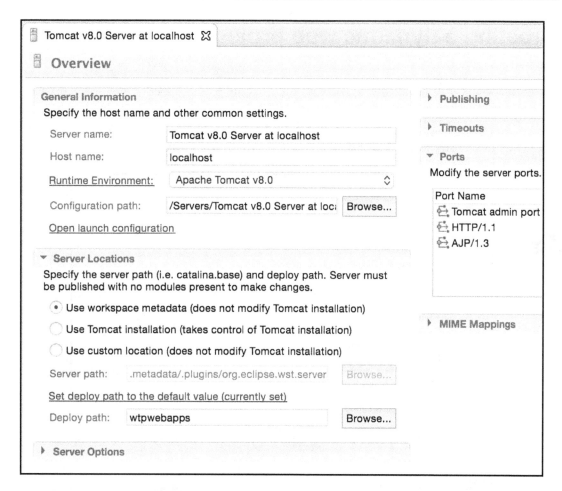

Figure 2.6: Tomcat settings

Note the options under **Server Locations**. Select the second option, **Use Tomcat installation**, if you want to use the actual Tomcat installation folders for configuration and for publishing applications from within Eclipse.

JavaServer Pages

We will start with a project to create a simple JSP. We will create a login JSP that submits data to itself and validates the user.

Creating a dynamic web project

We will perform the following steps to create a dynamic web project:

1. Select the **File** | **New** | **Other** menu. This opens the selection wizard. At the top of the wizard, you will find a textbox with a cross icon on the extreme right side.
2. Type web in the textbox. This is the filter box. Many wizards and views in Eclipse have such a filter textbox, which makes finding items very easy.

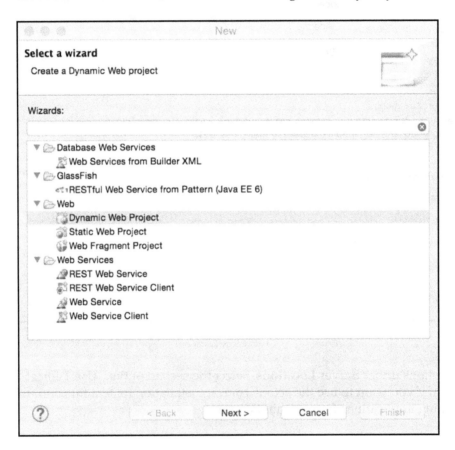

Figure 2.7: New selection wizard

3. Select **Dynamic Web Project** and click **Next** to open the **Dynamic Web Project** wizard. Enter project name, for example, LoginSampleWebApp. Note that the **Dynamic web module version** field in this page lists Servlet API version numbers. Select version 3.0 or greater. Click **Next**.

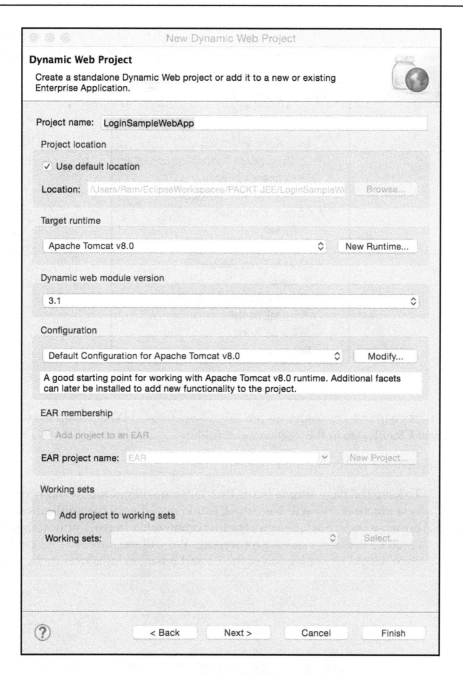

Figure 2.8: New Dynamic Web Project wizard

4. Click **Next** in the following pages and click **Finish** on the last page to create a `LoginSimpleWebApp` project. This project is also added to **Project Explorer**.

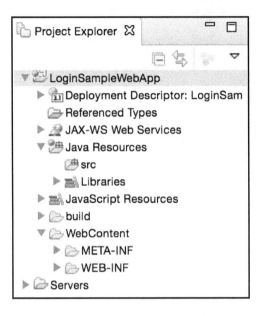

Figure 2.9: New web project

Java source files go in the `src` folder under `Java Resources`. Web resources such as the HTML, JS, and CSS files go in the `WebContent` folder.

In the next section, we will create a JSP page for login.

To keep the page simple in the first JSP, we will not follow many of the best practices. We will have the UI code mixed with the application business code. Such design is not recommended in real applications, but could be useful for quick prototyping. We will see how to write better JSP code with clear separation of the UI and business logic later in the chapter.

Creating JSP

We will perform the following steps to create the JSP:

1. Right-click on the `WebContent` folder and select **New** | **JSP File**. Name it `index.jsp`. The file will open in the editor with the split view. The top part shows the design view, and the bottom part shows the code. If the file is not opened in the split editor, right-click on `index.jsp` in the **Project Explorer** and select **Open With** | **Web Page Editor**.

Figure 2.10: The JSP editor

2. If you do not like the split view and want to see either the full design view or the full code view, then use appropriate toolbar buttons at the top right, as shown in the following screenshot:

Figure 2.11: The JSP editor display buttons

3. Change the title from `Insert title here` to `Login`.

4. Let's now see how Eclipse provides code assistance for HTML tags. Note that input fields must be in a `form` tag. We will add a `form` tag later. Inside the `body` tag, type the `User Name:` label. Then, type `<`. If you wait for a moment, Eclipse pops up the code assist window showing options for all the valid HTML tags. You can also invoke code assist manually.

5. Place a caret just after `<` and press *Ctrl + Spacebar*.

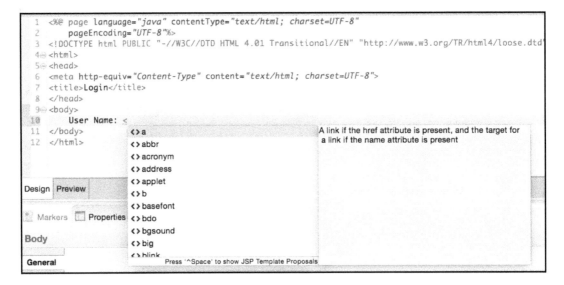

Figure 2.12: HTML code assist in JSP

Code assist works on partial text too; for example, if you invoke code assist after text `<i`, you will see a list of HTML tags starting with `i` (`i`, `iframe`, `img`, `input`, and so on). You can also use code assist for tag attributes and attribute values. For now, we want to insert the `input` field for username.

6. Select `input` from the code assist proposals, or type it.

7. After the `input` element is inserted, move the caret inside the closing > and invoke code assist again (*Ctrl/Cmd + Spacebar*). You will see the list of proposals for the attributes of the `input` tag.

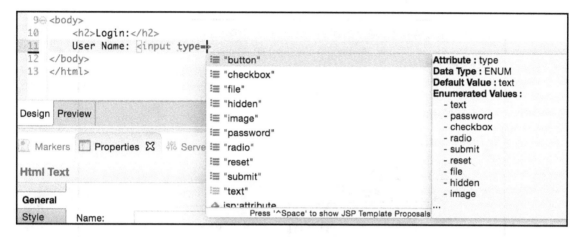

Figure 2.13: Code assist for the tag attribute value

8. Type the following code to create a login form:

```html
<body>
  <h2>Login:</h2>
  <form method="post">
    User Name: <input type="text" name="userName"><br>
    Password: <input type="password" name="password"><br>
    <button type="submit" name="submit">Submit</button>
    <button type="reset">Reset</button>
  </form>
</body>
```

Downloading the example code

You can download the example code files from your account at `http://www.packtpub.com` for all the Packt Publishing books that you have purchased. If you purchased this book elsewhere, you can visit `http://www.packtpub.com/support` and register to have the files emailed directly to you.

If you are using the split editor (design and source pages), you can see the login form rendered in the design view. If you want to see how the page would look in the web browser, click the **Preview** tab at the bottom of the editor. You will see that the web page is displayed in the browser view inside the editor. Therefore, you don't need to move out of Eclipse to test your web pages.

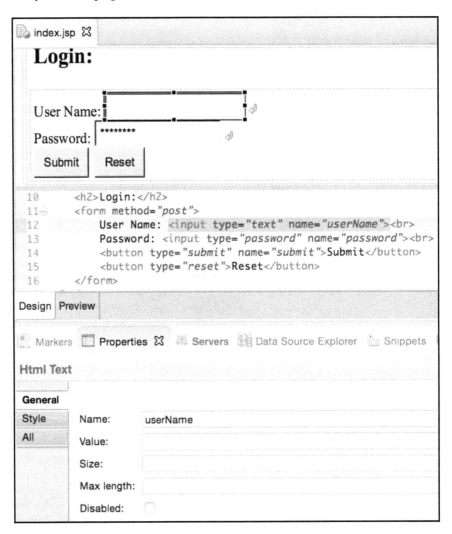

Figure 2.14: Design and Source views

If you click on any user interface control in the design view, you will see its properties in the **Properties** view (see *Figure 2.14*). You can edit properties, such as **Name** and **Value** of the selected element. Click on the **Style** tab of the **Properties** window to edit CSS styles of the element.

 We have not specified the action attribute in the previous form. This attribute specifies a URL to which the form data is to be posted when the user clicks the **Submit** button. If this attribute is not specified, then the request or the form data would be submitted to the same page; in this case, the form data would be submitted to index.jsp. We will now write the code to handle form data.

As mentioned in Chapter 1, *Introducing JEE and Eclipse*, you can write Java code and the client-side code (HTML, CSS, and JavaScript) in the same JSP. It is not considered good practice to mix Java code with HTML code, but we will do that anyway in this example to keep the code simpler. Later in the book, we will see how to make our code modular.

Java code is written in JSP between <% and %>; such Java code blocks in JSP are called **scriptlets**. You can also set page-level attributes in JSP. They are called **page directives** and are included between <%@ and %>. The JSP that we created already has a page directive to set the content type of the page. The content type tells the browser the type of response (in this case, html/text) returned by the server. The browser displays an appropriate response based on the content type:

```
<%@ page language="java" contentType="text/html; charset=UTF-8"
    pageEncoding="UTF-8"%>
```

In JSP you have access to a number of objects to help you process and generate the response, as described in the following table:

Object name	Type
request	HttpServletRequest (http://docs.oracle.com/javaee/7/api/javax/servlet/http/HttpServletRequest.html). Use this to get request parameters and other request-related data.
response	HttpServletResponse (http://docs.oracle.com/javaee/7/api/javax/servlet/http/HttpServletResponse.html). Use this to send a response.
out	JSPWriter (http://docs.oracle.com/javaee/7/api/javax/servlet/jsp/JspWriter.html). Use this to generate a text response.
session	HttpSession (http://docs.oracle.com/javaee/7/api/javax/servlet/http/HttpSession.html). Use this to get or put objects in the session.

application	ServletContext (http://docs.oracle.com/javaee/7/api/javax/servlet/ServletContext.html). Use this to get or put objects in the context, which are shared across all JSPs and servlets in the same application.

In this example, we are going to make use of request and out objects. We will first check whether the form is submitted using the POST method. If true, we will get values of username and password fields. If the credentials are valid (in this example, we are going to hardcode username and the password as admin), we will print a welcome message:

```
<%
  String errMsg = null;
  //first check whether the form was submitted
  if ("POST".equalsIgnoreCase(request.getMethod()) &&
   request.getParameter("submit") != null)
  {
    //form was submitted
    String userName = request.getParameter("userName");
    String password = request.getParameter("password");
    if ("admin".equalsIgnoreCase(userName) &&
     "admin".equalsIgnoreCase(password))
    {
      //valid user
      System.out.println("Welcome admin !");
    }
    else
    {
      //invalid user. Set error message
      errMsg = "Invalid user id or password. Please try again";
    }
  }
%>
```

We have used two built-in objects in the preceding code—request and out. We first check whether the form was submitted—"POST".equalsIgnoreCase(request.getMethod(). Then, we check whether the submit button was used to post the form—request.getParameter("submit") != null.

We then get the username and the password by calling the `request.getParameter` method. To keep the code simple, we compare them with the hardcoded values. In the real application, you would most probably validate credentials against a database or some naming and folder service. If the credentials are valid, we print a message by using the `out` (`JSPWriter`) object. If the credentials are not valid, we set an error message. We will print the error message, if any, just before the login form:

```
<h2>Login:</h2>
  <!-- Check error message. If it is set, then display it -->
  <%if (errMsg != null) { %>
    <span style="color: red;"><%=;"><%=;"><%=errMsg %></span>
  <%} %>
  <form method="post">
  ...
  </form>
```

Here, we start another Java code block by using `<%%>`. If an error message is not null, we display it by using the `span` tag. Notice how the value of the error message is printed—`<%=errMsg %>`. This is a short syntax for `<%out.print(errMsg);%>`. Also notice that the curly brace that started in the first Java code block is completed in the next and separate Java code block. Between these two code blocks you can add any HTML code and it will be included in the response only if the conditional expression in the `if` statement is evaluated to true.

Here is the complete code of the JSP we created in this section:

```
<%@ page language="java" contentType="text/html; charset=UTF-8"
    pageEncoding="UTF-8"%>
<!DOCTYPE html PUBLIC "-//W3C//DTD HTML 4.01 Transitional//EN"
 "http://www.w3.org/TR/html4/loose.dtd">
<html>
<head>
<meta http-equiv="Content-Type" content="text/html;
charset=UTF-8">
<title>Login</title>
</head>
<%
  String errMsg = null;
  //first check whether the form was submitted
  if ("POST".equalsIgnoreCase(request.getMethod()) &&
   request.getParameter("submit") != null)
  {
    //form was submitted
    String userName = request.getParameter("userName");
    String password = request.getParameter("password");
```

```
      if ("admin".equalsIgnoreCase(userName) &&
       "admin".equalsIgnoreCase(password))
      {
        //valid user
        out.println("Welcome admin !");
        return;
      }
      else
      {
        //invalid user. Set error message
        errMsg = "Invalid user id or password. Please try again";
      }
    }
%>
<body>
  <h2>Login:</h2>
  <!-- Check error message. If it is set, then display it -->
  <%if (errMsg != null) { %>
    <span style="color: red;"><%out.print(errMsg); %></span>
  <%} %>
  <form method="post">
    User Name: <input type="text" name="userName"><br>
    Password: <input type="password" name="password"><br>
    <button type="submit" name="submit">Submit</button>
    <button type="reset">Reset</button>
  </form>
</body>
</html>
```

Running JSP in Tomcat

To run the JSP we created in the previous section in the web browser, you will need to deploy the application in a servlet container. We have already seen how to configure Tomcat in Eclipse. Make sure that Tomcat is running by checking its status in the **Servers** view of Eclipse:

Figure 2.15: Tomcat started in the Servers view

There are two ways to add a project to a configured server so that the application can be run on the server:

1. Right-click on the server in the **Servers** view and select the **Add and Remove** option. Select your project from the list on the left (**Available** resources) and click **Add** to move it to the **Configured** list. Click **Finish**.

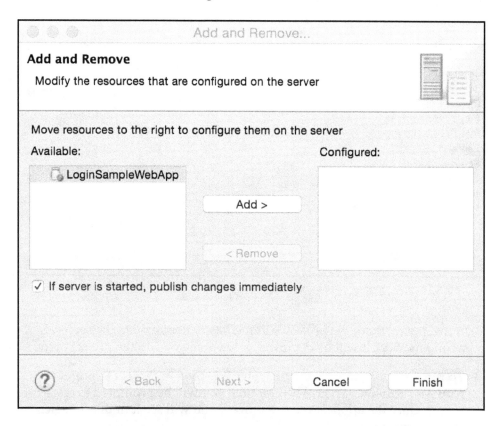

Figure 2.16: Add a project to the server

2. The other method to add a project to the server is to right-click on the project in **Project Explorer** and select **Properties**. This opens the **Project Properties** dialog box. Click on **Server** in the list and select the server in which you want to deploy this project. Click **OK** or **Apply**.

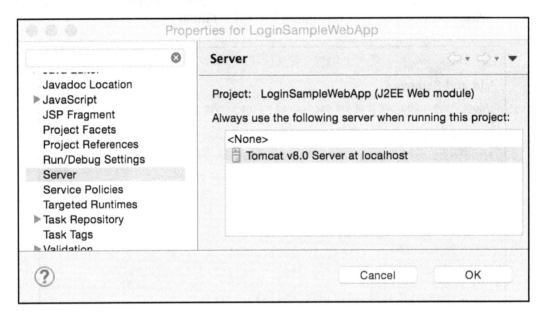

Figure 2.17: Select server in project properties

In the first method, the project is immediately deployed in the server. In the second method, it will be deployed only when you run the project in the server.

3. To run the application, right-click on the project in **Project Explorer** and select **Run As** | **Run on Server**. The first time you will be prompted to restart the server. Once the application is deployed, you will see it under the selected server in the **Servers** view:

Figure 2.18: Project deployed on the server

4. Enter some text other than admin in the username and password boxes and click **Submit**. You should see the error message and the same form should be displayed again.

Figure 2.19: Project running in the built-in browser in Eclipse

5. Now enter admin as username and password and then submit the form. You should see the welcome message.

JSPs are compiled dynamically to Java classes, so if you make any changes in the page, in most cases, you do not have to restart the server; just refresh the page, and Tomcat will recompile the page if it has changed and the modified page will be displayed. In cases when you need to restart the server to apply your changes, Eclipse will prompt you if you want to restart the server.

Using JavaBeans in JSP

The JSP that we created previously does not follow JSP best practices. In general, it is a bad idea to have scriptlets (Java code) in JSP. In most large organizations, UI designer and programmer are different roles performed by different people. Therefore, it is recommended that JSP contains mostly markup tags so that it is easy for designers to work on the page design. Java code should be in separate classes. It also makes sense from a reusability point of view to move Java code out of JSP.

You can delegate the processing of the business logic to JavaBeans from JSP. JavaBeans are simple Java objects with attributes and getters and setters methods. The naming convention for getter/setter methods in JavaBeans is the prefix `get`/`set` followed by the name of the attribute, with the first letter of each word in uppercase, also known as CamelCase. For example, if you have a class attribute named `firstName`, then the getter method will be `getFirstName` and the setter will be `setFirstName`.

JSP has a special tag for using JavaBeans—`jsp:useBean`:

```
<jsp:useBean id="name_of_variable" class="name_of_bean_class"
   scope="scope_of_bean"/>
```

Scope indicates the lifetime of the bean. Valid values are `application`, `page`, `request`, and `session`.

Scope name	Description
page	Bean can be used only in the current page.
request	Bean can be used in any page in the processing of the same request. One web request can be handled by multiple JSPs if one page forwards the request to another page.
session	Bean can be used in the same HTTP session. The session is useful if your application wants to save the user data per interaction with the application, for example, to save items in the shopping cart in an online store application.
application	Bean can be used in any page in the same web application. Typically, web applications are deployed in a web application container as **web application archive** (**WAR**) files. In the application scope, all JSPs in the WAR file can use JavaBeans.

We will move the code to validate users in our login example to the `JavaBean` class. First, we need to create a `JavaBean` class:

1. In **Project Explorer**, right-click on the `src` folder **New** | **Package** menu option.
2. Create a package named `packt.book.jee_eclipse.ch2.bean`.
3. Right-click on the package and select the **New** | **Class** menu option.
4. Create a class named `LoginBean`.

5. Create two private `String` members as follows:

```
public class LoginBean {
    private String userName;
    private String password;
}
```

6. Right-click anywhere inside the class (in the editor) and select the **Source** | **Generate Getters and Setters** menu option:

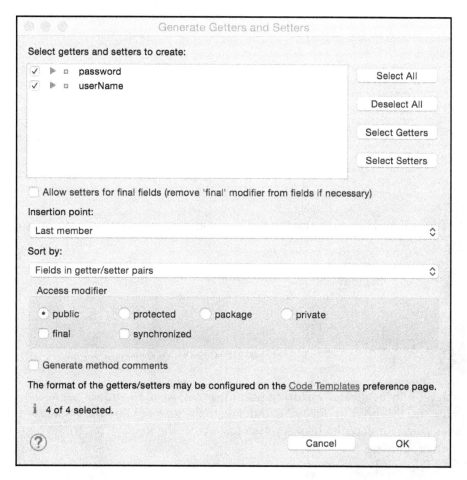

Figure 2.20: Generate getters and setters

7. We want to generate getters and setters for all members of the class. Therefore, click the **Select All** button and select **Last member** from the drop-down list for **Insertion point**, because we want to insert the getters and setters after declaring all member variables.

The `LoginBean` class should now be as follows:

```
public class LoginBean {
private String userName;
   private String password;
   public String getUserName() {
     return userName;
   }
   public void setUserName(String userName) {
     this.userName = userName;
   }
   public String getPassword() {
     return password;
   }
   public void setPassword(String password) {
     this.password = password;
   }
}
```

8. We will add one more method to it, to validate username and password:

```
public boolean isValidUser()
   {
     //Validation can happen here from a number of sources
     //for example, database and LDAP
     //We are just going to hardcode a valid username and
     //password here.
     return "admin".equals(this.userName) &&
             "admin".equals(this.password);
   }
```

This completes our JavaBean for storing user information and validation.
We will now use this bean in our JSP and delegate the task of validating users to this bean.
Open `index.jsp`. Replace the Java scriptlet just above the `<body>` tag in the preceding code with the following:

```
<%String errMsg = null; %>
<%if ("POST".equalsIgnoreCase(request.getMethod()) &&
request.getParameter("submit") != null) {%>
  <jsp:useBean id="loginBean"
   class="packt.book.jee_eclipse.ch2.bean.LoginBean">
     <jsp:setProperty name="loginBean" property="*"/>
```

```
</jsp:useBean>
<%
  if (loginBean.isValidUser())
  {
    //valid user
    out.println("<h2>Welcome admin !</h2>");
    out.println("You are successfully logged in");
  }
  else
  {

    errMsg = "Invalid user id or password. Please try again";


  }
%>
<%} %>
```

Before we discuss what has changed in the preceding code, note that you can invoke and get code assist for the attributes and values of `<jsp:*>` tags too. If you are not sure whether code assist is available, just press *Ctrl/Cmd + C*.

Figure 2.21: Code assist in JSP tags

Notice that Eclipse displays code assist for the JavaBean that we just added.

Let's now understand what we changed in the JSP:

- We created multiple scriptlets, one for declaration of the `errMsg` variable and two more for separate `if` blocks.
- We added a `<jsp:useBean` tag in the first `if` condition. The bean is created when a condition in the `if` statement is true, that is, when the form is posted by clicking the **Submit** button.

- We used the `<jsp:setProperty>` tag to set attributes of the bean:

  ```
  <jsp:setProperty name="loginBean" property="*"/>
  ```

  We are setting values of member variables of `loginBean`. Furthermore, we are setting values of all the member variables by specifying `property="*"`. However, where do we specify values? The values are specified implicitly because we have named members of `LoginBean` to be the same as the fields in the form. So, the JSP runtime gets parameters from the `request` object and assigns values to the JavaBean members with the same name.
  If names of the members of JavaBean do not match the request parameters, then you need to set the values explicitly:

  ```
  <jsp:setProperty name="loginBean" property="userName"
    value="<%=request.getParameter("userName")%>"/>
  <jsp:setProperty name="loginBean" property="password"
    value="<%=request.getParameter("password")%>"/>
  ```

- We then checked whether the user is valid by calling `loginBean.isValidUser()`. The code to handle error messages hasn't changed.

To test the page, perform the following steps:

1. Right-click on `index.jsp` in **Project Explorer**.
2. Select the **Run As** | **Run on Server** menu option. Eclipse will prompt you to restart the Tomcat server.
3. Click the **OK** button to restart the server.

The page will be displayed in the internal Eclipse browser. It should behave in the same way as in the previous example.

Although we have moved validation of users to `LoginBean`, we still have a lot of code in Java scriptlets. Ideally, we should have as few Java scriptlets as possible in JSP. We still have scriptlets for checking conditions and for variable assignments. We can write the same code by using tags so that it is consistent with the remaining tag-based code in JSP and will be easier for web designers to work with it. This can be achieved using **JSP Standard Tag Library (JSTL)**.

Using JSTL

JSTL tags can be used to replace much of the Java scriptlets in JSP. JSTL tags are classified in five broad groups:

- **Core**: Covers flow control and variable support among other things
- **XML**: Tags to process XML documents
- **i18n**: Tags to support internationalization
- **SQL**: Tags to access database
- **Functions**: Tags to perform some of the common string operations

 See `http://docs.oracle.com/javaee/5/tutorial/doc/bnake.html` for more details on JSTL.

We will modify the login JSP to use JSTL, so that there are no Java scriptlets in it:

1. Download JSTL libraries for APIs and their implementation. At the time of writing, the latest `.jar` files are `javax.servlet.jsp.jstl-api-1.2.1.jar` (`http://search.maven.org/remotecontent?filepath=javax/servlet/jsp/jstl/javax.servlet.jsp.jstl-api/1.2.1/javax.servlet.jsp.jstl-api-1.2.1.jar`) and `javax.servlet.jsp.jstl-1.2.1.jar` (`http://search.maven.org/remotecontent?filepath=org/glassfish/web/javax.servlet.jsp.jstl/1.2.1/javax.servlet.jsp.jstl-1.2.1.jar`). Make sure that these files are copied to `WEB-INF/lib`. All `.jar` files in this folder are added to the `classpath` of the web application.

2. We need to add a declaration for JSTL in our JSP. Add the following `taglib` declaration below the first page declaration (`<%@ page language="java" ...>`):

   ```
   <%@ taglib prefix="c" uri="http://java.sun.com/jsp/jstl/core" %>
   ```

   The `taglib` declaration contains the URL of the `tag` library and `prefix`. All tags in the `tag` library are accessed using `prefix` in JSP.

3. Replace `<%String errMsg = null; %>` with the `set` tag of JSTL:

```
<c:set var="errMsg" value="${null}"/>
<c:set var="displayForm" value="${true}"/>
```

We have enclosed the value in `${}`. This is called **Expression Language** (**EL**). You enclose the Java expression in JSTL in `${}`.

4. Replace the following code:

```
<%if ("POST".equalsIgnoreCase(request.getMethod()) &&
request.getParameter("submit") != null) {%>
```

With the `if` tag of JSTL:

```
<c:if test="${"POST".equalsIgnoreCase(pageContext.request
.method) && pageContext.request.getParameter("submit") !=
null}">
```

The `request` object is accessed in the JSTL tag via `pageContext`.

5. JavaBean tags go within the `if` tag. There is no change in this code:

```
<jsp:useBean id="loginBean"
  class="packt.book.jee_eclipse.ch2.bean.LoginBean">
  <jsp:setProperty name="loginBean" property="*"/>
</jsp:useBean>
```

6. We then add tags to call `loginBean.isValidUser()` and based on its return value, to set messages. However, we can't use the `if` tag of JSTL here, because we need to write the `else` statement too. JSTL does not have a tag for `else`. Instead, for multiple `if...else` statements, you need to use the `choose` statement, which is somewhat similar to the `switch` statement:

```
<c:choose>
  <c:when test="${!loginBean.isValidUser()}">
    <c:set var="errMsg" value="Invalid user id or password. Please
    try again"/>
  </c:when>
  <c:otherwise>
    <h2><c:out value="Welcome admin !"/></h2>
    <c:out value="You are successfully logged in"/>
    <c:set var="displayForm" value="${false}"/>
  </c:otherwise>
</c:choose>
```

If the user credentials are not valid, we set the error message. Or (in the `c:otherwise` tag), we print the welcome message and set the `displayForm` flag to `false`. We don't want to display the login form if the user is successfully logged in.

7. We will now replace another `if` scriptlet code by `<%if%>` tag. Replace the following code snippet:

```
<%if (errMsg != null) { %>
  <span style="color: red;"><%out.print(errMsg); %></span>
<%} %>
```

With the following code:

```
<c:if test="${errMsg != null}">
  <span style="color: red;">
    <c:out value="${errMsg}"></c:out>
  </span>
</c:if>
```

Note that we have used the `out` tag to print an error message.

8. Finally, we enclose the entire `<body>` content in another JSTL `if` tag:

```
<c:if test="${displayForm}">
<body>
   . . .
</body>
</c:if>
```

Here is the complete source code of the JSP:

```
<%@ page language="java" contentType="text/html; charset=UTF-8"
    pageEncoding="UTF-8"%>
<%@ taglib prefix="c" uri="http://java.sun.com/jsp/jstl/core" %>

<!DOCTYPE html PUBLIC "-//W3C//DTD HTML 4.01 Transitional//EN"
"http://www.w3.org/TR/html4/loose.dtd">
<html>
<head>
<meta http-equiv="Content-Type" content="text/html; charset=UTF-
  8">
<title>Login</title>
</head>

<c:set var="errMsg" value="${null}"/>
<c:set var="displayForm" value="${true}"/>
```

```
<c:if test="${"POST".equalsIgnoreCase(pageContext.request.method)
&& pageContext.request.getParameter("submit") != null}">
  <jsp:useBean id="loginBean"
   class="packt.book.jee_eclipse.ch2.bean.LoginBean">
    <jsp:setProperty name="loginBean" property="*"/>
  </jsp:useBean>
  <c:choose>
    <c:when test="${!loginBean.isValidUser()}">
      <c:set var="errMsg" value="Invalid user id or password.
       Please try again"/>
    </c:when>
    <c:otherwise>
    <h2><c:out value="Welcome admin !"/></h2>
      <c:out value="You are successfully logged in"/>
      <c:set var="displayForm" value="${false}"/>
    </c:otherwise>
  </c:choose>
</c:if>

<c:if test="${displayForm}">
<body>
  <h2>Login:</h2>
  <!-- Check error message. If it is set, then display it -->
  <c:if test="${errMsg != null}">
    <span style="color: red;">
      <c:out value="${errMsg}"></c:out>
    </span>
  </c:if>
  <form method="post">
    User Name: <input type="text" name="userName"><br>
    Password: <input type="password" name="password"><br>
    <button type="submit" name="submit">Submit</button>
    <button type="reset">Reset</button>
  </form>
</body>
</c:if>
</html>
```

As you can see, there are no Java scriptlets in the preceding code. All of them, from the previous code, are replaced by tags. This makes it easy for web designers to edit the page without worrying about Java scriptlets.

One last note before we leave the topic of JSP. In real-world applications, you would probably forward the request to another page after the user successfully logs in, instead of just displaying a welcome message on the same page. You could use the `<jsp:forward>` tag to achieve this.

Java Servlet

We will now see how to implement a login application using Java Servlet. Create a new **Dynamic Web Application** in Eclipse as described in the previous section. We will call this LoginServletApp:

1. Right-click on the src folder under Java Resources for the project in **Project Explorer**. Select the **New | Servlet** menu option.
2. In the **Create Servlet** wizard, enter package name as packt.book.jee_eclipse.book.servlet and class name as LoginServlet. Then, click **Finish**.

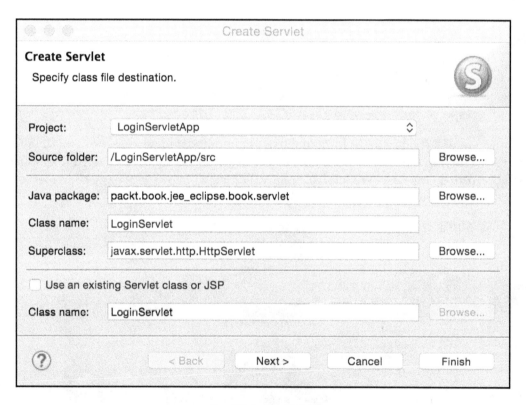

Figure 2.22: Create Servlet wizard

3. The servlet wizard creates the class for you. Notice the `@WebServlet("/LoginServlet")` annotation just above the class declaration. Before JEE 5, you had to declare servlets in `web.xml` in the `WEB-INF` folder. You can still do that, but you can skip this declaration if you use proper annotations. Using `WebServlet`, we are telling the servlet container that `LoginServlet` is a servlet, and we are mapping it to the `/LoginServlet` URL path. Thus, we are avoiding the following two entries in `web.xml` by using this annotation: `<servlet>` and `<servlet-mapping>`.

   We will now change the mapping from `/LoginServlet` to just `/login`. Therefore, we will modify the annotation as follows:

   ```
   @WebServlet("/login")
   public class LoginServlet extends HttpServlet {...}
   ```

4. The wizard also created the `doGet` and `doPost` methods. These methods are overridden from the following base class: `HttpServlet`. The `doGet` method is called to create response for the `Get` request and `doPost` is called to create a response for the `Post` request.

   We will create a login form in the `doGet` method and process the form data (`Post`) in the `doPost` method. However, because `doPost` may need to display the form, in case user credentials are invalid, we will write a `createForm` method, which could be called from both `doGet` and `doPost`.

5. Add a `createForm` method as follows:

   ```
   protected String createForm(String errMsg) {
    StringBuilder sb = new StringBuilder("<h2>Login</h2>");
   //check whether error message is to be displayed
     if (errMsg != null) {
       sb.append("<span style='color: red;'>")
         .append(errMsg)
         .append("</span>");
     }
     //create form
     sb.append("<form method='post'>n")
       .append("User Name: <input type='text'
       name='userName'><br>n")     .append("Password: <input
   type='password'
       name='password'><br>n")     .append("<button type='submit'
       name='submit'>Submit</button>n")
       .append("<button type='reset'>Reset</button>n")
       .append("</form>");
   ```

```
        return sb.toString();
    }
```

6. We will now modify a `doGet` method to call a `createForm` method and return the response:

```
protected void doGet(HttpServletRequest request,
  HttpServletResponse response)
    throws ServletException, IOException {
    response.getWriter().write(createForm(null));
}
```

We call the `getWrite` method on the `response` object and write the form content to it by calling the `createForm` function. Note that when we display the form, initially, there is no error message, so we pass a `null` argument to `createForm`.

7. We will modify `doPost` to process the form content when the user posts the form by clicking the **Submit** button:

```
protected void doPost(HttpServletRequest request,
HttpServletResponse response)
    throws ServletException, IOException {
      String userName = request.getParameter("userName");
      String password = request.getParameter("password");

    //create StringBuilder to hold response string
    StringBuilder responseStr = new StringBuilder();
    if ("admin".equals(userName) && "admin".equals(password)) {
      responseStr.append("<h2>Welcome admin !</h2>")
      .append("You are successfully logged in");
    }
    else {
      //invalid user credentials
      responseStr.append(createForm("Invalid user id or password.
      Please try again"));
    }

    response.getWriter().write(responseStr.toString());
}
```

We first get username and password from the request object by calling the request.getParameter method. If the credentials are valid, we add a welcome message to the response string; or else, we call createForm with an error message and add a return value (markup for the form) to the response string.

Finally, we get the Writer object from the response string and write the response.

8. Right-click on the LoginServlet.java file in **Project Explorer** and select the **Run As | Run on Server** option. We have not added this project to the Tomcat server. Therefore, Eclipse will ask if you want to use the configured server to run this servlet. Click the **Finish** button of the wizard.

9. Tomcat needs to restart because a new web application is deployed in the server. Eclipse will prompt you to restart the server. Click **OK**.

When the servlet is run in the internal browser of Eclipse, notice the URL; it ends with /login, which is the mapping that we specified in the servlet annotation. However, you will observe that instead of rendering the HTML form, the page displays the markup text. This is because we missed an important setting on the response object. We did not tell the browser the type of content we are returning, so the browser assumed it to be text and rendered it as plain text. We need to tell the browser that it is HTML content. We do this by calling response.setContentType("text/html") in both the doGet and the doPost methods. Here is the complete source code:

```
package packt.book.jee_eclipse.book.servlet;

// skipping imports to save space

/**
 * Servlet implementation class LoginServlet
 */
@WebServlet("/login")
public class LoginServlet extends HttpServlet {
  private static final long serialVersionUID = 1L;

  public LoginServlet() {
    super();
  }
  //Handles HTTP Get requests
  protected void doGet(HttpServletRequest request, HttpServletResponse response)
    throws ServletException, IOException {
  response.setContentType("text/html");
```

```
    response.getWriter().write(createForm(null));
  }
  //Handles HTTP POST requests
  protected void doPost(HttpServletRequest request,
   HttpServletResponse response)
      throws ServletException, IOException {
    String userName = request.getParameter("userName");
    String password = request.getParameter("password");

    //create StringBuilder to hold response string
    StringBuilder responseStr = new StringBuilder();
    if ("admin".equals(userName) && "admin".equals(password)) {
      responseStr.append("<h2>Welcome admin !</h2>")
        .append("You're are successfully logged in");
    } else {
      //invalid user credentials
      responseStr.append(createForm("Invalid user id or password.
       Please try again"));
    }
    response.setContentType("text/html");
    response.getWriter().write(responseStr.toString());
  }


  //Creates HTML Login form
  protected String createForm(String errMsg) {
    StringBuilder sb = new StringBuilder("<h2>Login</h2>");
    //check if error message to be displayed
    if (errMsg != null) {
      sb.append("<span style='color: red;'>")
        .append(errMsg)
        .append("</span>");
    }
    //create form
    sb.append("<form method='post'>n")
      .append("User Name: <input type='text'
      name='userName'><br>n")        .append("Password: <input
type='password'
      name='password'><br>n")        .append("<button type='submit'
      name='submit'>Submit</button>n")
      .append("<button type='reset'>Reset</button>n")
      .append("</form>");
    return sb.toString();
  }
}
```

As you can see, it is not very convenient to write HTML markup in servlet. Therefore, if you are creating a page with a lot of HTML markup, then it is better to use JSP or plain HTML. Servlets are good to process requests that do not need to generate too much markup, for example, controllers in **Model-View-Controller** (**MVC**) frameworks, for processing requests that generate a non-text response, or for creating a web service or WebSocket endpoints.

Creating WAR

Thus far, we have been running our web application from Eclipse, which does all the work of deploying the application to the Tomcat server. This works fine during development, but when you want to deploy it to test or production servers, you need to create a **web application archive** (**WAR**). We will see how to create a WAR from Eclipse. However, first we will un-deploy the existing applications from Tomcat.

1. Go to the **Servers** view, select the application, and right-click and select the **Remove** option:

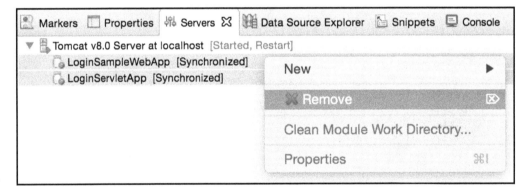

Figure 2.23 Un-deploy a web application from the server

2. Then, right-click on the project in **Project Explorer** and select **Export | WAR file**. Select the destination for the WAR file:

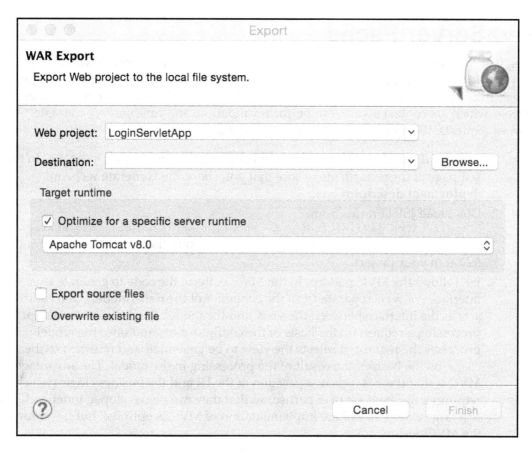

Figure 2.24 Export WAR

To deploy the WAR file to Tomcat, copy it to the `<tomcat_home>/webapps` folder. Then start the server if it is not already running. If Tomcat is already running, you don't need to restart it.

Tomcat monitors the `webapps` folder and any WAR file copied to it is automatically deployed. You can verify this by opening the URL of your application in the browser, for example, `http://localhost:8080/LoginServletApp/login`.

JavaServer Faces

When working with JSP, we saw that it is not a good idea to mix scriptlets with the HTML markup. We solved this problem by using JavaBean. JavaServer Faces takes this design further. In addition to supporting JavaBeans, JSF provides built-in tags for HTML user controls, which are context aware, can perform validation, and can preserve the state between requests. We will now create the login application using JSF:

1. Create a dynamic web application in Eclipse; let's name it `LoginJSFApp`. In the last page of the wizard, make sure that you check the **Generate web.xml deployment descriptor** box.

2. Download JSF libraries from
   `https://maven.java.net/content/repositories/releases/org/glassfish/javax.faces/2.2.9/javax.faces-2.2.9.jar` and copy them to the `WEB-INF/lib` folder in your project.

3. JSF follows the MVC pattern. In the MVC pattern, the code to generate user interface (view) is separate from the container of the data (model). The controller acts as the interface between the view and the model. It selects the model for processing a request on the basis of the configuration, and once the model processes the request, it selects the view to be generated and returned to the client, on the basis of the result of the processing in the model. The advantage of MVC is that there is a clear separation of the UI and the business logic (which requires a different set of expertise) so that they can be developed independently, to a large extent. In JSP the implementation of MVC is optional, but JSF enforces the MVC design.

Views are JSF created as `xhtml` files. The controller is a servlet from the JSF library and models are **managed beans** (JavaBeans).

We will first configure a controller for JSF. We will add the servlet configuration and mapping in `web.xml`. Open `web.xml` from the `WEB-INF` folder of the project (`web.xml` should have been created for you by the project wizard if you checked the **Generate web.xml deployment descriptor** box; step 1). Add the following XML snippet before `</web-app>`:

```xml
<servlet>
  <servlet-name>JSFServlet</servlet-name>
  <servlet-class>javax.faces.webapp.FacesServlet</servlet-class>
  <load-on-startup>1</load-on-startup>
</servlet>

<servlet-mapping>
```

```
    <servlet-name>JSFServlet</servlet-name>
    <url-pattern>*.xhtml</url-pattern>
 </servlet-mapping>
```

Note that you can get code assist when creating the preceding elements by pressing *Ctrl/Cmd + C*.

You can specify any name as `servlet-name`; just make sure that you use the same name in `servlet-mapping`. The class for the servlet is `javax.faces.webapp.FacesServlet`, which is in the JAR file that we downloaded as the JSF library and copied to `WEB-INF/lib`. Furthermore, we have mapped any request ending with `.xhtml` to this servlet.

Next, we will create a managed bean for our login page. This is the same as JavaBean that we had created earlier, but with the addition of JSF-specific annotations:

1. Right-click on the `src` folder under `Java Resources` for the project in **Project Explorer**.
2. Select the **New** | **Class** menu option.
3. Create JavaBean, `LoginBean`, as described in the *Using JavaBeans in JSP* section of this chapter.
4. Create two members for `userName` and `password`.
5. Create the getters and setters for them. Then, add two annotations as follows:

```java
package packt.book.jee_eclipse.bean;
import javax.faces.bean.ManagedBean;
import javax.faces.bean.RequestScoped;

@ManagedBean(name="loginBean")
@RequestScoped
public class LoginBean {
  private String userName;
  private String password;
  public String getUserName() {
    return userName;
  }
  public void setUserName(String userName) {
    this.userName = userName;
  }
  public String getPassword() {
    return password;
  }
  public void setPassword(String password) {
    this.password = password;
  }
}
```

(You can get code assist for annotations too. Type @ and press *Ctrl/Cmd + C*. Code assist works for the annotation `key-value` attribute pairs too, for example, for the `name` attribute of the `ManagedBean` annotation).

6. Create a new file called `index.xhtml` inside the `WebContent` folder of the project by selecting the **File** | **New** | **File** menu option. When using JSF, you need to add a few namespace declarations at the top of the file:

```
<html xmlns="http://www.w3.org/1999/xhtml"
    xmlns:f="http://java.sun.com/jsf/core"
    xmlns:h="http://java.sun.com/jsf/html">
```

Here, we are declaring namespaces for JSF built-in `tag` libraries. We will access tags in the core JSF `tag` library with the prefix `f` and HTML tags with the prefix `h`.

7. Add the title and start the `body` tag:

```
<head>
<title>Login</title>
</head>
<body>
    <h2>Login</h2>
```

There are corresponding JSF tags for the `head` and the `body`, but we do not use any attributes specific to JSF; therefore, we have used simple HTML tags.

8. We then add the code to display the error message, if it is not null:

```
<h:outputText value="#{loginBean.errorMsg}"
              rendered="#{loginBean.errorMsg != null}"
              style="color:red;"/>
```

Here, we use a tag specific to JSF and expression language to display the value of the error message. The `OutputText` tag is similar to the `c:out` tag that we saw in JSTL. We have also added a condition to render it only if the error message in the managed bean is not `null`. Additionally, we have set the color of this output text.

9. We have not added the `errorMsg` member to the managed bean yet. Therefore, let's add the declaration, the getter, and the setter. Open the `LoginBean` class and add the following code:

```
private String errorMsg;
public String getErrorMsg() {
  return errorMsg;
}
```

```
public void setErrorMsg(String errorMsg) {
   this.errorMsg = errorMsg;
}
```

Note that we access the managed bean in JSF by using value of the `name` attribute of the `ManagedBean` annotation. Furthermore, unlike JavaBean in JSP, we do not create it by using the `<jsp:useBean>` tag. The JSF runtime creates the bean if it is not already there in the required scope, in this case, the `Request` scope.

10. Let's go back to editing `index.xhtml`. We will now add the following form:

```
<h:form>
  User Name: <h:inputText id="userName"
                    value="#{loginBean.userName}"/><br/>
  Password: <h:inputSecret id="password"
                    value="#{loginBean.password}"/><br/>
  <h:commandButton value="Submit"
   action="#{loginBean.validate}"/>
</h:form>
```

Many things are happening here. First, we have used the `inputText` tag of JSF to create textboxes for username and password. We have set their values with the corresponding members of `loginBean`. We have used the `commandButton` tag of JSF to create a **Submit** button. When the user clicks the **Submit** button, we have set it to call the `loginBean.validate` method (using the `action` attribute).

11. We haven't defined a `validate` method in `loginBean`, so let's add that. Open the `LoginBean` class and add the following code:

```
public String validate()
{
  if ("admin".equals(userName) && "admin".equals(password)) {
    errorMsg = null;
    return "welcome";
  } else {
    errorMsg = "Invalid user id or password. Please try
     again";
    return null;
  }
}
```

Note that the `validate` method returns a string. How is the return value used? It is used for navigation purposes in JSF. The JSF runtime looks for the JSF file with the same name as the string value returned after evaluating the expression in the `action` attribute of `commandButton`. In the `validate` method, we return `welcome` if the user credentials are valid. In this case we are telling the JSF runtime to navigate to `welcome.xhtml`. If the credentials are invalid, we set the error message and return `null`, in which case, the JSF runtime displays the same page.

12. We will now add the `welcome.xhtml` page. It simply contains the welcome message:

```
<html xmlns="http://www.w3.org/1999/xhtml"
      xmlns:f="http://java.sun.com/jsf/core"
      xmlns:h="http://java.sun.com/jsf/html">
  <body>
    <h2>Welcome admin !</h2>
      You are successfully logged in
  </body>
</html>
```

Here is the complete source code of `index.html`:

```
<html xmlns="http://www.w3.org/1999/xhtml"
   xmlns:f="http://java.sun.com/jsf/core"
   xmlns:h="http://java.sun.com/jsf/html">

<head>
   <title>Login</title>
</head>
<body>
<h2>Login</h2>
<h:outputText value="#{loginBean.errorMsg}"
rendered="#{loginBean.errorMsg != null}"
style="color:red;"/>
<h:form>
   User Name: <h:inputText id="userName"
    value="#{loginBean.userName}"/><br/>     Password: <h:inputSecret
id="password"
     value="#{loginBean.password}"/><br/>
  <h:commandButton value="Submit" action="#{loginBean.validate}"/>
  </h:form>
</body>
</html>
```

Here is the source code of the `LoginBean` class:

```
package packt.book.jee_eclipse.bean;
import javax.faces.bean.ManagedBean;
import javax.faces.bean.RequestScoped;

@ManagedBean(name="loginBean")
@RequestScoped
public class LoginBean {
  private String userName;
  private String password;
  private String errorMsg;
  public String getUserName() {
    return userName;
  }
  public void setUserName(String userName) {
    this.userName = userName;
  }
  public String getPassword() {
    return password;
  }
  public void setPassword(String password) {
    this.password = password;
  }
  public String getErrorMsg() {
    return errorMsg;
  }
  public void setErrorMsg(String errorMsg) {
    this.errorMsg = errorMsg;
  }
  public String validate()
  {
    if ("admin".equals(userName) && "admin".equals(password)) {
      errorMsg = null;
      return "welcome";
    }
    else {
      errorMsg = "Invalid user id or password. Please try again";
      return null;
    }
  }
}
```

To run the application, right-click on `index.xhtml` in **Project Explorer** and select the **Run As | Run on Server** option.

JSF can do much more than what we have seen in this small example—it has the support to validate an input and create page templates too. However, these topics are beyond the scope of this book.

Visit `http://docs.oracle.com/cd/E11035_01/workshop102/webapplications/jsf/jsf-app-tutorial/Introduction.html` for a tutorial on JSF.

Using Maven for project management

In the projects that we have created thus far in this chapter, we have managed many project management tasks, such as downloading libraries on which our project depends, adding them to the appropriate folder so that the web application can find it, and exporting the project to create the WAR file for deployment. These are just some of the project management tasks that we have performed so far, but there are many more, which we will see in the subsequent chapters. It helps to have a tool do many of the project management tasks for us so that we can focus on application development. There are some well-known build management tools available for Java, for example, Apache Ant (`http://ant.apache.org/`) and Maven (`http://maven.apache.org/`).

In this section, we will see how to use Maven as a project management tool. By following the convention for creating the project structure and allowing projects to define the hierarchy, Maven makes project management easier than Ant. Ant is primarily a build tool, whereas Maven is a project management tool, which does build management too. See `http://maven.apache.org/what-is-maven.html` to understand what Maven can do.

In particular, Maven simplifies dependency management. In the JSF project earlier in this chapter, we first downloaded the appropriate `.jar` files for JSF and copied them to the `lib` folder. Maven can automate this. You can configure Maven settings in `pom.xml`. **POM** stands for **Project Object Model**.

Before we use Maven, it is important to understand how it works. Maven uses repositories. Repositories contain plugins for many well-known libraries/projects. A plugin includes the project configuration information, `.jar` files required to use this project in your own project, and any other supporting artifacts. The default Maven repository is a collection of plugins. You can find the list of plugins in the default Maven repository at `http://maven.apache.org/plugins/index.html`. You can also browse the content of the Maven repository at `http://search.maven.org/#browse`. Maven also maintains a local repository on your machine. This local repository contains only those plugins that your projects have specified dependencies on. On Windows, you will find the local repository at `C:/Users /<username>.m2`, and on macOS X, it is located at `~/.m2`.

You define plugins on which your project depends in the `dependencies` section of `pom.xml` (we will see the structure of `pom.xml` shortly when we create a Maven project). For example, we can specify a dependency on JSF. When you run the Maven tool, it first inspects all dependencies in `pom.xml`. It then checks whether the dependent plugins with the required versions are already downloaded in the local repository. If not, it downloads them from the central (remote) repository. You can also specify repositories to look in. If you do not specify any repository, then dependencies are searched in the central Maven repository.

We will create a Maven project and explore `pom.xml` in more detail. However, if you are curious to know what `pom.xml` is, then visit `http://maven.apache.org/pom.html#What_is_the_POM`.

Eclipse JEE version has Maven built-in, so you don't need to download it. However, if you plan to use Maven from outside Eclipse, then download it from `http://maven.apache.org/download.cgi`.

Maven views and preferences in Eclipse JEE

Before we create a Maven project, let's explore the views and preferences specific to Maven in Eclipse:

1. Select the **Window** I **Show View** I **Other...** menu.

2. Type `Maven` in the filter box. You will see two views for **Maven**:

Figure 2.25: Maven views

3. Select **Maven Repositories** view and click **OK**. This view is opened in the bottom tab window of Eclipse. You can see the location of the local and remote repositories.

4. Right-click on a global repository to see the options to index the repository:

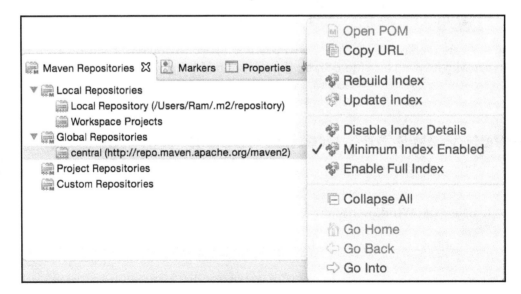

Figure 2.26: The Maven Repositories view

5. Open Eclipse **Preferences** and type Maven in the filter box to see all the Maven preferences:

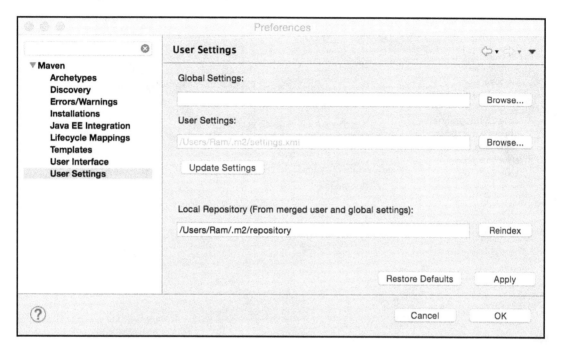

Figure 2.27: Maven preferences

You should set the Maven preferences to refresh repository indexes on startup, so that the latest libraries are available when you add dependencies to your project (we will learn how to add dependencies shortly).

6. Click on the **Maven** node in **Preferences** and set the following options:

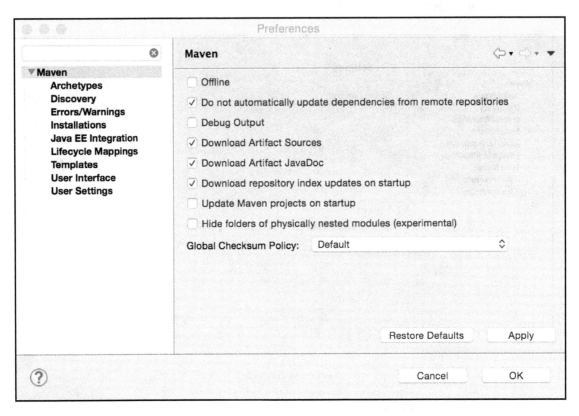

Figure 2.28: Maven preferences for updating indexes on startup

Creating a Maven project

In the following steps, we will see how to create a Maven project in Eclipse:

1. Select the **New** | **Maven Project** menu:

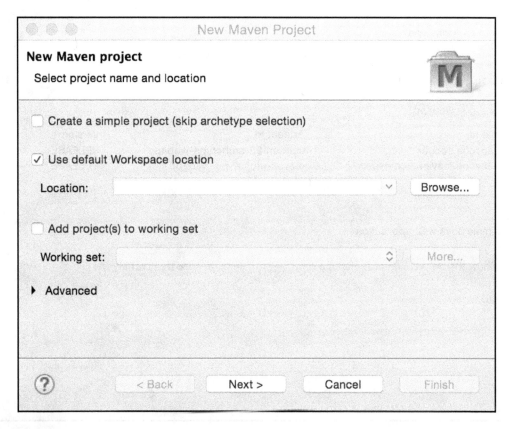

Figure 2.29: Maven New Project wizard

2. Accept all default options and click **Next**. Type `webapp` in the filter box and select **maven-archetype-webapp**:

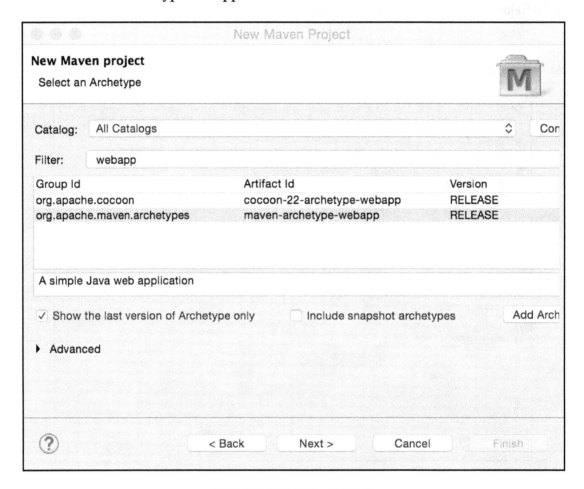

Figure 2.30: New Maven project - select archetype

Maven archetype

We selected **maven-archetype-webapp** in the preceding wizard. An archetype is a project template. When you use an archetype for your project, all the dependencies and other Maven project configurations defined in the template (archetype) are imported into your project.

See more information about Maven archetype at
`http://maven.apache.org/guides/introduction/introduction-to-arch`
`etypes.html`.

1. Continuing with the **New Maven Project** wizard, click on **Next**. In the **Group Id**
   field, enter `packt.book.jee_eclipse`. In the **Artifact Id** field, enter
   `maven_jsf_web_app`:

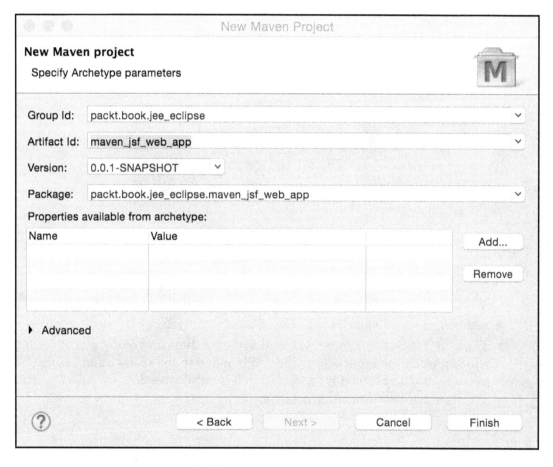

Figure 2.31: New Maven project - archetype parameters

2. Click on **Finish**. A `maven_jsf_web_app` project is added in **Project Explorer**.

Exploring the POM

Open `pom.xml` in the editor and go to the **pom.xml** tab. The file should have the following content:

```xml
<project xmlns="http://maven.apache.org/POM/4.0.0"
xmlns:xsi="http://www.w3.org/2001/XMLSchema-instance"
  xsi:schemaLocation="http://maven.apache.org/POM/4.0.0
   http://maven.apache.org/maven-v4_0_0.xsd">
  <modelVersion>4.0.0</modelVersion>
  <groupId>packt.book.jee_eclipse</groupId>
  <artifactId>maven_jsf_web_app</artifactId>
  <packaging>war</packaging>
  <version>0.0.1-SNAPSHOT</version>
  <name>maven_jsf_web_app Maven Webapp</name>
  <url>http://maven.apache.org</url>
  <dependencies>
    <dependency>
      <groupId>junit</groupId>
      <artifactId>junit</artifactId>
      <version>3.8.1</version>
      <scope>test</scope>
    </dependency>
  </dependencies>
  <build>
    <finalName>maven_jsf_web_app</finalName>
  </build>
</project>
```

Let's have a look at the different tags in detail, that are used in the preceding code snippet:

- `modelVersion`: This in the `pom.xml` file is the version of Maven.
- `groupId`: This is the common ID used in the business unit or organization under which projects are grouped together. Although it is not necessary to use the package structure format for group ID, it is generally used.
- `artifactId`: This is the project name.

- version: This is version number of the project. Version numbers are important when specifying dependencies. You can have multiple versions of a project, and you can specify different version dependencies in different projects. Maven also appends the version number to JAR, WAR, or EAR files that it creates for the project.
- packaging: This tells Maven what kind of final output we want when the project is built. In this book, we will be using JAR, WAR, and EAR packaging types, although more types exist.
- name: This is actually the name of the project, but Eclipse shows artifactid as the project name in **Project Explorer**.
- url: This is the URL of your project if you are hosting the project information on the web. The default is Maven's URL.
- dependencies: This section is where we specify the libraries (or other Maven artifacts) that the project depends on. The archetype that we selected for this project has added the default dependency of JUnit to our project. We will learn more about JUnit in chapter 5, *Unit Testing*.
- finalName: This tag in the build tag indicates the name of the output file (JAR, WAR, or EAR) that Maven generates for your project.

Adding Maven dependencies

The archetype that we selected for the project does not include some of the dependencies required for a JEE web project. Therefore, you might see error markers in index.jsp. We will fix this by adding dependencies for the JEE libraries:

1. With pom.xml open in the editor, click on the **Dependencies** tab.
2. Click the **Add** button. This opens the **Select Dependency** dialog.
3. In the filter box, type javax.servlet (we want to use servlet APIs in the project).

4. Select the latest version of the API and click the **OK** button.

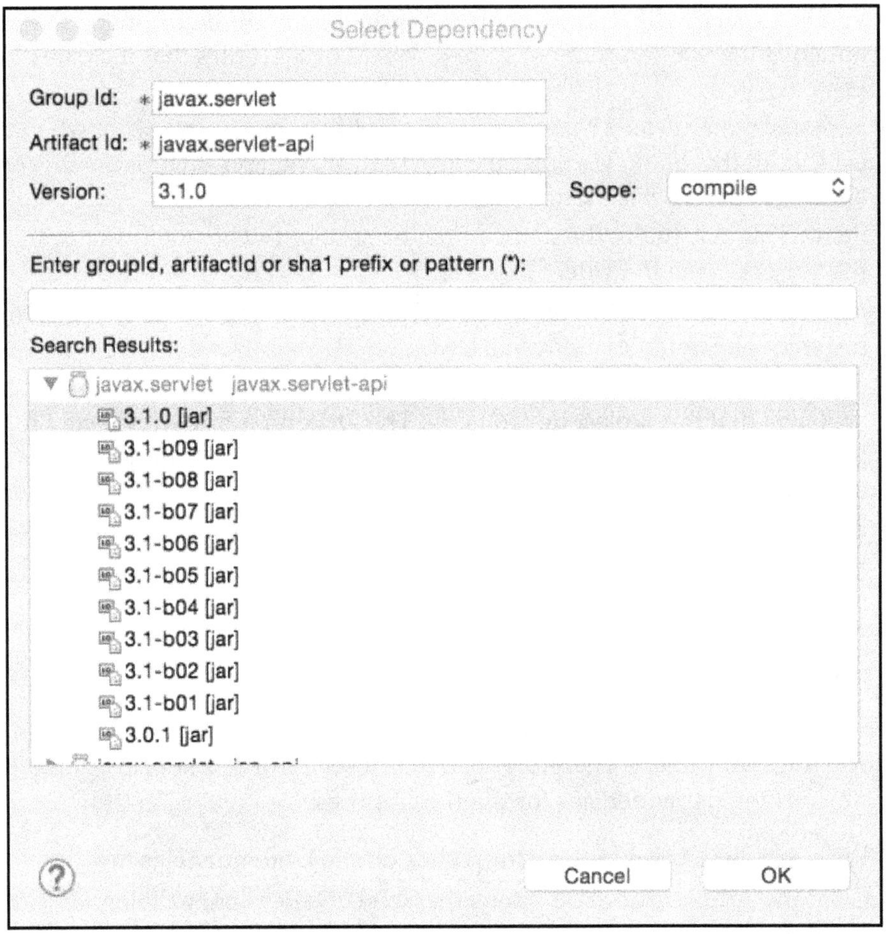

Figure 2.32: Adding servlet API dependency

However, we need JAR files for servlet APIs only at the compile time; at runtime, these APIs are provided by Tomcat. We can indicate this by specifying the scope of the dependency; in this case, setting it to provided, which tells Maven to evaluate this dependency for compilation only and not to package it in the WAR file. See `http://maven.apache.org/guides/introduction/introduction-to-dependency-mechanism.html` for more information on dependency scopes.

5. To set scope of the dependency, select dependency from the **Dependencies** tab of the POM editor.

6. Click the **Properties** button. Then, select the **provided** scope from the drop-down list:

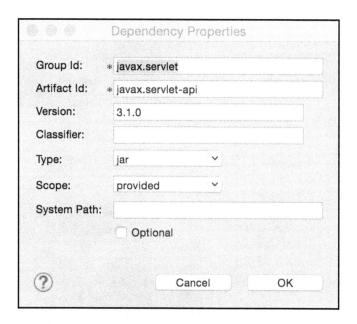

Figure 2.33: Setting the Maven dependency scope

7. Now we need to add dependencies for JSF APIs and their implementation. Click the **Add** button again and type `jsf` in the search box.

8. From the list, select `jsf-api` with **Group Id** `com.sun.faces` and click the **OK** button:

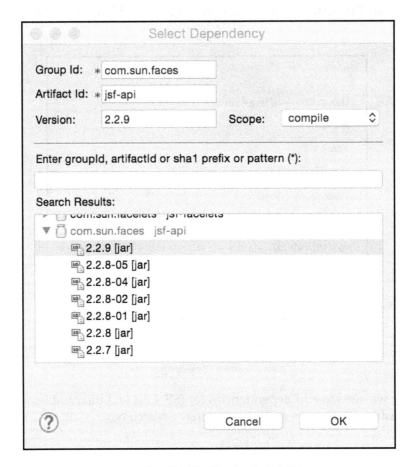

Figure 2.34: Adding Maven dependencies for JSF

9. Similarly, add a dependency for `jsf-impl` with **Group Id** `com.sun.faces`. The dependencies section in your `pom.xml` should look as follows:

```
<dependencies>
    <dependency>
        <groupId>junit</groupId>
        <artifactId>junit</artifactId>
        <version>3.8.1</version>
        <scope>test</scope>
    </dependency>
    <dependency>
        <groupId>javax.servlet</groupId>
        <artifactId>javax.servlet-api</artifactId>
        <version>3.1.0</version>
        <scope>provided</scope>
    </dependency>
    <dependency>
        <groupId>com.sun.faces</groupId>
        <artifactId>jsf-api</artifactId>
        <version>2.2.16</version>
    </dependency>
    <dependency>
        <groupId>com.sun.faces</groupId>
        <artifactId>jsf-impl</artifactId>
        <version>2.2.16</version>
    </dependency>
</dependencies>
```

If Tomcat throws an exception for not finding `javax.faces.webapp.FacesServlet` then you may have to download `jsf-api-2.2.16.jar` (http://central.maven.org/maven2/com/sun/faces/jsf-impl/2.2.16/jsf-impl-2.2.16.jar) and `jsf-impl-2.2.16.jar` (http://central.maven.org/maven2/com/sun/faces/jsf-impl/2.2.16/jsf-impl-2.2.16.jar) and copy them to the `<tomcat-install-folder>/lib` folder.

Maven project structure

The Maven project wizard creates `src` and `target` folders under the main project folder. As the name suggests, all source files go under `src`. However, Java package structure starts under the `main` folder. By convention, Maven expects Java source files under the `java` folder. Therefore, create a `java` folder under `src/main`. The Java package structure starts from the `java` folder, that is, `src/main/java/<java-packages>`. Web content such as HTML, JS, CSS, and JSP goes in the `webapp` folder under `src/main`. Compiled classes and other output files generated by the Maven build process are stored in the `target` folder:

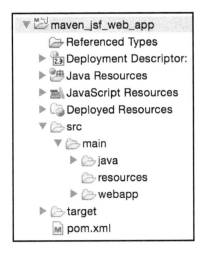

Figure 2.35: Maven web application project structure

The source code for our login JSF page is the same as in the previous example of `LoginJSFApp`. Therefore, copy the `packt` folder from the `src` folder of that project to the `src/main/java` folder of this Maven project. This adds `LoginBean.java` to the project. Then, copy `web.xml` from the `WEB-INF` folder to the `src/main/webapp/WEB-INF` folder of this project. Copy `index.xhtml` and `welcome.xhtml` to the `src/main/webapp` folder:

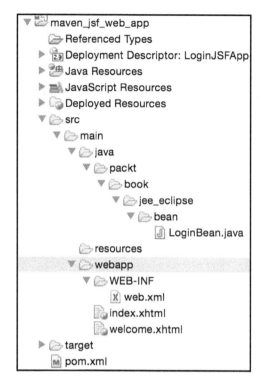

Figure 2.36: Project structure after adding source files

No change is required in the source code. To run the application, right-click on `index.xhtml` and select **Run As | Run on Server**.

We will be using Maven for project management in the rest of this book.

Creating a WAR file using Maven

In a previous example, we created the WAR file using the **Export** option of Eclipse. In a Maven project you can create a WAR by invoking the **Maven Install** plugin. Right-click on the project and select the **Run As | Maven install** option. The WAR file is created in the `target` folder. You can then deploy the WAR file in Tomcat by copying it to the `webapps` folder of Tomcat.

Summary

In this chapter, we learned how to configure Tomcat in Eclipse. We learned how the same web page can be implemented using three different technologies, namely JSP, Servlet, and JSF. All of them can be used for developing any dynamic web application. However, JSP and JSF are better suited for more UI-intensive pages, and servlets are better suited for controllers and as endpoints for web services and WebSockets. JSF enforces the MVC design and provides many additional services compared to JSP.

We also learned how to use Maven for many project management tasks.

In the next chapter, we will learn how to configure and use source control management systems, particularly SVN and Git.

Source Control Management in Eclipse 3

In the previous chapter, we learned how to create simple web applications using JSP, JSF, and servlets. We also learned how to use Maven for build and project management.

In this chapter, we will learn how to integrate Eclipse with SVN and Git. The chapter covers the following topics:

- Installing Eclipse plugins for SVN and Git
- Performing source control tasks such as checking out files, committing changes, and so on from Eclipse
- Synchronizing projects with remote repositories

Source Control Management (SCM) is an essential part of software development. By using SCM tools, you make sure that you have access to versions of your code at important milestones. SCM also helps to manage the source code when you are working in a team, by providing you with tools to make sure you do not overwrite the work done by others. Whether your project is small or large, whether you are working alone or in a large team, using SCM would benefit you.

Eclipse has had support for integrating various SCM tools for a long time—this includes support for CVS, Microsoft SourceSafe, Perforce, and **Subversion (SVN)**. The recent versions of Eclipse have built-in support for Git too.

We will start by learning how to use SVN from Eclipse.

The Eclipse subversion plugin

In this section, we will learn how to install and use the SVN Eclipse plugin. We will create a small project and see how to check in a project to SVN from within Eclipse. We will also see how to sync with the existing SVN repository.

You will need access to an SVN repository to follow the steps in this chapter. If you do not have access to an SVN repository, you can choose from some of the free SVN offerings online. This book does not promote or suggest using any particular online SVN hosting, but for the purpose of explaining SVN Eclipse plugin features, the author has used `https://riouxsvn.com`. However, the plugin would work the same way with any SVN server.

Installing the Eclipse Subversion plugin

1. Open the **Eclipse Marketplace** by selecting the **Help | Eclipse Marketplace** menu. Search for `subversion`:

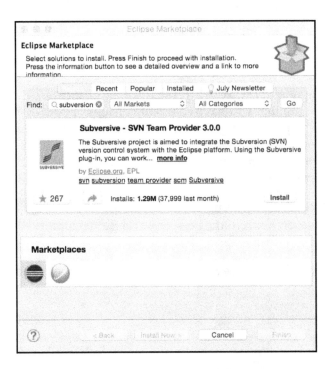

Figure 3.1: Installing the Subversion plugin

2. Install the plugin. Before we configure an SVN repository in Eclipse, we need to select/install an **SVN Connector**. Go to Eclipse **Preferences** and type svn in the filter box. Then, go to the **SVN Connector** tab:

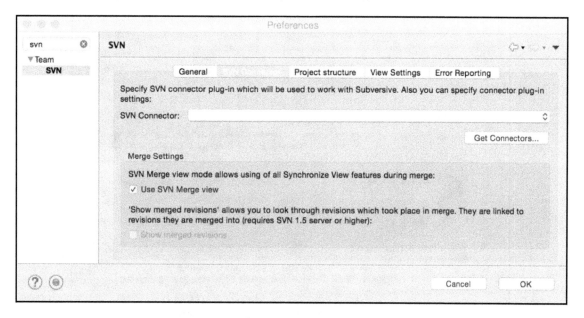

Figure 3.2: SVN Connector preferences

If no connectors are installed, then you will see a **Get Connectors...** button. Click the button.

3. Eclipse displays a number of available connectors. We will choose the **SVN Kit** connector and install it (click the **Finish** button):

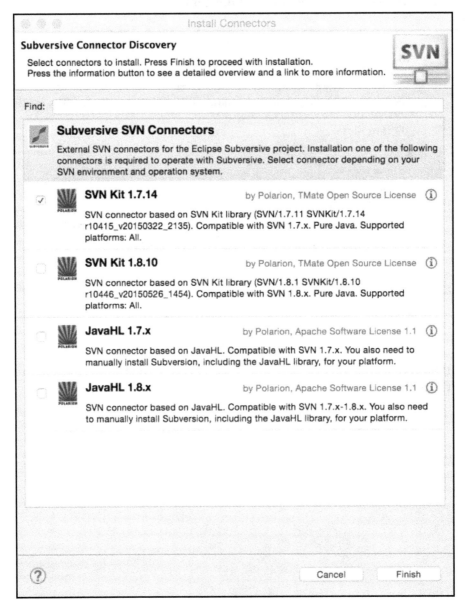

Figure 3.3: The SVN Connector Discovery wizard

4. We will now configure an existing SVN repository in Eclipse. Select the **Window | Open Perspective | Other** menu and then select the **SVN Repository Exploring** perspective:

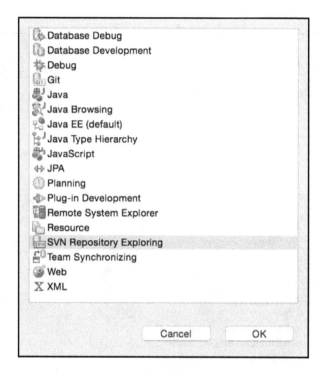

Figure 3.4: Open SVN perspective

Adding projects to an SVN repository

Perform the following steps to add projects to an SVN repository:

1. Right-click in the **SVN Repositories** view and select **New | Repository Location**.

2. Enter the **URL** of your SVN repository, your username, and password. If you need to set SSH or SSL information to connect to your SVN repository, then click on the appropriate tab and enter the information. Click **Finish** to add the repository to Eclipse:

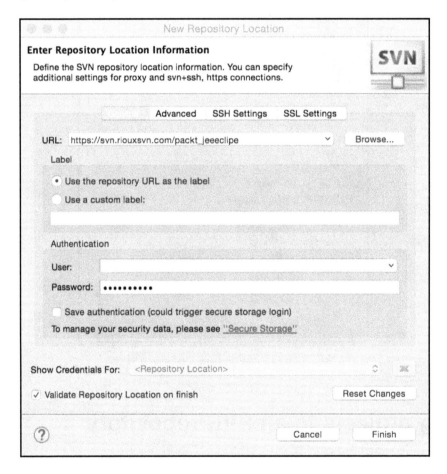

Figure 3.5: Configuring an SVN repository

Let's now create a simple Java project that we would check into the SVN repository. In this chapter, it is not important what code you write in the project; we are going to use the project only to understand how to check in project files to SVN and then see how to sync the project.

1. Create a simple Java project as shown in the following screenshot:

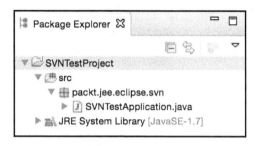

Figure 3.6: A sample project for SVN testing

2. The project has one source file. We will now check in this project in SVN. Right-click on the project and select **Team** | **Share Project...**.

3. Select **SVN** and click the **Next** button. The wizard gives you options to either create a new SVN repository or select an already configured SVN repository:

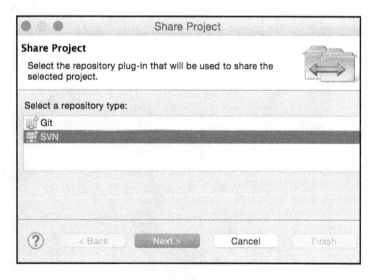

Figure 3.7: Share Project with SVN repository

4. We are going to use the already configured repository. So, select the repository:

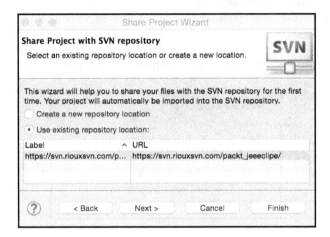

Figure 3.8: Selecting an SVN repository or creating a new one

5. We can click **Next** and configure the advanced option, but we will keep the configuration simple and click **Finish**. You will be prompted to check in existing files in the project:

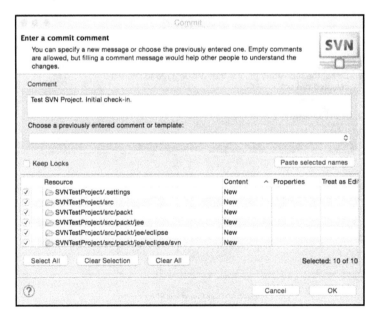

Figure 3.9: Share Project with SVN repository

6. Select the files you want to check in and enter the check-in comments. Then click **OK**. To see the checked in files in the SVN repository, switch to the **SVN Repository Exploring** perspective and then to the **SVN Repositories** view:

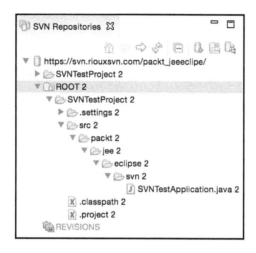

Figure 3.10: Checked in files in the SVN Repositories view

Committing changes to an SVN repository

Let's now modify a file and check in the changes. Switch back to the **Java** perspective and open SVNTestApplication.java from **Package Explorer** or **Navigator**. Modify the file and save the changes. To compare the files or the folders in your working directory with those in the repository, right-click on file/folder/project in **Navigator** and select **Compare With | Latest from Repository**.

Now that we have modified `SVNTestApplication.java`, let's see how it differs from the one in the repository:

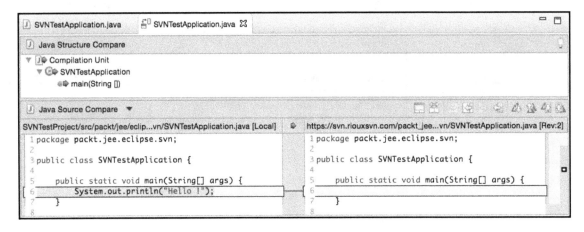

Figure 3.11: Comparing SVN files

Let's add a new file now, say `readme.txt`, in the root of the project. To add the file to the repository, right-click on the file and select **Team** | **Add to Version Control...**:

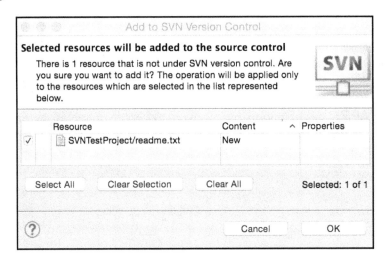

Figure 3.12: Adding files to an SVN repository

Synchronizing with an SVN repository

To synchronize your local project with the remote repository, right-click on the project and select **Team** | **Synchronize with Repository**. This will update the project with files in the remote repository, show files that are new in the local folder, and also show the changed files:

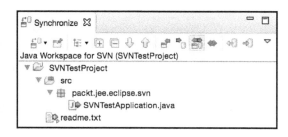

Figure 3.13: The Synchronize view

You can filter the list as incoming mode (changes from the remote repository), outgoing mode (changes in your working directory), or both. As you can see in *Figure 3.13*, we have two files that are changed in the working directory; one modified and one new. To commit the changes, right-click on the project and select **Commit....** If you want to commit from **Navigator** or **Package Explorer**, then right-click on the project and select **Team** | **Commit....** Enter the check-in comment and click **OK**. To update the project (receive all the changes from the remote repository), right-click on the project and select **Team** | **Update**.

To see the revision history of the file or folder, right-click **Navigator** or **Package Explorer** and select **Team** | **Show History**:

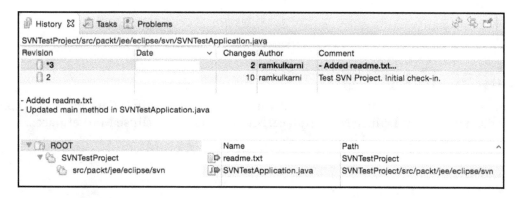

Figure 3.14: SVN file revision history

Checking out a project from SVN

It is easy to check out projects from an SVN repository into a new workspace. In the **SVN Repositories** view, click on the project you want to check out and select the **Check Out** option:

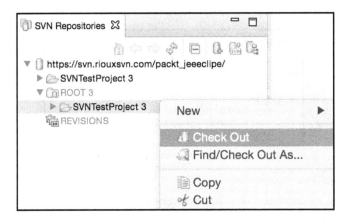

Figure 3.15: SVN file revision history

This option checks out the project in the current workspace. You can also use the **Import** project option to check out the project from SVN. Select the **File | Import** menu option and then select the **SVN | Project from SVN** option.

 There are many other features of SVN that you can use from Eclipse. Refer to http://www.eclipse.org/subversive/documentation.php.

Eclipse Git plugin

Recent versions of Eclipse are pre-installed with Eclipse **Git plugin** (**EGit**). If not, you can install the plugin from **Eclipse Marketplace**. Select the **Help | Eclipse Marketplace...** option and type egit in the **Find** textbox:

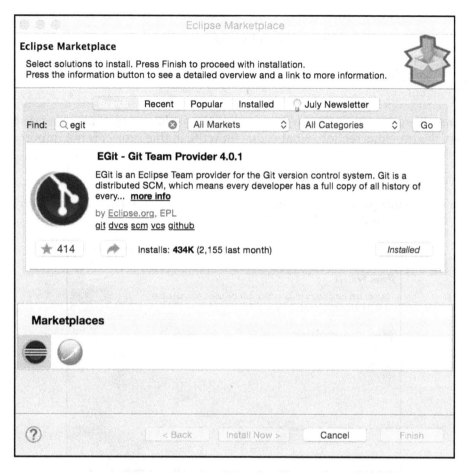

Figure 3.16: Searching the EGit plugin in Eclipse Marketplace

If the plugin is already installed, it will be marked as **Installed**.

Adding a project to Git

Git is a distributed repository. Unlike some of the other source management systems, Git maintains the complete local repository too. So you can perform activities such as check-out and check-in in the local repository without connecting to any remote repository. When you are ready to move your code to a remote repository, you can connect to it and push your files to the remote repository.

> If you are new to Git, take a look at the following documentation and tutorial:
> `https://git-scm.com/doc` and `https://www.atlassian.com/git/tutorials/`.

To learn how to add a project to Git, let's create a simple Java project in the workspace. Again as in the previous section, what code you write in this project is not important for now:

1. Create a Java class in the project.
2. To add this project to Git, right-click on the project in **Package Explorer** or **Navigator** and select **Team** | **Share Project...**:

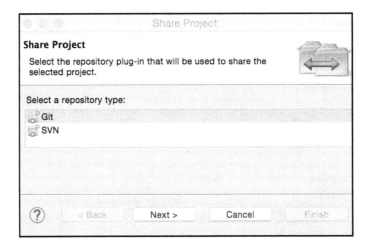

Figure 3.17: Sharing an Eclipse project with Git

3. Select **Git** and click **Next**. Check the box **Use or create repository in parent folder of project**.

4. Select the project (check the box for the project) and click the **Create Repository** button. Then click **Finish**:

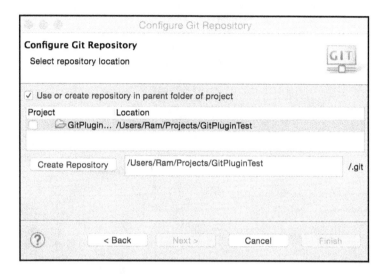

Figure 3.18: Creating a Git repository for a project

5. This creates a new Git repository in the project folder. Switch to the **Git** perspective (or open the **Git Repositories** view from the **Window | Show View | Other** option) and you should see the project listed in the **Git Repositories** view (see the following screenshot):

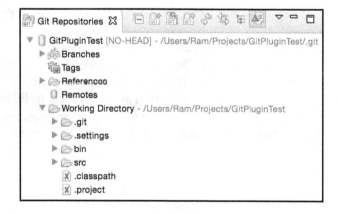

Figure 3.19: Git Repositories view

Committing files in the Git repository

In Git, new or modified files are staged for commit. To see the staged files, click on the **Git Staging** tab in the **Git** perspective:

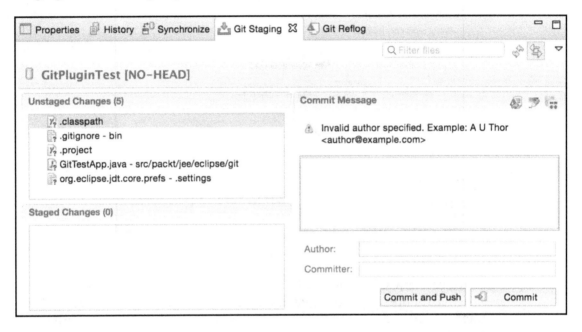

Figure 3.20: The Git Staging view

If you do not want to add a file to the Git repository, then right-click on that file (or multiple files selection) and select the **Ignore** option. Before you commit files to Git, you need to move **Unstaged Changes** to **Staged Changes**. We are going to add all the files to Git. So select all the files in the **Unstaged Changes** view and drag and drop them in the **Staged Changes** view. It is also recommended to set **Author** name and **Committer**. It is usually in `Name <email>` format. To set this option at global level in Eclipse (so that you do not have to set these fields at every commit), go to Eclipse **Preferences** and search for `Git`. Then go to the **Team | Git | Configuration** page and click the **Add Entry...** button:

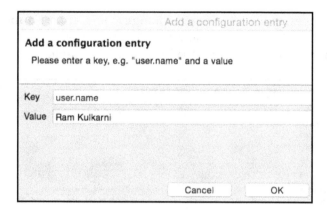

Figure 3.21: Adding a Git configuration entry

Similarly, add the `user.email` entry:

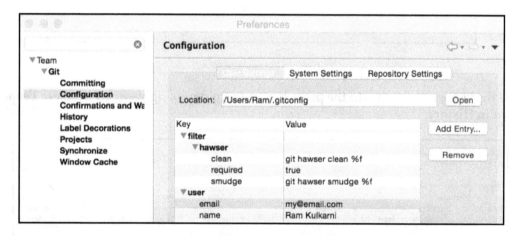

Figure 3.22: Git configurations in Preferences

Coming back to the **Git Staging** view, enter **Author**, **Committer**, and **Commit Message**. Then click the **Commit** button.

Viewing file differences after modifications

Let's modify the single Java class created in the previous project. If you go to the **Git Staging** view after making changes to the file, you will see that the file appears in the **Unstaged Changes** list. To see what changes have been made to the file since the last commit, double-click on the file in the **Git Staging** view.

To commit these changes, move it to **Staged Changes** view, enter **Commit Message**, and click the **Commit** button. You can also view the file differences by clicking on the file in **Package Explorer** and selecting **Compare With** | **Head Revision**:

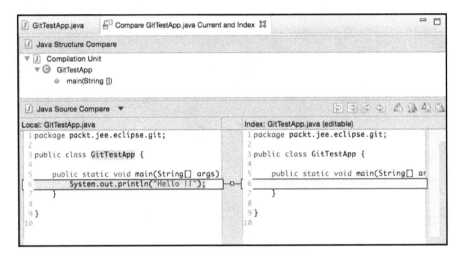

Figure 3.23: Viewing a file difference

To see the history of changes to the project or file(s)/folder(s), right-click and select **Team** | **Shown in History**:

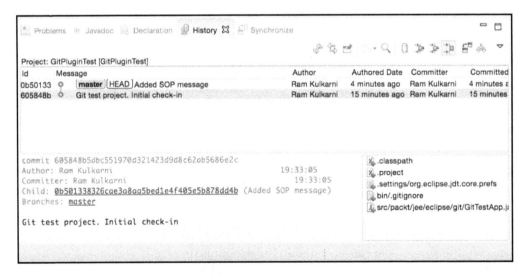

Figure 3.24: Git History view

Creating a new branch

It is typical when you are using source control management to create separate branches for features or even for bug fixes. The idea is that the main or the master branch should always have the working code and you do development on the branches that may not be stable. When you finish a feature or fix a bug and know that the branch is stable, then you merge the code from that branch to the master branch.

To create a new branch, go to the **Git Repositories** view and right-click on the repository you want to branch. Then select the **Switch To | New Branch...** option:

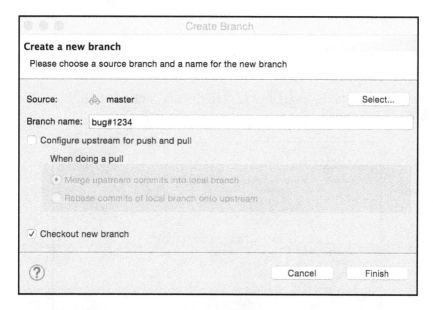

Figure 3.25: Creating a new branch

Note that the **Checkout new branch** box should be checked. Because of this option, the new branch becomes the active branch once it is created. Any changes you commit are going to be in this branch and the master branch remains unaffected. Click **Finish** to create the branch.

Let's make some changes to the code, say in the `main` method of the `GitTestApp` class:

```
public class GitTestApp {

  public static void main(String[] args) {
    System.out.println("Hello Git, from branch bug#1234 !!");
  }
}
```

Commit the preceding changes to the new branch.

Now let's check out the master branch. Right-click on the repository in the **Git Repositories** view and select **Switch To | master**. Open the file you modified in the new branch. You will observe that the changes you made to the file are not present. As mentioned previously, any changes you do to branches are not committed to the master branch. You have to explicitly merge the changes.

To merge the changes from branch **bug#1234** to the master branch, right-click on the repository in the **Git Repositories** view and select **Merge...**:

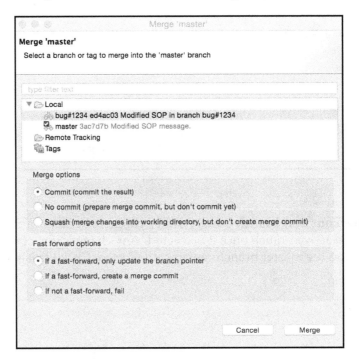

Figure 3.26: Merge Git braches

Select branch **bug#1234**. This branch will be merged in the master branch. Click **Merge**. Git will display a summary of the merge. Click **OK** to complete the merge operation. Now the file in the master branch will contain the changes done in branch **bug#1234**.

We have merged all the changes from branch **bug#1234** to the master and we no longer need it. So, let's delete branch **bug#1234**. Expand the **Branches** node in the **Git Repositories** view and right-click on the branch to be deleted (the selected branch should not be the active branch when deleting). Then select the **Delete Branch** menu option:

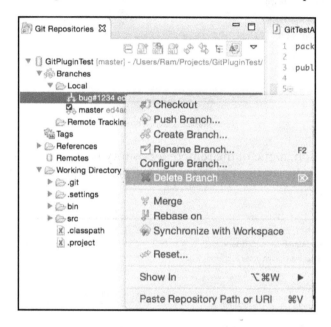

Figure 3.27: Deleting Git branch

Committing a project to a remote repository

So far, we have been working in the local Git repository. But you may want to push your project to a remote repository if you want to share your code and/or make sure that you do not lose your local changes. So in this section, we will learn how to push a local project to a remote Git repository. If you do not have access to a Git repository, you could create one at `http://www.github.com`.

1. Create a new repository in the remote Git server, named `GitPluginTest`.

2. In the **Git Repositories** view, right-click on the **Remotes** node and select the **Create Remote...** option:

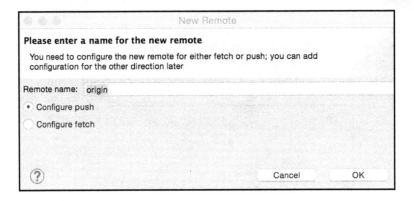

Figure 3.28: Adding a remote Git repository

3. By convention, name of the remote repository is `origin`. Click **OK**. In the next page, set up the configuration for push. Click on the **Change** button next to the URI textbox:

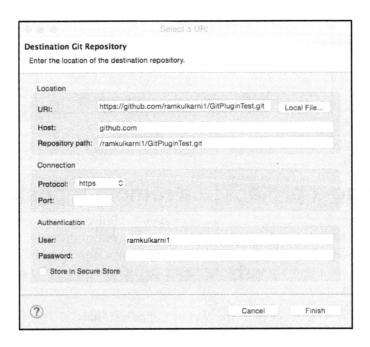

Figure 3.29: Setting up a remote Git URI

4. Enter the URI of the remote Git repository. The wizard extracts host, repository path, and protocol from the URI. Enter your user ID and password and click **Finish**:

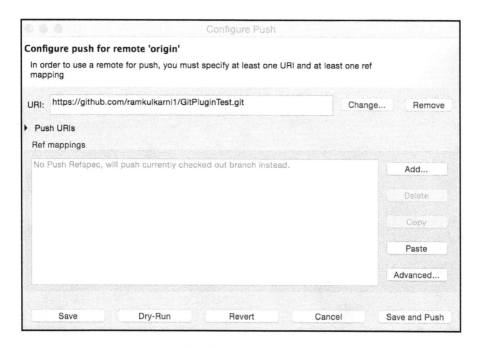

Figure 3.30: Configuring a Git push

5. Click **Save and Push**. This sends files in the local master branch to the remote Git repository.

Pulling changes from a remote repository

As you work in a team, your team members will also be making changes to the remote repository. When you want to get the changes done in the remote repository to your local repository, you use the **Pull** option. But before you perform the **Pull** operation, you need to configure it.

In **Package Explorer**, right-click on the project and select **Team | Remote | Configure Fetch from Upstream...**:

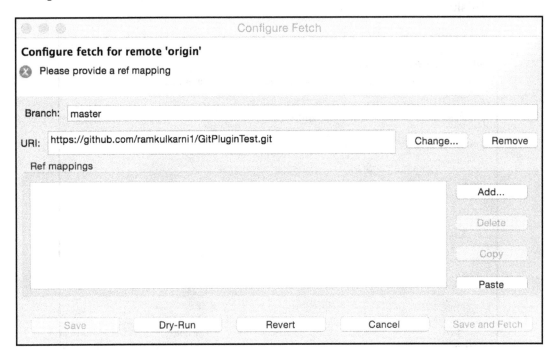

Figure 3.31: Configuring Git Fetch

 In Git, both **Pull** and **Fetch** can get the changes from a remote repository. However, the **Fetch** operation does not merge the changes in the local repository. The **Pull** operation first fetches the changes and then merges in the local repository. If you want to inspect the files before you merge, then select the **Fetch** option.

We need to map the local master branch with a branch in the remote repository. This tells the **Pull** operation to fetch the changes from the branch in the remote repository and merge it in the given (in this case, master) local repository. Click the **Add...** button:

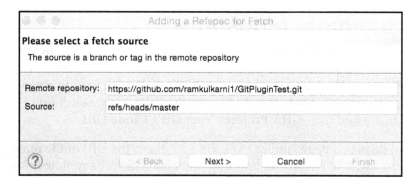

Figure 3.32: Configuring Git Fetch

Start typing the name of the branch in the source textbox and the wizard will get the branch information from the remote repository and auto complete it. Click **Next** and then **Finish**. This takes you back to the **Configure Fetch** page with mapping of the branches added to it:

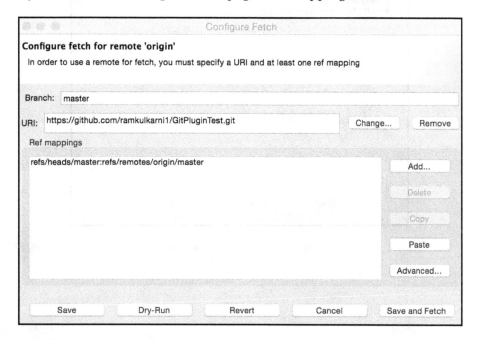

Figure 3.33: Configuring Git Fetch with mapping added

Click **Save and Fetch** to pull the changes from the remote repository.

Cloning a remote repository

We have learned how to start development using a local Git repository and then push changes to a remote repository. Let's now learn how we can get an existing remote Git repository and create a local copy; in other words, we will learn how to clone a remote Git repository. The easiest option is to import the remote Git project. Select **File** | **Import...** from the main menu and then **Git** | **Projects from Git** | **Clone URI**.

The wizard will display a page similar to *Figure 3.29*. Enter the URI of the remote repository, username, and password, and then click **Next**. Select a remote branch and click **Next**:

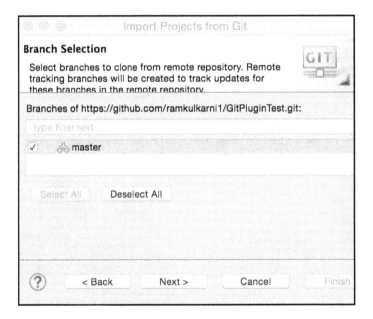

Figure 3.34: Selecting a remote branch to clone

Click the **Next** button in the branch selection page:

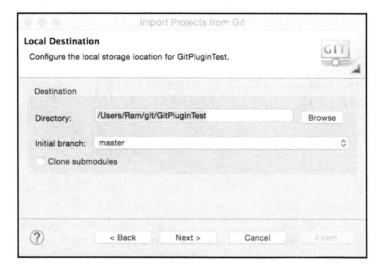

Figure 3.35: Selecting the location of the cloned project

Select the location where the project is to be saved and click **Next**:

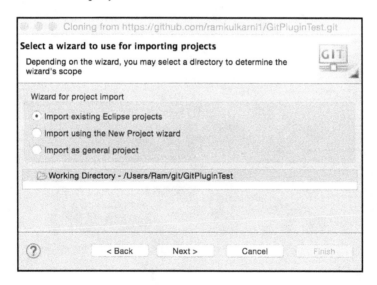

Figure 3.36: Options to import the cloned project

There are three options to import the cloned project. If the remote repository contains the entire Eclipse project, then select **Import existing Eclipse projects**, or else select either of the remaining two options. Since we have checked in the Eclipse project in the remote repository, we will select the first option. Click **Next** and then **Finish**.

> For more information about the Eclipse Git plugin, refer to
> `https://wiki.eclipse.org/EGit/User_Guide`.

Summary

There are Eclipse plugins available for a wide variety of SCM systems. In this chapter, we learned how to use Eclipse plugins for SVN and Git. Using these plugins you can perform many of the typical SCM operations, such as checking out source, comparing versions, and committing changes, right within the Eclipse IDE. This provides great convenience and can improve your productivity.

In the next chapter, we will see how to create JEE Database applications using JDBC and JDO.

4
Creating JEE Database Applications

In the previous chapter, we learned how to use source control management software from Eclipse. Specifically, we learned how to use SVN and Git from Eclipse. In this chapter, we will get back to discussing JEE application development. Most web applications today require access to the database. In this chapter, we will learn two ways to access databases from JEE web applications: using JDBC APIs, and using JPA APIs.

JDBC4 has been part of JDK since version 1.1. It provides uniform APIs to access different relational databases. Between JDBC APIs and the database sits the JDBC driver for that database (either provided by the vendor of the database or a third-party vendor). JDBC translates common API calls to database-specific calls. The results returned from the database are also converted into objects of common data access classes. Although JDBC APIs require you to write a lot more code to access the database, it is still popular in JEE web applications because of its simplicity, flexibility of using database-specific SQL statements, and low learning curve.

JPA is the result of **Java Specification Request** 220 (which stands for **JSR**). One of the problems of using JDBC APIs directly is converting object representation of data to relation data. Object representation is in your JEE application, which needs to be mapped to tables and columns in the relational database. The process is reversed when handling data returned from the relational database. If there is a way to automatically map object-oriented representation of data in web applications to relational data, it would save a lot of developer time. This is also called **object-relational mapping (ORM)**. Hibernate (`http://hibernate.org/`) is a very popular framework for ORM in Java applications.

Many of the concepts of such popular third-party ORM frameworks were incorporated in JPA. Just as JDBC provides uniform APIs for accessing relational databases, JPA provides uniform APIs for accessing ORM libraries. Third-party ORM frameworks provide implementations of JPA on top of their own framework. The JPA implementation may use the JDBC APIs underneath.

We will explore many features of JDBC and JPA in this chapter as we build applications using these frameworks. In fact, we will build the same application, once using JDBC and then using JPA.

The application that we are going to build is for student-course management. The goal is to take an example that can show how to model relationships between tables and use them in JEE applications. We will use a MySQL database and Tomcat web application container. Although this chapter is about database programming in JEE, we will revisit some of the things we learned about JSTL and JSF in Chapter 2, *Creating a Simple JEE Web Application*. We will use them to create user interfaces for our database web application. Make sure that you have configured Tomcat in Eclipse as described in Chapter 2, *Creating a Simple JEE Web Application*.

We will cover the following topics:

- Core JDBC concepts
- Using JDBC to access the database
- Using JDBC connection pool
- Core JPA concepts
- Using JPA to map entities (classes) to tables in the database
- Configuring relationships between JPA entities

Let's first create a database and tables for this application.

Creating database schema

There are many ways of creating database tables and relationships in MySQL:

- You can use **data description language** (DDL) statements directly at MySQL Command Prompt from the Terminal
- You can use MySQL Workbench and create tables directly
- You can create an entity-relationship diagram in MySQL Workbench, export it to create a DDL script, and then run this script to create tables and relationships

We will use the third option. If you just want to get the script to create tables and want to skip creating the ER diagram, then jump to the *Script to create tables and relationships* section of this chapter.

If you have not already installed MySQL and MySQL Workbench, then refer to `Chapter 1`, *Introducing JEE and Eclipse*, for instructions:

1. Open MySQL Workbench. Select the **File** | **New Model** menu. A blank model will be created with the option to create ER diagrams:

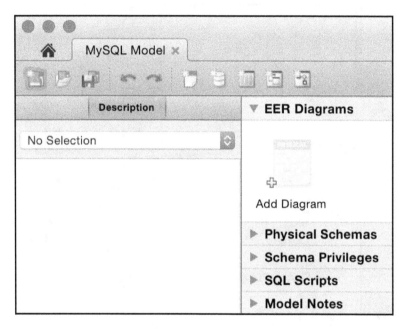

Figure 4.1: Creating a new MySQL Workbench model

2. Double-click the **Add Diagram** icon; a blank ER diagram will be opened:

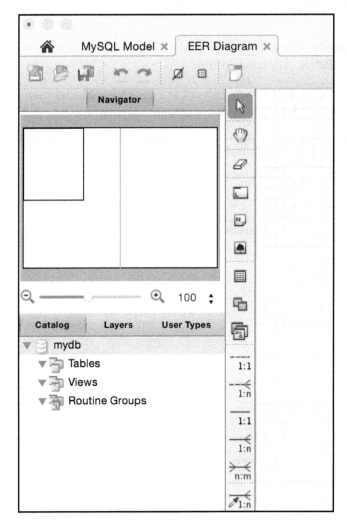

Figure 4.2: Creating a new ER diagram

3. By default, the new schema is named `mydb`. Double-click on it to open properties of the schema. Rename the schema`course_management`:

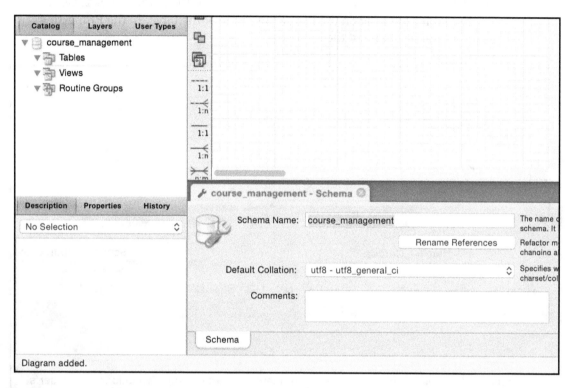

Figure 4.3: Renaming the schema

4. Hover over the toolbar buttons on the left-hand side of the page, and you will see tool tips about their functions. Click on the button for a new table and then click on the blank page. This will insert a new table with the name `table1`. Double-click the table icon to open the **Properties** page of the table. In the **Properties** page, change the name of the table to `Course`:

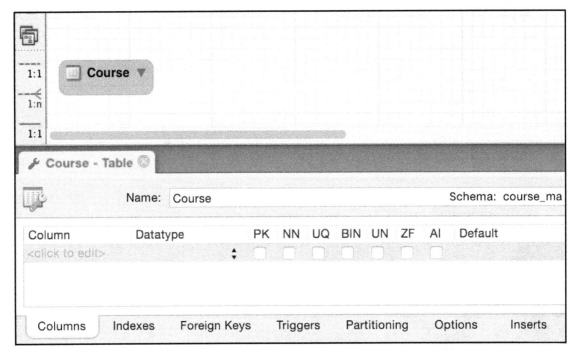

Figure 4.4: Creating a table in ER diagram

5. We will now create columns of the table. Double-click on the first column and name it **id**. Check the **PK (primary key)**, **NN (not null)**, and **AI (auto increment)** checkboxes. Add other columns as shown in the following screenshot:

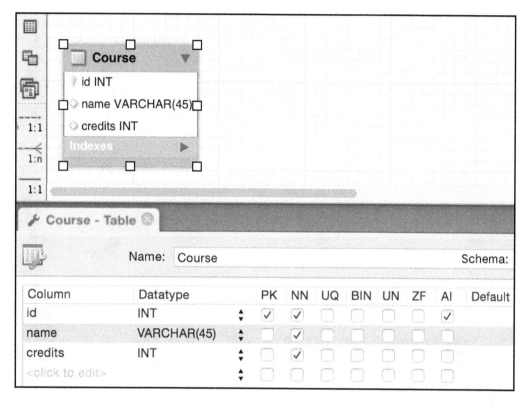

Figure 4.5: Creating columns in a table in the ER diagram

6. Create other tables, namely `Student` and `Teacher`, as shown in the following screenshot:

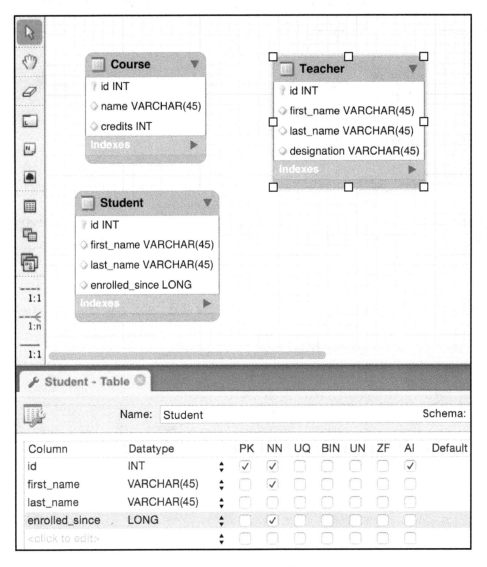

Figure 4.6: Creating additional tables

Note that if you want to edit column properties of any table, then double-click the table in the ER diagram. Just selecting a table by a single click would not change the table selection in the **Properties** page. All columns in all tables are required (not null), except the `last_name` column in `Student` and `Teacher` tables.

We will now create relationships between the tables. One course can have many students, and students can take many courses. So, there is a many-to-many relationship between `Course` and `Student`.

We will assume that one course is taught by only one teacher. However, a teacher can teach more than one course. Therefore, there is a many-to-one relationship between `Course` and `Teacher`.

Let's now model these relationships in the ER diagram:

1. First, we will create a non-identifying relationship between `Course` and `Teacher`.
2. Click on the non-identifying one-to-many button in the toolbar (dotted lines and **1:n**).
3. Then, click on the `Course` table first and then on the `Teacher` table. It will create a relationship as shown in *Figure 4.7*. Note that a foreign key `Teacher_id` is created in the `Course` table. We don't want to make a `Teacher_id` field required in `Course`. A course can exist without a teacher in our application. Therefore, double-click on the link joining `Course` and `Teacher` tables.
4. Then, click on the **Foreign Key** tab.

5. On the **Referenced Table** side, uncheck the **Mandatory** checkbox:

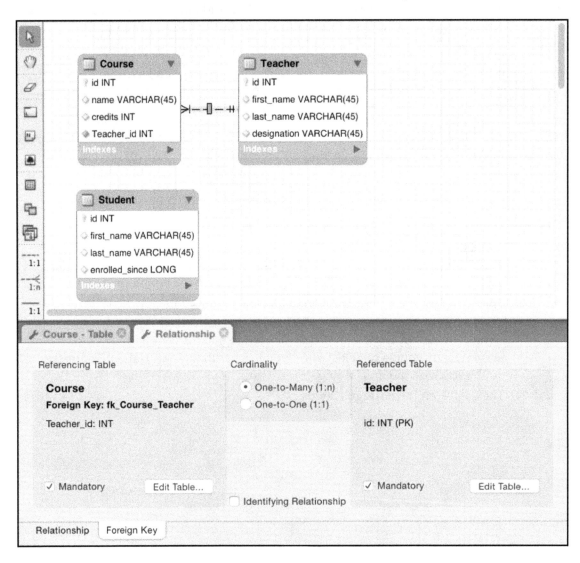

Figure 4.7: Creating a one-to-many relationship between tables

Creation of a many-to-many relationship requires a link table to be created. To create a many-to-many relationship between `Course` and `Student`, click on the icon for many-to-many (**n:m**) and then click on the `Course` table and `Student` table. This will create a third table (link table) called `Course_has_Student`. We will rename this table `Course_Student`. The final diagram is as shown in the following screenshot:

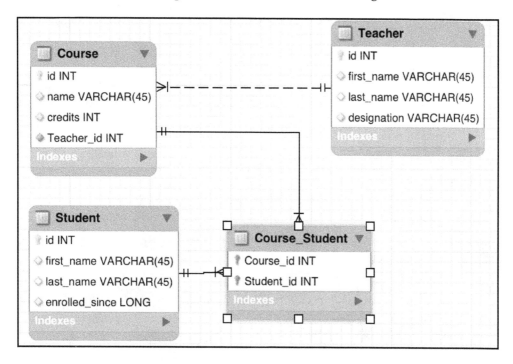

Figure 4.8: ER diagram for the course management example

Follow these steps to create DDL scripts from the ER diagram:

1. Select the **File | Export | Forward Engineer SQL Create Script...** menu.
2. On the **SQL Export Options** page, select checkboxes for two options:
   - **Generate DROP Statements Before Each CREATE Statement**
   - **Generate DROP SCHEMA**
3. Specify the **Output SQL Script File** path if you want to save the script.
4. On the last page of the **Export** wizard, you will see the script generated by MySQL Workbench. Copy this script by clicking the **Copy to Clipboard** button.

Script to create tables and relationships

The following is the DDL script to create tables and relationships for the course management example:

```
-- MySQL Script generated by MySQL Workbench
-- Sun Mar  8 18:17:07 2015
-- Model: New Model    Version: 1.0
-- MySQL Workbench Forward Engineering

SET @OLD_UNIQUE_CHECKS=@@UNIQUE_CHECKS, UNIQUE_CHECKS=0;
SET @OLD_FOREIGN_KEY_CHECKS=@@FOREIGN_KEY_CHECKS, FOREIGN_KEY_CHECKS=0;
SET @OLD_SQL_MODE=@@SQL_MODE, SQL_MODE='TRADITIONAL,ALLOW_INVALID_DATES';


-- -----------------------------------------------------
-- Schema course_management
-- -----------------------------------------------------
DROP SCHEMA IF EXISTS `course_management` ;


-- -----------------------------------------------------
-- Schema course_management
-- -----------------------------------------------------
CREATE SCHEMA IF NOT EXISTS `course_management` DEFAULT CHARACTER SET utf8
COLLATE utf8_general_ci ;
USE `course_management` ;


-- -----------------------------------------------------
-- Table `course_management`.`Teacher`
-- -----------------------------------------------------
DROP TABLE IF EXISTS `course_management`.`Teacher` ;

CREATE TABLE IF NOT EXISTS `course_management`.`Teacher` (
  `id` INT NOT NULL AUTO_INCREMENT,
  `first_name` VARCHAR(45) NOT NULL,
  `last_name` VARCHAR(45) NULL,
  `designation` VARCHAR(45) NOT NULL,
  PRIMARY KEY (`id`))
ENGINE = InnoDB;


-- -----------------------------------------------------
-- Table `course_management`.`Course`
-- -----------------------------------------------------
DROP TABLE IF EXISTS `course_management`.`Course` ;

CREATE TABLE IF NOT EXISTS `course_management`.`Course` (
  `id` INT NOT NULL AUTO_INCREMENT,
```

```
  `name` VARCHAR(45) NOT NULL,
  `credits` INT NOT NULL,
  `Teacher_id` INT NULL,
  PRIMARY KEY (`id`),
  INDEX `fk_Course_Teacher_idx` (`Teacher_id` ASC),
  CONSTRAINT `fk_Course_Teacher`
    FOREIGN KEY (`Teacher_id`)
    REFERENCES `course_management`.`Teacher` (`id`)
    ON DELETE NO ACTION
    ON UPDATE NO ACTION)
ENGINE = InnoDB;


-- -------------------------------------------------------
-- Table `course_management`.`Student`
-- -------------------------------------------------------
DROP TABLE IF EXISTS `course_management`.`Student` ;

CREATE TABLE IF NOT EXISTS `course_management`.`Student` (
  `id` INT NOT NULL AUTO_INCREMENT,
  `first_name` VARCHAR(45) NOT NULL,
  `last_name` VARCHAR(45) NULL,
  `enrolled_since` MEDIUMTEXT NOT NULL,
  PRIMARY KEY (`id`))
ENGINE = InnoDB;


-- -------------------------------------------------------
-- Table `course_management`.`Course_Student`
-- -------------------------------------------------------
DROP TABLE IF EXISTS `course_management`.`Course_Student` ;

CREATE TABLE IF NOT EXISTS `course_management`.`Course_Student` (
  `Course_id` INT NOT NULL,
  `Student_id` INT NOT NULL,
  PRIMARY KEY (`Course_id`, `Student_id`),
  INDEX `fk_Course_has_Student_Student1_idx` (`Student_id` ASC),
  INDEX `fk_Course_has_Student_Course1_idx` (`Course_id` ASC),
  CONSTRAINT `fk_Course_has_Student_Course1`
    FOREIGN KEY (`Course_id`)
    REFERENCES `course_management`.`Course` (`id`)
    ON DELETE NO ACTION
    ON UPDATE NO ACTION,
  CONSTRAINT `fk_Course_has_Student_Student1`
    FOREIGN KEY (`Student_id`)
    REFERENCES `course_management`.`Student` (`id`)
    ON DELETE NO ACTION
    ON UPDATE NO ACTION)
```

```
ENGINE = InnoDB;


SET SQL_MODE=@OLD_SQL_MODE;
SET FOREIGN_KEY_CHECKS=@OLD_FOREIGN_KEY_CHECKS;
SET UNIQUE_CHECKS=@OLD_UNIQUE_CHECKS;
```

Creating tables in MySQL

Let's now create tables and relationships in the MySQL database by using the script created in the previous section.

Make sure that MySQL is running and there is an open connection to the server from MySQL Workbench (see `Chapter 1`, *Introducing JEE and Eclipse*, for more details):

1. Create a new query tab (the first button in the toolbar) and paste the preceding script.
2. Execute the query.
3. At the end of the execution, refresh schemas in the left-hand pane. You should see the **course_management** schema and the tables created in it.

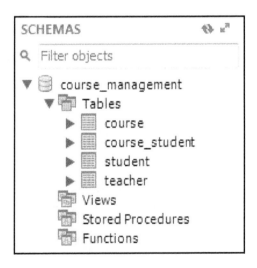

Figure 4.9: MySQL schema for the course management example

Creating a database application using JDBC

In this section, we will use JDBC to create a simple course management web application. We will use the MySQL schema created in the previous section. Furthermore, we will create the web application using Tomcat; we have already seen how to create one in Chapter 2, *Creating a Simple JEE Web Application*. We have also learned how to use JSTL and JSF in the same chapter. In this section, we will use JSTL and JDBC to create the course management application, and in the next section, we will use JSF and JPA to create the same application. We will use Maven (as described in Chapter 2, *Creating a Simple JEE Web Application*) for project management, and of course, our IDE is going to be Eclipse JEE.

Creating a project and setting up Maven dependencies

We will perform the following steps to create the Maven project for our application:

1. Create a Maven web project as described in Chapter 2, *Creating a Simple JEE Web Application*.
2. Name the project CourseManagementJDBC.
3. Add dependencies for servlet and JSP, but do not add a dependency for JSF.

4. To add the dependency for JSTL, open `pom.xml` and go to the **Dependencies** tab. Click on the **Add...** button. Type `javax.servlet` in the search box and select **jstl**:

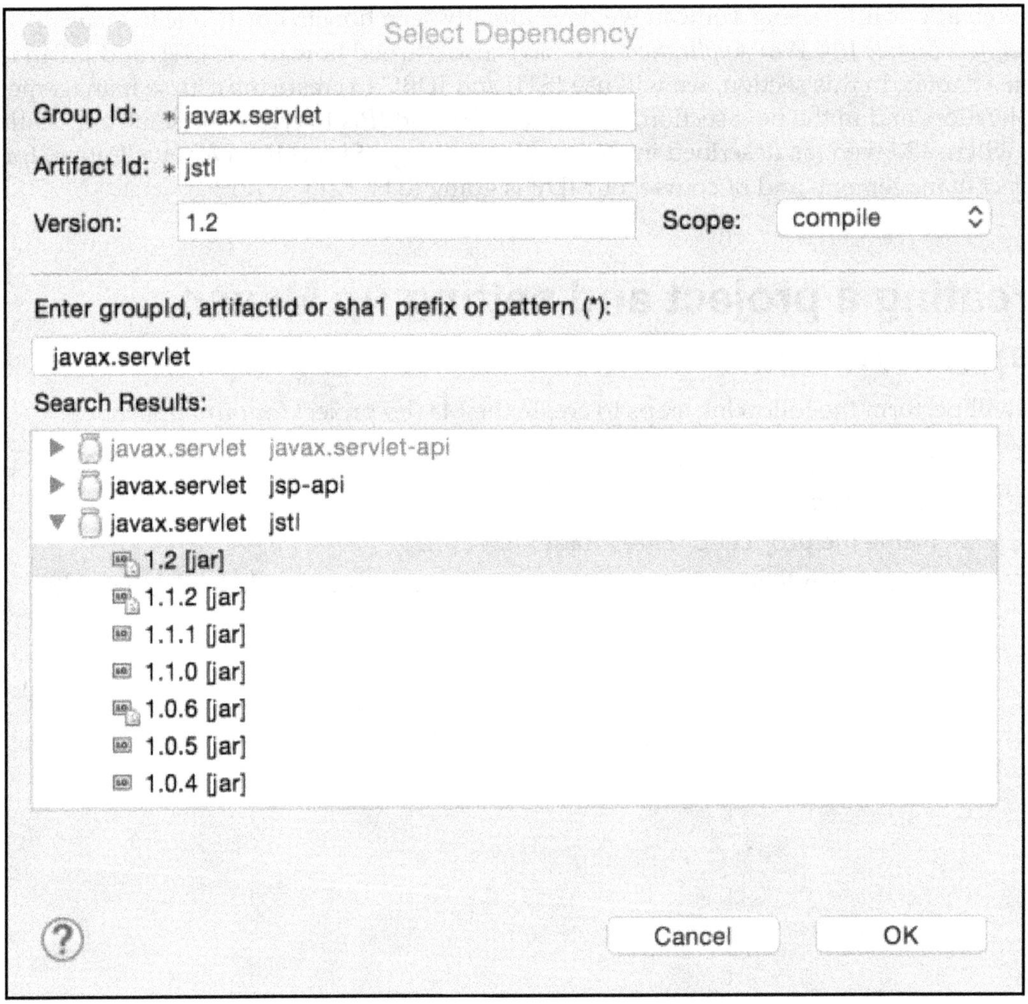

Figure 4.10: Adding a dependency for jstl

5. Add the dependency for the MySQL JDBC driver too:

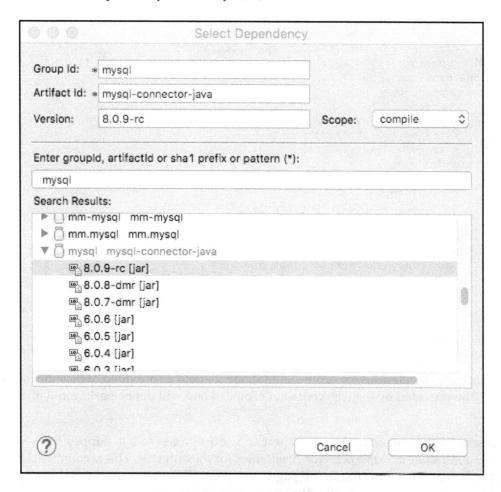

Figure 4.11: Adding dependency for the MySQL JDBC driver

Here is the `pom.xml` file after adding dependencies:

```
<project xmlns="http://maven.apache.org/POM/4.0.0"
  xmlns:xsi="http://www.w3.org/2001/XMLSchema-instance"
  xsi:schemaLocation="http://maven.apache.org/POM/4.0.0
http://maven.apache.org/xsd/maven-4.0.0.xsd">
 <modelVersion>4.0.0</modelVersion>
 <groupId>packt.book.jee.eclipse</groupId>
 <artifactId>CourseManagementJDBC</artifactId>
 <version>1</version>
```

```
        <packaging>war</packaging>
        <dependencies>
          <dependency>
            <groupId>javax.servlet</groupId>
            <artifactId>javax.servlet-api</artifactId>
            <version>3.1.0</version>
      <scope>provided</scope>
          </dependency>
          <dependency>
            <groupId>javax.servlet</groupId>
            <artifactId>jstl</artifactId>
            <version>1.2</version>
          </dependency>
          <dependency>
            <groupId>mysql</groupId>
            <artifactId>mysql-connector-java</artifactId>
            <version>8.0.9-rc</version>
          </dependency>
          <dependency>
            <groupId>javax.servlet.jsp</groupId>
            <artifactId>jsp-api</artifactId>
            <version>2.2</version>
            <scope>provided</scope>
          </dependency>
        </dependencies>
      </project>
```

Note that the dependencies for servlet and JSP are marked as provided, which means that they will be provided by the web container (Tomcat) and will not be packaged with the application.

The description of how to configure Tomcat and add a project to it is skipped here. Refer to Chapter 2, *Creating a Simple JEE Web Application*, for these details. This section will also not repeat information on how to run JSP pages and about JSTL that were covered in Chapter 2, *Creating a Simple JEE Web Application*.

Creating JavaBeans for data storage

We will first create JavaBean classes for Student, Course, and Teacher. Since both student and teacher are people, we will create a new class called Person and have Student and Teacher classes extend it. Create these JavaBeans in the packt.book.jee.eclipse.ch4.beans package as follows.

The code for the `Course` bean will be as follows:

```
package packt.book.jee.eclipse.ch4.bean;

public class Course {
  private int id;
  private String name;
  private int credits;
  public int getId() {
    return id;
  }
  public void setId(int id) {
    this.id = id;
  }
  public String getName() {
    return name;
  }
  public void setName(String name) {
    this.name = name;
  }
  public int getCredits() {
    return credits;
  }
  public void setCredits(int credits) {
    this.credits = credits;
  }
}
```

The code for the `Person` bean will be as follows:

```
package packt.book.jee.eclipse.ch4.bean;

public class Person {
  private int id;
  private String firstName;
  private String lastName;

  public int getId() {
    return id;
  }
  public void setId(int id) {
    this.id = id;
  }
  public String getFirstName() {
    return firstName;
  }
  public void setFirstName(String firstName) {
    this.firstName = firstName;
```

```
    }
    public String getLastName() {
       return lastName;
    }
    public void setLastName(String lastName) {
       this.lastName = lastName;
    }
  }
```

The code for the Student bean will be as follows:

```
package packt.book.jee.eclipse.ch4.bean;

public class Student extends Person {
  private long enrolledsince;

  public long getEnrolledsince() {
     return enrolledsince;
  }

  public void setEnrolledsince(long enrolledsince) {
     this.enrolledsince = enrolledsince;
  }
}
```

The Teacher bean will be as follows:

```
package packt.book.jee.eclipse.ch4.bean;

public class Teacher extends Person {
  private String designation;

  public String getDesignation() {
     return designation;
  }

  public void setDesignation(String designation) {
     this.designation = designation;
  }
}
```

Creating JSP to add a course

Let's now create a JSP page to add new courses. Right-click on the project in **Package Explorer** and select the **New | Other...** option. Type jsp in the filter box and select **JSP File**. Name the file addCourse.jsp. Eclipse will create the file in the src/main/webapp folder of the project.

Type the following code in addCourse.jsp:

```jsp
<%@ page language="java" contentType="text/html; charset=UTF-8"
    pageEncoding="UTF-8"%>
<%@ taglib prefix="c" uri="http://java.sun.com/jsp/jstl/core" %>

<!DOCTYPE html PUBLIC "-//W3C//DTD HTML 4.01 Transitional//EN"
"http://www.w3.org/TR/html4/loose.dtd">
<html>
<head>
<meta http-equiv="Content-Type" content="text/html; charset=UTF-8">
<title>Add Course</title>
</head>
<body>
  <c:set var="errMsg" value="${null}"/>
  <c:set var="displayForm" value="${true}"/>
    <c:if test="${\"POST\".equalsIgnoreCase(pageContext.request.method)
        && pageContext.request.getParameter(\"submit\") != null}">
    <jsp:useBean id="courseBean"
class="packt.book.jee.eclipse.ch4.bean.Course">
      <c:catch var="beanStorageException">
        <jsp:setProperty name="courseBean" property="*" />
      </c:catch>
    </jsp:useBean>
    <c:choose>
      <c:when test="${!courseBean.isValidCourse() || beanStorageException
!= null}">
        <c:set var="errMsg" value="Invalid course details. Please
          try again"/>
      </c:when>
      <c:otherwise>
        <c:redirect url="listCourse.jsp"/>
      </c:otherwise>
    </c:choose>
  </c:if>

  <h2>Add Course:</h2>
  <c:if test="${errMsg != null}">
    <span style="color: red;">
      <c:out value="${errMsg}"></c:out>
```

```
    </span>
  </c:if>
  <form method="post">
    Name: <input type="text" name="name"> <br>
    Credits : <input type="text" name="credits"> <br>
    <button type="submit" name="submit">Add</button>
  </form>

</body>
</html>
```

Most of the code should be familiar, if you have read Chapter 2, *Creating a Simple JEE Web Application* (see the *Using JSTL* section). We have a form to add courses. At the top of the file, we check whether the post request is made; if so, store content of the form in courseBean (make sure that names of the form field are the same as the members defined in the bean). The new tag that we have used here is <c:catch>. It is like a *try-catch* block in Java. Any exception thrown from within the body of <c:catch> is assigned to the variable name declared in the var attribute. Here, we are not doing anything with beanStorageException; we are suppressing the exception. When an exception is thrown, the credits field of the Course bean will remain set to zero and it will be caught in the courseBean.isValidCourse method. If the course data is valid, then we redirect the request to the listCourse.jsp page using the JSTL <c:redirect> tag.

We need to add the isValidCourse method in the Course bean. Therefore, open the class in the editor and add the following method:

```
public boolean isValidCourse() {
  return name != null && credits != 0;
}
```

We also need to create listCourse.jsp. For now, just create a simple JSP with no JSTL/Java code and with only one header in the body tag:

```
<h2>Courses:</h2>
```

Right-click on addCourse.jsp in **Package Explorer** and select **Run As** | **Run on Server**. If you have configured Tomcat properly and added your project in Tomcat (as described in Chapter 2, *Creating a Simple JEE Web Application*), then you should see the JSP page running in the internal Eclipse browser. Test the page with both valid and invalid data (a wrong credit value; for example, a non-numeric value). If the data entered is valid, then you would be redirected to listCourse.jsp, or else the same page would be displayed with the error message.

Before we start writing JDBC code, let's learn some fundamental concepts of JDBC.

JDBC concepts

Before performing any operations in JDBC, we need to establish a connection to the database. Here are some of the important classes/interfaces in JDBC for executing SQL statements:

JDBC class/interface	Description
`java.sql.Connection`	Represents the connection between the application and the backend database. Must for performing any action on the database.
`java.sql.DriverManager`	Manages JDBC drivers used in the application. Call the `DriverManager.getConnection` static method to obtain the connection.
`java.sql.Statement`	Used for executing static SQL statements.
`java.sql.PreparedStatement`	Used for preparing parameterized SQL statements. SQL statements are pre-compiled and can be executed repeatedly with different parameters.
`Java.sqlCallableStatement`	Used for executing a stored procedure.
`java.sql.ResultSet`	Represents a row in the database table in the result returned after execution of an SQL query by `Statement` or `PreparedStatement`.

You can find all the interfaces for JDBC at 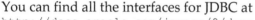 `http://docs.oracle.com/javase/8/docs/api/java/sql/package-frame.html`.

Many of these are interfaces, and implementations of these interfaces are provided by the JDBC drivers.

Creating database connections

Make sure that the JDBC driver for the database you want to connect to is downloaded and is in the classpath. In our project, we have already ensured this by adding a dependency in Maven. Maven downloads the driver and adds it to the class path of our web application.

It is always a good practice to make sure that the JDBC driver class is available when the application is running. If it is not, we can set a suitable error message and not perform any JDBC operations. The name of the MySQL JDBC driver class is `com.mysql.cj.jdbc.Driver`:

```
try {
    Class.forName("com.mysql.cj.jdbc.Driver");
}
catch (ClassNotFoundException e) {
    //log excetion
    //either throw application specific exception or return
    return;
}
```

Then, get the connection by calling the `DriverManager.getConnection` method:

```
try {
    Connection con =
    DriverManager.getConnection("jdbc:mysql://localhost:3306/schema_name?" +
        "user=your_user_name&password=your_password");
//perform DB operations and then close the connection
    con.close();
}
catch (SQLException e) {
    //handle exception
}
```

The argument to `DriverManager.getConnection` is called a connection URL. It is specific to the JDBC driver. So, check the documentation of the JDBC driver to understand how to create a connection URL. The URL format in the preceding code snippet is for MySQL. See `https://dev.mysql.com/doc/connector-j/8.0/en/connector-j-reference-configuration-properties.html`.

The connection URL contains the following details: hostname of the MySQL database server, port on which it is running (default is 3306), and the schema name (database name that you want to connect to). You can pass username and password to connect to the database as URL parameters.

Creating a connection is an expensive operation. Also, database servers allow a certain maximum number of connections to it, so connections should be created sparingly. It is advisable to cache database connections and reuse. However, make sure that you close the connection when you no longer need it, for example, in the `final` blocks of your code. Later, we will see how to create a pool of connections so that we create a limited number of connections, take them out of the pool when required, perform the required operations, and return them to the pool so that they can be reused.

Executing SQL statements

Use `Statement` for executing static SQL (having no parameters) and `PreparedStatement` for executing parameterized statements.

To avoid the risk of SQL injection, refer to `https://www.owasp.org/index.php/SQL_injection`.

To execute any `Statement`, you first need to create the statement using the `Connection` object. You can then perform any SQL operation, such as `create`, `update`, `delete`, and `select`. The `Select` statement (query) returns a `ResultSet` object. Iterate over the `ResultSet` object to get individual rows.

For example, the following code gets all rows from the `Course` table:

```
Statement stmt = null;
ResultSet rs = null;
try {
  stmt = con.createStatement();
  rs = stmt.executeQuery("select * from Course");

  List<Course> courses = new ArrayList<Course>();
  //Depending on the database that you connect to, you may have to
  //call rs.first() before calling rs.next(). In the case of a MySQL
  //database, it is not necessary to call rs.first()
  while (rs.next()) {
    Course course = new Course();
    course.setId(rs.getInt("id"));
    course.setName(rs.getString("name"));
    course.setCredits(rs.getInt("credits"));
    courses.add(course);
  }
}
catch (SQLException e) {
  //handle exception
  e.printStackTrace();
}
finally {
  try {
    if (rs != null)
    rs.close();
    if (stmt != null)
    stmt.close();
  }
```

```
    catch (SQLException e) {
      //handle exception
    }
  }
}
```

Things to note:

- Call `Connection.createStatement` `()` to create an instance of `Statement`.
- `Statement.executeQuery` returns `ResultSet`. If the SQL statement is not a query, for example `create`, `update`, and `delete` statements, then call `Statement.execute` (which returns `true` if the statement is executed successfully; or else, `false`) or call `Statement.executeUpdate` (which returns the number of rows affected or zero if none is affected).
- Pass the SQL statement to the `Statement.executeQuery` function. This can be any valid SQL string understood by the database.
- Iterate over `ResultSet` by calling the `next` method, until it returns `false`.
- Call different variations of `get` methods (depending on the data type of the column) to obtain values of columns in the current row that the `ResultSet` is pointing to. You can either pass positional index of the column in SQL that you passed to `executeQuery` or column names as used in the database table or alias specified in the SQL statement. For example, we would use the following code if we had specified column names in the SQL:

  ```
  rs = stmt.executeQuery("select id, name, credits as courseCredit
  from Course");
  ```

  Then, we could retrieve column values as follows:

  ```
  course.setId(rs.getInt(1));
  course.setName(rs.getString(2));
  course.setCredits(rs.getInt("courseCredit"));
  ```

- Make sure you close `ResultSet` and `Statement`.

Instead of getting all courses, if you want to get a specific course, you would want to use `PreparedStatement`:

```
PreparedStatement stmt = null;
int courseId = 10;
ResultSet rs = null;
try {
  stmt = con.prepareStatement("select * from Course where id =
   ?");
  stmt.setInt(1, courseId);
```

```
      rs = stmt.executeQuery();

      Course course = null;
      if (rs.next()) {
        course = new Course();
        course.setId(rs.getInt("id"));
        course.setName(rs.getString("name"));
        course.setCredits(rs.getInt("credits"));
      }
    }
    catch (SQLException e) {
      //handle exception
      e.printStackTrace();
    }
    finally {
      try {
        if (rs != null)
        rs.close();
        if (stmt != null
        stmt.close();
      }
    catch (SQLException e) {
        //handle exception
      }
    }
```

In this example, we are trying to get the course with ID 10. We first get an instance of `PreparedStatement` by calling `Connection.prepareStatement`. Note that you need to pass an SQL statement as an argument to this function. Parameters in the query are replaced by the ? placeholder. We then set the value of the parameter by calling `stmt.setInt`. The first argument is the position of the parameter (it starts from 1) and the second argument is the value. There are many variations of the `set` method for different data types.

Handling transactions

If you want to perform multiple changes to the database as a single unit, that is, either all changes should be done or none, then you need to start a transaction in JDBC. You start a transaction by calling `Connection. setAutoCommit(false)`. Once all operations are executed successfully, commit the changes to the database by calling `Connection.commit`. If for any reason you want to abort the transaction, call `Connection.rollback()`. Changes are not done in the database until you call `Connection.commit`.

Here is an example of inserting a bunch of courses into the database. Although in a real application, it may not make sense to abort a transaction when one of the courses is not inserted, here we assume that either all courses must be inserted into the database or none:

```
PreparedStatement stmt = con.prepareStatement("insert into Course (id,
name, credits) values (?,?,?)");

con.setAutoCommit(false);
try {
  for (Course course : courses) {
    stmt.setInt(1, course.getId());
    stmt.setString(2, course.getName());
    stmt.setInt(3, course.getCredits());
    stmt.execute();
  }
  //commit the transaction now
  con.commit();
}
catch (SQLException e) {
  //rollback commit
  con.rollback();
}
```

There is more to learn about transactions than explained here. Refer to Oracle's JDBC tutorial at `http://docs.oracle.com/javase/tutorial/jdbc/basics/transactions.html`.

Using a JDBC database connection pool

As mentioned before, a JDBC database connection is an expensive operation and connection objects should be reused. Connection pools are used for this purpose. Most web containers provide their own implementation of a connection pool along with ways to configure it using JNDI. Tomcat also lets you configure a connection pool using JNDI. The advantage of configuring a connection pool using JNDI is that the database configuration parameters, such as hostname and port, remain outside the source code and can be easily modified. See `http://tomcat.apache.org/tomcat-8.0-doc/jdbc-pool.html`.

However, a Tomcat connection pool can also be used without JNDI, as described in the preceding link. In this example, we will use a connection pool without JNDI. The advantage is that you can use the connection pool implementation provided by a third party; your application then becomes easily portable to other web containers. With JNDI, you can also port your application, as long as you create the JNDI context and resources in the web container that you are switching to.

We will add the dependency of the Tomcat connection pool library to Maven's `pom.xml`. Open the `pom.xml` file and add the following dependencies (see `Chapter 2`, *Creating a Simple JEE Web Application*, to know how to add dependencies to Maven):

```xml
<dependency>
  <groupId>org.apache.tomcat</groupId>
  <artifactId>tomcat-jdbc</artifactId>
  <version>9.0.6</version>
</dependency>
```

Note that you can use any other implementation of the JDBC connection pool. One such connection pool library is HikariCP (`https://github.com/brettwooldridge/HikariCP`).

We also want to move the database properties out of the code. Therefore, create a file called `db.properties` in `src/main/resources`. Maven puts all files in this folder in the classpath of the application. Add the following properties in `db.properties`:

```
db_host=localhost
db_port=3306
db_name=course_management
db_user_name=your_user_name
db_password=your_password
db_driver_class_name=com.mysql.cj.jdbc.Driver
```

We will create a singleton class to create JDBC connections using the Tomcat connection pool. Create a `packt.book.jee.eclipse.ch4.db.connection` package and create a `DatabaseConnectionFactory` class in it:

```java
package packt.book.jee.eclipse.ch4.db.connection;

// skipping imports to save space here

/**
 * Singleton Factory class to create JDBC database connections
 *
 */
public class DatabaseConnectionFactory {
  //singleton instance
```

```
private static DatabaseConnectionFactory conFactory = new
 DatabaseConnectionFactory();

private DataSource dataSource = null;

//Make the construction private
private DatabaseConnectionFactory() {}

/**
 * Must be called before any other method in this class.
 * Initializes the data source and saves it in an instance
 variable
 *
 * @throws IOException
 */
public synchronized void init() throws IOException {
  //Check if init was already called
if (dataSource != null)
  return;

  //load db.properties file first
  InputStream inStream =
this.getClass().getClassLoader().getResourceAsStream("db.properties");
  Properties dbProperties = new Properties();
  dbProperties.load(inStream);
  inStream.close();

  //create Tomcat specific pool properties
  PoolProperties p = new PoolProperties();
p.setUrl("jdbc:mysql://" + dbProperties.getProperty("db_host") +
":" + dbProperties.getProperty("db_port") + "/" +
dbProperties.getProperty("db_name"));

p.setDriverClassName(dbProperties.getProperty("db_driver_class_name"));
  p.setUsername(dbProperties.getProperty("db_user_name"));
  p.setPassword(dbProperties.getProperty("db_password"));
  p.setMaxActive(10);

  dataSource = new DataSource();
  dataSource.setPoolProperties(p);
}

//Provides access to singleton instance
public static DatabaseConnectionFactory getConnectionFactory() {
  return conFactory;
}

//returns database connection object
```

```
  public Connection getConnection () throws SQLException {
    if (dataSource == null)
      throw new SQLException("Error initializing datasource");
    return dataSource.getConnection();
  }
}
```

We must call the `init` method of `DatabaseConnectionFactory` before getting connections from it. We will create a servlet and load it on startup. Then, we will call `DatabaseConnectionFactory.init` from the `init` method of the servlet.

Create package `packt.book.jee.eclipse.ch4.servlet` and then create an `InitServlet` class in it:

```
package packt.book.jee.eclipse.ch4.servlet;
import java.io.IOException;
import javax.servlet.ServletConfig;
import javax.servlet.ServletException;
import javax.servlet.annotation.WebServlet;
import javax.servlet.http.HttpServlet;

import packt.book.jee.eclipse.ch4.db.connection.DatabaseConnectionFactory;

@WebServlet(value="/initServlet", loadOnStartup=1)
public class InitServlet extends HttpServlet {
  private static final long serialVersionUID = 1L;

  public InitServlet() {
    super();
  }

  public void init(ServletConfig config) throws ServletException {
    try {
      DatabaseConnectionFactory.getConnectionFactory().init();
    }
    catch (IOException e) {
      config.getServletContext().log(e.getLocalizedMessage(),e);
    }
  }
}
```

Note that we have used the `@WebServlet` annotation to mark this class as a servlet and the `loadOnStartup` attribute is set to 1, to tell the web container to load this servlet on startup.

Now we can call the following statement to get a `Connection` object from anywhere in the application:

```
Connection con =
DatabaseConnectionFactory.getConnectionFactory().getConnection();
```

If there are no more connections available in the pool, then the `getConnection` method throws an exception (in particular, in the case of the `Tomcat` datasource, it throws `PoolExhaustedException`). When you close the connection that was obtained from the connection pool, the connection is returned to the pool for reuse.

Saving courses in database tables using JDBC

Now that we have figured out how to use the JDBC connection pool and get a connection from it, let's write the code to save a course to the database.

We will create **Course Data Access Object** (**CourseDAO**), which will have functions required to directly interact with the database. We are thus separating the code to access the database from the UI and business code.

Create `package packt.book.jee.eclipse.ch4.dao`. Create a class called `CourseDAO` in it:

```
package packt.book.jee.eclipse.ch4.dao;

import java.sql.Connection;
import java.sql.PreparedStatement;
import java.sql.ResultSet;
import java.sql.SQLException;
import java.sql.Statement;

import packt.book.jee.eclipse.ch4.bean.Course;
import packt.book.jee.eclipse.ch4.db.connection.DatabaseConnectionFactory;

public class CourseDAO {

  public static void addCourse (Course course) throws SQLException
    {
      //get connection from connection pool
      Connection con =
```

```
DatabaseConnectionFactory.getConnectionFactory().getConnection();
    try {
        final String sql = "insert into Course (name, credits)
        values (?,?)";        //create the prepared statement with an option
to get auto-
        generated keys         PreparedStatement stmt =
con.prepareStatement(sql,
        Statement.RETURN_GENERATED_KEYS);
        //set parameters
        stmt.setString(1, course.getName());
        stmt.setInt(2, course.getCredits());

        stmt.execute();

        //Get auto-generated keys
        ResultSet rs = stmt.getGeneratedKeys();

        if (rs.next())
          course.setId(rs.getInt(1));

        rs.close();
        stmt.close();
    }
    finally {
        con.close();
    }
  }
}
```

We have already seen how to insert a record using JDBC. The only new thing in the preceding code is to get the autogenerated ID. Recall that the id column in the Course table is autogenerated. This is the reason that we did not specify it in the insert SQL:

```
String sql = "insert into Course (name, credits) values (?,?)";
```

When we prepare a statement, we are telling the driver to get the autogenerated ID. After the row is inserted into the table, we get the autogenerated ID by calling the following:

```
ResultSet rs = stmt.getGeneratedKeys();
```

We have already created addCourse.jsp. Somehow addCourse.jsp needs to send the form data to CourseDAO in order to save the data in the database. addCourse.jsp already has access to the Course bean and saves the form data in it. So, it makes sense for the Course bean to interface between addCourse.jsp and CourseDAO. Let's modify the Course bean to add an instance of CourseDAO as a member variable and then create a function to add a course (instance of CourseDAO) to the database:

```
public class Course {
. . . .

  private CourseDAO courseDAO = new CourseDAO();

. . .

  public void addCourse() throws SQLException {
    courseDAO.addCourse(this);
  }
}
```

We will then modify addCourse.jsp to call the addCourse method of the Course bean. We will have to add this code after the form is submitted and the data is validated:

```
<c:catch var="addCourseException">
  ${courseBean.addCourse()}
</c:catch>
<c:choose>
  <c:when test="${addCourseException != null}">
    <c:set var="errMsg" value="${addCourseException.message}"/>
  </c:when>
  <c:otherwise>
    <c:redirect url="listCourse.jsp"/>
  </c:otherwise>
</c:choose>
```

One thing to note in the preceding code is the following statement:

```
${courseBean.addCourse()}
```

You can insert **Expression Language** (**EL**) in JSP as discussed previously. This method does not return anything (it is a void method). Therefore, we didn't use the <c:set> tag. Furthermore, note that the call is made within the <c:catch> tag. If any SQLException is thrown from the method, then it will be assigned to the addCourseException variable. We then check whether addCourseException is set in the <c:when> tag. If the value is not null, then it means that the exception was thrown. We set the error message, which is later displayed on the same page. If no error is thrown, then the request is redirected to listCourse.jsp. Here is the complete code of addCourse.jsp:

```jsp
<%@ page language="java" contentType="text/html; charset=UTF-8"
    pageEncoding="UTF-8"%>
<%@ taglib prefix="c" uri="http://java.sun.com/jsp/jstl/core" %>

<!DOCTYPE html PUBLIC "-//W3C//DTD HTML 4.01 Transitional//EN"
 "http://www.w3.org/TR/html4/loose.dtd">
<html>
<head>
<meta http-equiv="Content-Type" content="text/html; charset=UTF-8">
<title>Insert title here</title>
</head>
<body>
  <c:set var="errMsg" value="${null}"/>
  <c:set var="displayForm" value="${true}"/>
  <c:if
 test="${"POST".equalsIgnoreCase(pageContext.request.method)
&& pageContext.request.getParameter("submit") != null}">
  <jsp:useBean id="courseBean"
   class="packt.book.jee.eclipse.ch4.bean.Course">
    <c:catch var="beanStorageException">
    <jsp:setProperty name="courseBean" property="*" />
    </c:catch>
    </jsp:useBean>
    <c:choose>
      <c:when test="${!courseBean.isValidCourse() ||
      beanStorageException != null}">         <c:set var="errMsg"
value="Invalid course details. Please
        try again"/>
      </c:when>
      <c:otherwise>
        <c:catch var="addCourseException">
        ${courseBean.addCourse()}
        </c:catch>
        <c:choose>
          <c:when test="${addCourseException != null}">
          <c:set var="errMsg"
           value="${addCourseException.message}"/>
```

```
      </c:when>
      <c:otherwise>
        <c:redirect url="listCourse.jsp"/>
      </c:otherwise>
    </c:choose>
  </c:otherwise>
</c:choose>
</c:if>

<h2>Add Course:</h2>
<c:if test="${errMsg != null}">
  <span style="color: red;">
    <c:out value="${errMsg}"></c:out>
  </span>
</c:if>
<form method="post">
  Name: <input type="text" name="name"> <br>
  Credits : <input type="text" name="credits"> <br>
  <button type="submit" name="submit">Add</button>
</form>

</body>
</html>
```

Run the page, either in Eclipse or outside (see Chapter 2, *Creating a Simple JEE Web Application,* to know how to run JSP in Eclipse and view it in Eclipse's internal browser) and add a couple of courses.

Getting courses from database tables using JDBC

We will now modify listCourses.jsp to display the courses that we have added using addCourse.jsp. However, we first need to add a method in CourseDAO to get all courses from the database.

Note that the `Course` table has a one-to-many relationship with `Teacher`. It stores the teacher ID in it. Further, the teacher ID is not a required field, so a course can exist in the `Course` table with null `teacher_id`. To get all the details of a course, we need to get the teacher for the course too. However, we cannot create a simple join in an SQL query to get the details of a course and of the teacher for each course, because a teacher may not have been set for the course. In such cases, we use the *left outer join*, which returns all records from the table on the left-hand side of the join, but only matching records from the table on the right-hand side of the join. Here is the SQL statement to get all courses and teachers for each course:

```
select course.id as courseId, course.name as courseName,
   course.credits as credits, Teacher.id as teacherId,
   Teacher.first_name as firstName, Teacher.last_name as lastName,
   Teacher.designation designation
from Course left outer join Teacher on
course.Teacher_id = Teacher.id
order by course.name
```

We will use the preceding query in `CourseDAO` to get all courses. Open the `CourseDAO` class and add the following method:

```
public List<Course> getCourses () throws SQLException {
   //get connection from connection pool
   Connection con =
 DatabaseConnectionFactory.getConnectionFactory().getConnection();

   List<Course> courses = new ArrayList<Course>();
   Statement stmt = null;
   ResultSet rs = null;
   try {
      stmt = con.createStatement();

      //create SQL statement using left outer join
      StringBuilder sb = new StringBuilder("select course.id as
         courseId, course.name as courseName,")       .append("course.credits as
credits, Teacher.id as teacherId,
         Teacher.first_name as firstName, ")       .append("Teacher.last_name
as lastName, Teacher.designation
         designation ")
         .append("from Course left outer join Teacher on ")
         .append("course.Teacher_id = Teacher.id ")
         .append("order by course.name");

//execute the query
      rs = stmt.executeQuery(sb.toString());
```

```
//iterate over result set and create Course objects
//add them to course list
    while (rs.next()) {
        Course course = new Course();
        course.setId(rs.getInt("courseId"));
        course.setName(rs.getString("courseName"));
        course.setCredits(rs.getInt("credits"));
        courses.add(course);

        int teacherId = rs.getInt("teacherId");
//check whether teacher id was null in the table
        if (rs.wasNull()) //no teacher set for this course.
            continue;
        Teacher teacher = new Teacher();
        teacher.setId(teacherId);
        teacher.setFirstName(rs.getString("firstName"));
        teacher.setLastName(rs.getString("lastName"));
        teacher.setDesignation(rs.getString("designation"));
        course.setTeacher(teacher);
    }

    return courses;
   }
finally {
   try {if (rs != null) rs.close();} catch (SQLException e) {}
   try {if (stmt != null) stmt.close();} catch (SQLException e) {}
   try {con.close();} catch (SQLException e) {}
   }
}
```

We have used `Statement` to execute the query because it is a static query. We have used `StringBuilder` to build the SQL statement because it is a relatively large query (compared to those that we have written so far) and we would like to avoid concatenation of string objects, because Strings are immutable. After executing the query, we iterate over the resultset and create a `Course` object and add it to the list of courses, which is returned at the end.

One interesting thing here is the use of `ResultSet.wasNull`. We want to check whether the `teacher_id` field in the `Course` table for that particular row was null. Therefore, immediately after calling `rs.getInt("teacherId")`, we check whether the value fetched by `ResultSet` was null by calling `rs.wasNull`. If `teacher_id` was null, then the teacher was not set for that course, so we continue the loop, skipping the code to create a `Teacher` object.

In the final block, we catch an exception when closing ResultSet, Statement, and Connection and ignore it.

Let's now add a method in the Course bean to fetch courses by calling the getCourses method of CourseDAO. Open the Course bean and add the following method:

```
public List<Course> getCourses() throws SQLException {
  return courseDAO.getCourses();
}
```

We are now ready to modify listCourse.jsp to display courses. Open the JSP and replace the existing code with the following:

```
<%@ page language="java" contentType="text/html; charset=UTF-8"
    pageEncoding="UTF-8"%>
<%@ taglib prefix="c" uri="http://java.sun.com/jsp/jstl/core" %>

<!DOCTYPE html PUBLIC "-//W3C//DTD HTML 4.01 Transitional//EN"
"http://www.w3.org/TR/html4/loose.dtd">
<html>
<head>
<meta http-equiv="Content-Type" content="text/html; charset=UTF-8">
<title>Courses</title>
</head>
<body>
  <c:catch var="err">
    <jsp:useBean id="courseBean"
     class="packt.book.jee.eclipse.ch4.bean.Course"/>
    <c:set var="courses" value="${courseBean.getCourses()}"/>
  </c:catch>
  <c:choose>
    <c:when test="${err != null}">
      <c:set var="errMsg" value="${err.message}"/>
    </c:when>
    <c:otherwise>
    </c:otherwise>
  </c:choose>
  <h2>Courses:</h2>
  <c:if test="${errMsg != null}">
    <span style="color: red;">
      <c:out value="${errMsg}"></c:out>
    </span>
  </c:if>
  <table>
    <tr>
      <th>Id</th>
      <th>Name</th>
```

```
      <th>Credits</th>
      <th>Teacher</th>
   </tr>
   <c:forEach items="${courses}" var="course">
     <tr>
       <td>${course.id}</td>
       <td>${course.name}</td>
       <td>${course.credits}</td>
       <c:choose>
         <c:when test="${course.teacher != null}">
           <td>${course.teacher.firstName}</td>
         </c:when>
         <c:otherwise>
           <td></td>
         </c:otherwise>
       </c:choose>
     </tr>
   </c:forEach>
  </table>
 </body>
 </html>
```

Most of the code should be easy to understand because we have used similar code in previous examples. At the beginning of the script, we create a `Course` bean and get all the courses and assign the course list to a variable called `courses`:

```
<c:catch var="err">
    <jsp:useBean id="courseBean"
     class="packt.book.jee.eclipse.ch4.bean.Course"/>
    <c:set var="courses" value="${courseBean.getCourses()}"/>
</c:catch>
```

To display courses, we create a HTML table and set its headers. A new thing in the preceding code is the use of the `<c:forEach>` JSTL tag to iterate over the list. The `forEach` tag takes the following two attributes:

- List of objects
- Variable name of a single item when iterating over the list

In the preceding case, the list of objects is provided by the `courses` variable that we set at the beginning of the script and we identify a single item in the list with the variable name `course`. We then display the course details and teacher for the course, if any.

Writing code to add `Teacher` and `Student` and list them is left to readers as an exercise. The code would be very similar to that for `course`, but with different table and class names.

Completing add course functionality

We still haven't completed the functionality for adding a new course; we need to provide an option to assign a teacher to a course when adding a new course. Assuming that you have implemented `TeacherDAO` and created `addTeacher` and `getTeachers` methods in the `Teacher` bean, we can now complete the add course functionality.

First, modify `addCourse` in `CourseADO` to save the teacher ID for each course, if it is not zero. The SQL statement to insert course changes is as follows:

```
String sql = "insert into Course (name, credits, Teacher_id) values
(?,?,?)";
```

We have added the `Teacher_id` column and the corresponding parameter holder `?`. We will set `Teacher_id` to null if it is zero; or else the actual value:

```
if (course.getTeacherId() == 0)
   stmt.setNull(3, Types.INTEGER);
else
   stmt.setInt(3, course.getTeacherId());
```

We will then modify the `Course` bean to save the teacher ID that will be passed along with the `POST` request from the HTML form:

```
public class Course {

  private int teacherId;
  public int getTeacherId() {
    return teacherId;
}

  public void setTeacherId(int teacherId) {
    this.teacherId = teacherId;
  }
}
```

Next, we will modify addCourse.jsp to display the drop-down list of teachers when adding a new course. We first need to get the list of teachers. Therefore, we will create a Teacher bean and call the getTeachers method on it. We will do this just before the **Add Course** header:

```
<jsp:useBean id="teacherBean"
class="packt.book.jee.eclipse.ch4.bean.Teacher"/>
<c:catch var="teacherBeanErr">
<c:set var="teachers" value="${teacherBean.getTeachers()}"/>
</c:catch>
<c:if test="${teacherBeanErr != null}">
  <c:set var="errMsg" value="${err.message}"/>
</c:if>
```

Finally, we will display the HTML drop-down list in the form and populate it with teacher names:

```
Teacher :
<select name="teacherId">
<c:forEach items="${teachers}" var="teacher">
<option value="${teacher.id}">${teacher.firstName}
</option>
</c:forEach>
</select>
```

Download the accompanying code for this chapter to see the complete source code of CourseDAO and addCourse.jsp.

With this, we conclude our discussion on using JDBC to create a web application that uses a database. With the examples that you have seen so far, you should be in a good position to complete the remaining application by adding functionality to modify and delete records in the database. The update and delete SQL statements can be executed by Statement or PreparedStatement, just as insert statements are executed using these two classes.

Using Eclipse Data Source Explorer

It is sometimes useful if you can see data in database tables from your IDE and can modify it. This is possible in Eclipse JEE using **Data Source Explorer**. This view is displayed in a tab at the lower pane, just below editors, in the **Java EE** perspective. If you do not see the view, or have closed the view, you can reopen it by selecting the **Window | Show View | Other** menu. Type data source in the filter textbox and you should see the view name under the **Data Management** group. Open the view:

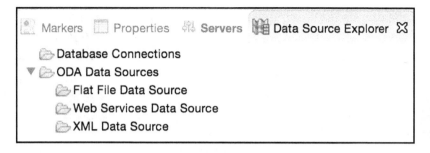

Figure 4.12: Data Source Explorer

Right-click on the **Database Connections** node and select **New**. From the list, select **MySQL**:

Figure 4.13: Select the MySQL Connection Profile

Click **Next**. If the drivers list is empty, you haven't configured the driver yet. Click on the icon next to the drop-down list for drivers to open the configuration page:

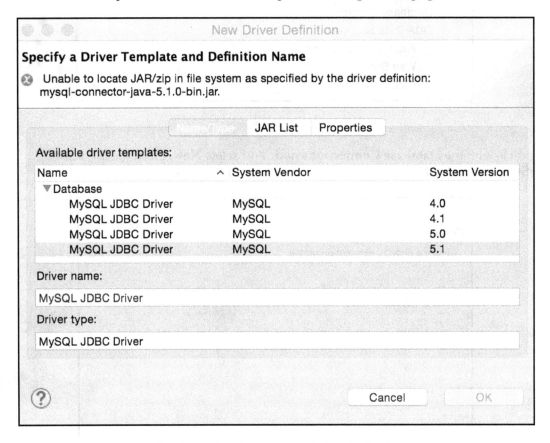

Figure 4.14: Selecting Database Driver in JDBC New Driver Definition page

Select the appropriate MySQL version and click on the **JAR List** tab:

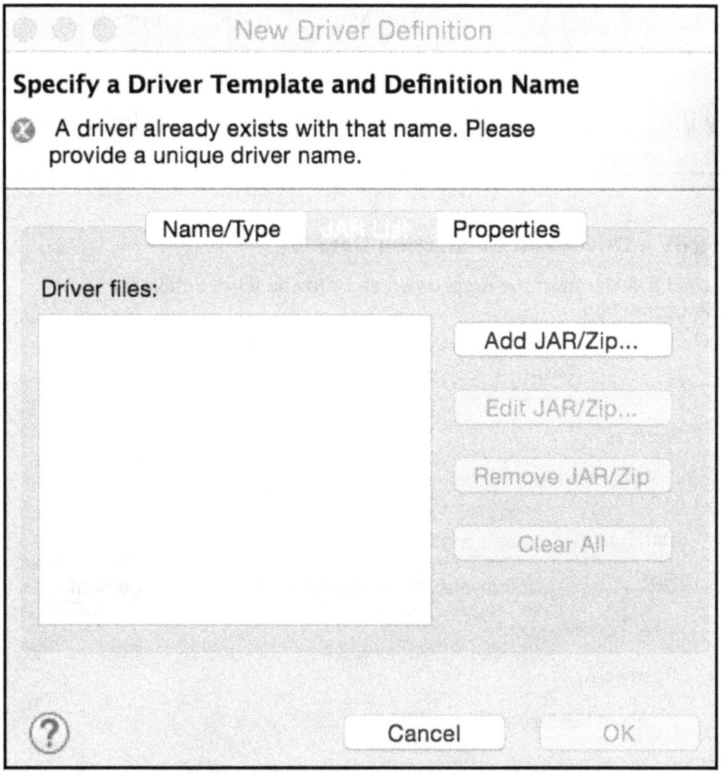

Figure 4.15: Adding Driver Files in JDBC New Driver Definition page

Remove any files from the **Driver files** list. Click on the **Add JAR/Zip...** button. This opens the **File Open** dialog. Select the JAR file for the MySQL driver version that you have selected. Since Maven has already downloaded the JAR file for you, you can select it from the local Maven repository. On OS X and Linux, the path is `~/.m2/repository/mysql/mysql-connector-java/<version_num>/mysql_connector_java_version_num/mysql-connector-java-version_num.jar` (`version_num` is a placeholder for the actual version number in the path). On Windows, you can find the Maven repository at `C:\Users\{your-username}\.m2` and then, the relative path for the MySQL driver is the same as that in OS X.

If you have trouble finding the JAR in the local Maven repository, you can download the JAR file (for the MySQL JDBC driver) from `http://dev.mysql.com/downloads/connector/j/`.

Once you specify the correct driver JAR file, you need to set the following properties:

Figure 4.16: Setting JDBC driver properties

Click **Next** and then **Finish**. A new database connection will be added in **Data Source Explorer**. You can now browse the database schema and tables:

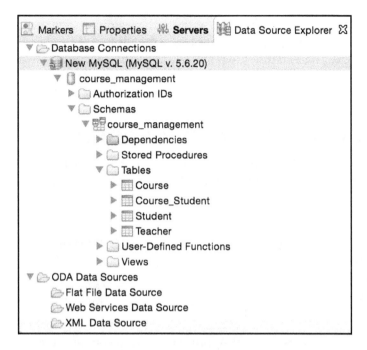

Figure 4.17: Browsing tables in Data Source Explorer

Right-click on any table to see the menu options available for different actions:

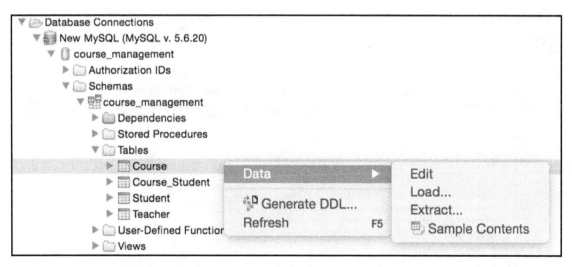

Figure 4.18: Table menu options in Data Source Explorer

Select the **Edit** menu to open a page in the editor where you can see the existing records in the table. You can also modify or add new data in the same page. Select the **Load** option to load data from an external file into the table. Select the **Extract** option to export data from the table.

Creating database applications using JPA

In the previous section, we learned how to create the *Course Management* application using JDBC and JSTL. In this section, we will build the same application using JPA and JSF. We have learned how to create a web application using JSF in Chapter 2, *Creating a Simple JEE Web Application*. We will use much of that knowledge in this section.

As mentioned at the beginning of this chapter, JPA is an ORM framework, which is now part of the JEE specification. At the time of writing, it is in version 2.2. We will learn a lot about JPA as we develop our application.

Create the Maven project called CourseManagementJPA with group ID packt.book.jee_eclipse and artifact ID CourseManagementJPA. Eclipse JEE has great tools for creating applications using JPA, but you need to convert your project to a JPA project. We will see how to do this later in this section.

Creating user interfaces for adding courses using JSF

Before we write any data access code using JPA, let's first create the user interface using JSF. As we have learned in Chapter 2, *Creating a Simple JEE Web Application*, we need to add Maven dependencies for JSF. Add the following dependencies in pom.xml:

```
<dependencies>
  <dependency>
    <groupId>javax.servlet</groupId>
    <artifactId>javax.servlet-api</artifactId>
    <version>3.1.0</version>
    <scope>provided</scope>
  </dependency>
  <dependency>
    <groupId>com.sun.faces</groupId>
    <artifactId>jsf-api</artifactId>
    <version>2.2.16</version>
  </dependency>
```

```
<dependency>
  <groupId>com.sun.faces</groupId>
  <artifactId>jsf-impl</artifactId>
  <version>2.2.16</version>
</dependency>
</dependencies>
```

When you run the application later, if Tomcat throws an exception for not finding `javax.faces.webapp.FacesServlet` then you may have to download `jsf-api-2.2.16.jar` (http://central.maven.org/maven2/com/sun/faces/jsf-impl/2.2.16/jsf-impl-2.2.16.jar), and `jsf-impl-2.2.16.jar` (http://central.maven.org/maven2/com/sun/faces/jsf-impl/2.2.16/jsf-impl-2.2.16.jar), and copy them to the `<tomcat-install-folder>/lib` folder. Set scopes for these two libraries as provided: `<scope>provided</scope>` in `pom.xml`. Then clean the project (**Run As** | **Maven Clean**) and install it again (**Run As** | **Maven Install**).

We need to add `web.xml`, add a declaration for the JSF servlet in it, and add the servlet mapping. Eclipse provides you a very easy way to add `web.xml` (which should be in the `WEB-INF` folder). Right-click on the project and select the **Java EE Tools** | **Generate Deployment Descriptor Stub** menu. This creates the `WEB-INF` folder under `src/main/webapp` and creates `web.xml` in the `WEB-INF` folder with the default content. Now, add the following servlet and mapping:

```
<servlet>
  <servlet-name>JSFServlet</servlet-name>
  <servlet-class>javax.faces.webapp.FacesServlet</servlet-class>
  <load-on-startup>1</load-on-startup>
</servlet>
<servlet-mapping>
  <servlet-name>JSFServlet</servlet-name>
  <url-pattern>*.xhtml</url-pattern>
</servlet-mapping>
```

Let's now create JavaBeans for `Course`, `Teacher`, `Student`, and `Person`, just as we created them in the previous example for JDBC. Create a `packt.book.jee.eclipse.ch4.jpa.bean` package and create the following JavaBeans.

Here is the source code of the `Course` bean (in `Course.java`):

```
package packt.book.jee.eclipse.ch4.jpa.bean;

import java.io.Serializable;
import javax.faces.bean.ManagedBean;
import javax.faces.bean.RequestScoped;

@ManagedBean (name="course")
@RequestScoped
public class Course implements Serializable {
  private static final long serialVersionUID = 1L;

  private int id;
  private String name;
  private int credits;
  private Teacher teacher;

  public int getId() {
    return id;
  }
  public void setId(int id) {
    this.id = id;
  }
  public String getName() {
    return name;
  }
  public void setName(String name) {
    this.name = name;
  }
  public int getCredits() {
    return credits;
  }
  public void setCredits(int credits) {
    this.credits = credits;
  }
  public boolean isValidCourse() {
    return name != null && credits != 0;
  }
  public Teacher getTeacher() {
    return teacher;
  }
  public void setTeacher(Teacher teacher) {
    this.teacher = teacher;
  }
}
```

Here is the source code of the `Person` bean (in `Person.java`):

```java
package packt.book.jee.eclipse.ch4.jpa.bean;

import java.io.Serializable;

public class Person implements Serializable{
  private static final long serialVersionUID = 1L;

  private int id;
  private String firstName;
  private String lastName;

  public int getId() {
    return id;
  }
  public void setId(int id) {
    this.id = id;
  }
  public String getFirstName() {
    return firstName;
  }
  public void setFirstName(String firstName) {
    this.firstName = firstName;
  }
  public String getLastName() {
    return lastName;
  }
  public void setLastName(String lastName) {
    this.lastName = lastName;
  }
}
```

Here is the source code of the `Student` bean (in `Student.java`):

```java
package packt.book.jee.eclipse.ch4.jpa.bean;

import javax.faces.bean.ManagedBean;
import javax.faces.bean.RequestScoped;
import java.util.Date;


@ManagedBean (name="student")
@RequestScoped
public class Student extends Person {
  private static final long serialVersionUID = 1L;

  private Date enrolledsince;
```

```
public Date getEnrolledsince() {
    return enrolledsince;
}

public void setEnrolledsince(Date enrolledsince) {
    this.enrolledsince = enrolledsince;
}
}
```

And, finally, here is the source code of the `Teacher` bean (in `Teacher.java`):

```
package packt.book.jee.eclipse.ch4.jpa.bean;

import javax.faces.bean.ManagedBean;
import javax.faces.bean.RequestScoped;

@ManagedBean (name="teacher")
@RequestScoped
public class Teacher extends Person {
    private static final long serialVersionUID = 1L;

    private String designation;

    public String getDesignation() {
        return designation;
    }

    public void setDesignation(String designation) {
        this.designation = designation;
    }
    public boolean isValidTeacher() {
        return getFirstName() != null;
    }
}
```

 All are JSF managed beans in `RequestScope`. Refer to the JSF discussion in `Chapter 2`, *Creating a Simple JEE Web Application*, for more about managed beans and scopes.

These beans are now ready to use in JSF pages. Create a JSF page and name it `addCourse.xhtml` and add the following content:

```
<html xmlns="http://www.w3.org/1999/xhtml"
    xmlns:f="http://java.sun.com/jsf/core"
    xmlns:h="http://java.sun.com/jsf/html">
```

```
<h2>Add Course:</h2>
<h:form>
  <h:outputLabel value="Name:" for="name"/>
    <h:inputText value="#{course.name}" id="name"/> <br/>
  <h:outputLabel value="Credits:" for="credits"/>
    <h:inputText value="#{course.credits}" id="credits"/>
  <br/>
  <h:commandButton value="Add" action="
   #{courseServiceBean.addCourse} "/>
</h:form>

</html>
```

The page uses JSF tags and managed beans to get and set values. Notice the value of the `action` attribute of the `h:commandButton` tag—it is the `courseServiceBean.addCourse` method, which will be called when the **Add** button is clicked. In the application that we created using JDBC, we wrote code to interact with DAOs in the JavaBeans. For example, the `Course` bean had the `addCourse` method. However, in the JPA project we will handle it differently. We will create service bean classes (they are also managed beans, just like `Course`) to interact with the data access objects and have the `Course` bean contain only the values set by the user.

Create a package named `packt.book.jee.eclipse.ch4.jpa.service_bean`. Create the class named `CourseServiceBean` in this package with the following code:

```
package packt.book.jee.eclipse.ch4.jpa.service_bean;

import javax.faces.bean.ManagedBean;
import javax.faces.bean.ManagedProperty;
import javax.faces.bean.RequestScoped;

import packt.book.jee.eclipse.ch4.jpa.bean.Course;

@ManagedBean(name="courseServiceBean")
@RequestScoped
public class CourseServiceBean {
  @ManagedProperty(value="#{course}")
  private Course course;

  private String errMsg= null;

  public Course getCourse() {
    return course;
  }

  public void setCourse(Course course) {
```

```
      this.course = course;
   }

   public String getErrMsg() {
     return errMsg;
   }

   public void setErrMsg(String errMsg) {
     this.errMsg = errMsg;
   }

   public String addCourse() {
     return "listCourse";
   }
 }
}
```

CourseServiceBean is a managed bean and it contains the errMsg field (to store any error message during the processing of requests), the addCourse method, and the course field (which is annotated with @ManagedProperty).

The ManagedProperty annotation tells the JSF implementation to inject another bean (specified as the value attribute) in the current bean. Here, we expect CourseServiceBean to have access to the course bean at runtime, without instantiating it. This is part of the **dependency injection (DI)** framework supported by Java EE. We will learn more about the DI framework in Java EE in later chapters. The addCourse function doesn't do much at this point, it just returns the "listCourse" string. If you want to execute addCourse.xhtml at this point, create a listCourse.xml file with some placeholder content and test addCourse.xhtml. We will add more content to listCourse.xml later in this section.

JPA concepts

JPA is an ORM framework in JEE. It provides a set of APIs that the JPA implementation providers are expected to implement. There are many JPA providers, such as **EclipseLink** (https://eclipse.org/eclipselink/), **Hibernate JPA** (http://hibernate.org/orm/), and **OpenJPA** (http://openjpa.apache.org/). Before we start writing the persistence code using JPA, it is important to understand basic concepts of JPA.

Entity

Entity represents a single object instance that is typically related to one table. Any **Plain Old Java Object** (**POJO**) can be converted to an entity by annotating the class with `@Entity`. Members of the class are mapped to columns of a table in the database. Entity classes are simple Java classes, so they can extend or include other Java classes or even another JPA entity. We will see an example of this in our application. You can also specify validation rules for members of the Entity class; for example, you can mark a member as not null using the `@NotNull` annotation. These annotations are provided by Java EE Bean Validation APIs. See `https://javaee.github.io/tutorial/bean-validation002.html#GIRCZ` for a list of validation annotations.

EntityManager

`EntityManager` provides the persistence context in which the entities exist. The persistence context also allows you to manage transactions. Using `EntityManager` APIs, you can perform query and write operations on entities. The entity manager can be web-container-managed (in which case an instance of `EntityManager` is injected by the container), or application-managed. In this chapter, we are going to look at application-managed entity managers. We will visit container-managed entity managers in Chapter 7, *Creating JEE Applications with EJB*, when we learn about EJBs. The persistence unit of the entity manager defines the database connectivity information and groups entities that become part of the persistence unit. It is defined in the configuration file called `persistence.xml` and is expected to be in `META-INF` in the class path.

`EntityManager` has its own persistence context, which is a cache of entities. Updates to entities are first done in the cache and then pushed to the database when a transaction is committed or when the data is explicitly pushed to the database.

When an application is managing `EntityManager`, it is advisable to have only one instance of `EntityManager` for a persistence unit.

EntityManagerFactory

`EntityManagerFactory` creates `EntityManager`. `EntityManagerFactory` itself is obtained by calling a static `Persistence.createEntityManagerFactory` method. An argument to this function is a `persistence-unit` name that you have specified in `persistence.xml`.

Creating a JPA application

The following are the typical steps in creating a JPA application:

1. Create a database schema (tables and relationships). Optionally, you can create tables and relationships from JPA entities. We will see an example of this. However, it should be mentioned here that although creating tables from JPA entities is fine for development, it is not recommended in the production environment; doing so may result in a non-optimized database model.

2. Create `persistence.xml` and specify the database configurations.

3. Create entities and relationships.

4. Get an instance of `EntityManagerFactory` by calling `Persistence.createEntityManagerFactory`.

5. Create an instance of `EntityManager` from `EntityManagerFactory`.

6. Start a transaction on `EntityManager` if you are performing `insert` or `update` operations on the entity.

7. Perform operations on the entity.

8. Commit the transaction.

Here is an example snippet:

```
EntityManagerFactory factory =
 Persistance.Persistence.createEntityManagerFactory("course_management")
EntityManager entityManager = factory.createEntityManager();
EntityTransaction txn = entityManager.getTransaction();
txn.begin();
entityManager. persist(course);
txn.commit();
```

You can find a description of JPA annotations at `http://www.eclipse.org/eclipselink/documentation/2.7/jpa/extensions/annotations_ref.htm`.

JPA tools in Eclipse EE make adding many of the annotations very easy, as we will see in this section.

Creating a new MySQL schema

For this example, we will create a separate MySQL schema (we won't use the same schema that we created for the JDBC application, although it is possible to do so). Open MySQL Workbench and connect to your MySQL database (see Chapter 1, *Introducing JEE and Eclipse,* if you do not know how to connect to the MySQL database from MySQL Workbench).

Right-click in the **Schema** window and select **Create Schema...**:

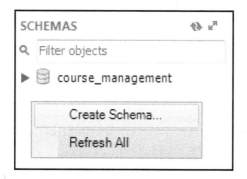

Figure 4.19: Creating a new MySQL schema

Name the new schema course_management_jpa and click **Apply**. We are going to use this schema for the JPA application.

Setting up a Maven dependency for JPA

In this example, we will use the EclipseLink (https://eclipse.org/eclipselink/) JPA implementation. We will use the MySQL JDBC driver and Bean Validation framework for validating members of entities. Finally, we will use Java annotations provided by JSR0250. So, let's add Maven dependencies for all these:

```xml
<dependency>
  <groupId>org.eclipse.persistence</groupId>
  <artifactId>eclipselink</artifactId>
  <version>2.5.2</version>
</dependency>
<dependency>
  <groupId>mysql</groupId>
  <artifactId>mysql-connector-java</artifactId>
  <version>5.1.34</version>
</dependency>
<dependency>
  <groupId>javax.validation</groupId>
  <artifactId>validation-api</artifactId>
  <version>1.1.0.Final</version>
</dependency>
<dependency>
  <groupId>javax.annotation</groupId>
  <artifactId>jsr250-api</artifactId>
  <version>1.0</version>
</dependency>
```

Converting a project into a JPA project

Many JPA tools become active in Eclipse JEE only if the project is a JPA project. Although we have created a Maven project, it is easy to add an Eclipse JPA facet to it:

1. Right-click on the project and select **Configure** | **Convert to JPA Project**:

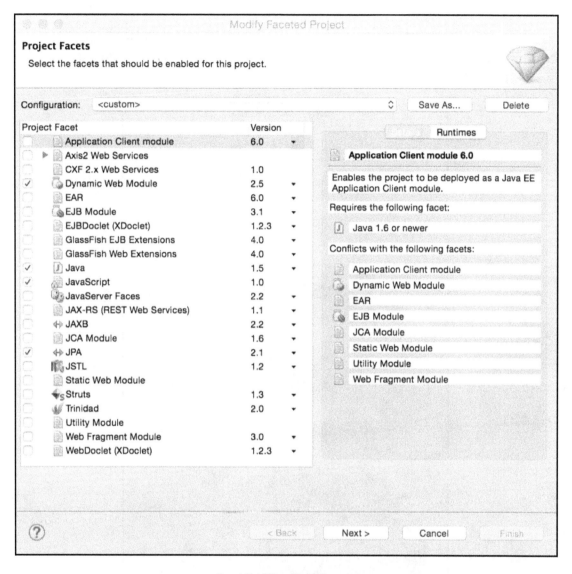

Figure 4.20: Addding a JPA facet to a project

2. Make sure JPA is selected.

3. On the next page, select **EclipseLink 2.5.x** as the platform.

4. For the JPA implementation type, select **Disable Library Configuration**.

5. The drop-down list for **Connection** lists any connections you might have
   configured in **Data Source Explorer**. For now, do not select any connection. At
   the bottom of the page, select the **Discover annotated classes automatically**
   option:

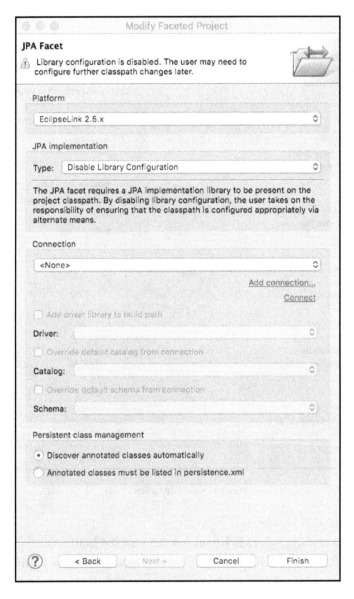

Figure 4.21: Configuring a JPA facet

6. Click **Finish**.

7. Notice that the **JPA Content** group is created under the project and `persistence.xml` is created in it. Open `persistence.xml` in the editor.

8. Click on the **Connection** tab and change **Transaction type** to **Resource Local**. We have selected **Resource Local** because, in this chapter, we are going to manage `EntityManager`. If you want the JEE container to manage `EntityManager`, then you should set **Transaction type** to **JTA**. We will see an example of the JTA transaction type in `Chapter 7`, *Creating JEE Application with EJB*.

9. Enter EclipseLink connection pool attributes as shown in the following screenshot and save the file:

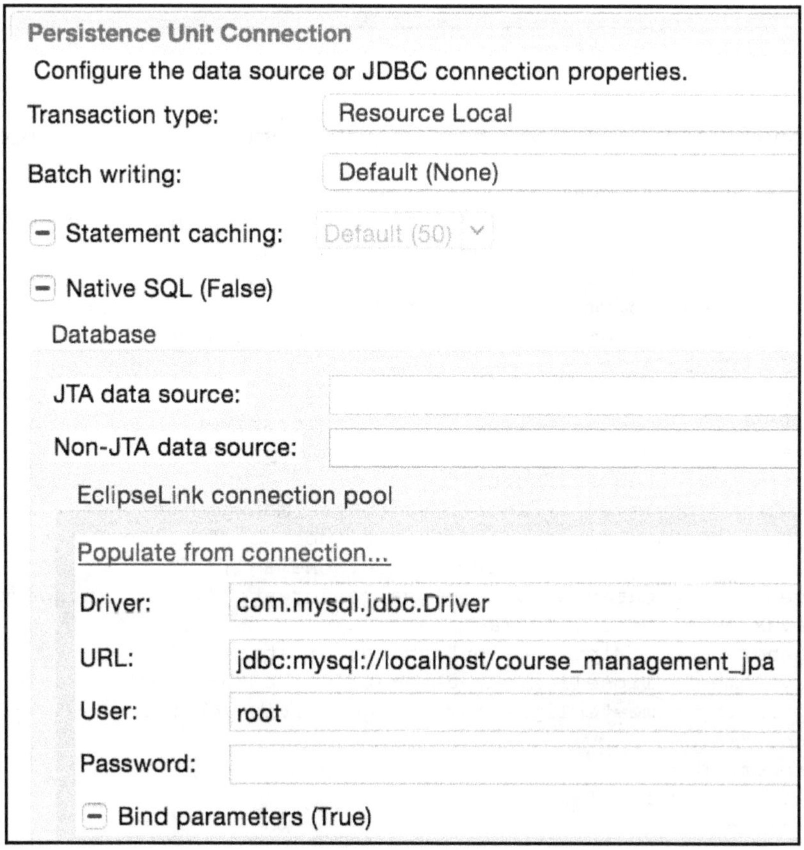

Persistence Unit Connection
Configure the data source or JDBC connection properties.

Transaction type:	Resource Local
Batch writing:	Default (None)
− Statement caching:	Default (50) ⌄

− Native SQL (False)

Database

JTA data source:	
Non-JTA data source:	

EclipseLink connection pool

Populate from connection...

Driver:	com.mysql.jdbc.Driver
URL:	jdbc:mysql://localhost/course_management_jpa
User:	root
Password:	

− Bind parameters (True)

Figure 4.22: Setting up Persistence Unit Connection

10. Next, click on the **Schema Generation** tab. Here, we will set the options to generate database tables and relationships from entities. Select the options as shown in the following screenshot:

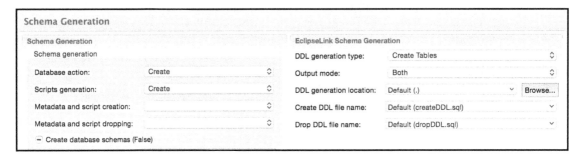

Figure 4.23: Setting up Schema Generation options of Persistence Unit

Here is the content of the `persistence.xml` file after setting the preceding options:

```
<?xml version="1.0" encoding="UTF-8"?>
<persistence version="2.1" xmlns="http://xmlns.jcp.org/xml/ns/persistence"
xmlns:xsi="http://www.w3.org/2001/XMLSchema-instance"
xsi:schemaLocation="http://xmlns.jcp.org/xml/ns/persistence
http://xmlns.jcp.org/xml/ns/persistence/persistence_2_1.xsd">
  <persistence-unit name="CourseManagementJPA" transaction-
type="RESOURCE_LOCAL">
    <properties>
      <property name="javax.persistence.jdbc.driver"
        value="com.mysql.jdbc.Driver"/>        <property
name="javax.persistence.jdbc.url"
        value="jdbc:mysql://localhost/course_management_jpa"/>
      <property name="javax.persistence.jdbc.user" value="root"/>
      <property name="javax.persistence.schema-
        generation.database.action" value="create"/>        <property
name="javax.persistence.schema-
        generation.scripts.action" value="create"/>
<property name="eclipselink.ddl-generation" value="create- tables"/>
      <property name="eclipselink.ddl-generation.output-mode"
value="both"/>
    </properties>
  </persistence-unit>
</persistence>
```

Creating entities

We have already created JavaBeans for `Course`, `Person`, `Student`, and `Teacher`. We will now convert them to JPA entities using the `@Entity` annotation. Open `Course.java` and add the following annotations:

```
@ManagedBean (name="course")
@RequestScoped
@Entity
public class Course implements Serializable
```

The same bean can act as a managed bean for JSF and an entity for JPA. Note that if the name of the class is different from the table name in the database, you will need to specify a `name` attribute of the `@Entity` annotation. For example, if our `Course` table were called `SchoolCourse`, then the entity declaration would be as follows:

```
@Entity (name="SchoolCourse")
```

To specify the primary key of the `Entity`, use the `@Id` annotation. In the `Course` table, `id` is the primary key and is autogenerated. To indicate autogeneration of the value, use the `@GeneratedValue` annotation. Use the `@column` annotation to indicate that the member variable corresponds to a column in the table. So, the annotations for `id` are as follows:

```
@Id
@GeneratedValue (strategy=GenerationType.IDENTITY)
@Column (name="id")
private int id;
```

You can specify validations for a column using Bean Validation framework annotations, as mentioned earlier. For example, the course name should not be null:

```
@NotNull
@Column (name="name")
private String name;
```

Furthermore, the minimum value of credits should be 1:

```
@Min (1)
@Column (name="credits")
private int credits;
```

In the preceding examples, the `@Column` annotation is not required to specify the name of the column if the field name is the same as the column name.

If you are using JPA entities to create tables and want to exactly specify the type of columns, then you can use the `columnDefinition` attribute of the `@Column` annotation; for example, to specify a column of type `varchar` with length 20, you could use `@Column(columnDefinition="VARCHAR(20)")`.

Refer to `https://javaee.github.io/javaee-spec/javadocs/javax/persistence/Column.html` to see all the attributes of the `@Column` annotation.

We will add more annotations to `Course Entity` as needed later. For now, let's turn our attention to the `Person` class. This class is the parent class of the `Student` and `Teacher` classes. However, in the database, there is no `Person` table and all the fields of `Person` and `Student` are in the `Student` table; and the same for the `Teacher` table. So, how do we model this in JPA? Well, JPA supports inheritance of entities and provides control over how they should be mapped to database tables. Open the `Person` class and add the following annotations:

```
@Entity
@Inheritance(strategy=TABLE_PER_CLASS)
public abstract class Person implements Serializable { ...
```

We are not only identifying the `Person` class as `Entity`, but we are also indicating that it is used for inheritance (using `@Inheritance`). The inheritance strategy decides how tables are mapped to classes. There are three possible strategies:

- `SINGLE_TABLE`: In this case, fields of parent and child classes would be mapped to the table of the parent class. If we use this strategy, then the fields of `Person`, `Student`, and `Teacher` will be mapped to the table for the `Person` entity.
- `TABLE_PER_CLASS`: In this case, each concrete class (non-abstract class) is mapped to a table in the database. All fields of the parent class are also mapped to the table for the child class. For example, all fields of `Person` and `Student` will be mapped to columns in the `Student` table. Since `Person` is marked as abstract, no table will be mapped by the `Person` class. It exists only to provide inheritance support in the application.

- JOINED: In this case, the parent and its children are mapped to separate tables. For example, Person will be mapped to the Person table, and Student and Teacher will be mapped to the corresponding tables in the database.

As per the schema that we created for the JDBC application, we have Student and Teacher tables with all the required columns and there is no Person table. Therefore, we have selected the TABLE_PER_CLASS strategy here.

 See more information about entity inheritance in JPA at https://javaee. github.io/tutorial/persistence-intro003.html#BNBQN.

The fields id, firstName, and lastName in the Person table are shared by Student and Teacher. Therefore, we need to mark them as columns in the tables and set the primary key. So, add the following annotations to the fields in the Person class:

```
@Id
@GeneratedValue(strategy=GenerationType.IDENTITY)
@Column(name="id")
private int id;

@Column(name = "first_name")
@NotNull
private String firstName;

@Column(name = "last_name")
private String lastName;
```

Here, column names in the table do not match class fields. Therefore, we have to specify the name attribute in @Column annotations.

Let's now mark the Student class as Entity:

```
@Entity
@ManagedBean (name="student")
@RequestScoped
public class Student extends Person implements Serializable
```

The `Student` class has a `Date` field called `enrolledSince`, which is of
the `java.util.Date` type. However, JDBC and JPA use the `java.sql.Date` type. If you
want JPA to automatically convert `java.sql.Date` to `java.util.Date`, then you need to
mark the field with the `@Temporal` annotation:

```
@Temporal(DATE)
@Column(name="enrolled_since")
private Date enrolledSince;
```

Open the `Teacher` class and add the `@Entity` annotation to it:

```
@Entity
@ManagedBean (name="teacher")
@RequestScoped
public class Teacher extends Person implements Serializable
```

Then, map the `designation` field in the class:

```
@NotNull
@Column(name="designation")
private String designation;
```

We have now added annotations for all tables and their fields that do not participate in
table relationships. We will now model the relationships between tables in our classes.

Configuring entity relationships

First, we will model the relationship between `Course` and `Teacher`. There is a one-to-many
relationship between them: one teacher may teach a number of courses. Open
`Course.java` in the editor. Open the JPA perspective in Eclipse JEE (**Window** | **Open
Perspective** | **JPA** menu).

Configuring many-to-one relationships

With `Course.java` open in the editor, click on the **JPA Details** tab in the lower window
(just below the editor window). In `Course.java`, click on the `teacher` member variable.
The **JPA Details** tab shows the details of this attribute:

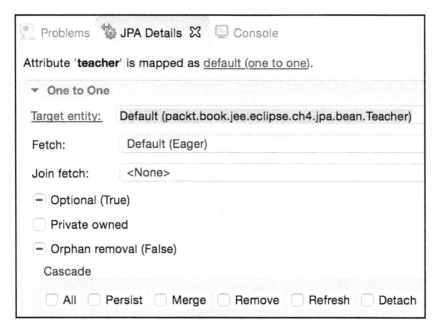

Figure 4.24: JPA details of an entity attribute

Target entity is auto-selected (as `Teacher`) because we have marked `Teacher` as an entity and the type of the `teacher` field is `Teacher`.

However, Eclipse has assumed a one-to-one relationship between `Course` and `Teacher`, which is not correct. There is a many-to-one relationship between `Course` and `Teacher`. To change this, click on the (**one_to_one**) hyperlink at the top of the **JPA Details** view and select the **Many To One** in **Mapping Type Selection** dialog box.

Select only **Merge** and **Refresh** cascade options; otherwise, duplicate entries will be added in the `Teacher` table for every `Teacher` that you selected for a `Course`.

See `https://javaee.github.io/tutorial/persistence-intro002.html#BNBQH` for more details on entity relationships and cascade options.

When you select **Merge** and **Refresh** cascade options, the `cascade` attribute added to the annotation is added to the `teacher` field in the `Course` entity:

```
@ManyToOne(cascade = { MERGE, REFRESH })
private Teacher teacher;
```

Scroll down the **JPA Details** page to see **Joining Strategy**. This determines how columns in `Course` and `Teacher` tables are joined:

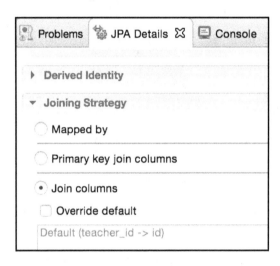

Figure 4.25: Editing Joining Strategy in an entity relationship

Note that the default joining strategy is that the `teacher_id` column in the `Course` table maps to the `id` column in the `Teacher` table. Eclipse has just guessed `teacher_id` (the appended `id` to the `teacher` field in the `Course` entity), but if we had a different join column in the `Course` table, for example, `teacherId`, then we would need to override the default join columns. Click on the **Override default** checkbox and then on the **Edit** button on the right-hand side of the textbox:

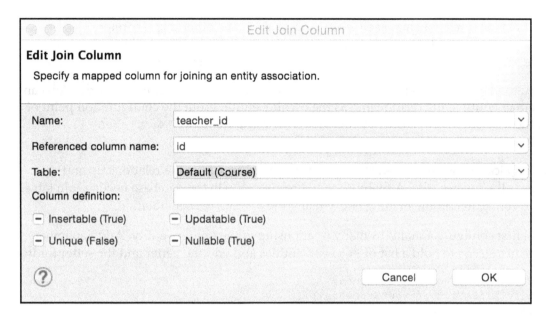

Figure 4.26: Editing Join Column

In our case, the default options match the table columns, so we will keep them unchanged. When you select the **Override default** checkbox, the `@JoinColumn` annotation is added to the `teacher` field in the `Course` entity:

```
@JoinColumn(name = "teacher_id", referencedColumnName = "id")
@ManyToOne(cascade = { MERGE, REFRESH })
private Teacher teacher;
```

All the required annotations for the `teacher` field are now added.

Configuring many-to-many relationships

We will now configure `Course` and `Student` entities for a many-to-many relationship (a course can have many students, and one student can take many courses).

Many-to-many relations could be unidirectional or bidirectional. For example, you may only want to track students enrolled in the courses (so the `Course` entity will have a list of students) and not students taking the courses (the `Student` entity does not keep a list of courses). This is an unidirectional relationship where only the `Course` entity knows about the students, but the `Student` entity does not know about the courses).

In a bidirectional relationship, each entity knows about the other one. Therefore, the Course entity will keep a list of students and the Student entity will keep a list of courses. We will configure the bidirectional relationship in this example.

A many-to-many relationship also has one owning side and the other inverse side. You can mark either entity in the relationship as the owning entity. From the configuration point of view, the inverse side is marked by the mappedBy attribute to the @ManyToMany annotation.

In our application, we will make Student as the owning side of the relationship and Course as the inverse side. A many-to-many relationship in the database needs a join table, which is configured in the owning entity using the @JoinTable annotation.

We will first configure a many-to-many relationship in the Course entity. Add a member variable in Course to hold a list of Student entities and add the getter and the setter for it:

```
private List<Student> students;
public List<Student> getStudents() {
  return students;
}
public void setStudents(List<Student> students) {
  this.students = students;
}
```

Then, click on the students field (added previously) and notice the settings in the **JPA Details** view:

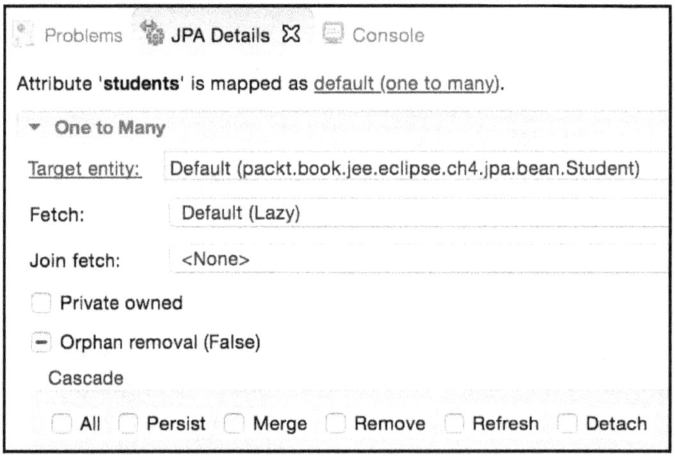

Figure 4.27: Default JPA details for the students field in Course Entity

Because the `students` field is a list of `Student` entities, Eclipse has assumed a one-to-many relationship (see the link at the top of the **JPA Details** view). We need to change this. Click on the **one_to_many** link and select **Many To Many**.

Check the **Merge** and **Refresh** cascade options. Since we are putting a `Course` entity on the inverse side of the relationship, select **Mapped By** as **Joining Strategy**. Enter `courses` in the **Attributes** text field. The compiler will show an error for this because we don't have a `courses` field in the `Student` entity yet. We will fix this shortly. The JPA settings for the `students` field should be as shown in the following screenshot:

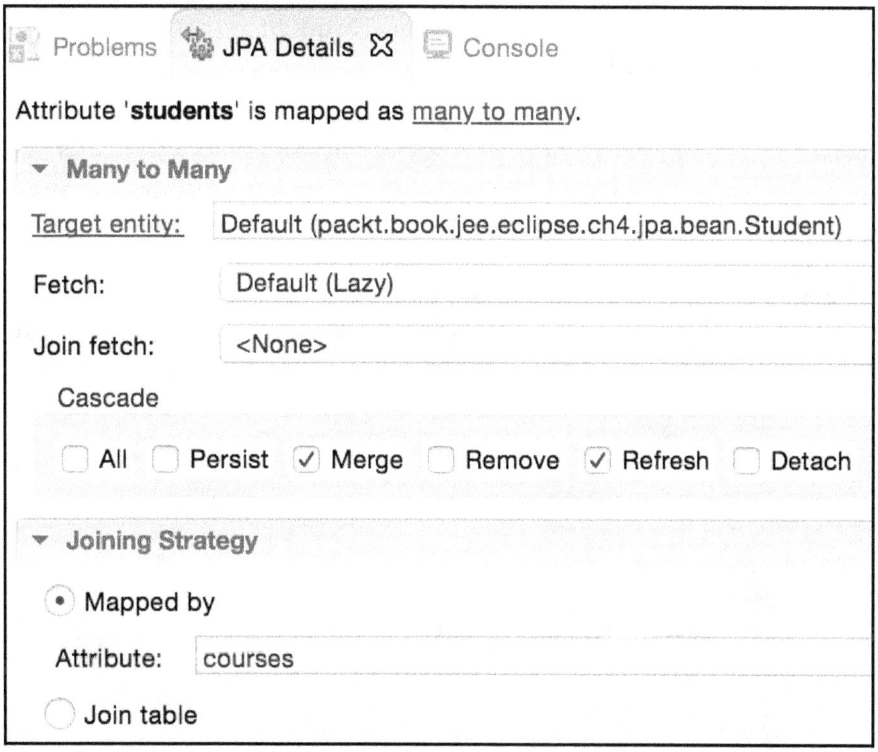

Figure 4.28: Modified JPA settings for the students field in Course Entity

Annotations for the `students` field in the `Course` entity should be as follows:

```
@ManyToMany(cascade = { MERGE, REFRESH }, mappedBy = "courses")
private List<Student> students;
```

Open `Student.java` in the editor. Add the `courses` field and the getter and the setter for it. Click on the `courses` field in the file and change the relationship from **one-to-many** to **many-to-many** in **JPA Details** view (as described previously for the `students` field in the `Course` entity). Select the **Merge** and **Refresh** cascade options. In the **Joining Strategy** section, make sure that the **Join table** option is selected. Eclipse creates the default join table by concatenating the owning table and the inverse table, separated by an underscore (in this case `Student_Course`). Change this to **Course_Student** to make it consistent with the schema that we created for the JDBC application.

In the **Join columns** section, select the **Override default** checkbox. Eclipse has named the join columns `students_id->id`, but in the **Course_Student** table we created in the JDBC application, we had a column named `student_id`. So, click the **Edit** button and change the name to **student_id**.

Similarly, change **Inverse join columns** from `courses_id->id` to `course_id->id`. After these changes, the **JPA Details** for the `courses` field should be as shown in the following screenshot:

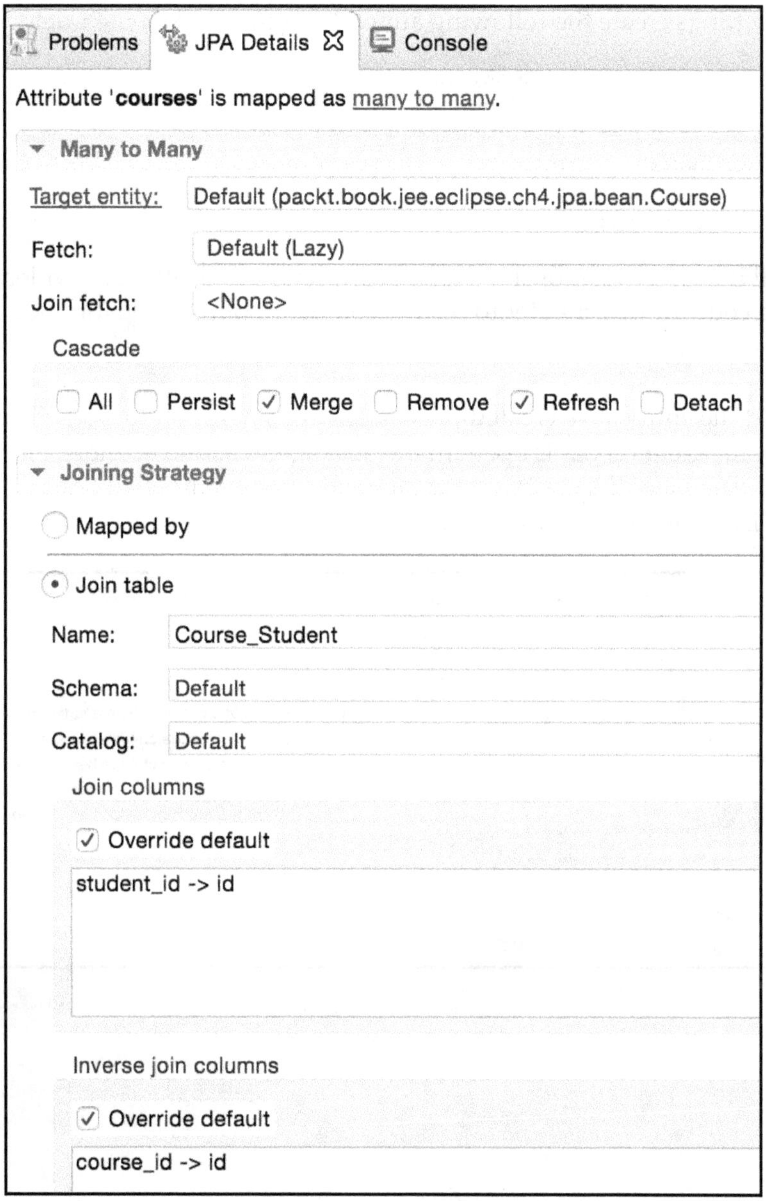

Figure 4.29: JPA Details for the courses field in Student entity

The previous settings create the following annotations for the `courses` field:

```
@ManyToMany(cascade = { MERGE, REFRESH })
@JoinTable(name = "Course_Student", joinColumns = @JoinColumn(name =
"student_id", referencedColumnName = "id"), inverseJoinColumns =
 @JoinColumn(name = "course_id", referencedColumnName = "id"))

List<Course> courses;
```

We have set all the entity relationships required for our application. Download the accompanying code for this chapter to see the complete source code for `Course`, `Student`, and `Teacher` entities.

We need to add the entities we created previously in `persistence.xml`. Open the file and make sure that the **General** tab is open. In the **Managed Classes** session, click the **Add** button. Type the name of the entity you want to add (for example, `Student`) and select the class from the list. Add all the four entities we have created:

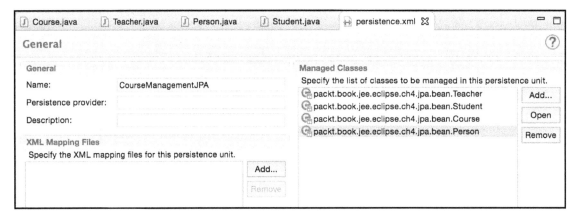

Figure 4.30: Add entities in persistence.xml

Creating database tables from entities

Follow these steps to create database tables from entities and relationships that we have modeled:

1. Right-click on the project and select **JPA Tool** | **Generate Tables from Entities**:

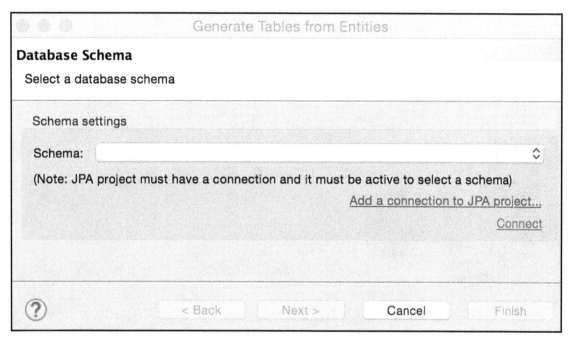

Figure 4.31: JPA Details for the courses field in Student entity

2. Because we haven't configured any schema for our JPA project, the **Schema** drop-down will be empty. Click the **Add a connection to JPA project** link:

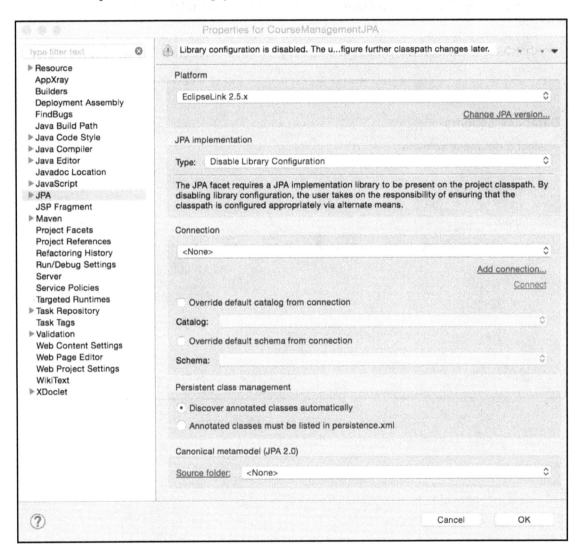

Figure 4.32: JPA project properties

3. Click the **Add connection** link and create a connection to the `course_management_jpa` schema we created earlier. We have already seen how to create a connection to the MySQL schema in the *Using Eclipse Data Source Explorer* section of this chapter.

4. Select `course_management_jpa` in the drop-down list shown in *Figure 4.31* and click **Next**:

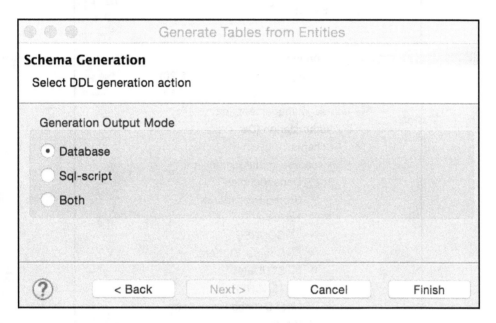

Figure 4.33: Schema Generation from entities

5. Click **Finish**.

Eclipse generates DDL scripts for creating tables and relationships and executes these scripts in the selected schema. Once the script is run successfully, open the **Data Source Explorer** view (see the *Using Eclipse Data Source Explorer* section of this chapter) and browse tables in **course_management_jpa** connection. Make sure that tables and fields are created according to the entities we have created:

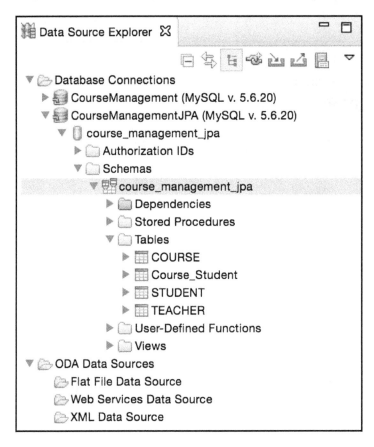

Figure 4.34: Tables created from JPA entities

This feature of Eclipse and JPA makes it very easy to update the database as you modify your entities.

Using JPA APIs to manage data

We will now create classes that use JPA APIs to manage data for our course management application. We will create service classes for **Course**, **Teacher**, and **Student** entities and add methods that directly access the database through JPA APIs.

As mentioned in the *JPA concepts* section, it is a good practice to cache an instance of EntityManagerFactory in our application. Furthermore, managed beans of JSF act as a link between the UI and the backend code, and as a conduit to transfer data between the UI and the data access objects. Therefore, they must have an instance of the data access objects (which use JPA to access data from the database). To cache an instance of EntityManagerFactory, we will create another managed bean, whose only job is to make the EntityManagerFactory instance available to other managed beans.

Create an EntityManagerFactoryBean class in the packt.book.jee.eclipse.ch4.jpa.service_bean package. This package contains all the managed beans. EntityManagerFactoryBean creates an instance of EntityManagerFactory in the constructor and provides a getter method:

```
package packt.book.jee.eclipse.ch4.jpa.service_bean;

import javax.faces.bean.ApplicationScoped;
import javax.faces.bean.ManagedBean;
import javax.persistence.EntityManagerFactory;
import javax.persistence.Persistence;

//Load this bean eagerly, i.e., before any request is made
@ManagedBean(name="emFactoryBean", eager=true)
@ApplicationScoped
public class EntityManagerFactoryBean {

  private EntityManagerFactory entityManagerFactory;

  public EntityManagerFactoryBean() {
    entityManagerFactory =
  Persistence.createEntityManagerFactory("CourseManagementJPA");
  }

  public EntityManagerFactory getEntityManagerFactory() {
    return entityManagerFactory;
  }

}
```

Note the argument passed in the following:

```
entityManagerFactory =
  Persistence.createEntityManagerFactory("CourseManagementJPA");
```

It is the name of the persistence unit in `persistence.xml`.

Now let's create service classes that actually use the JPA APIs to access database tables.

Create a package called `packt.book.jee.eclipse.ch4.jpa.service`. Create the class named `CourseService`. Every service class will need access to `EntityManagerFactory`. So, create a private member variable as follows:

```
private EntityManagerFactory factory;
```

The constructor takes an instance of `EntityManagerFactoryBean` and gets the reference of `EntityManagerFactory` from it:

```
public CourseService(EntityManagerFactoryBean factoryBean) {
   this.factory = factoryBean.getEntityManagerFactory();
}
```

Let's now add a function to get all `courses` from the database:

```
public List<Course> getCourses() {
   EntityManager em = factory.createEntityManager();
   CriteriaBuilder cb = em.getCriteriaBuilder();
   CriteriaQuery<Course> cq = cb.createQuery(Course.class);
   TypedQuery<Course> tq = em.createQuery(cq);
   List<Course> courses = tq.getResultList();
   em.close();
   return courses;
}
```

Note how `CriteriaBuilder`, `CriteriaQuery`, and `TypesQuery` are used to get all the courses. It is a type-safe way to execute the query.

See `https://javaee.github.io/tutorial/persistence-criteria.html#GJITV` for detailed discussion on how to use the JPA criteria APIs.

We could have done the same thing using **Java Persistence Query Language** (**JQL**)—http://www.oracle.com/technetwork/articles/vasiliev-jpql-087123.html—but it is not type-safe. However, here is an example of using JQL to write the getCourses function:

```
public List<Course> getCourses() {
  EntityManager em = factory.createEntityManager();
  List<Course> courses = em.createQuery("select crs from Course
crs").getResultList();
  em.close();
  return courses;
}
```

Add a method to insert the course into the database:

```
public void addCourse (Course course) {
  EntityManager em = factory.createEntityManager();
  EntityTransaction txn = em.getTransaction();
  txn.begin();
  em.persist(course);
  txn.commit();
}
```

The code is quite simple. We get the entity manager and then start a transaction, because it is an update operation. Then, we call the persist method on EntityManager by passing an instance of Course to save. Then, we commit the transaction. The methods to update and delete are also simple. Here is the entire source code of CourseService:

```
package packt.book.jee.eclipse.ch4.jpa.service;

// imports skipped

import packt.book.jee.eclipse.ch4.jpa.bean.Course;
import
packt.book.jee.eclipse.ch4.jpa.service_bean.EntityManagerFactoryBean;

public class CourseService {
  private EntityManagerFactory factory;

  public CourseService(EntityManagerFactoryBean factoryBean) {
    factory = factoryBean.getEntityManagerFactory();
  }

  public List<Course> getCourses() {
    EntityManager em = factory.createEntityManager();
    CriteriaBuilder cb = em.getCriteriaBuilder();
```

```
        CriteriaQuery<Course> cq = cb.createQuery(Course.class);
        TypedQuery<Course> tq = em.createQuery(cq);
        List<Course> courses = tq.getResultList();
        em.close();
        return courses;
    }

public void addCourse (Course course) {
    EntityManager em = factory.createEntityManager();
    EntityTransaction txn = em.getTransaction();
    txn.begin();
    em.persist(course);
    txn.commit();
}

    public void updateCourse (Course course) {
      EntityManager em = factory.createEntityManager();
      EntityTransaction txn = em.getTransaction();
      txn.begin();
      em.merge(course);
      txn.commit();
    }

    public Course getCourse (int id) {
      EntityManager em = factory.createEntityManager();
      return em.find(Course.class, id);
    }

    public void deleteCourse (Course course) {
      EntityManager em = factory.createEntityManager();
      EntityTransaction txn = em.getTransaction();
      txn.begin();
      Course mergedCourse = em.find(Course.class, course.getId());
      em.remove(mergedCourse);
      txn.commit();
    }
  }
```

Let's now create `StudentService` and `TeacherService` classes with the following methods:

```
public class StudentService {
  private EntityManagerFactory factory;

  public StudentService (EntityManagerFactoryBean factoryBean) {
    factory = factoryBean.getEntityManagerFactory();
  }

  public void addStudent (Student student) {
    EntityManager em = factory.createEntityManager();
    EntityTransaction txn = em.getTransaction();
    txn.begin();
    em.persist(student);
    txn.commit();
  }

  public List<Student> getStudents() {
    EntityManager em = factory.createEntityManager();
    CriteriaBuilder cb = em.getCriteriaBuilder();
    CriteriaQuery<Student> cq = cb.createQuery(Student.class);
    TypedQuery<Student> tq = em.createQuery(cq);
    List<Student> students = tq.getResultList();
    em.close();
    return students;
  }

}

public class TeacherService {
  private EntityManagerFactory factory;

  public TeacherService (EntityManagerFactoryBean factoryBean) {
    factory = factoryBean.getEntityManagerFactory();
  }

  public void addTeacher (Teacher teacher) {
    EntityManager em = factory.createEntityManager();
    EntityTransaction txn = em.getTransaction();
    txn.begin();
    em.persist(teacher);
    txn.commit();
  }

  public List<Teacher> getTeacher() {
    EntityManager em = factory.createEntityManager();
```

```
        CriteriaBuilder cb = em.getCriteriaBuilder();
        CriteriaQuery<Teacher> cq = cb.createQuery(Teacher.class);
        TypedQuery<Teacher> tq = em.createQuery(cq);
        List<Teacher> teachers = tq.getResultList();
        em.close();
        return teachers;
    }

   public Teacher getTeacher (int id) {
       EntityManager em = factory.createEntityManager();
       return em.find(Teacher.class, id);
   }
}
```

Wiring user interface with JPA service classes

Now that we have all data access classes ready, we need to connect the user interface that
we have created for adding courses, addCourse.xhtml, to pass data and get data from the
JPA service classes. As mentioned previously, we are going to do this using managed
beans, in this case, CourseServiceBean.

CourseServiceBean will need to create an instance of CourseService and call
the addCourse method. Open CourseServiceBean and create a member variable as
follows:

```
    private CourseService courseService ;
```

We also need an instance of the EntityManagerFactoryBean managed bean that we
created earlier:

```
    @ManagedProperty(value="#{emFactoryBean}")
    private EntityManagerFactoryBean factoryBean;
```

The factoryBean instance is injected by the JSF runtime and is available only after the
managed bean is completely constructed. However, for this bean to be injected, we need to
provide a setter method. Therefore, add a setter method for factoryBean. We can have JSF
call a method of our bean after it is fully constructed by annotating the method with
@PostConstruct. So, let's create a method called postConstruct:

```
    @PostConstruct
    public void init() {
      courseService = new CourseService(factoryBean);
    }
```

Then, modify the `addCourse` method to call our service method:

```
public String addCourse() {
  courseService.addCourse(course);
  return "listCourse";
}
```

Since the `listCourse.xhtml` page will need to get a list of courses, let's also add the `getCourses` method in `CourseServiceBean`:

```
public List<Course> getCourses() {
  return courseService.getCourses();
}
```

Here is `CourseServiceBean` after the preceding changes:

```
@ManagedBean(name="courseServiceBean")
@RequestScoped
public class CourseServiceBean {

  private CourseService courseService ;

  @ManagedProperty(value="#{emFactoryBean}")
  private EntityManagerFactoryBean factoryBean;

  @ManagedProperty(value="#{course}")
  private Course course;

  private String errMsg= null;

  @PostConstruct
  public void init() {
    courseService = new CourseService(factoryBean);
  }

  public void setFactoryBean(EntityManagerFactoryBean factoryBean)
    {
    this.factoryBean = factoryBean;
  }

  public Course getCourse() {
    return course;
  }

  public void setCourse(Course course) {
    this.course = course;
  }
```

```
public String getErrMsg() {
  return errMsg;
}

public void setErrMsg(String errMsg) {
  this.errMsg = errMsg;
}

public String addCourse() {
  courseService.addCourse(course);
  return "listCourse";
}

public List<Course> getCourses() {
  return courseService.getCourses();
}

}
```

Finally, we will write the code to display a list of courses in `listCourse.xhtml`:

```
<html xmlns="http://www.w3.org/1999/xhtml"
    xmlns:f="http://java.sun.com/jsf/core"
    xmlns:h="http://java.sun.com/jsf/html"
    xmlns:c="http://java.sun.com/jsp/jstl/core">

  <h2>Courses:</h2>
  <h:form>
    <h:messages style="color:red"/>
    <h:dataTable value="#{courseServiceBean.courses}"
     var="course">
      <h:column>
        <f:facet name="header">ID</f:facet>
        <h:outputText value="#{course.id}"/>
      </h:column>
      <h:column>
        <f:facet name="header">Name</f:facet>
        <h:outputText value="#{course.name}"/>
      </h:column>
      <h:column>
        <f:facet name="header">Credits</f:facet>
        <h:outputText value="#{course.credits}"
         style="float:right" />
      </h:column>
    </h:dataTable>
  </h:form>

  <h:panelGroup rendered="#{courseServiceBean.courses.size() ==
```

```
    0}">
      <h3>No courses found</h3>
    </h:panelGroup>

    <c:if test="#{courseServiceBean.courses.size() > 0}">
      <b>Total number of courses
        <h:outputText value="#{courseServiceBean.courses.size()}"/>
      </b>
    </c:if>
    <p/>
    <h:button value="Add" outcome="addCourse"/>
  </html>
```

Because of space constraints, we will not discuss how to add functionality to delete/update courses, or to create a course with the Teacher field selected. Please download the source code for the examples discussed in this chapter to see completed projects.

Summary

In this chapter, we learned how to build web applications that require accessing data from a relational database. First, we built a simple *Course Management* application using JDBC and JSTL, and then, the same application was built using JPA and JSF.

JPA is preferred to JDBC because you end up writing a lot less code. The code to map object data to relational data is created for you by the JPA implementation. However, JDBC is still being used in many web applications because it is simpler to use. Although JPA has a moderate learning curve, JPA tools in Eclipse EE can make using JPA APIs a bit easier, particularly configuring entities, relationships, and persistence.xml.

In the next chapter, we will deviate a bit from our discussion on JEE and see how to write and run unit tests for Java applications. We will also see how to measure code coverage after running the unit tests.

5
Unit Testing

In the last chapter, we learned how to create a web application that uses a database. In this chapter, we will learn how to write and execute unit tests in Eclipse for JEE applications. We will cover the following topics in this chapter:

- Creating and executing unit tests using Eclipse JEE
- Executing unit tests from Eclipse IDE
- Mocking external dependencies for unit tests
- Calculating unit test coverage

Testing the software that you develop is a very important part of the overall software development cycle. There are many types of testing; each one has a specific purpose, and each one varies in scope. Some examples of testing are functional testing, integration testing, scenario testing, and unit testing.

Of all these types, unit tests are the narrowest in scope and are typically coded and executed by developers. Each unit test is meant to test a specific and small piece of functionality (typically, a method in a class), and is expected to execute without any external dependencies. Here are some of the reasons why you should write efficient unit tests:

- To catch bugs early. If you find a bug in functional or integration testing, which have a much wider scope of testing, then it might be difficult to isolate the code that caused the bug. It is much easier to catch and fix bugs in unit testing, because unit tests, by definition, work in a narrower scope, and if a test fails, you will find out exactly where to go to fix the issue.
- Unit tests can help you catch any regression that you might have introduced when editing the code. There are good tools and libraries available for automating the execution of unit tests. For example, using build tools such as Ant and Maven, you can execute unit tests at the end of a successful build, so that you will immediately find out if the changes you have made have broken any previously working code.

As mentioned previously, writing unit tests and executing them is typically the responsibility of the developer. Therefore, most IDEs have good built-in support for writing and executing unit tests. Eclipse JEE is no exception. It has built-in support for JUnit, which is a popular unit testing framework for Java.

In this chapter, we will see how to write and execute JUnit tests for the *Course Management* web application that we built in `Chapter 4`, *Creating JEE Database Applications*. However, first, here is a quick introduction to JUnit.

Introducing JUnit

JUnit test classes are Java classes separate from the classes you want to test. Each test class can contain many test cases, which are just methods marked to be executed when JUnit tests are executed. A test suite is a collection of test classes.

The convention is to assign the test class the same name as that of the class you want to test, and append `Test` to that name. For example, if you wanted to test the `Course` class from the previous chapter, then you would create a JUnit test class and name it `CourseTest`. Test case (method) names start with `test`, followed by the name of the method in the class that you want to test; for example, if you wanted to test the `validate` method in the `Course` class, then you would create the `testValidate` method in the `CourseTest` class. Test classes are also created in the same package as the package in which the classes to be tested are present. In Maven projects, test classes are typically created under the `src/test/java` folder. The convention is to create the same package structure in the `test` folder as in the `src/main/java` folder.

JUnit supports annotations to mark unit tests and test suites. Here is a simple test case for the `Course` class:

```
/**
 * Test for {@link Course}
 */
Class CourseTest {
  @Test
  public void testValidate() {
    Course course = new Course();
    Assert.assertFalse(course.validate());
    course.setName("course1")
    Assert.assetFalse(course.validate());
    Course.setCredits(-5);
    Assert.assetFalse(course.validate());
    course.setCredits(5);
```

```
        Assert.assertTrue(course.validate());
    }
}
```

Let's assume that the `validate` method checks that the course `name` is not null and that `credits` is greater than zero.

The preceding test case is marked with the `@Test` annotation. It creates an instance of the `Course` class, and then calls the `Assert.assertFalse` method to make sure that the `validate` method returns `false`, because `name` and `credits` are not set, and they will have their default values, which are `null` and `0`, respectively. `Assert` is a class provided by the JUnit library, and has many assert methods to test many conditions (see `http://junit.sourceforge.net/javadoc/org/junit/Assert.html` for more information).

The test case, then, only sets the name, and does the same validation again, expecting the `validate` method to return `false`, because the credits are still zero. Finally, the test case sets both the name and credits, and calls the `Assert.assertTrue` method to ensure that `course.validate()` returns `true`. If any of the assertions fail, then the test case fails.

Other than `@Test`, you can use the following annotations provided by JUnit:

- `@Before` and `@After`: Methods annotated with these annotations are executed before and after each test. You may want to initialize resources in `@Before` and free them in `@After`.
- `@BeforeClass` and `@AfterClass`: Similar to `@Before` and `@After`, but instead of being called per test, these methods are called once per test class. A method with the `@BeforeClass` annotation is called before any of the test cases in that class are executed, and one with `@AfterClass` is called after all the test cases are executed.

 You can find more annotations for JUnit at `https://junit.org/junit4/javadoc/latest/org/junit/package-summary.html`.

Creating and executing unit tests using Eclipse JEE

To understand how to write unit tests, let's take the JDBC version of the *Course Management* application that we developed in Chapter 4, *Creating JEE Database Applications*. Let's start with a simple test case for validating a course. The following is the source code of Course.java:

```java
package packt.book.jee.eclipse.ch5.bean;

import java.sql.SQLException;
import java.util.List;

import packt.book.jee.eclipse.ch5.dao.CourseDAO;

public class Course {
    private int id;
    private String name;
    private int credits;
    private Teacher teacher;
    private int teacherId;
    private CourseDAO courseDAO = new CourseDAO();

    public int getId() {
        return id;
    }
    public void setId(int id) {
        this.id = id;
    }
    public String getName() {
        return name;
    }
    public void setName(String name) {
        this.name = name;
    }
    public int getCredits() {
        return credits;
    }
    public void setCredits(int credits) {
        this.credits = credits;
    }
    public boolean isValidCourse() {
        return name != null && credits != 0;
    }
    public Teacher getTeacher() {
```

```
    return teacher;
  }
  public void setTeacher(Teacher teacher) {
    this.teacher = teacher;
  }
  public void addCourse() throws SQLException {
    courseDAO.addCourse(this);
  }
  public List<Course> getCourses() throws SQLException {
    return courseDAO.getCourses();
  }
  public int getTeacherId() {
    return teacherId;
  }
  public void setTeacherId(int teacherId) {
    this.teacherId = teacherId;
  }
}
```

Creating unit test cases

Maven projects follow certain conventions; the entire application source in a Maven project is in the `src/main/java` folder, and unit tests are expected to be in the `src/test/java` folder. In fact, when you create a Maven project in Eclipse, it creates the `src/test/java` folder for you. We are going to create our test cases in this folder. We are going to create the same package structure for the test classes as that for the application source; that is, to test the `packt.book.jee.eclipse.ch5.bean.Course` class, we will create the `packt.book.jee.eclipse.ch5.bean` package under the `src/test/java` folder and then create a JUnit test class called `CourseTest`, as follows:

1. Right-click on the `src/test/java` folder in **Package Explorer** in Eclipse and select **New** | **JUnit Test Case** (if you do not find this option in the menu, select **New** | **Other**, and type `junit` into the **Filter** textbox. Then, select the **JUnit Test Case** option).
2. Enter the package name as `packt.book.jee.eclipse.ch5.bean` and the class name as `CourseTest`.

3. Click on the **Browse...** button next to the **Class under test** textbox. Type `course` into the **Filter** textbox and select the `Course` class:

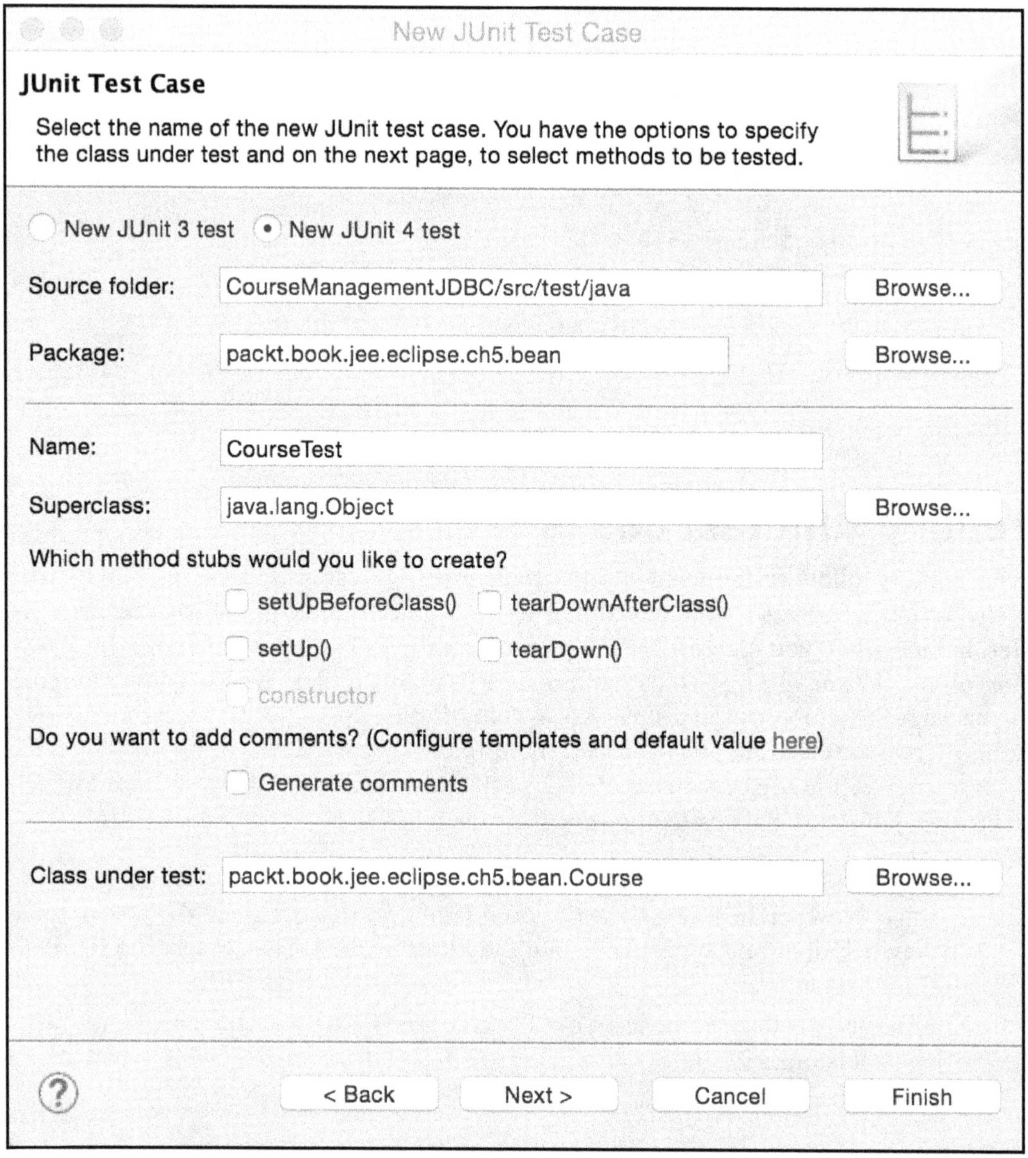

JUnit Test Case

Select the name of the new JUnit test case. You have the options to specify the class under test and on the next page, to select methods to be tested.

○ New JUnit 3 test ● New JUnit 4 test

Source folder: CourseManagementJDBC/src/test/java   Browse...

Package: packt.book.jee.eclipse.ch5.bean   Browse...

Name: CourseTest

Superclass: java.lang.Object   Browse...

Which method stubs would you like to create?

☐ setUpBeforeClass()   ☐ tearDownAfterClass()

☐ setUp()   ☐ tearDown()

☐ constructor

Do you want to add comments? (Configure templates and default value here)

☐ Generate comments

Class under test: packt.book.jee.eclipse.ch5.bean.Course   Browse...

< Back   Next >   Cancel   Finish

Figure 5.1: JUnit test case wizard

4. Click **Next**. The page shows methods in the class (`Course`) for which we want to create the test cases. Select the methods that you want to create test cases for.

5. We don't want to test getters and setters because they are simple methods and don't do much other than just getting or setting member variables. Presently, we will create a test case for only one method: `isValidTestCase`. Select the checkbox for this method:

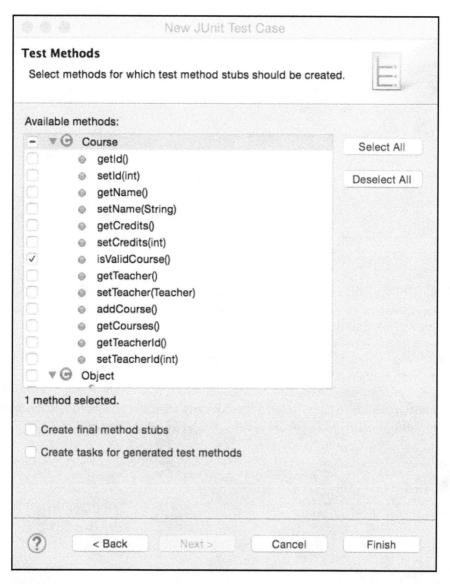

Figure 5.2: Select methods for test cases

6. Click **Finish**. Eclipse checks whether JUnit libraries are included in your project, and if not, prompts you to include them:

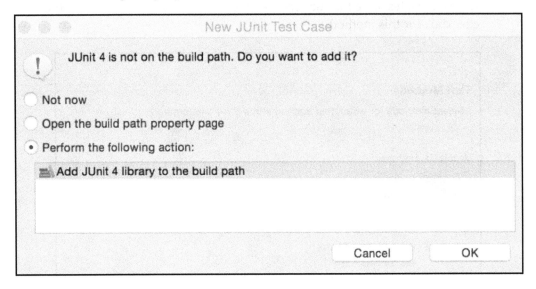

Figure 5.3: Include JUnit libraries in project

7. Click **OK**. Eclipse creates the package and the test class with one method/test case called `testIsValidCourse`. Note that the method is annotated with `@Test`, indicating that it is a JUnit test case.

How do we test whether `isValidCourse` works as expected? We create an instance of the `Course` class, set some values that we know are valid/invalid, call the `isValidateCourse` method, and compare the results with the expected results. JUnit provides many methods in the `Assert` class to compare the actual results obtained by calling test methods with the expected results. So, let's add the test code to the `testIsValidCourse` method:

```
package packt.book.jee.eclipse.ch5.bean;
import org.junit.Assert;
import org.junit.Test;
public class CourseTest {

  @Test
  public void testIsValidCourse() {
    Course course = new Course();
    //First validate without any values set
    Assert.assertFalse(course.isValidCourse());
```

```
    //set  name
    course.setName("course1");
    Assert.assertFalse(course.isValidCourse());
    //set zero credits
    course.setCredits(0);
    Assert.assertFalse(course.isValidCourse());
    //now set valid credits
    course.setCredits(4);
    Assert.assertTrue(course.isValidCourse());
  }


}
```

We first create an instance of the Course class, and without setting any of its values, call the isValidCourse method. We know that it is not a valid course because the name and credits are the required fields in a valid course. So, we check whether the returned value of isValidCourse is false by calling the Assert.assertFalse method. We then set the name and check again, expecting the instance to be an invalid course. Then, we set a 0 credits value for Course, and, finally, we set 4 credits for Course. Now, isValidCourse is expected to return true because both the name and credits are valid. We verify this by calling Assert.assertTrue.

Running unit test cases

Let's run this test case in Eclipse. Right-click on the file, or anywhere in the project in **Package Explorer**, and select the **Run As | JUnit Test** menu. Eclipse finds all unit tests in the project, executes them, and shows the results in the **JUnit** view:

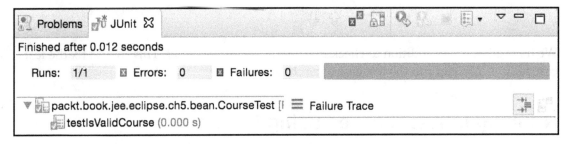

Figure 5.4: JUnit results view

This view shows a summary of the test cases run. In this case, it has run one test case, which was successful. The green bar shows that all test cases were executed successfully.

Now, let's add one more check into the method:

```
@Test
public void testIsValidCourse() {
    ...
    //set empty course name
    course.setName("");
    Assert.assertFalse(course.isValidCourse());
}
```

Then, run the test case again:

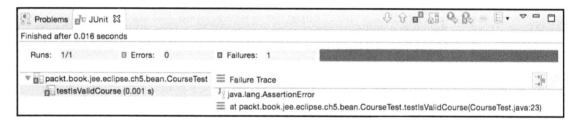

Figure 5.5: JUnit results view showing the failed test

The test case failed because `course.isValidCourse()` returned `true` when the course name was set to an empty string, while the test case expected the instance to be an invalid course. So, we need to modify the `isValidCourse` method of the `Course` class to fix this failure:

```
public boolean isValidCourse() {
    return name != null && credits != 0 && name.trim().length() > 0;
}
```

We have added the condition to check the length of the `name` field. This should fix the test case failure. You can run the test case again to verify.

Running unit test cases using Maven

You can run unit test cases using Maven, too. In fact, the install target of Maven also runs unit tests. However, it is possible to run only unit tests. To do this, right-click on the project in **Package Explorer** and select **Run As | Maven test**.

You might see the following error in the console:

```
java.lang.NoClassDefFoundError: org/junit/Assert
  at packt.book.jee.eclipse.ch5.bean.CourseTest.testIsValidCourse
(CourseTest.java:10)
Caused by: java.lang.ClassNotFoundException: org.junit.Assert
  at java.net.URLClassLoader$1.run(URLClassLoader.java:366)
  at java.net.URLClassLoader$1.run(URLClassLoader.java:355)
  at java.security.AccessController.doPrivileged(Native Method)
```

The reason for this error is that we haven't added a dependency on JUnit for our Maven project. Add the following dependency in `pom.xml`:

```xml
<dependency>
    <groupId>junit</groupId>
    <artifactId>junit</artifactId>
    <version>4.12</version>
</dependency>
```

Refer to the *Using Maven for project management* section in `Chapter 2`, *Creating a Simple JEE Web Application*, to learn how to add dependencies to a Maven project.

Run the Maven test again; this time, the test should pass.

Mocking external dependencies for unit tests

Unit tests are meant to execute without any external dependencies. We can certainly write methods at a granular level, such that the core business logic methods are totally separate from methods that have external dependencies. However, sometimes this is not practical, and we may have to write unit tests for code that are closely dependent on methods that access external systems.

For example, let's assume that we have to add a method in our `Course` bean to add students to the course. We will also mandate that the course has an upper limit on the number of students that it can enroll, and once this limit is reached, no more students can be enrolled. Let's add the following method to our `Course` bean:

```java
public void addStudent (Student student)
    throws EnrolmentFullException, SQLException {
  //get current enrolement first
  int currentEnrolment = courseDAO.getNumStudentsInCourse(id);
  if (currentEnrolment >= getMaxStudents())
```

```
     throw new EnrolmentFullException("Course if full. Enrolment closed");
   courseDAO.enrolStudentInCourse(id, student.getId());
}
```

The `addStudent` method first finds the current enrollment in the course. For this, it queries the database using the `CourseDAO` class. It then checks whether the current enrollment is less than the maximum enrollment. Then, it calls the `enrollStudentInCourse` method of `CourseDAO`.

The `addStudent` method has an external dependency. It depends on successful access to an external database. We can write a unit test for this function as follows:

```
@Test
public void testAddStudent() {
   //create course
   Course course = new Course();
   course.setId(1);
   course.setName("course1");
   course.setMaxStudents(2);
   //create student
   Student student = new Student();
   student.setFirstName("Student1");
   student.setId(1);
   //now add student
   try {
      course.addStudent(student);
   } catch (Exception e) {
      Assert.fail(e.getMessage());
   }
}
```

The `testAddStudent` method is meant to check whether `addStudent` method works fine when all external dependencies are satisfied; in this case, it means that a database connection is established, the database server is up and running, and the tables are configured properly. If we want to verify that the functionality to enroll a student on a course works by taking into account all dependencies, then we should write a functional test. Unit tests only need to check whether code that does not depend on external dependencies works fine; in this case, it is a trivial check to verify that the total enrollment is less than the maximum allowed enrollment. This is a simple example, but in real applications you might have a lot more complex code to test.

The problem with the previous unit test is that we may have false failures, from the perspective of unit testing, because the database could be down or might not be configured correctly. One solution is to mock external dependencies; we can mock calls to the database (in this case, calls to `CourseDAO`). Instead of making real calls to the database, we can create stubs that will return some mock data or perform a mock operation. For example, we can write a mock function that returns some hardcoded value for the `getNumStudentsInCourse` method of `CourseDAO`. However, we don't want to modify the application source code to add mock methods. Fortunately, there are open source frameworks that let us mock dependencies in unit tests. Next, we will see how to mock dependencies using a popular framework called Mockito (`http://mockito.org/`).

Using Mockito

At a very high level, we can use Mockito to do two things:

- Provide wrapper implementations over dependent methods in the application class
- Verify that these wrapper implementations are called

We specify the wrapper implementation using a static method of Mockito:

```
Mockito.when(object_name.method_name(params)).thenReturn(return_value);
```

Further, we verify whether the wrapper method was called by calling another static method of Mockito:

```
Mockito.verify(object_name, Mockito.atLeastOnce()).method_name(params);
```

To use Mockito in our project, we need to add a dependency on it in our `pom.xml`:

```
<dependency>
  <groupId>org.mockito</groupId>
  <artifactId>mockito-core</artifactId>
  <version>2.17.0</version>
</dependency>
```

Before we start writing a unit test case using Mockito, we will make a small change in the Course class. Currently, CourseDAO in the Course class is private and there are no setters for it. Add the setter method (setCourseDAO) in the Course class:

```
public void setCourseDAO(CourseDAO courseDAO) {
    this.courseDAO = courseDAO;
}
```

Now, let's rewrite our test case using Mockito.

First, we need to tell Mockito which method calls we want to mock and what action should be taken in the mocked function (for example, return a specific value). In our example, we would like to mock the methods in CourseDAO that are called from the Course.addStudent method, because methods in CourseDAO access the database, and we want our unit tests to be independent of the data access code. Therefore, we create a mocked (wrapper) instance of CourseDAO using Mockito:

```
CourseDAO courseDAO = Mockito.mock(CourseDAO.class);
```

Then, we tell Mockito which specific methods in this object to mock. We want to mock getNumStudentsInCourse and getNumStudentsInCourseas follows:

```
try {
Mockito.when(courseDAO.getNumStudentsInCourse(1)).thenReturn(60);
Mockito.doNothing().when(courseDAO).enrollStudentInCourse(1, 1);
} catch (SQLException e) {
  Assert.fail(e.getMessage());
}
```

The code is in a try...catch block because the getNumStudentsInCourse and getNumStudentsInCourse methods throw SQLException. This will not happen when we mock the method because the mocked method will not call any SQL code. However, since the signature of these methods indicates that SQLException can be thrown from these methods, we have to call them in try...catch to avoid compiler errors.

The first statement in the try block tells Mockito that when the getNumStudentsInCourse method is called on the courseDAO object with the parameter 1 (course ID), it should return 60 from the mocked method.

The second statement tells Mockito that when enrollStudentInCourse is called on the courseDAO object with the arguments 1 (course ID) and 1 (student ID), it should do nothing. We don't really want to insert any record into the database from the unit test code.

We will now create the `Course` and `Student` objects and call the `addStudent` method of `Course`. This code is similar to the one we wrote in the preceding test case:

```
Course course = new Course();
course.setCourseDAO(courseDAO);

course.setId(1);
course.setName("course1");
course.setMaxStudents(60);
//create student
Student student = new Student();
student.setFirstName("Student1");
student.setId(1);
//now add student
course.addStudent(student);
```

Note that the course ID and student ID that we used when creating the `Course` and `Student` objects, respectively, should match the arguments we passed to `getNumStudentsInCourse` and `enrollStudentInCourse` when mocking the methods.

We have set that the maximum number of students to be allowed in this course to 60. When mocking `getNumStudentsInCourse`, we asked Mockito to also return 60. Therefore, the `addStudent` method should throw an exception because the course is full. We will verify this by adding the `@Test` annotation later.

At the end of the test, we want to verify that the mocked method was actually called:

```
try {
  Mockito.verify(courseDAO,
Mockito.atLeastOnce()).getNumStudentsInCourse(1);
} catch (SQLException e) {
  Assert.fail(e.getMessage());
}
```

The preceding code verifies that `getNumStudentsInCourse` of `courseDAO` was called at least once by Mockito, when running this test.

Here is the complete test case, including the `@Test` annotation attribute, to make sure that the function throws an exception:

```
@Test (expected = EnrollmentFullException.class)
public void testAddStudentWithEnrollmentFull() throws Exception
  {
    CourseDAO courseDAO = Mockito.mock(CourseDAO.class);
    try {
Mockito.when(courseDAO.getNumStudentsInCourse(1)).thenReturn(60);
```

```
Mockito.doNothing().when(courseDAO).enrollStudentInCourse(1, 1);
    } catch (SQLException e) {
      Assert.fail(e.getMessage());
    }
    Course course = new Course();
    course.setCourseDAO(courseDAO);

    course.setId(1);
    course.setName("course1");
    course.setMaxStudents(60);
    //create student
    Student student = new Student();
    student.setFirstName("Student1");
    student.setId(1);
    //now add student
    course.addStudent(student);

    try {
      Mockito.verify(courseDAO,
        Mockito.atLeastOnce()).getNumStudentsInCourse(1);
    } catch (SQLException e) {
      Assert.fail(e.getMessage());
    }

    //If no exception was thrown then the test case was successful
    //No need of Assert here
  }
```

Now, run the unit tests. All tests should pass.

Here is a similar test case that makes Mockito return the current enrollment number of 59, and makes sure that the student is enrolled successfully:

```
@Test
public void testAddStudentWithEnrollmentOpen() throws Exception
  {
    CourseDAO courseDAO = Mockito.mock(CourseDAO.class);
    try {
Mockito.when(courseDAO.getNumStudentsInCourse(1)).thenReturn(59);
Mockito.doNothing().when(courseDAO).enrollStudentInCourse(1, 1);
    } catch (SQLException e) {
      Assert.fail(e.getMessage());
    }
    Course course = new Course();
    course.setCourseDAO(courseDAO);

    course.setId(1);
```

```
course.setName("course1");
course.setMaxStudents(60);
//create student
Student student = new Student();
student.setFirstName("Student1");
student.setId(1);
//now add student
course.addStudent(student);

try {
    Mockito.verify(courseDAO,
        Mockito.atLeastOnce()).getNumStudentsInCourse(1);
Mockito.verify(courseDAO,
        Mockito.atLeastOnce()).enrollStudentInCourse(1,1);
} catch (SQLException e) {
    Assert.fail(e.getMessage());
}

//If no exception was thrown then the test case was successful
//No need of Assert here
}
```

Note that this test case does not expect any exceptions to be thrown (if an exception is thrown, then the test case fails). We can also verify that the mocked `enrollStudentInCourse` method is called. We did not verify this in the previous test case because an exception was thrown before calling this method in the `Course.addStudent` method.

There are many topics of JUnit that we have not covered in this section. You are encouraged to read the JUnit documentation at `https://github.com/junit-team/junit4/wiki`. In particular, the following topics might be of interest to you:

- JUnit test suites. You can aggregate test cases from different test classes in a suite. Find more information about test suites at `https://github.com/junit-team/junit4/wiki/Aggregating-tests-in-suites`.
- Parameterized test cases; find information at `https://github.com/junit-team/junit4/wiki/Parameterized-tests`.
- If you are using Apache Ant for building your project, then take a look at the JUnit Ant task at `https://ant.apache.org/manual/Tasks/junit.html`.

Calculating unit test coverage

Unit tests tell you whether your application code behaves as expected. Unit tests are important to maintain code quality and catch errors early in the development cycle. However, this goal is at risk if you do not write enough unit tests to test your application code, or if you have not tested all possible input conditions in the test cases and the exception paths. To measure the quality and adequacy of your test cases, you need to calculate the coverage of your test cases. In simple terms, coverage tells you what percentage of your application code was touched by running your unit tests. There are different measures to calculate coverage:

- Number of lines covered
- Number of branches covered (created using the `if`, `else`, `elseif`, `switch`, and `try`/`catch` statements)
- Number of functions covered

Together, these three measures give a fair measurement of the quality of your unit tests. There are many code coverage tools for Java. In this chapter, we will take a look at an open source code coverage tool called JaCoCo (`http://www.eclemma.org/jacoco/`). JaCoCo also has an Eclipse plugin (`http://www.eclemma.org/`), and we can measure code coverage from right within Eclipse.

You can install the JaCoCo plugin using the update URL (`http://update.eclemma.org/`) or from **Eclipse Marketplace**. To install it using the update site, select the **Help | Install New Software...** menu. Click on the **Add** button and enter the name of the update site (you can give any name) and the update URL:

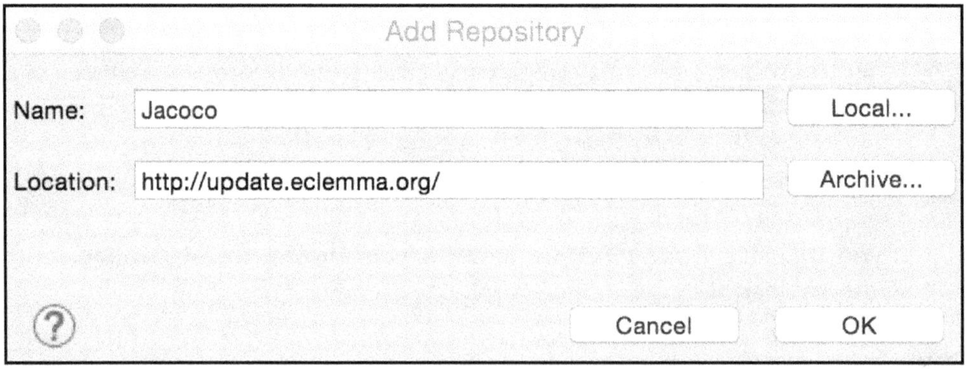

Figure 5.6: Add an update site for JaCoCo

Then, follow the instructions to install the plugin.

Alternatively, you can install it from the marketplace. Select the **Help** | **Eclipse Marketplace...** menu. Type `EclEmma` into the **Find** textbox, and click the **Go** button:

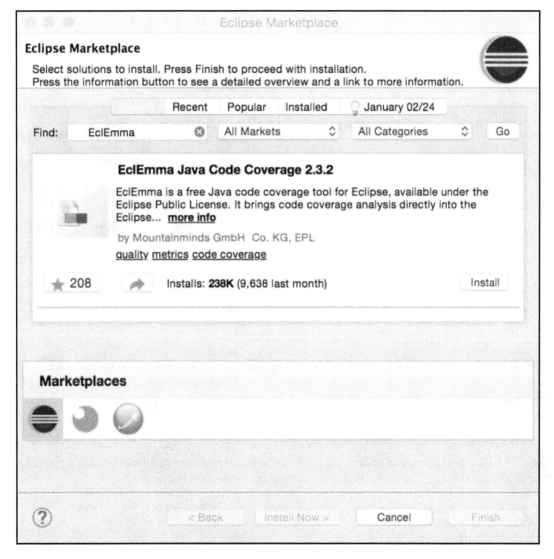

Figure 5.7: Install EclEmma code coverage plugin from Eclipse Marketplace

Click the **Install** button and follow the instructions.

To verify that the plugin is installed properly, open **Window** I **Show View** I **Other**. Type coverage into the **Filter** textbox and make sure that the **Coverage** (under the **Java** category) view is available. Open the view.

To run a unit test with coverage, right-click on the project in **Package Explorer** and select **Coverage As** I **JUnit Test**. After the tests have run, the coverage information is displayed in the **Coverage** view:

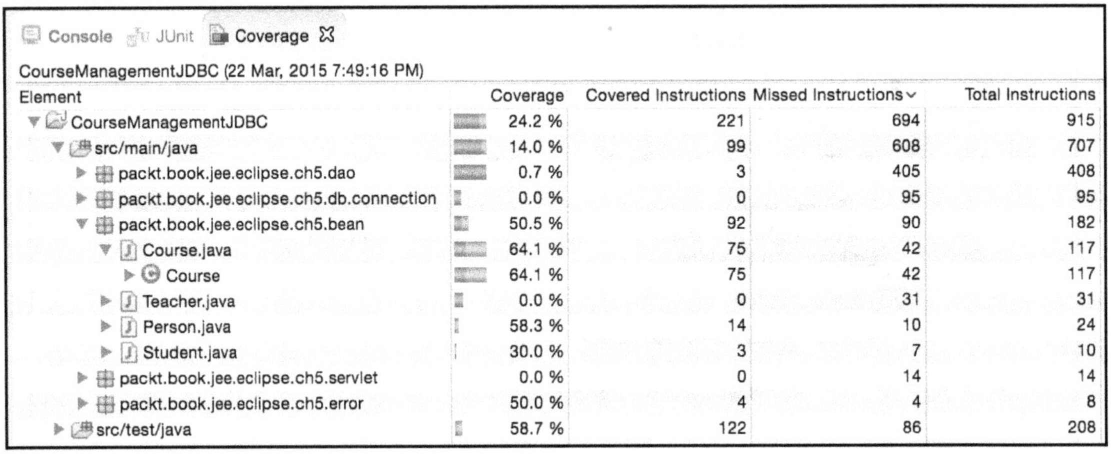

Element	Coverage	Covered Instructions	Missed Instructions ∨	Total Instructions
▼ 🗁 CourseManagementJDBC	24.2 %	221	694	915
▼ 🔗 src/main/java	14.0 %	99	608	707
▶ 🌐 packt.book.jee.eclipse.ch5.dao	0.7 %	3	405	408
▶ 🌐 packt.book.jee.eclipse.ch5.db.connection	0.0 %	0	95	95
▼ 🌐 packt.book.jee.eclipse.ch5.bean	50.5 %	92	90	182
▼ 🗋 Course.java	64.1 %	75	42	117
▶ 🔵 Course	64.1 %	75	42	117
▶ 🗋 Teacher.java	0.0 %	0	31	31
▶ 🗋 Person.java	58.3 %	14	10	24
▶ 🗋 Student.java	30.0 %	3	7	10
▶ 🌐 packt.book.jee.eclipse.ch5.servlet	0.0 %	0	14	14
▶ 🌐 packt.book.jee.eclipse.ch5.error	50.0 %	4	4	8
▶ 🔗 src/test/java	58.7 %	122	86	208

Console JUnit **Coverage** ✕

CourseManagementJDBC (22 Mar, 2015 7:49:16 PM)

Figure 5.8: Coverage results

How can you interpret these results? Overall, at the project level the coverage is **24.2%**. This means that out of all the code that we have written in this application, our unit test case has touched only **24.2%**. Then, there is the coverage percentage at the package level and at the class level.

Double-click on Course.java in the **Coverage** view to see which lines are covered in this file. The following screenshot shows a part of the file where the red lines indicate the code that is not covered, and the green lines indicate the code that is covered:

```
60⊝    public int getTeacherId() {
61          return teacherId;
62     }
63⊝    public void setTeacherId(int teacherId) {
64          this.teacherId = teacherId;
65     }
66⊝    public int getMinStudents() {
67          return minStudents;
68     }
69⊝    public void setMinStudents(int minStudents) {
70          this.minStudents = minStudents;
71     }
72⊝    public int getMaxStudents() {
73          return maxStudents;
74     }
75⊝    public void setMaxStudents(int maxStudents) {
76          this.maxStudents = maxStudents;
77     }
78⊝    public void addStudent (Student student)
79             throws EnrollmentFullException, SQLException {
80        //get current enrollement first
81        int currentEnrollment = courseDAO.getNumStudentsInCourse(id);
82        if (currentEnrollment >= getMaxStudents())
83            throw new EnrollmentFullException("Course if full. Enrollment closed");
84        courseDAO.enrollStudentInCourse(id, student.getId());
85     }
```

Figure 5.9: Line coverage details

We have written unit tests for addStudent, and the coverage of this class is **100%**, which is good. We haven't used all getters and setters in our unit tests, so some of them are not covered.

As you can see, the coverage results help you understand places in your code for which unit tests are not written, or which are partially covered by the unit tests. Based on this data, you can add unit tests for the code that is not covered. Of course, you may not want all lines to be covered if the code is very simple, such as the getters and setters in the preceding class, if the code is very simple.

In *Figure 5.8*, observe that the coverage tool has analyzed the test classes too. Typically, we don't want to measure coverage on test classes; we want to measure the coverage of the application code by running the test classes. To exclude the test classes from this analysis, right-click on the project and select **Coverage As | Coverage Configurations...**. Click on the **Coverage** tab and select only **CourseManagementJDBC - src/main/java**:

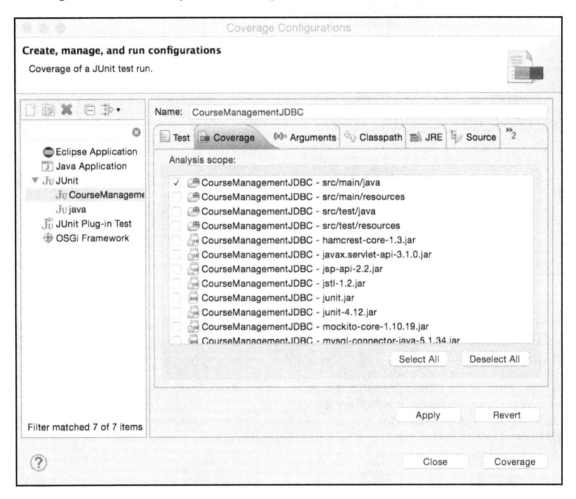

Figure 5.10: Coverage configurations

Click **Coverage** to run coverage with the new settings. You will see in the **Coverage** view that the test classes do not appear in the report, and that the overall test coverage on the project has also dropped.

If you want to run coverage using Maven, then refer to `http://www.eclemma.org/jacoco/trunk/doc/maven.html`. Specifically, take a look at `pom.xml` (`http://jacoco.org/jacoco/trunk/doc/examples/build/pom-it.xml`), which creates reports for JUnit and JaCoCo coverage.

Summary

Writing unit tests is an important part of the application development process. Unit tests help you catch bugs in your application at very early stages; they also help you catch any regression because of subsequent code changes. JUnit and Eclipse provide an easy way to integrate unit tests into your development workflow. Eclipse also creates a nice report in the JUnit view, which makes it easy to identify the failed tests and jump to the line in the code where the test failed.

Unit tests are meant to be executed without any external dependencies. Libraries such as Mockito help you to mock any external dependencies.

Use coverage tools such as JaCoCo to find out the quality of the unit tests that you have written. Coverage tools tell you the percentage of the application code that is covered by your unit tests. You can also see in each class which lines are covered by your unit tests and which are not. Such a report can help you to decide whether you need to write more unit test cases or modify the existing unit test cases to cover important code that your unit tests have not tested.

In the next chapter, we will see how to debug Java applications from Eclipse. The chapter will also explain how to connect to a remote JEE server for debugging.

Debugging the JEE Application

6

In the previous chapter, we learned how to write and run unit tests for Java applications using Eclipse and JUnit. In this chapter, we are going to learn how to use Eclipse to debug JEE applications. Debugging is an unavoidable part of application development. Unless the application is very simple, the chances are that it is not going to work as expected on the very first attempt and you will spend some time trying to find out the reasons why. In very complex applications, application developers may end up spending more time debugging than writing application code. Problems may not necessarily exist in your code, but may exist in the external system that your application depends on. Debugging a complex piece of software requires skill, which can be developed with experience. However, it also needs good support from the application runtime and IDE.

There are different ways to debug an application. You may just put `System.out.println()` statements in your code and print values of the variables, or just a message stating that execution of the application has reached a certain point. If the application is small or simple, this may work, but this may not be a good idea when debugging large and complex applications. You also need to remember to remove such debug statements before moving the code to staging or production. If you have written unit tests and if some of the unit tests fail, then that may give you some idea about the problems in your code. However, in many cases, you may want to monitor the execution of code at line level or function level and check the values of the variables at that line or in that function. This requires support from the language runtime and a good IDE that helps you visualize and control the debugging process. Fortunately, Java has an excellent debugger, and Eclipse JEE provides great support for debugging Java code.

In this chapter, we are going to learn how to debug JEE applications using Eclipse JEE. We will use the same *Course Management* application that we built in Chapter 4, *Creating JEE Database Applications*, for debugging. The debugging technique described in this chapter can be applied to remotely debug any Java application, and is not necessarily restricted to the JEE applications.

In this chapter, we are going to cover the following topics:

- Setting up Eclipse to debug JEE applications remotely
- Understanding how to perform different different debugging actions, such as setting breakpoints, inspecting variables and expressions, and stepping through the code
- Connecting the debugger from Eclipse to an externally running JEE application server

Debugging a remote Java application

You may have debugged standalone Java applications from Eclipse. You set breakpoints in the code, run the application in the **Debug** mode from Eclipse, and then debug the application by stepping through the code. Debugging remote Java applications is a bit different, particularly when it comes to how you launch the debugger. In the case of local application, the debugger launches the application. In the case of remote application, it is already launched and you need to connect the debugger to it. In general, if you want to allow remote debugging for the application, you need to run the application using the following parameters:

```
-Xdebug -Xrunjdwp:transport=dt_socket,address=9001,server=y,suspend=n
```

- Xdebug enables debugging
- Xrunjdwp runs the debugger implementation of the **Java Debug Wire Protocol (JDWP)**

Instead of −Xdebug −Xrunjdwp, you can also use −agentlib:jdwp for JDK 1.5 and above, for example:

−agentlib:jdwp=transport= dt_socket,address=9001,server=y,suspend=n

Let's understand the parameters used here in detail:

- `transport=dt_socket`: This starts a socket server at `address=9001` (this can be any free port) to receive debugger commands and send responses.
- `server=y`: This tells the JVM if the application is a server or a client, in the context of debugger communication. Use the `y` value for remote applications.
- `suspend=n`: This tells the JVM to not wait for the debugger client to attach to it. If the value is `y`, then the JVM will wait before executing the main class until a debugger client attaches to it. Setting the `y` value for this option may be useful in cases where you want to debug, for example, the initialization code of servlets that are loaded upon startup of the web container. In such cases, if you do not choose to suspend the application till the debugger connects to it, the code that you want to debug may get executed before the debugger client attaches to it.

Debugging a web application using Tomcat in Eclipse EE

We have already learned how to configure Tomcat in Eclipse EE and deploy web applications in it from Eclipse (refer to the *Configuring Tomcat in Eclipse* and *Running JSP in Tomcat* sections in Chapter 2, *Creating a Simple JEE Web Application*). We will use the *Course Management* application that we created in Chapter 4, *Creating JEE Database Applications* (JDBC version), for debugging.

Starting Tomcat in Debug mode

If you want to debug a remote Java process, you need to start the process using debug parameters. However, if you have configured Tomcat in Eclipse EE, you don't need to do this manually. Eclipse takes care of launching Tomcat in **Debug** mode. To start Tomcat in **Debug** mode, select the server in the **Servers** view and click the **Debug** button. Alternatively, right-click on the server and select **Debug** from the menu. Make sure that the project you want to debug is already added to Tomcat; in this case, the project is `CourseManagementJDBC`:

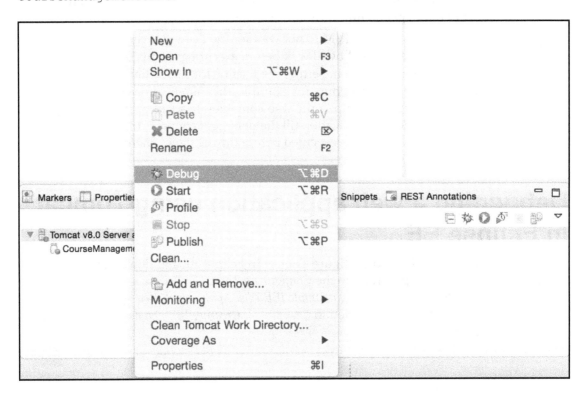

Figure 6.1: Starting Tomcat in Debug mode

Once Tomcat is started in **Debug** mode, its status changes to **Debugging**:

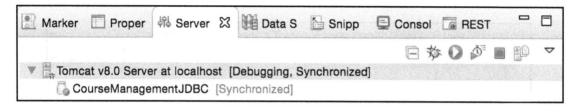

Figure 6.2: Tomcat running in Debug mode

Setting breakpoints

Now, let's set breakpoints in the code before we launch the `CourseManagement`
application. Open `CourseDAO` from the `CourseManagementJDBC` project and double-click
in the left margin of the first line in the `getCourses` method:

```java
47
48    public List<Course> getCourses () throws SQLException {
49        //get connection from connection pool
50        Connection con = DatabaseConnectionFactory.getConnectionFactory().getConnection();
51
52        List<Course> courses = new ArrayList<Course>();
53        Statement stmt = null;
54        ResultSet rs = null;
55        try {
56            stmt = con.createStatement();
57
58            StringBuilder sb = new StringBuilder("select course.id as courseId, course.name as c(
59                .append("course.credits as credits, Teacher.id as teacherId, Teacher.first_name (
60                .append("Teacher.last_name as lastName, Teacher.designation designation ")
61                .append("from Course left outer join Teacher on ")
62                .append("course.Teacher_id = Teacher.id ")
63                .append("order by course.name");
64
```

Figure 6.3: Setting a breakpoint

Another way to set a breakpoint at a line is to right-click in the left margin and select **Toggle Breakpoint**:

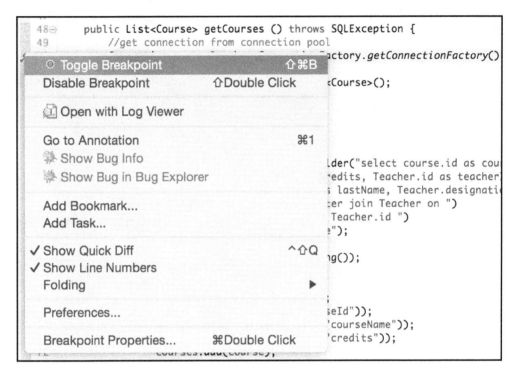

Figure 6.4: Toggling breakpoints using the menu

You can also set breakpoints at the method level. Just place the caret inside any method, and select the **Run | Toggle Method Breakpoint** menu. This is equivalent to setting the breakpoint at the first line of the method. This is preferred over setting a breakpoint at the first line of the method when you always want to stop at the beginning of the method. The debugger will always stop at the first statement in the method, even if you later insert code at the beginning of the method.

Another useful breakpoint option is to set it when any exception occurs during program execution. Often, you may not want to set a breakpoint at a specific location, but may want to investigate why an exception is happening. If you do not have access to the stack trace of the exception, you can just set a breakpoint for the exception and run the program again. Next time, the execution will stop at the code location where the exception occurred. This makes it easy to debug exceptions. To set a breakpoint for an exception, select **Run** | **Add Java Exception Breakpoint...** and select the Exception class from the list:

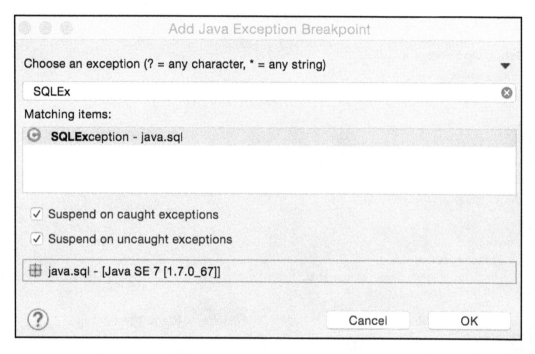

Figure 6.5: Setting a breakpoint at an exception

Running the application in Debug mode

Now, let's run the `listCourse.jsp` page in **Debug** mode:

1. In **Project Navigator**, go to `src/main/webapp/listCourse.jsp` and right-click on the file. Select **Debug As** | **Debug on Server**. Eclipse may prompt you to use the existing debug server:

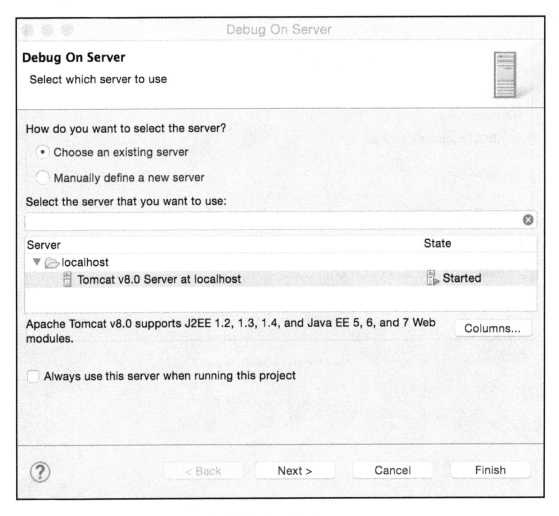

Figure 6.6: Choosing an existing debug server

2. Click **Finish**. Eclipse will ask you if you want to switch to the **Debug** perspective (refer to `Chapter 1`, *Introducing JEE and Eclipse,* for a discussion on Eclipse perspectives):

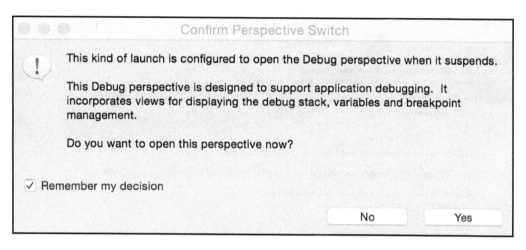

Figure 6.7: Auto-switching to the Debug perspective

3. Select the **Remember my decision** option and click the **Yes** button. Eclipse will switch to the **Debug** perspective. Eclipse will try to open the page in the internal Eclipse browser, but it won't display the page immediately. Recall that `listCourse.jsp` calls `Course.getCourses()`, which in turn calls `CourseDAO.getCourses()`. We have set a breakpoint in the `CourseDAO.getCourses()` method, so the execution of the page stops there:

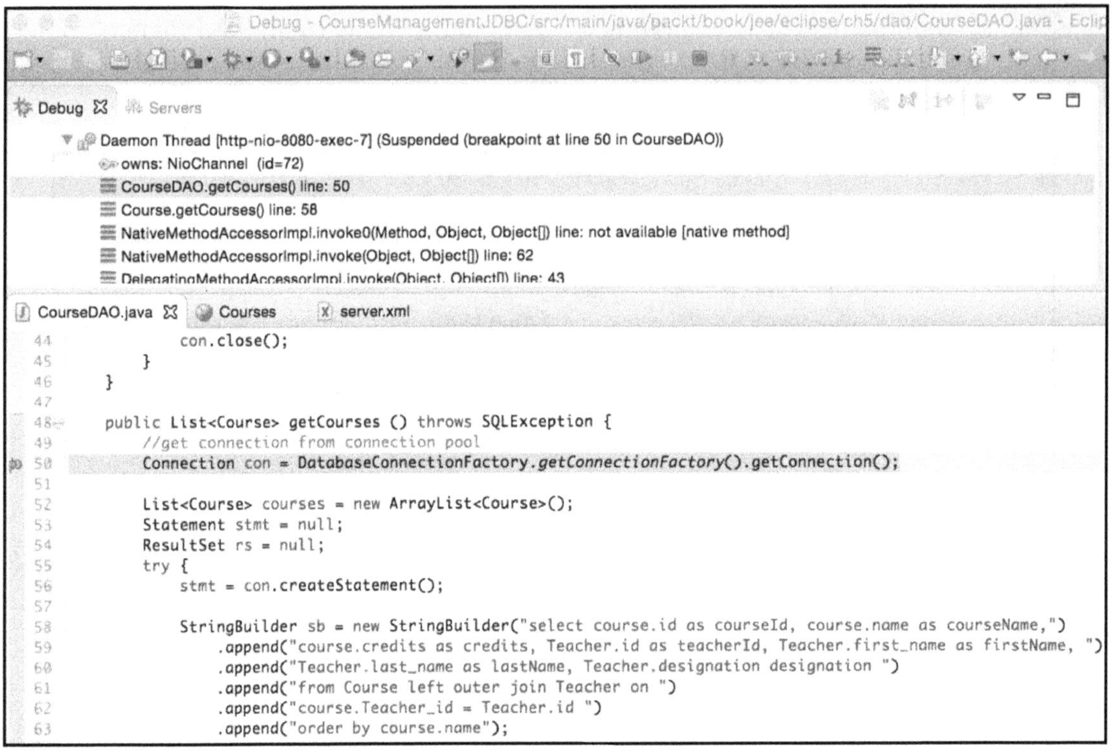

Figure 6.8: The debugger paused at a breakpoint

Performing step operations and inspecting variables

You can now perform different step operations (step over, step in, and step out) using the toolbar icons at the top, or using keyboard shortcuts. Open the drop-down on the **Run** menu to learn about the menu and toolbar shortcuts for debugging. Typically, you would inspect variables or perform step operations to verify whether the execution flow is correct and then continue the execution by clicking the **Resume** button or by using the menu/keyboard shortcut.

In the **Debug** tab (refer to *Figure 6.8*), you can see all the threads and inspect the stack frames of each thread when the debugger is suspended. Stack frames of a thread show you the path of a program execution in that thread until the point that the debugger was suspended after hitting a breakpoint or due to step operations. In a multithreaded application, such as a Tomcat web container, more than one thread might have been suspended at a time and each might have different stack frames. When debugging a multithreaded application, make sure that you have selected the required thread in the **Debug** tab before selecting options to step over/in/out or resume.

Often, you step into a method and realize that the values are not what you expect and you want to rerun statements in the current method to investigate them. In such cases, you can drop to any previous stack frame and start over.

For example, let's say that in the preceding example we step into the `DatabaseConnectionFactory.getConnectionFactory().getConnection` method. When we step in, the debugger first steps into the `getConnectionFactory` method, and in the next step-in operation, it steps into the `getConnection` method. Suppose, when we are in the `getConnection` method that we want to go back and check what happened in the `getConnectionFactory` method for something that we might have missed earlier (although in this simple example, not much happens in the `getConnectionFactory` method; it should just serve as an example). We can go back to the `getCourses` method and start over the execution of `getConnectionFactory` and `getConnection`. In the **Debug** tab, right-click on the `CourseDAO.getCourses()` stack frame and select **Drop to Frame**, as shown in the following screenshot:

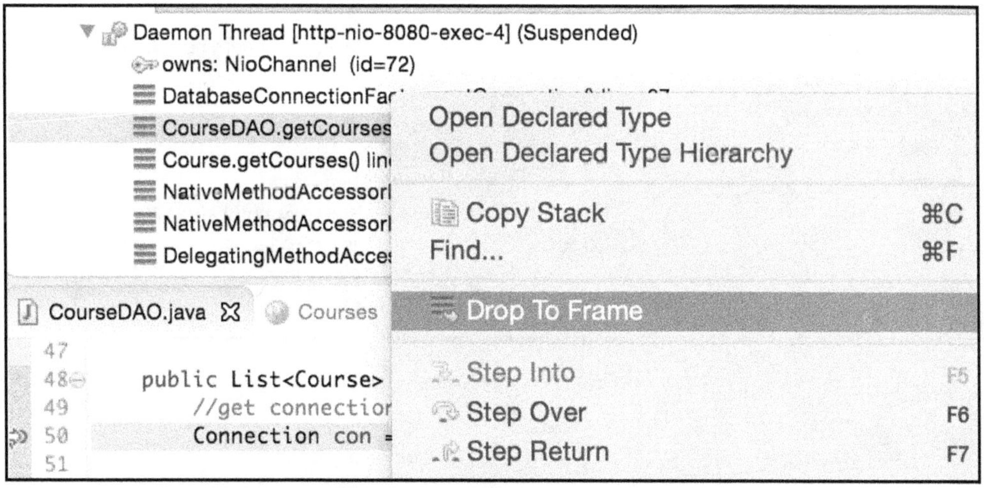

Figure 6.9 Drop to Frame

The debugger discards all the stack frames above the selected frame, and the execution drops back to the selected frame; in this case, in the `getCourses` method of the `CourseDAO` class. You can then step over again into the `getConnection` method. Note that only stack variables and their values are discarded when you drop to frame. Any changes made to reference objects that are not on the stack are not rolled back.

Inspecting variable values

Now let's step over a few statements till we are in the `while` loop to create course objects from the data returned by the result set. In the top-right window, you will find the **Variables** view, which displays variables applicable at that point of execution:

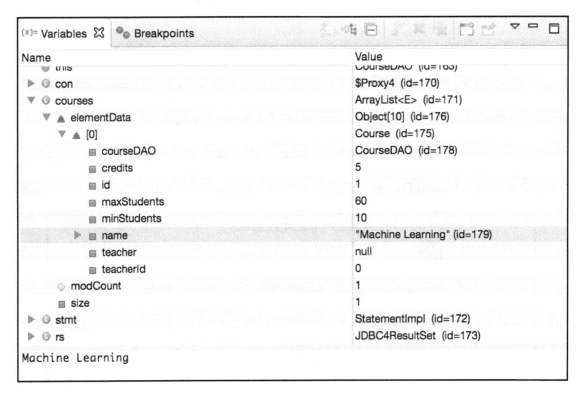

Figure 6.10: The debugger paused at breakpoint

You can inspect variables in the previous method calls too by changing the selection in the **Debug** tab: click on any previous method call (stack frame) and the **Variables** view will display variables that are valid for the selected method. You can change the value of any variable, including values of the member variables of the objects. For example, in *Figure 6.8*, we can change the value of the course name from `"Machine Learning"` to `"Machine Learning - Part1"`. To change the variable value, right-click on the variable in the **Variables** view and select **Change Value**:

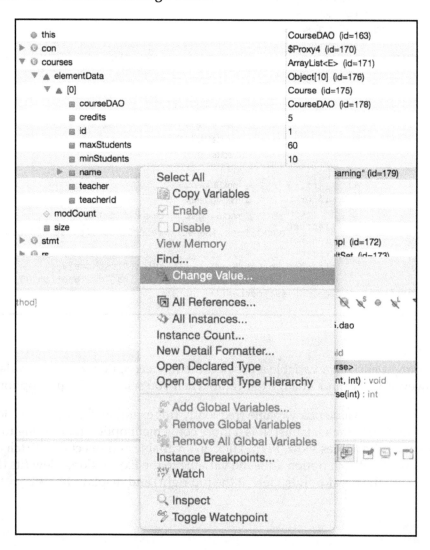

Figure 6.11: Changing the variable's value during debugging

You don't have to go to the **Variables** view to check a variable's value every time. There is a quick way: just hover the cursor over the variable in the editor and Eclipse will pop up a window showing the variable's value:

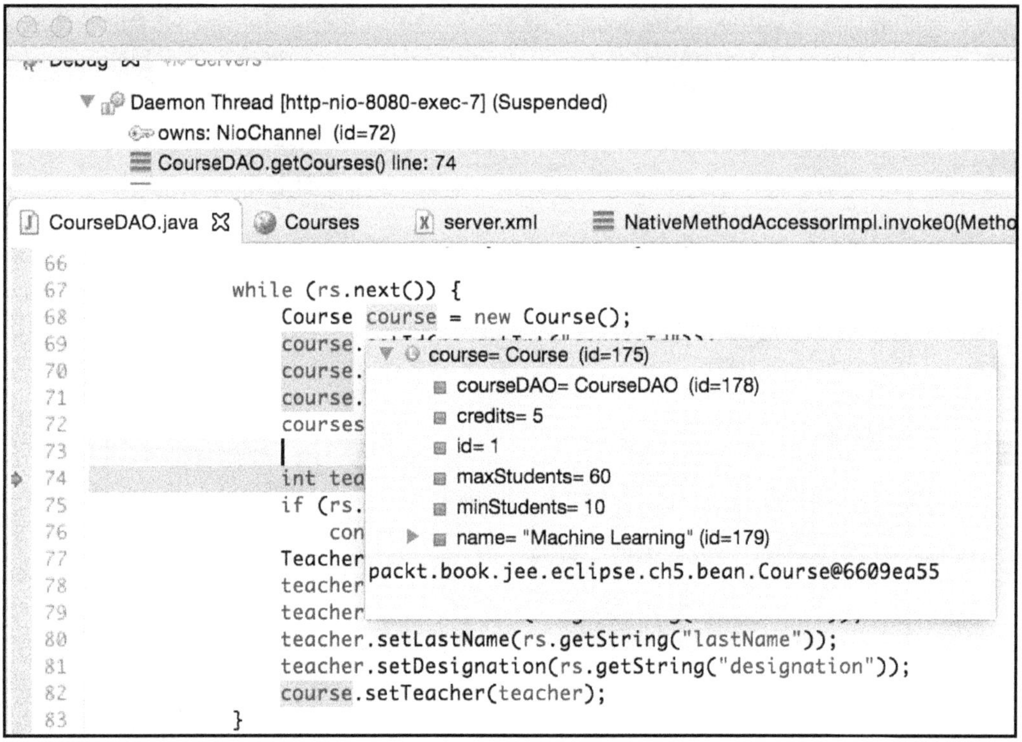

Figure 6.12: Inspecting the variable

You can also right-click on a variable and select the **Inspect** option to see the variable's values. However, you cannot change the value when you select the **Inspect** option.

If you want to see the value of a variable frequently (for example, a variable in a loop), you can add the variable to the watchlist. It is a more convenient option than trying to search for the variable in the **Variables** view. Right-click on a variable and select the **Watch** option from the menu. The **Watch** option adds the variable to the **Expressions** view (its default location is next to the **Breakpoints** view at the top right) and displays its value:

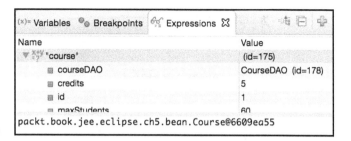

Figure 6.13: Inspecting a variable

The use of the **Expressions** view is not limited to watching variable values. You can watch any valid Java expression, such as arithmetic expressions, or even method calls. Click on the plus icon in the **Expressions** view and add an expression.

Debugging an application in an externally configured Tomcat

Thus far, we have debugged our application using Tomcat configured within Eclipse. When we launched Tomcat in **Debug** mode, Eclipse took care of adding the JVM parameters for debugging to the Tomcat launch script. In this section, we will see how to launch an external (to Eclipse) Tomcat instance and connect to it from Eclipse. Although we are going to debug a remote instance of Tomcat, information in this section can be used for connecting to any remotely running Java program that is launched in **Debug** mode. We have already seen the debug parameters to pass when launching a remote application in **Debug** mode.

Launching Tomcat externally in **Debug** mode is not too difficult. Tomcat startup scripts already have an option to start the server in **Debug** mode; you just need to pass the appropriate parameters. From the Command Prompt, select the <TOMCAT_HOME>/bin folder and type the following command in Windows:

```
>catalina.bat jpda start
```

Launching Tomcat in **Debug** mode in Mac OSX and Linux:

```
$./catalina.sh jpda start
```

Passing the jpda argument sets the default values to all the required debug parameters. The default debug port is 8000. If you want to change it, either modify catalin.bat/catalin.sh or set the environment variable JPDA_ADDRESS as follows:

Setting `JPDA_ADDRESS` environment variable in Windows:

> `>set JPDA_ADDRESS=9001`

Setting `JPDA_ADDRESS` environment variable in OSX and Linux:

> `$export JPDA_ADDRESS=9001`

Similarly, you can set `JPDA_SUSPEND` to `y` or `n` to control whether the debugger should wait for the client to connect before executing the `main` class.

To connect the debugger from Eclipse to a remote instance, select the **Run | Debug Configurations...** menu. Right-click on the **Remote Java Application** node in the list view on the left and select **New**:

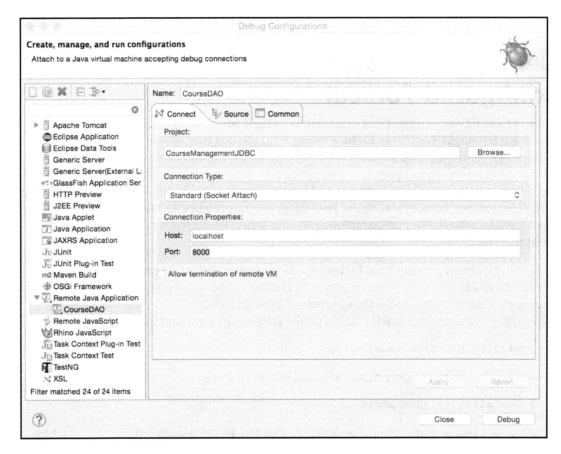

Figure 6.14: Inspecting a variable

Set the appropriate **Project** and **Port** (the same as what you selected to start Tomcat in **Debug** mode, that is, the default: 8000) and click **Debug**. If the debugger connection is successful, Eclipse will switch to the debug perspective. From here on out, the process of debugging is the same as that explained earlier.

Using the debugger to know the status of program execution

We have seen how to use the debugger to verify the execution flow of a program (using the step operations) and to inspect variables. You can also use the debugger to know what the status of the running program is. For example, a web request is taking too long and you want to know where exactly the execution is stuck. You can use the debugger to find this. It is similar to taking the thread dump of a running program, but is much easier than the methods used to get the thread dump. Let's assume that our `CourseDAO.getCourses` method is taking a long time to execute. Let's simulate this by using a couple of `Thread.sleep` calls, as shown in the following code snippet:

```
public List<Course> getCourses () throws SQLException {
  //get connection from connection pool
  Connection con =
DatabaseConnectionFactory.getConnectionFactory().getConnection();

  try {
    Thread.sleep(5000);
  } catch (InterruptedException e) {}


  List<Course> courses = new ArrayList<Course>();
  Statement stmt = null;
  ResultSet rs = null;
  try {
    stmt = con.createStatement();

    StringBuilder sb = new StringBuilder("select course.id as
      courseId, course.name as courseName,")        .append("course.credits as
credits, Teacher.id as teacherId,
        Teacher.first_name as firstName, ")        .append("Teacher.last_name
as lastName, Teacher.designation
        designation ")
      .append("from Course left outer join Teacher on ")
      .append("course.Teacher_id = Teacher.id ")
      .append("order by course.name");
```

```
      rs = stmt.executeQuery(sb.toString());

    while (rs.next()) {
      Course course = new Course();
      course.setId(rs.getInt("courseId"));
      course.setName(rs.getString("courseName"));
      course.setCredits(rs.getInt("credits"));
      courses.add(course);

      int teacherId = rs.getInt("teacherId");
      if (rs.wasNull()) //no teacher set for this course.
        continue;
      Teacher teacher = new Teacher();
      teacher.setId(teacherId);
      teacher.setFirstName(rs.getString("firstName"));
      teacher.setLastName(rs.getString("lastName"));
      teacher.setDesignation(rs.getString("designation"));
      course.setTeacher(teacher);
    }

    try {
      Thread.sleep(5000);
    } catch (InterruptedException e) {}


    return courses;
  } finally {
    try {if (rs != null) rs.close();} catch (SQLException e) {}
    try {if (stmt != null) stmt.close();} catch (SQLException e)
{}
    try {con.close();} catch (SQLException e) {}
  }
}
```

Start Tomcat in **Debug** mode, and run `listCourses.jsp` in **Debug** mode. Because we have inserted `Thread.sleep` statements, the request will take time. Go to the **Debug** view, which is where threads and stack frames are displayed. Click on the first node under the Tomcat debug configuration node and select the **Suspend** option, as shown in the following screenshot:

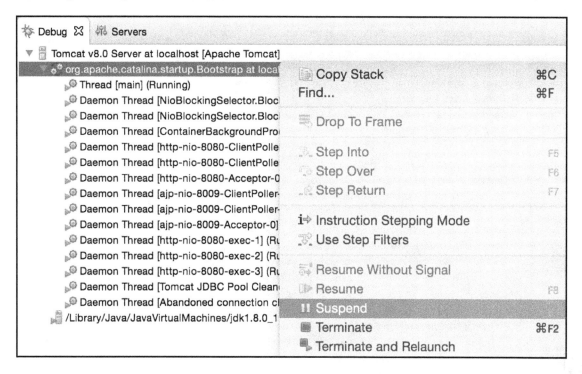

Figure 6.15: Suspending program execution

The debugger pauses execution of all threads in the program. You can then see the status of each thread by expanding the thread nodes. You will find one of the threads executing the `CourseDAO.getCourse` method and the statement that it was executing before being suspended:

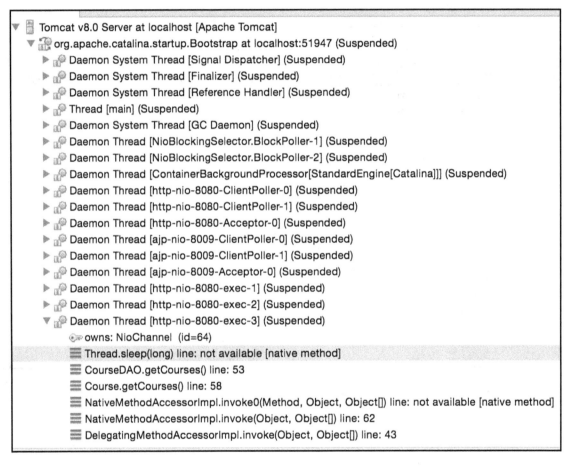

▼ 🖥 Tomcat v8.0 Server at localhost [Apache Tomcat]
  ▼ 🖳 org.apache.catalina.startup.Bootstrap at localhost:51947 (Suspended)
    ▶ 🖫 Daemon System Thread [Signal Dispatcher] (Suspended)
    ▶ 🖫 Daemon System Thread [Finalizer] (Suspended)
    ▶ 🖫 Daemon System Thread [Reference Handler] (Suspended)
    ▶ 🖫 Thread [main] (Suspended)
    ▶ 🖫 Daemon System Thread [GC Daemon] (Suspended)
    ▶ 🖫 Daemon Thread [NioBlockingSelector.BlockPoller-1] (Suspended)
    ▶ 🖫 Daemon Thread [NioBlockingSelector.BlockPoller-2] (Suspended)
    ▶ 🖫 Daemon Thread [ContainerBackgroundProcessor[StandardEngine[Catalina]]] (Suspended)
    ▶ 🖫 Daemon Thread [http-nio-8080-ClientPoller-0] (Suspended)
    ▶ 🖫 Daemon Thread [http-nio-8080-ClientPoller-1] (Suspended)
    ▶ 🖫 Daemon Thread [http-nio-8080-Acceptor-0] (Suspended)
    ▶ 🖫 Daemon Thread [ajp-nio-8009-ClientPoller-0] (Suspended)
    ▶ 🖫 Daemon Thread [ajp-nio-8009-ClientPoller-1] (Suspended)
    ▶ 🖫 Daemon Thread [ajp-nio-8009-Acceptor-0] (Suspended)
    ▶ 🖫 Daemon Thread [http-nio-8080-exec-1] (Suspended)
    ▶ 🖫 Daemon Thread [http-nio-8080-exec-2] (Suspended)
    ▼ 🖫 Daemon Thread [http-nio-8080-exec-3] (Suspended)
      ☞ owns: NioChannel (id=64)
      ☰ Thread.sleep(long) line: not available [native method]
      ☰ CourseDAO.getCourses() line: 53
      ☰ Course.getCourses() line: 58
      ☰ NativeMethodAccessorImpl.invoke0(Method, Object, Object[]) line: not available [native method]
      ☰ NativeMethodAccessorImpl.invoke(Object, Object[]) line: 62
      ☰ DelegatingMethodAccessorImpl.invoke(Object, Object[]) line: 43

Figure 6.16: The status of suspended threads

From the preceding screenshot, you can see that the execution of the thread is suspended in the `CourseDAO.getCourses` method of the `Thread.sleep` statement. You can even inspect variables at each stack frame when the program is suspended. By suspending the program and inspecting the state of threads and stack frames, you may be able to find bottlenecks in your application.

Summary

Good support for debugging from language runtime and IDE can considerably reduce the time spent in debugging. Java runtime and Eclipse provide excellent support for debugging local and remote applications. To debug a remote application, launch it with debug parameters for JVM and connect the Eclipse debugger to it. You can then debug the remote application just as you would debug the local one, that is, set breakpoints, perform step operations, and inspect variables. You can also change variable values in the application when its execution is suspended.

In the next chapter, we will see how to develop JEE applications using EJBs and use the GlassFish server. Although this chapter explained the debugging of JEE applications deployed in Tomcat, you can use the same techniques in the GlassFish server.

7
Creating JEE Applications with EJB

In the last chapter, we learned some techniques to debug JEE applications from Eclipse. In this chapter, we will shift our focus back to JEE application development and learn how to create and use **Enterprise JavaBeans** (**EJB**). If you recall the architecture of database applications in Chapter 4, *Creating JEE Database Applications*, we had JSP or a JSF page calling a JSP bean or a managed bean. The beans then called DAOs to execute the data access code. This separated code for the user interface, the business logic, and the database nicely. This would work for small or medium applications, but may prove to be a bottleneck in large enterprise applications; the application may not scale very well. If processing of the business logic is time consuming then it would make more sense to distribute it on different servers for better scalability and resilience. If code for the user interface, the business logic, and the data access is all on the same machine, then it may affect scalability of the application; that is, it may not perform well under the load.

Using EJB for implementing the business logic is ideal in scenarios where you want components processing the business logic to be distributed across different servers. However, this is just one of the advantages of EJB. Even if you use EJBs on the same server as the web application, you may gain from a number of services that the EJB container provides; you can specify the security constraints for calling EJB methods declaratively (using annotations) and can easily specify transaction boundaries (specify a set of method calls from a part of one transaction) using annotations. Furthermore, the container handles the life cycle of EJBs, including pooling of certain types of EJB objects so that more objects can be created when load on the application increases.

In Chapter 4, *Creating JEE Database Applications*, we created a *Course Management* web application using simple JavaBeans. In this chapter, we will create the same application using EJBs and deploy it on the GlassFish Server. However, before that we need to understand some basic concepts of EJBs.

We will cover the following broad topics:

- Understanding different types of EJBs and how they can be accessed from different client deployment scenarios
- Configuring GlassFish Server for testing EJB applications in Eclipse
- Creating and testing EJB projects from Eclipse with and without Maven

Types of EJB

EJB can be of the following types according to the EJB3 specification:

- Session bean:

    - Stateful session bean
    - Stateless session bean
    - Singleton session bean

- Message-driven bean

We will discuss **message-driven bean** (**MDB**) in detail in a Chapter 10, *Asynchronous Programming with JMS*, when we learn about asynchronous processing of requests in the JEE application. In this chapter, we will focus on session beans.

Session beans

In general, session beans are meant to contain methods to execute the main business logic of the enterprise application. Any **Plain Old Java Object** (**POJO**) can be annotated with the appropriate EJB3-specific annotations to make it a session bean. Session beans come in three types.

Stateful session beans

One stateful session bean serves requests for one client only. There is one-to-one mapping between the stateful session bean and the client. Therefore, stateful beans can hold the state data for the client between multiple method calls. In our *Course Management* application, we could use a stateful bean for holding student data (student profile and courses taken by her/him) after a student logs in. The state maintained by the stateful bean is lost when the server restarts or when the session times out. Since there is one stateful bean per client, using a stateful bean might impact scalability of the application.

We use the `@Stateful` annotation on the class to mark it as a stateful session bean.

Stateless session beans

A stateless session bean does not hold any state information for the client. Therefore, one session bean can be shared across multiple clients. The EJB container maintains pools of stateless beans, and when a client request comes, it takes a bean out of the pool, executes methods, and returns the bean to the pool again. Stateless session beans provide excellent scalability because they can be shared and they need not be created for each client.

We use the `@Stateless` annotation on the class to mark it as a stateless session bean.

Singleton session beans

As the name suggests, there is only one instance of a singleton bean class in the EJB container (this is true in the clustered environment too; each EJB container will have one instance of a singleton bean). This means that they are shared by multiple clients, and they are not pooled by EJB containers (because there can be only one instance). Since a singleton session bean is a shared resource, we need to manage concurrency in it. Java EE provides two concurrency management options for singleton session beans, namely container-managed concurrency and bean-managed concurrency. Container-managed concurrency can be easily specified by annotations.

See `https://javaee.github.io/tutorial/ejb-basicexamples003.html#GIPSZ` for more information on managing concurrency in singleton session beans.

The use of a singleton bean could have an impact on the scalability of the application if there are resource contentions.

We use the `@Singleton` annotation on the class to mark it as a singleton session bean.

Accessing session beans from a client

Session beans can be designed to be accessed locally (client and bean in the same application), remotely (from a client running in a different application or JVM), or both. In the case of remote access, session beans are required to implement a remote interface. For local access, session beans can implement a local interface or implement no interface (no-interface view of a session bean). The remote and local interfaces that the session bean implements are sometimes also called **business interfaces** because they typically expose the primary business functionality.

Creating a no-interface session bean

To create a session bean with the no-interface view, create a POJO and annotate it with the appropriate EJB annotation type and `@LocalBean`. For example, we can create a local stateful `Student` bean as follows:

```
import javax.ejb.LocalBean;
import javax.ejb.Singleton;

@Singleton
@LocalBean
public class Student {
...
}
```

Accessing session beans using dependency injection

You can access session beans either using the `@EJB` annotation (which injects the bean in the client class) or by performing the **Java Naming and Directory Interface (JNDI)** lookup. EJB containers are required to make JNDI URLs of the EJBs available to clients.

Injecting session beans using `@EJB` works only for managed components, that is, components of the application whose life cycle is managed by the EJB container. When a component is managed by the container, it is created (instantiated) and destroyed by the container. You do not create managed components using the `new` operator. JEE-managed components that support direct injection of EJBs are servlets, managed beans of JSF pages, and EJBs themselves (one EJB can have another EJB injected into it). Unfortunately, you cannot have a web container inject EJBs in JSPs or JSP beans. Furthermore, you cannot have EJBs injected into any custom classes that you create and that are instantiated using the `new` operator. Later in the chapter, we will see how to use JNDI to access EJBs from objects that are not managed by the container.

We could use a student bean (created previously) from a managed bean of a JSF as follows:

```
import javax.ejb.EJB;
import javax.faces.bean.ManagedBean;

@ManagedBean
public class StudentJSFBean {
  @EJB
  private Student studentEJB;
}
```

Note that if you create an EJB with no-interface view, then all `public` methods in that EJB will be exposed to the client. If you want to control the methods that could be called by the client, then you should implement a business interface.

Creating session beans using local business interface

Business interface for the EJB is a simple Java interface annotated either with `@Remote` or `@Local`. Therefore, we can create a local interface for a student bean as follows:

```
import java.util.List;
import javax.ejb.Local;

@Local
public interface StudentLocal {
  public List<Course> getCourses();
}
```

Furthermore, we can implement a session bean as follows:

```
import java.util.List;
import javax.ejb.Local;
import javax.ejb.Stateful;
```

```
@Stateful
@Local
public class Student implements StudentLocal {
  @Override
  public List<CourseDTO> getCourses() {
    //get courses are return
  ...
  }
}
```

The client can access the `Student` EJB only through the local interface:

```
import javax.ejb.EJB;
import javax.faces.bean.ManagedBean;

@ManagedBean
public class StudentJSFBean {
  @EJB
  private StudentLocal student;
}
```

A session bean can implement multiple business interfaces.

Accessing session beans using JNDI lookup

Although accessing EJB using dependency injection is the easiest way, it works only if the container manages the class that accesses the EJB. If you want to access EJB from a POJO that is not a managed bean, then dependency injection will not work. Another scenario where dependency injection does not work is when EJB is deployed in a separate JVM (could be on a remote server). In such cases, you will have to access the EJB using JNDI lookup (visit `https://docs.oracle.com/javase/tutorial/jndi/` for more information on JNDI).

JEE applications could be packaged in **Enterprise Application aRchive** (**EAR**), which contains a `.jar` file for EJBs and a `.war` file for web applications (and a `lib` folder containing libraries required for both). If, for example, the name of the EAR file is `CourseManagement.ear` and the name of the EJB JAR in it is `CourseManagementEJBs.jar`, then the name of the application is `CourseManagement` (name of the EAR file) and the module name is `CourseManagementEJBs`. The EJB container uses these names to create JNDI URL for looking up EJBs. A global JNDI URL for EJB is created as follows:

```
"java:global/<application_name>/<module_name>/<bean_name>![<bean_interface>
]"
```

Let's have a look at the different parameters used in the preceding code snippets:

- `java:global`: This indicates that it is a global JNDI URL.
- `<application_name>`: This is typically the name of the EAR file.
- `<module_name>`: This is the name of the EJB JAR.
- `<bean_name>`: This is the name of the EJB bean class.
- `<bean_interface>`: This is optional if EJB has a no-interface view, or if EJB implements only one business interface. Otherwise it is a fully qualified name of the business interface.

EJB containers are required to publish two more variations of JNDI URLs for each EJB. These are not global URLs, which means that they can't be used to access EJBs from clients that are not in the same JEE application (in the same EAR):

- `java:app/[<module_name>]/<bean_name>![<bean_interface>]`
- `java:module/<bean_name>![<bean_interface>]`

The first URL can be used if the EJB client is in the same application, and the second URL can be used if the client is in the same module (the same `.jar` file as the EJB).

Before you look up any URL in a JNDI server, you need to create `InitialContext`, which includes, among other things, information such as the hostname of the JNDI server and the port on which it is running. If you create `InitialContext` in the same server, then there is no need to specify these attributes:

```
InitialContext initCtx = new InitialContext();
Object obj = initCtx.lookup("jndi_url");
```

We can use the following JNDI URLs to access a no-interface (`LocalBean`) Student EJB (assuming that the name of the EAR file is `CourseManagement` and the name of the `.jar` file for EJBs is `CourseManagementEJBs`):

URL	When to use
`java:global/CourseManagement/CourseManagementEJBs/Student`	The client can be anywhere in the EAR file, because we use the global URL. Note that we haven't specified the interface name because we are assuming that the student bean provides a no-interface view in this example.

	The client can be anywhere in the EAR. We skipped application name because the client is expected to be in the same application, because the namespace of the URL is `java:app`.
`java:app/CourseManagementEJBs/Student`	
`java:module/Student`	The client must be in the same `.jar` file as EJB.

We can use the following JNDI URLs for accessing `Student` EJB that implemented a local interface called `StudentLocal`:

URL	When to use
`java:global/CourseManagement/` `CourseManagementEJBs/Student!packt.jee.book.ch6.StudentLocal`	The client can be anywhere in the EAR file, because we use a global URL.
`java:global/CourseManagement/ CourseManagementEJBs/Student`	The client can be anywhere in the EAR. We skipped the interface name because the bean implements only one business interface. Note that the object returned from this call will be of `StudentLocal` type, and not `Student` type.

`java:app/CourseManagementEJBs/Student`
Or
`java:app/CourseManagementEJBs/Student!packt.jee.book.ch6.StudentLocal`
	The client can be anywhere in the EAR. We skipped the application name because the JNDI namespace is `java:app`.

`java:module/Student`
Or
`java:module/Student!packt.jee.book.ch6.StudentLocal`
	The client must be in the same EAR as the EJB.

Here is an example of how we can call the student bean with a local business interface from one of the objects (that is not managed by the web container) in our web application:

```
InitialContext ctx = new InitialContext();
StudentLocal student = (StudentLocal) ctx.loopup
  ("java:app/CourseManagementEJBs/Student");
return student.getCourses(id) ; //get courses from Student EJB
```

Creating session beans using remote business interface

If the session bean that you create is going to be accessed by a client object that is not in the same JVM as the bean, then the bean needs to implement a remote business interface. You create a remote business interface by annotating the class with @Remote:

```
import java.util.List;
import javax.ejb.Remote;

@Remote
public interface StudentRemote {
    public List<CourseDTO> getCourses();
}
```

The EJB implementing the remote interface is also annotated with @Remote:

```
@Stateful
@Remote
public class Student implements StudentRemote {
    @Override
    public List<CourseDTO> getCourses() {
        //get courses are return
...
    }
}
```

Remote EJBs can be injected into managed objects in the same application using the `@EJB` annotation. For example, a JSF bean can access the previously mentioned student bean (in the same application) as follows:

```
import javax.ejb.EJB;
import javax.faces.bean.ManagedBean;

@ManagedBean
public class StudentJSFBean {
  @EJB
  private StudentRemote student;
}
```

Accessing remote session beans

For accessing a remote `Student` EJB, we can use the following JNDI URLs:

URL	When to use
`java:global/CourseManagement/` `CourseManagementEJBs/Student!packt.jee.book.ch6.StudentRemote`	The client can be in the same application or remote. In the case of a remote client, we need to set up proper `InitialContext` parameters.
`java:global/CourseManagement/CourseManagementEJBs/Student`	The client can be in the same application or remote. We skipped the interface name because the bean implements only one business interface.

`java:app/CourseManagementEJBs/Student`
Or
`java:app/CourseManagementEJBs/Student!packt.jee.book.ch6.StudentRemote`
	The client can be anywhere in the EAR. We skipped the application name because the JNDI namespace is `java:app`.

URL	When to use

`java:module/Student`
`Or`
`java:module/Student!packt.jee.book.ch6.StudentRemote`
	The client must be in the same EAR as the EJB.

To access EJBs from a remote client, you need to use the JNDI lookup method. Furthermore, you need to set up `InitialContext` with certain properties; some of them are JEE application server specific. If the remote EJB and the client are both deployed in GlassFish (different instances of GlassFish), then you can look up the remote EJB as follows:

```
Properties jndiProperties = new Properties();
jndiProperties.setProperty("org.omg.CORBA.ORBInitialHost",
  "<remote_host>");
//target ORB port. default is 3700 in GlassFish
jndiProperties.setProperty("org.omg.CORBA.ORBInitialPort",
  "3700");

InitialContext ctx = new InitialContext(jndiProperties);
StudentRemote student =
  (StudentRemote)ctx.lookup("java:app/CourseManagementEJBs/Student");
return student.getCourses();
```

Configuring the GlassFish Server in Eclipse

We are going to use the GlassFish application server in this chapter. We have already seen how to install GlassFish in the *Installing GlassFish Server* section of `Chapter 1`, *Introducing JEE and Eclipse*.

We will first configure the GlassFish Server in Eclipse JEE:

1. To configure the GlassFish Server in Eclipse EE, make sure that you are in the **Java EE** perspective in Eclipse. Right-click on the **Servers** view and select **New** | **Server**. It you do not see the GlassFish Server group in the list of server types, then expand Oracle node and select and install **GlassFish Tools**:

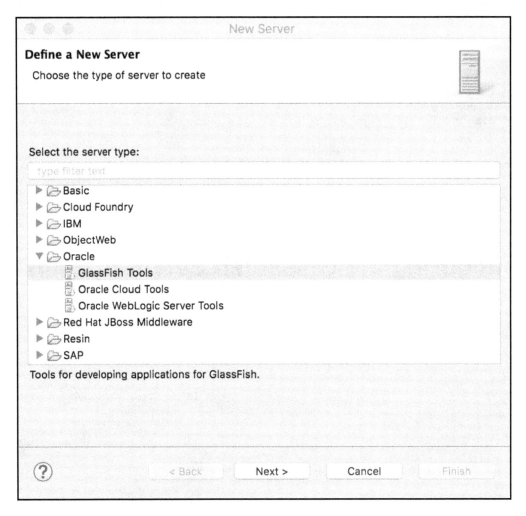

Figure 7.1: Installing GlassFish Tools

2. If you have already installed **GlassFish Tools**, or if GlassFish Server type is available in the list, then expand that and select the **GlassFish** option:

Figure 7.2: Creating GlassFish Server instance in Eclipse

3. Click **Next**. Enter the path of the GlassFish Server on your local machine in the **Domain path** field. Enter admin name and password, if applicable, and click **Next**:

Figure 7.3: Defining GlassFish Server properties

4. The next page allows you to deploy the existing Java EE projects in GlassFish. We don't have any projects to add at this point, so just click **Finish**.

5. The server is added to the **Servers** view. Right-click on the server and select **Start**. If the server is installed and configured properly, then the server status should change to **Started**.

6. To open the admin page of the server, right-click on the server and select **GlassFish** | **View Admin Console**. The admin page is opened in the built-in Eclipse browser. You can browse to the server home page by opening the `http://localhost:8080` URL. 8080 is the default GlassFish port.

Creating a Course Management application using EJB

Let's now create the *Course Management* application that we created in Chapter 4, *Creating JEE Database Applications,* this time using EJBs. In Chapter 4, *Creating JEE Database Applications*, we created service classes (which were POJOs) for writing the business logic. We will replace them with EJBs. We will start by creating Eclipse projects for EJBs.

Creating EJB projects in Eclipse

EJBs are packaged in a JAR file. Web applications are packaged in a **Web Application aRchive** (**WAR**). If EJBs are to be accessed remotely, then the client needs to have access to business interfaces. Therefore, EJB business interfaces and shared objects are packaged in a separate JAR, called EJB client JAR. Furthermore, if EJBs and web applications are to be deployed as one single application, then they need to be packaged in an EAR.

So, in most cases the application with EJBs is not a single project, but four different projects:

- EJB project that creates EJB JAR
- EJB client project that contains business classes and shared (between EJB and client) classes
- Web project that generates WAR
- EAR project that generates EAR containing EBJ JAR, EJB client JAR, and WAR

You can create each of these projects independently and integrate them. However, Eclipse gives you the option to create EJB projects, EJB client projects, and EAR projects with one wizard:

> 1. Select **File | New | EJB Project**. Type `CourseManagementEJBs` in the **Project name** textbox:

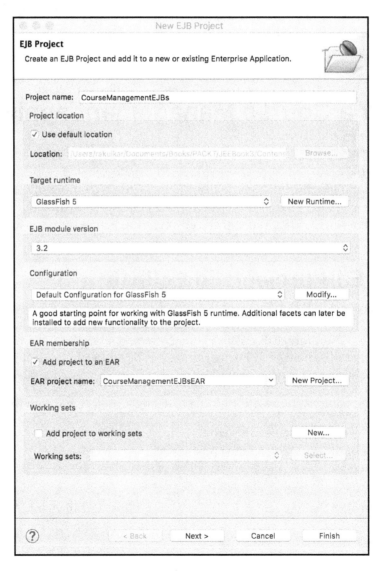

Figure 7.4: New EJB Project wizard

Make sure **Target runtime** is **GlassFish 5** and **EJB module version** is **3.2** or later. From the **Configuration** drop-down list, select **Default Configuration for GlassFish 5**. In the **EAR membership** group, check the **Add project to an EAR** box.

2. Select **Next**. On the next page, specify source and output folders for the classes. Leave the defaults unchanged on this page:

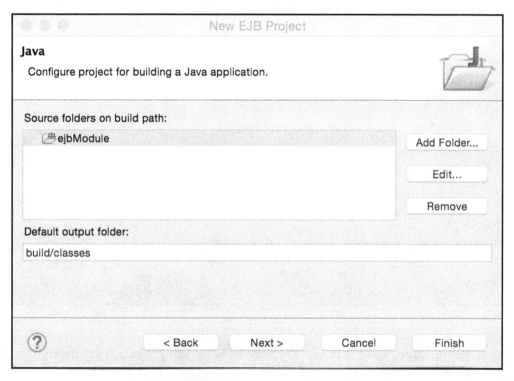

Figure 7.5: Select source and output folders

3. The source Java files in this project would be created in the `ejbModule` folder. Click **Next**:

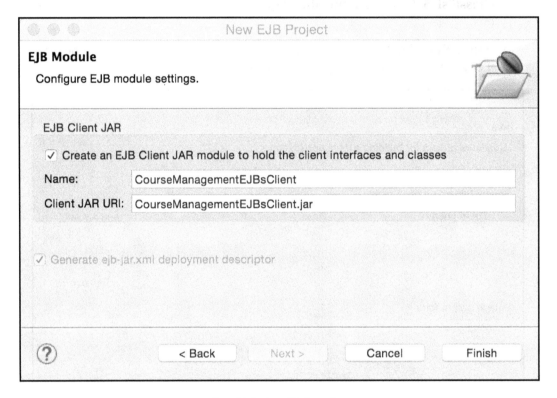

4. Eclipse gives you the option to create an EJB client project. Select the option and click **Finish**.
5. Since we are building a web application, we will create a web project. Select **File | Dynamic Web Project**. Set the project name as `CourseManagementWeb`:

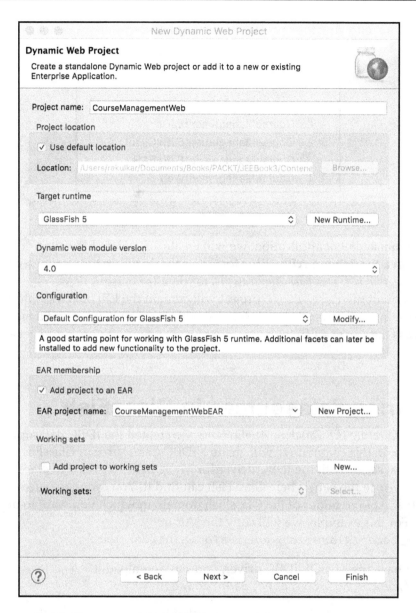

Figure 7.7: New Dynamic Web Project

6. Select the **Add Project to an EAR** checkbox. Since we have only one EAR project in the workspace, Eclipse selects this project from the drop-down list. Click **Finish**.

We now have the following four projects in the workspace:

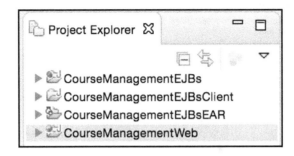

Figure 7.8: Course Management projects

In the course management application, we will create a stateless EJB called `CourseBean`. We will use **Java Persistence APIs** (JPA) for data access and create a `Course` entity. See Chapter 4, *Creating JEE Database Applications*, for details on using JPAs.

The `CourseManagementEJBClient` project will contain the EJB business interface and shared classes. In `CourseManagementWeb`, we will create a JSF page and a managed bean that will access the `Course` EJB in the `CourseManagementEJBs` project to get a list of courses.

Configuring datasources in GlassFish

In Chapter 4, *Creating JEE Database Applications,* we created the JDBC datasource locally in the application. In this chapter, we will create a JDBC datasource in GlassFish. GlassFish Server is not packaged with the JDBC driver for MySQL. So, we need to place the `.jar` file for `MySQLDriver` in the path where GlassFish can find it. You can place such external libraries in the `lib/ext` folder of the GlassFish domain in which you want to deploy your application. For this example, we will copy the JAR in `<glassfish_home>/glassfish/domains/domain1/lib/ext`.

If you do not have the MySQL JDBC driver, you can download it from `http://dev.mysql.com/downloads/connector/j/`:

1. Open the GlassFish admin console, either by right-clicking on the server in the **Servers** view and selecting **GlassFish | View Admin Console** (this opens the admin console inside Eclipse) or browsing to `http://localhost:4848` (4848 is the default port to which the GlassFish admin console application listens). In the admin console, select **Resources | JDBC | JDBC Connection Pools**. Click the **New** button on the **JDBC Connection Pool** page:

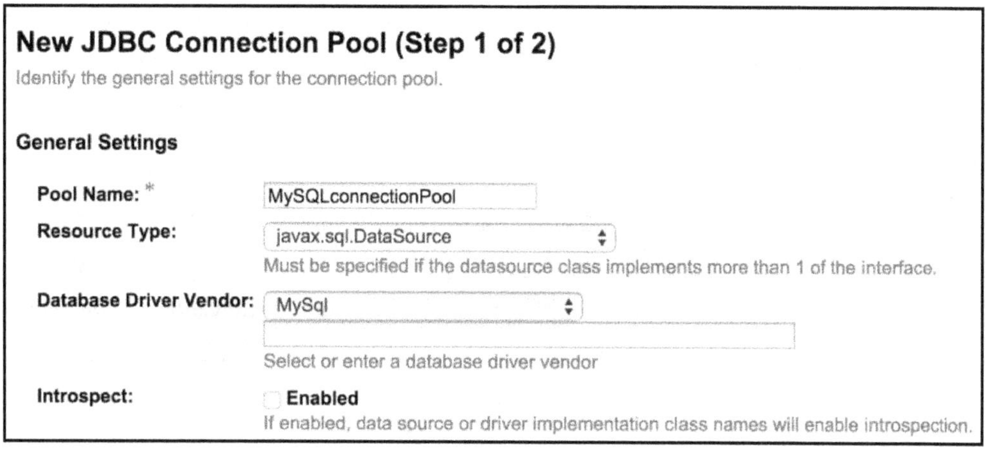

New JDBC Connection Pool (Step 1 of 2)

Identify the general settings for the connection pool.

General Settings

Pool Name: *

> MySQLconnectionPool

Resource Type:

> javax.sql.DataSource

Must be specified if the datasource class implements more than 1 of the interface.

Database Driver Vendor:

> MySql

Select or enter a database driver vendor

Introspect:

> ☐ **Enabled**
> If enabled, data source or driver implementation class names will enable introspection.

Figure 7.9: Create JDBC Connection Pool in GlassFish

2. Set **Pool Name** as `MySQLconnectionPool` and select **javax.sql.DataSource** as **Resource Type**. Select **MySql** from the **Database Driver Vendor** list and click **Next**. In the next page, select the correct **Datasource Classname** (**com.mysql.jdbc.jdbc2.optional.MysqlDatasource**):

New JDBC Connection Pool (Step 2 of 2)

Identify the general settings for the connection pool. Datasource Classname or Driver Classname must be

General Settings

Pool Name: MySQLconnectionPool

Resource Type: javax.sql.DataSource

Database Driver Vendor: MySql

Datasource Classname:

> com.mysql.jdbc.jdbc2.optional.MysqlDataSource

Select or enter vendor-specific classname that implements the DataSource

Driver Classname:

Select or enter vendor-specific classname that implements the java.sql.Driv

Ping:

> ☐ **Enabled**
> When enabled, the pool is pinged during creation or reconfiguration to ident

Description:

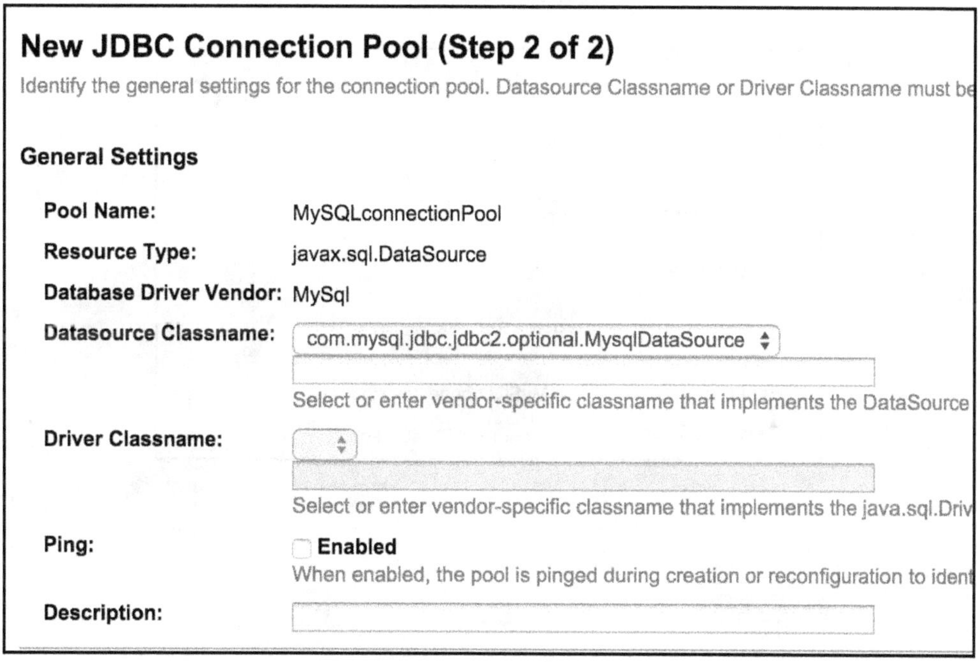

Figure 7.10: JDBC Connection Pool settings in GlassFish

3. We need to set the hostname, port, username, and password of MySQL. In the admin page, scroll down to the **Additional Properties** section and set the following properties:

Properties	Values
Port/PortNumber	3306
DatabaseName	`<schemaname_of_coursemanagement>`, for example, `course_management`. See `Chapter 4`, *Creating JEE Database Applications*, for details on creating the MySQL schema for the *Course Management* database.
Password	MySQL database password.
URL/Url	`jdbc:mysql://:3306/<database_name>`, for example, `jdbc:mysql://:3306/course_management`
ServerName	`localhost`
User	MySQL username

4. Click **Finish**. The new connection pool is added to the list in the left pane. Click on the newly added connection pool. In the **General** tab, click on the **Ping** button and make sure that the ping is successful:

Figure 7.11: Test JDBC Connection Pool in GlassFish

5. Next, we need to create a JNDI resource for this connection pool so that it can be accessed from the client application. Select the **Resources** | **JDBC** | **JDBC Resources** node in the left pane. Click the **New** button to create a new JDBC resource:

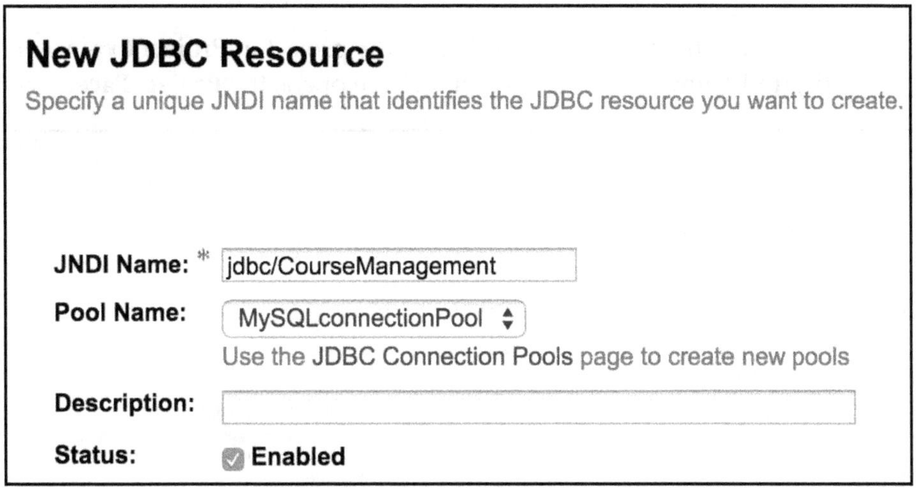

New JDBC Resource

Specify a unique JNDI name that identifies the JDBC resource you want to create.

JNDI Name: * jdbc/CourseManagement

Pool Name: MySQLconnectionPool ‡
Use the JDBC Connection Pools page to create new pools

Description:

Status: ☑ **Enabled**

Figure 7.12: Test JDBC Connection Pool in GlassFish

6. Set **JNDI Name** as `jdbc/CourseManagement`. From the **Pool Name** drop-down list, select the connection pool that we created for MySQL, `MySQLconnectionPool`. Click **Save**.

Configuring JPA in an Eclipse project

We will now configure our EJB project to use JPA to access the MySQL database. We have already learned how to enable JPA for an Eclipse project in Chapter 4, *Creating JEE Database Applications*. However, we will briefly cover the steps again here:

1. Right-click on the CourseManagementEJBs project in **Project Explorer** and select **Configure** | **Convert to JPA Project**. Eclipse opens the **Project Facets** window:

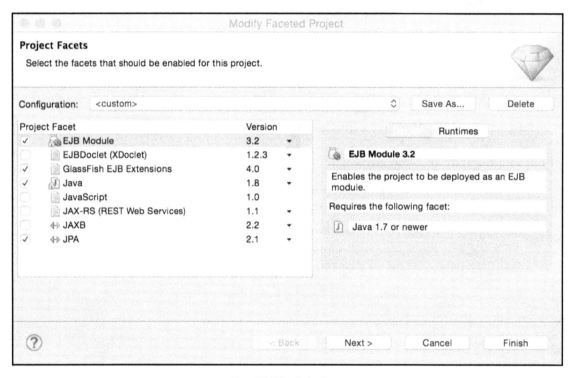

Figure 7.13: Eclipse Project Facets

2. Click **Next** to go to the **JPA Facet** page:

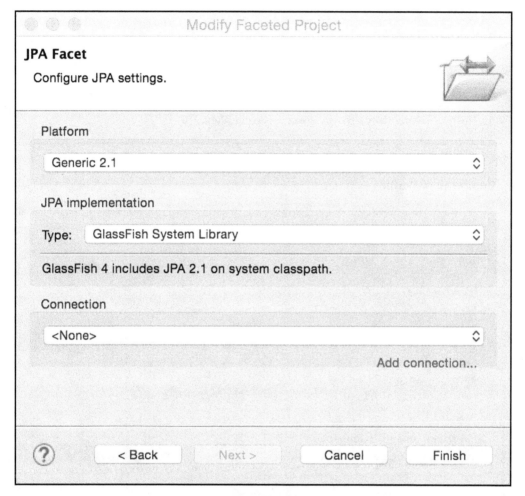

Figure 7.14: JPA Facet

Keep the default values unchanged, and click **Finish**. Eclipse adds persistence.xml, required by JPA, to the project under the **JPA Content** group in **Project Explorer**. We need to configure the JPA datasource in persistence.xml. Open persistence.xml and click on the **Connection** tab. Set **Transaction Type** to JTA. In the **JTA datasource** textbox, type the JNDI name that we set up for our MySQL database in the previous section, which was jdbc/CourseManagement. Save the file. Note that the actual location of persistence.xml is ejbModule/META-INF.

Let's now create a database connection in Eclipse and link it with JPA properties of the project so that we can create JPA entities from the database tables. Right-click on the `CourseManagementEJBs` project and select **Properties**. This opens the **Project Properties** window. Click on the **JPA** node to see the details page. Click on the **Add connection** link just below the **Connection** drop-down box. We have already seen how to set up a database connection in the *Using Eclipse Data Source Explorer* section of `Chapter 4`, *Creating JEE Database Applications*. However, we will quickly recap the steps:

1. In the **Connection Profile** window, select MySQL:

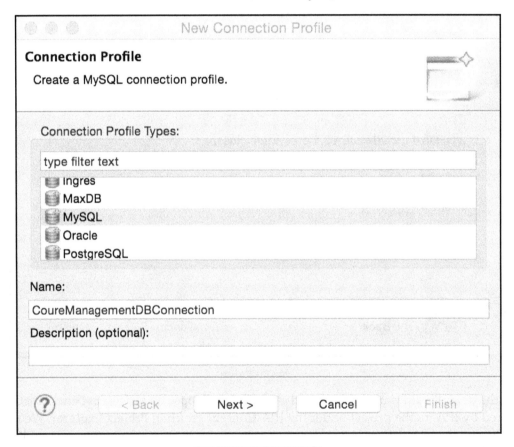

Figure 7.15: New DB Connection Profile

2. Type `CourseManagementDBConnection` in the name textbox and click **Next**. In the **New Connection Profile** window, click on the **new connection profile** button (the circle next to the **Drivers** drop-down box) to open the **New Driver Definition** window. Select the appropriate **MySQL JDBC Driver** version and click on the **JAR List** tab. In the case of any error, remove any existing `.jar` and click on the **Add JAR/Zip** button. Browse to the MySQL JDBC driver JAR that we saved in the `<glassfish_home>/glassfish/domains/domain1/lib/ext` folder. Click **OK**. Back in the **New Connection Profile** window, enter the database name, modify the connection URL, and enter **User name** and **Password**:

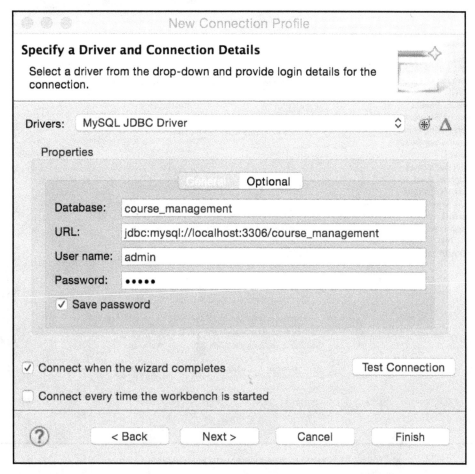

Figure 7.16: Configuring MySQL database connection

3. Select the **Save password** checkbox. Click the **Test Connection** button and make sure that the test is successful. Click the **Finish** button. Back in the JPA properties page, the new connection is added and appropriate schema is selected:

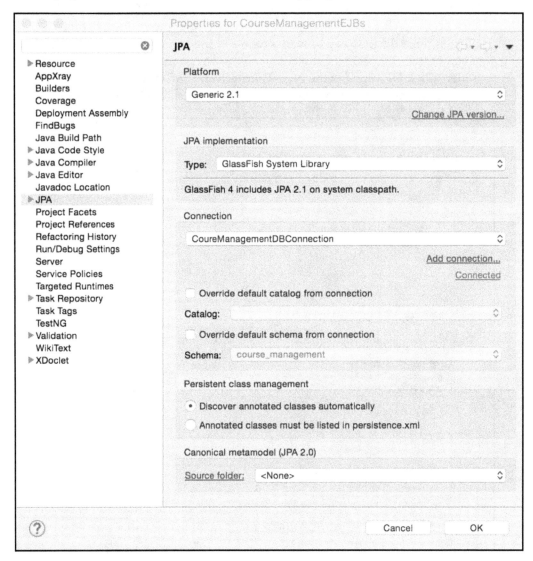

Figure 7.17: Connection added to JPA project properties

4. Click **OK** to save the changes.

Creating a JPA entity

We will now create the entity class for Course, using Eclipse JPA tools:

1. Right-click on the CourseManagementEJBs project and select **JPA Tool |
   Generate Entities from Tables**:

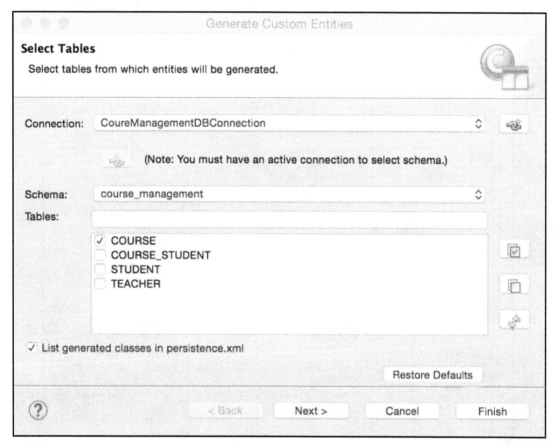

Figure 7.18: Creating entity from tables

2. Select the **Course** table and click **Next**. Click **Next** in the **Table Associations** window. On the next page, select identity as **Key generator**:

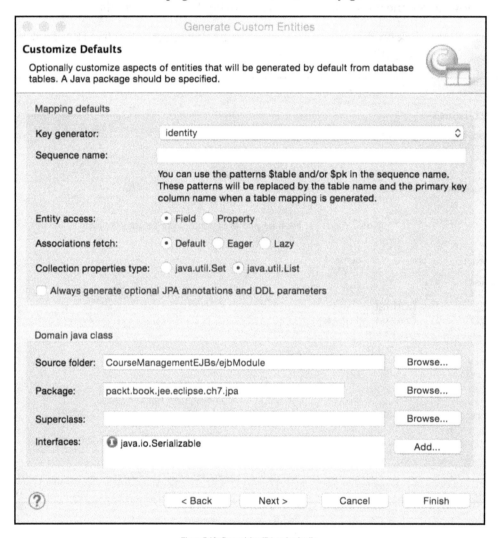

Figure 7.19: Customizing JPA entity details

3. Enter the package name. We do not want to change anything on the next page, so click **Finish**. Notice that the wizard creates a findAll query for the class that we can use to get all courses:

```
@Entity
@NamedQuery(name="Course.findAll", query="SELECT c FROM
```

```
    Course c")
public class Course implements Serializable { ...}
```

Creating stateless EJB

We will now create the stateless EJB for our application:

1. Right-click on the `ejbModule` folder in the `CourseManagementEJBs` project in **Project Explorer** and select **New | Session Bean (3.x)**. Type `packt.book.jee.eclipse.ch7.ejb` in the **Java package** textbox and `CourseBean` in **Class name**. Select the **Remote** checkbox:

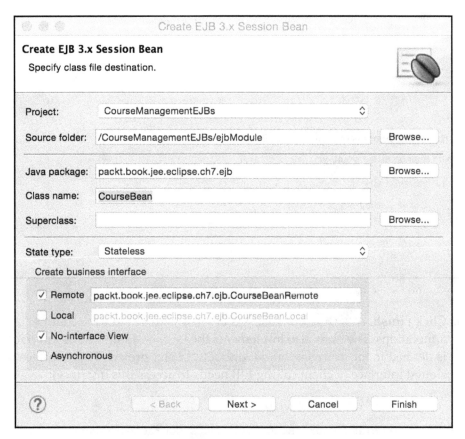

Figure 7.20: Creating a stateless session bean

2. Click **Next**. No change is required on the next page:

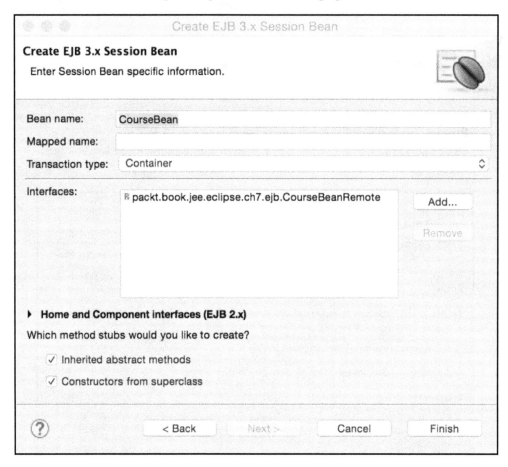

Figure 7.21: Stateless session bean information

3. Click **Finish**. A `CourseBean` class is created with `@Stateless` and `@Localbean` annotations. The class also implements the `CourseBeanRemote` interface, which is defined in the `CourseManagementEJBClient` project. This interface is a shared interface (a client calling EJB needs to access this interface):

```
@Stateless
@LocalBean
public class CourseBean implements CourseBeanRemote {
    public CourseBean() {
    }
}
```

The interface is annotated with `@Remote`:

```
@Remote
public interface CourseBeanRemote {

}
```

Now, the question is how do we return `Course` information from our EJB? The EJB will call JPA APIs to get instances of the `Course` entity, but do we want EJB to return instances of the `Course` entity or should it return instances of lightweight **data transfer object (DTO)**? Each has its own advantages. If we return a `Course` entity, then we do not need to transfer data between objects; which we will have to do in the case of DTO (transfer data from the entity to the corresponding DTO). However, passing entities between layers may not be a good idea if the EJB client is not in the same application, and you may not want to expose your data model to external applications. Furthermore, by passing back JPA entities you are forcing the client application to depend on JPA libraries in its implementation.

DTOs are lightweight, and you can expose only those fields that you want your clients to use. However, you will have to transfer data between entities and DTOs.

If your EJBs are going to be used by the client in the same application, then it could be easier to transfer entities to the client from the EJBs. However, if your client is not part of the same EJB application, or when you want to expose the EJB as a web service (we will learn how to create web services in `Chapter 9`, *Creating Web Services*), then you may need to use DTOs.

In our application, we will see examples of both the approaches, that is, an EJB method returning JPA entities as well as DTOs. Remember that we have created `CourseBean` as a remote as well as a local bean (no-interface view). Implementation of the remote interface method will return DTOs and that of the local method will return JPA entities.

Let's now add the `getCourses` method to the EJB. We will create `CourseDTO`, a data transfer object, which is a POJO, and returns instances of the DTO from the `getCourses` method. This DTO needs to be in the `CourseManagementEJBsClient` project because it will be shared between the EJB and its client.

Create the following class in the `packt.book.jee.eclipse.ch7.dto` package in the `CourseManagementEJBsClient` project:

```
package packt.book.jee.eclipse.ch7.dto;

public class CourseDTO {
    private int id;
    private int credits;
```

```
    private String name;
    public int getId() {
      return id;
    }
    public void setId(int id) {
      this.id = id;
    }
    public int getCredits() {
      return credits;
    }
    public void setCredits(int credits) {
      this.credits = credits;
    }
    public String getName() {
      return name;
    }
    public void setName(String name) {
      this.name = name;
    }
}
```

Add the following method to `CourseBeanRemote`:

```
public List<CourseDTO> getCourses();
```

We need to implement this method in `CourseBean` EJB. To get the courses from the database, the EJB needs to first get an instance of `EntityManager`. Recall that in chapter 4, *Creating JEE Database Applications*, we created `EntityManagerFactory` and got an instance of `EntityManager` from it. Then, we passed that instance to the service class, which actually got the data from the database using JPA APIs.

JEE application servers make injecting `EntityManager` very easy. You just need to create the `EntityManager` field in the EJB class and annotate it with `@PersistenceContext(unitName="<name_as_specified_in_persistence.xml>")`. The `unitName` attribute is optional if there is only one persistence unit defined in `persistence.xml`. Open the `CourseBean` class and add the following declaration:

```
@PersistenceContext
EntityManager entityManager;
```

EJBs are managed objects, and the EJB container injects `EntityManager` after EJBs are created.

TIP

Auto injection of objects is a part of JEE features called **Context and Dependency Injection (CDI)**. See `https://javaee.github.io/tutorial/cdi-basic.html#GIWHB` for information on CDI.

Let's now add a method to `CourseBean` EJB that will return a list of `Course` entities. We will name this method `getCourseEntities`. This method will be called by the `getCourses` method in the same EJB, which will then convert the list of entities to DTOs. The method `getCourseEntities` can also be called by any web application, because the EJB exposes no-interface view (using the `@LocalBean` annotation):

```
public List<Course> getCourseEntities() {
//Use named query created in Course entity using @NameQuery
 annotation.       TypedQuery<Course> courseQuery =
 entityManager.createNamedQuery("Course.findAll", Course.class);
      return courseQuery.getResultList();
}
```

After implementing the `getCourses` method (defined in our remote business interface called `CourseBeanRemote`), we have `CourseBean`, as follows:

```
@Stateless
@LocalBean
public class CourseBean implements CourseBeanRemote {
  @PersistenceContext
  EntityManager entityManager;

    public CourseBean() {
    }

    public List<Course> getCourseEntities() {
      //Use named query created in Course entity using @NameQuery
       annotation.       TypedQuery<Course> courseQuery =
 entityManager.createNamedQuery("Course.findAll", Course.class);
      return courseQuery.getResultList();
    }

  @Override
  public List<CourseDTO> getCourses() {
    //get course entities first
    List<Course> courseEntities = getCourseEntities();

    //create list of course DTOs. This is the result we will
     return
    List<CourseDTO> courses = new ArrayList<CourseDTO>();
```

```
    for (Course courseEntity : courseEntities) {
      //Create CourseDTO from Course entity
      CourseDTO course = new CourseDTO();
      course.setId(courseEntity.getId());
      course.setName(courseEntity.getName());
      course.setCredits(course.getCredits());
      courses.add(course);
    }
    return courses;
  }
}
```

Creating JSF and managed beans

We will now create a JSF page to display courses in the `CourseManagementWeb` project.
We will also create a managed bean that will call the `getCourses` method of `CourseEJB`.
See the *Java Server Faces* section in `Chapter 2`, *Creating a Simple JEE Web Application*, for
details about JSF.

As explained in `Chapter 2`, *Creating a Simple JEE Web Application*, we need to add JSF
Servlet and mapping to `web.xml`. Open `web.xml` from the `CourseManagementWeb` project.
You can open this file either by double-clicking the **Deployment
Descriptor: CourseManagementWeb** node (under the project in **Project Explorer**) or from
the `WebContent/Web-INF` folder (again, under the project in **Project Explorer**). Add the
following servlet declaration and mapping (within the `web-app` node):

```
<servlet>
  <servlet-name>JSFServlet</servlet-name>
  <servlet-class>javax.faces.webapp.FacesServlet</servlet-class>
  <load-on-startup>1</load-on-startup>
</servlet>

<servlet-mapping>
  <servlet-name>JSFServlet</servlet-name>
  <url-pattern>*.xhtml</url-pattern>
</servlet-mapping>
```

The `CourseManagementWeb` project needs to access the business interface of EJB, which is
in `CourseManagementEJBsClient`. So, we need to add the reference of
`CourseManagementEJBsClient` to `CourseManagementWeb`. Open the project properties
of `CourseManagementWeb` (right-click on the `CourseManagementWeb` project and select
Properties) and select **Java Build Path**. Click on the **Projects** tab, and then click
the **Add...** button. Select `CourseManagementEJBsClient` from the list and click **OK**:

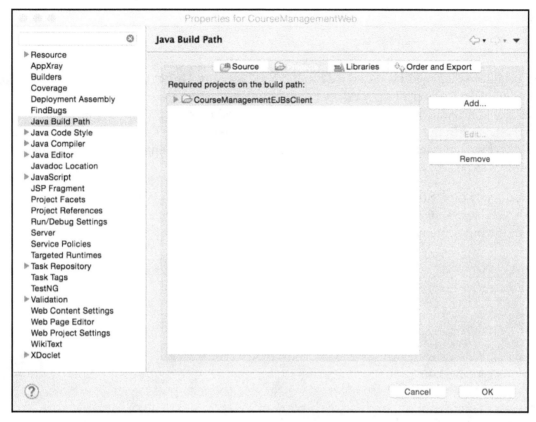

Figure 7.22: Adding project reference

Now, let's create a managed bean for the JSF that we are going to create later. Create a `CourseJSFBean` class in the `packt.book.jee.eclipse.ch7.web.bean` package in the `CourseManagementWeb` project (Java source files go in the `src` folder under the **Java Resources** group):

```
import java.util.List;
import javax.ejb.EJB;
import javax.faces.bean.ManagedBean;
import packt.book.jee.eclipse.ch7.dto.CourseDTO;
import packt.book.jee.eclipse.ch7.ejb.CourseBeanRemote;

@ManagedBean(name="Course")
public class CourseJSFBean {
  @EJB
  CourseBeanRemote courseBean;
```

```
    public List<CourseDTO> getCourses() {
      return courseBean.getCourses();
    }
  }
```

JSF beans are managed beans, so we can have the container inject EJBs using the `@EJB` annotation. In the preceding code we have referenced `CourseBean` with its remote interface, `CourseBeanRemote`. We then created a method called `getCourses`, which calls the method with the same name on `Course` EJB and returns the list of `CourseDTO` objects. Note that we have set the `name` attribute in the `@ManagedBean` annotation. This managed bean would be accessed from JSF as variable `Course`.

We will now create the JSF page, `course.xhtml`. Right-click on **WebContent** group in the `CourseManagementWeb` project, and select **New** | **File**. Create `courses.xhtml` with the following content:

```
<html xmlns="http://www.w3.org/1999/xhtml"
  xmlns:f="http://java.sun.com/jsf/core"
  xmlns:h="http://java.sun.com/jsf/html">

<head>
  <title>Courses</title>
</head>
<body>
  <h2>Courses</h2>
  <h:dataTable value="#{Course.courses}" var="course">
      <h:column>
      <f:facet name="header">Name</f:facet>
      #{course.name}
    </h:column>
      <h:column>
      <f:facet name="header">Credits</f:facet>
      #{course.credits}
    </h:column>
  </h:dataTable>
</body>
</html>
```

The page uses the `dataTable` tag (`https://docs.oracle.com/javaee/7/javaserver-faces-2-2/vdldocs-jsp/h/dataTable.html`), which receives the data to populate from the `Course` managed bean (which is actually the `CourseJSFBean` class). `Course.courses` in the expression language syntax is a short-form for `Course.getCourses()`. This results in a call to the `getCourses` method of the `CourseJSFBean` class.

Each element of the list returned by `Course.courses`, which is `List` of `CourseDTO`, is represented by the `course` variable (in the `var` attribute value). We then display the name and credits of each course in the table using the `column` child tag.

Running the example

Before we can run the example, we need to start the GlassFish Server and deploy our JEE application in it:

1. Start the GlassFish Server.
2. Once it is started, right-click on the GlassFish Server in the **Servers** view and select the **Add and Remove...** menu option:

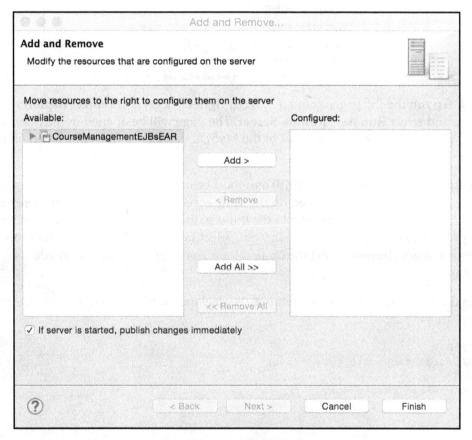

Figure 7.23: Adding a project to GlassFish for deployment

3. Select the EAR project and click on the **Add** button. Then, click **Finish**. The selected EAR application will be deployed in the server:

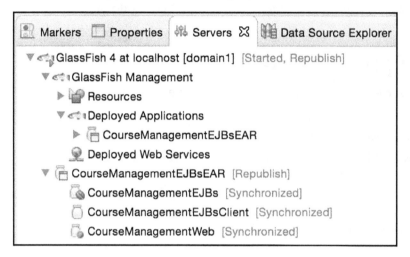

Figure 7.24: Application deployed in GlassFish

4. To run the JSF page, `course.xhtml`, right-click on it in **Project Explorer** and select **Run As | Run on Server**. The page will be opened in the internal Eclipse browser and courses in the MySQL database will be displayed on the page.

Note that we can use `CourseBean` (EJB) as a local bean in `CourseJSFBean`, because they are in the same application deployed on the same server. To do this, add a reference of the `CourseManagementEJBs` project in the build path of `CourseManagementWeb` (open the project properties of `CourseManagementWeb`, select **Java Build Path**, select the **Projects** tab, and click the **Add...** button. Select the `CourseManagementEJBs` project and add its reference).

Then, in the `CourseJSFBean` class, remove the declaration of `CourseBeanRemote` and add one for `CourseBean`:

```
//@EJB
//CourseBeanRemote courseBean;
@EJB
CourseBean courseBean;
```

When you make any changes in the code, the EAR project needs to be redeployed in the GlassFish Server. In **Servers** view, you can see whether redeployment is needed by checking the status of the server. If it is **[Started, Synchronized]**, then no redeployment is needed. However, if it is **[Started, Republish]**, then redeployment is required. Just click on the server node and select the **Publish** menu option.

Creating EAR for deployment outside Eclipse

In the last section, we learned how to deploy an application to GlassFish from Eclipse. This works fine during development, but finally you will need to create the EAR file for deployment to an external server. To create the EAR file from the project, right-click on the EAR project (in our example, it is CourseManagementEJBsEAR) and select **Export | EAR file**:

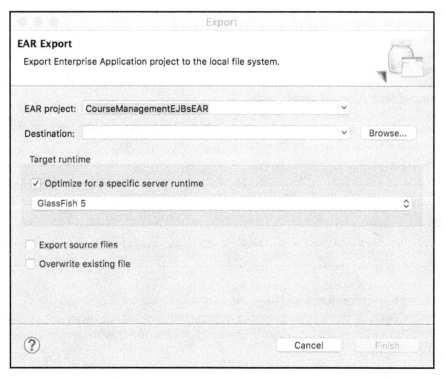

Figure 7.25: Exporting to EAR file

Select the destination folder and click **Finish**. This file can then be deployed in GlassFish using the management console or by copying it to the autodeploy folder in GlassFish.

Creating a JEE project using Maven

In this section, we will learn how to create JEE projects with EJBs using Maven. Creating Maven projects may be preferable to Eclipse JEE projects because builds can be automated. We have seen many details of creating EJBs, JPA entities, and other classes in the previous section, so we won't repeat all that information here. We have also learned how to create Maven projects in Chapter 2, *Creating a Simple JEE Web Application*, and Chapter 3, *Source Control Management in Eclipse*, so the basic details of creating a Maven project will not be repeated either. We will focus mainly on how to create EJB projects using Maven. We will create the following projects:

- CourseManagementMavenEJBs: This project contains EJBs
- CourseManagementMavenEJBClient: This project contains shared interfaces and objects between an EJB project and the client projects
- CourseManagementMavenWAR: This is a web project containing a JSF page and a managed bean
- CourseManagementMavenEAR: This project creates the EAR file that can be deployed in GlassFish
- CourseManagement: This project is the overall parent project that builds all the previously mentioned projects

We still start with CourseManagementMavenEJBs. This project should generate the EJB JAR file. Let's create a Maven project with the following details:

Field	Value
Group ID	packt.book.jee.eclipse.ch7.maven
Artifact ID	CourseManagementMavenEJBClient
Version	1
Packaging	jar

We need to add the dependency of JEE APIs to our EJB project. Let's add the dependency of javax.javaee-api. Since we are going to deploy this project in GlassFish, which comes with its own JEE implementation and libraries, we will scope this dependency as provided. Add the following in pom.xml:

```xml
<dependencies>
  <dependency>
    <groupId>javax</groupId>
    <artifactId>javaee-api</artifactId>
    <version>8.0</version>
```

```
        <scope>provided</scope>
    </dependency>
</dependencies>
```

When we create the EJBs in this project, we need to create local or remote business interfaces in a shared project (client project). Therefore, we will create `CourseManagementMavenEJBClient` with the following details:

Field	Values
Group ID	**packt.book.jee.eclipse.ch7.maven**
Artifact ID	**CourseManagementMavenEJBs**
Version	**1**
Packaging	**jar**

This shared project also needs to access EJB annotations. So, add the same dependency for `javax.javaee-api` that we added previously to the `pom.xml` file of the `CourseManagementMavenEJBClient` project.

We will create a `packt.book.jee.eclipse.ch7.ejb` package in this project and create a remote interface. Create a `CourseBeanRemote` interface (just as we created in the *Creating stateless EJB* section of this chapter). Furthermore, create a `CourseDTO` class in the `packt.book.jee.eclipse.ch7.dto` package. This class is the same as the one that we created in the *Creating stateless EJB* section.

We are going to create a `Course` JPA entity in the `CourseManagementMavenEJBs` project. Before we do that, let's convert this project to a JPA project. Right-click on the project in **Package Explorer** and select **Configure | Convert to JPA Project**. In the JPA configuration wizard, select the following JPA facet details:

Fields	Values
Platform	**Generic 2.1**
JPA Implementation	**Disable Library Configuration**

JPA wizard creates a `META-INF` folder in the `src` folder of the project and creates `persistence.xml`. Open `persistence.xml` and click on the **Connection** tab. We have already created the MySQL datasource in GlassFish (see the *Configuring datasource in GlassFish* section). Enter the JNDI name of the datasource, `jdbc/CourseManagement`, in the **JTA data source** field.

Create a `Course` entity in `packt.book.jee.eclipse.ch7.jpa`, as described in the *Creating JPA entity* section. Before we create the EJB in this project, let's add an EJB facet to this project. Right-click on the project and select **Properties**. Click on the **Project Facets** group and select the **EJB Module** checkbox. Set version to the latest one (at the time of writing, the latest version was 3.2). We will now create the implementation class of the remote session bean interface that we created previously. Right-click on the `CourseManagementMavenEJBs` project and select the **New | Session Bean** menu. Create the EJB class with the following details:

Fields	Values
Java package	packt.book.jee.eclipse.ch7.ejb
Class name	CourseBean
State type	Stateless

Do not select any business interface, because we have already created the business interface in the `CourseManagementMavenEJBClient` project. Click **Next**. On the next page, select `CourseBeanRemote`. Eclipse will show errors at this point because `CourseManagementMavenEJBs` does not know about `CourseManagementMavenEJBClient`, which contains the `CourseBeanRemote` interface, used by `CourseBean` in the EJB project. Adding the Maven dependency (in `pom.xml`) for `CourseManagementMavenEJBClient` in `CourseManagementMavenEJBs` and implementing the `getCourses` method in the EJB class should fix the compilation errors. Now complete the implementation of the `CourseBean` class as described in the *Creating stateless EJB* section of this chapter. Make sure that EJB is marked as `Remote`:

```
@Stateless
@Remote
public class CourseBean implements CourseBeanRemote {
...
}
```

Let's create a web application project for course management using Maven. Create a Maven project with the following details:

Fields	Values
Group ID	packt.book.jee.eclipse.ch7.maven
Artifact ID	CourseManagementMavenWebApp
Version	1
Packaging	war

To create `web.xml` in this project, right-click on the project and select **Java EE Tools** | **Generate Deployment Descriptor Stub**. The `web.xml` file is created in the `src/main/webapp/WEB-INF` folder. Open `web.xml` and add the servlet definition and mapping for JSF (see the *Creating JSF and managed bean* section of this chapter). Add the dependency of the `CourseManagementMavenEJBClient` project and `javax.javaee-api` in `pom.xml` of the `CourseManagementMavenWebApp` project so that the web project has access to the EJB business interface declared in the shared project and also to EJB annotations.

Let's now create a `CourseJSFBean` class in the web project as described in the *Creating JSF and managed bean* section. Note that this will reference the remote interface of the EJB in the managed bean, as follows:

```
@ManagedBean(name="Course")
public class CourseJSFBean {
  @EJB
  CourseBeanRemote courseBean;

  public List<CourseDTO> getCourses() {
    return courseBean.getCourses();
  }
}
```

Create `course.xhtml` in the `webapp` folder as described in the *Creating JSF and managed bean* section.

Let's now create a `CourseManagementMavenEAR` project with the following details:

Fields	Values
Group ID	**packt.book.jee.eclipse.ch7.maven**
Artifact ID	**CourseManagementMavenEAR**
Version	**1**
Packaging	**ear**

You will have to type `ear` in the **Packaging file**; there is no `ear` option in the drop-down list. Add dependencies of `web`, `ejb`, and `client` projects to `pom.xml`, as follows:

```
<dependencies>
  <dependency>
    <groupId>packt.book.jee.eclipse.ch7.maven</groupId>
    <artifactId>CourseManagementMavenEJBClient</artifactId>
    <version>1</version>
  <type>jar</type>
```

```
      </dependency>
      <dependency>
        <groupId>packt.book.jee.eclipse.ch7.maven</groupId>
        <artifactId>CourseManagementMavenEJBs</artifactId>
        <version>1</version>
        <type>ejb</type>
      </dependency>
      <dependency>
        <groupId>packt.book.jee.eclipse.ch7.maven</groupId>
        <artifactId>CourseManagementMavenWebApp</artifactId>
        <version>1</version>
        <type>war</type>
      </dependency>
    </dependencies>
```

Make sure to set `<type>` of each dependency properly. You also need to update JNDI URLs for any name changes.

Maven does not have built-in support to package EAR. However, there is a Maven plugin for EAR. You can find details of this plugin at `https://maven.apache.org/plugins/maven-ear-plugin/` and `https://maven.apache.org/plugins/maven-ear-plugin/modules.html`. We need to add this plugin to our `pom.xml` and configure its parameters. Our EAR file will contain the JAR for the EJB project, the client project, and the WAR for the web project. Right-click on `pom.xml` of the EAR project, and select **Maven** | **Add Plugin**. Type ear in the **Filter** box, and select the latest plugin version under **maven-ear-plugin**. Make sure that you also install the **maven-acr-plugin** plugin. Configure the EAR plugin in the `pom.xml` details, as follows:

```
    <build>
      <plugins>
        <plugin>
          <groupId>org.apache.maven.plugins</groupId>
          <artifactId>maven-acr-plugin</artifactId>
          <version>1.0</version>
          <extensions>true</extensions>
        </plugin>

        <plugin>
          <groupId>org.apache.maven.plugins</groupId>
          <artifactId>maven-ear-plugin</artifactId>
          <version>2.10</version>
          <configuration>
            <version>6</version>
          <defaultLibBundleDir>lib</defaultLibBundleDir>
          <modules>
```

```
<webModule>
<groupId>packt.book.jee.eclipse.ch7.maven</groupId>
<artifactId>CourseManagementMavenWebApp</artifactId>
</webModule>
<ejbModule>
<groupId>packt.book.jee.eclipse.ch7.maven</groupId>
<artifactId>CourseManagementMavenEJBs</artifactId>
</ejbModule>
< jarModule >
<groupId>packt.book.jee.eclipse.ch7.maven</groupId>
<artifactId>CourseManagementMavenEJBClient</artifactId>
</ jarModule >
</modules>
</configuration>
</plugin>
</plugins>
</build>
```

After modifying `pom.xml`, sometimes Eclipse may display the following error:

```
Project configuration is not up-to-date with pom.xml. Run Maven->Update
Project or use Quick Fix...
```

In such cases, right-click on the project and select **Maven** | **Update Project**.

The last project that we create in this section is `CourseManagement`, which will be the container project for all other EJB projects. When this project is installed, it should build and install all the contained projects. Create a Maven project with the following details:

Fields	Values
Group ID	packt.book.jee.eclipse.ch7.maven
Artifact ID	CourseManagement
Version	1
Packaging	Pom

Open `pom.xml` and click on the **Overview** tab. Expand the **Modules** group, and add all the other projects as modules. The following modules should be listed in `pom.xml`:

```
<modules>
    <module>../CourseManagementMavenEAR</module>
    <module>../CourseManagementMavenEJBClient</module>
    <module>../CourseManagementMavenEJBs</module>
    <module>../CourseManagementMavenWebApp</module>
</modules>
```

Right-click on the `CourseManagement` project and select **Run As** | **Maven Install**. This builds all EJB projects, and an EAR file is created in the target folder of the `CourseManagementMavenEAR` project. You can deploy this EAR in GlassFish from its management console, or you can right-click on the configured GlassFish Server in the **Servers** view of Eclipse, select the **Add and Remove...** option, and deploy the EAR project from within Eclipse. Browse to `http://localhost:8080/CourseManagementMavenWebApp/course.xhtml` to see the list of courses displayed by the `course.xhtml` JSF page.

Summary

EJBs are ideal for writing business logic in web applications. They can act as the perfect bridge between web interface components such as JSF, servlet, or JSP and data access objects such as JDO. EJBs can be distributed across multiple JEE application servers (this could improve application scalability), and their life cycle is managed by the container. EJBs can be easily injected into managed objects or can be looked up using JNDI.

Eclipse JEE makes creating and consuming EJBs very easy. Just like we saw how Tomcat can be configured and managed within Eclipse, JEE application servers, such as GlassFish, can also be managed from within Eclipse.

In the next chapter, we will learn how to create web applications using Spring MVC. Although Spring is not part of JEE, it is a popular framework to implement the MVC pattern in JEE web applications. Spring can also work with many of the JEE specifications.

8
Creating Web Applications with Spring MVC

In the last chapter, we learned how to create JEE applications using EJBs. In this chapter, we are going to divert a bit from the core JEE specifications and learn Spring MVC.

Although this book is about JEE and Eclipse, and Spring MVC is not a part of JEE, it would be worthwhile to understand the Spring MVC framework. Spring MVC is a very popular framework for creating web applications and can be used with other JEE technologies, such as servlet, JSP, JPA, and EJBs.

JEE does support MVC out of the box, if you use JSF. Refer to *Java Server Faces* in `Chapter 2, Creating a Simple JEE Web Application*, for details. However, there is a difference in the design of JSF and Spring MVC. JSF is a component-based MVC framework. It is designed so that the user interface designer can create pages by assembling reusable components that are either provided by JSF or custom-developed. Spring MVC is a request-response-based MVC framework. If you are familiar with writing JSP or servlets, then Spring MVC would be an easier framework to use than JSF. You can find a good description of component-based MVC (as implemented by JSF) and request-response-based MVC (as implemented by Spring MVC) by Ed Burns at
`http://www.oracle.com/technetwork/articles/java/mvc-2280472.html`. JSR 371 for MVC was supposed to be part of JEE 8, but this JSR was later withdrawn from JEE 8 specifications. You can find more information about JSR 371 (also called MVC 1.0) at `https://www.mvc-spec.org/`.

Before we see how Spring MVC works, we need to understand what the MVC framework is. **MVC** stands for **Model-View-Controller**. We are going to refer to the MVC framework in the context of Java web applications only, although it should be mentioned here that the MVC pattern is often used in desktop applications too:

- **Model**: The Model contains data that is used by the View to create the output. In the example that we have been following in this book, the *Course Management* application, if you have a `Course` class that contains information about the course to be displayed on a page, then the `Course` object can be called the Model. Some definitions of MVC also include classes that implement business logic in the Model layer. For example, a `CourseService` class that takes a `Course` object and calls `CourseDAO` to save the `Course` in the database could also be considered a part of the Model layer.

- **View**: The View is a page that is displayed to the user. A JSP that displays a list of courses could be considered a part of the View layer. The View holds a reference to the Model object and uses the data it contains to create the page that the user sees in the browser.

- **Controller:** The Controller is the glue between Model and View. It handles requests/actions from the web client (for example, the browser), calls the Model to handle business logic, and makes Model objects available to the View to create the page (user interface) to be returned to the client. The Controller could be a servlet, as in the case of JSF, or could be POJOs (as in the case of Spring MVC). When Controllers are POJOs, typically they get called by `DispatcherServlet`. `DispatherServlet` is a servlet that receives the request and dispatches it to one of the Controllers, based on the configuration. We will see example of this later in the chapter.

MVC provides separation of concerns; that is, the code for the user interface and the business logic are separate. Because of this, the UI and the business layer can be modified independently to a great extent. Of course, since the UI usually displays the data generated by the business layer, it may not always be possible to make changes to each of the layers independent of the others. Developers of appropriate skills can work on each layer independently. A UI expert need not be too worried about how the business layer is implemented and vice versa.

In this chapter, we will cover the following topics:

- Introduction to Spring dependency injection
- Configuring Spring beans and injecting them into the application
- Creating Spring MVC applications using the Eclipse plugin and JEE specifications such as JDBC, JPA, and JSP

Dependency injection

Spring MVC is a part of the overall Spring Framework. The core feature of the Spring Framework is **dependency injection (DI)**. Almost all other features of the Spring Framework use DI. Objects managed by the dependency injection framework are not directly instantiated in the code (using, for example, the `new` operator). Let's call them *managed objects*. These objects are created by a DI framework, such as Spring. Because these objects are created by a framework, the framework has a lot more flexibility in deciding how to set values in the object and from where to get them. For example, your **Data Access Object (DAO)** class might need an instance of a database connection factory object. However, instead of instantiating it in the DAO class, you just tell the DI framework that when it instantiates the DAO, it has to set the value of a member variable for the connection pool factory. Of course, the parameters for the connection pool factory will have to be configured somewhere and be known to the DI framework.

When a class instantiates another class, there is tight dependency between them. Such design could be a problem if you want to test classes independently of others. For example, you may want to test a class that has business logic, but one that also refers to a DAO, which in turn depends on a JDBC connection object. When testing the first class, you will have to instantiate the DAO and configure the connection pool. As we saw in Chapter 5, *Unit Testing*, unit tests should be able to run without any external dependencies. One way to achieve this is by using DI. Instead of instantiating the DAO class, our class could refer to an interface that is implemented by the DAO and have the DI framework inject the implementation of this interface at runtime. When you are unit testing this class, the DI framework can be configured to inject a mock object that implements the required interface. Thus, DI enables loose coupling between objects.

Dependency injection in Spring

Because DI is at the core of the Spring Framework, let's spend some time understanding how it works in Spring. We will create a standalone application for this purpose. Create a simple Maven project. Add the following dependency for the Spring Framework:

```
<dependency>
  <groupId>org.springframework</groupId>
  <artifactId>spring-context</artifactId>
  <version>5.0.5.RELEASE</version>
</dependency>
```

Replace the preceding version number with the latest version of Spring. Classes managed by the DI container of Spring are called beans or components. You can either declare beans in an XML file or you can annotate the class. We will use annotations in this chapter. However, even though we use annotations, we need to specify the minimum configuration in an XML file. So, create an XML file in the src/main/resource folder of your project and name it context.xml. The reason that we are creating this file in the src/main.resource folder is that the files in this folder are made available in the classpath. Next, add the following content to context.xml:

```
<?xml version="1.0" encoding="UTF-8"?>
<beans xmlns="http://www.springframework.org/schema/beans"
    xmlns:xsi="http://www.w3.org/2001/XMLSchema-instance"
    xmlns:context="http://www.springframework.org/schema/context"
  xsi:schemaLocation="http://www.springframework.org/schema/beans
        http://www.springframework.org/schema/beans/spring-beans.xsd
        http://www.springframework.org/schema/context
        http://www.springframework.org/schema/context/spring-context.xsd">
        <context:component-scan base-package="packt.jee.eclipse.spring"/>
</beans>
```

By using the <context:component-scan> tag, we are telling the Spring Framework to scan the base-package folder and then look for the classes annotated with @Component and recognize them as managed classes so that they can be made available when injecting dependencies. In the preceding example, all classes in the packt.jee.eclipse.spring package (and its sub-packages) would be scanned to identify components.

Information read from the configuration file must be saved in an object. In Spring, it is saved in an instance of the ApplicationContext interface. There are different implementations of ApplicationContext. We will be using the ClassPathXmlApplicationContext class, which looks for the configuration XML file in the classpath.

We will now create two Spring components. The first one is `CourseDAO`, and the second is `CourseService`. Although we won't write any business logic in these classes (the purpose of this example is to understand how DI works in Spring), assume that `CourseDAO` could have the code to access the database and `CourseService` calls `CourseDAO` to perform the database operations. So, `CourseService` is dependent on `CourseDAO`. To keep the code simple, we will not create any interface for `CourseDAO` but will have the direct dependency. Create the `CourseDAO` class as follows:

```
package packt.jee.eclipse.spring;

import org.springframework.stereotype.Component;

@Component
public class CourseDAO {

}
```

We will have no methods in `CourseDAO`, but as mentioned before, it could have methods to access the database. `@Component` marks this class as managed by Spring. Now, create the `CourseService` class. This class needs an instance of `CourseDAO`:

```
package packt.jee.eclipse.spring;

import org.springframework.beans.factory.annotation.Autowired;
import org.springframework.stereotype.Component;

@Component
public class CourseService {

  @Autowired
  private CourseDAO courseDAO;

  public CourseDAO getCourseDAO() {
    return courseDAO;
  }
}
```

We have declared a member variable called `courseDAO` and annotated it with `@Autowired`. This tells Spring to look for a component in its context (of `CourseDAO` type) and assign that to the `courseDAO` member.

We will now create the main class. It creates `ApplicationContext`, gets the `CourseService` bean, calls the `getCourseDAO` method, and then checks whether it was injected properly. Create the `SpringMain` class:

```
package packt.jee.eclipse.spring;

import org.springframework.context.ApplicationContext;
import org.springframework.context.support.ClassPathXmlApplicationContext;

public class SpringMain {

  public static void main (String[] args) {
    //create ApplicationContext
    ApplicationContext ctx = new
     ClassPathXmlApplicationContext("context.xml");
    //Get bean
    CourseService courseService = (CourseService)
     ctx.getBean("courseService");
    //Get and print CourseDAO. It should not be null
    System.out.println("CourseDAO = " +
     courseService.getCourseDAO());
  }
}
```

We first create an instance of `ClassPathXmlApplicationContext`. The configuration XML file is passed as an argument to the constructor. We then get the `courseService` bean/component. Note the naming convention when specifying the bean name; it is the class name with the first letter in lowercase. We then get and print the value of `CourseDAO`. The value won't show any meaningful information, but if the value is not null, then it would mean that the Spring DI container has injected it properly. Note that we have not instantiated `CourseDAO`; it is the Spring DI container that instantiates and injects this object.

In the preceding code, we saw an example of injecting objects at the member declaration (this is also called property injection). We can have this object injected in the constructors too:

```
@Component
public class CourseService {

  private CourseDAO courseDAO;

  @Autowired
  public CourseService (CourseDAO courseDAO) {
    this.courseDAO = coueseDAO;
  }
```

```
public CourseDAO getCourseDAO() {
   return courseDAO;
   }
}
```

Note that the @Autowired annotation is moved to the constructor, and the single constructor argument is auto-injected. You can also have the object injected in a setter:

```
@Component
public class CourseService {

   private CourseDAO courseDAO;

   @Autowired
   public void setCourseDAO (CourseDAO courseDAO) {
      this.courseDAO = courseDAO;
   }

   public CourseDAO getCourseDAO() {
      return courseDAO;
   }
}
```

Component scopes

You can specify the scope for your components in Spring MVC. The default scope is singleton, which means that there will be only one instance of the component in the context. Every request for this component will be served with the same instance. The other scopes are as follows:

- **Prototype**: Each request for the component is served with a new instance of that class.
- **Request**: Valid for web applications. Single instance of a component class created for each HTTP request.
- **Session**: Single instance of a component class created for each HTTP session. Used in web applications.
- **Global session**: Single instance of a component class created for the global HTTP session. Used in portlet applications.
- **Application**: Single instance of a component class in the web application. The instance is shared by all sessions in that application.

See `https://docs.spring.io/spring/docs/current/spring-framework-reference/core.html#beans-factory-scopes` for more information on component scopes in Spring.

If the component to be injected was not instantiated at the time it was requested, then Spring creates an instance of the component. In the previous example, we have not specified the scope of the `CourseDAO` component, so the same instance would be injected if there is another request for injecting `CourseDAO`. You can specify the scope in the `@Component` annotation. You can also specify the component name if you want to override the default name that Spring gives to the component.

To see if a single instance of a component is injected when no scope is specified, let's change the `main` method in the `SpringMain` class and make two calls to the `getBean` method:

```java
public static void main (String[] args) {
  //create ApplicationContext
  ApplicationContext ctx = new
   ClassPathXmlApplicationContext("context.xml");
  //call and print ctx.getBean first time
  System.out.println("Course Service 1 - " +
   ctx.getBean("courseService"));    System.out.println("Course Service 2
- " +
   ctx.getBean("courseService"));
}
```

Run the application and you should see the same instance of the `courseService` bean printed. Let's change the scope of the `CourseService` component:

```java
@Component
@Scope(ConfigurableBeanFactory.SCOPE_PROTOTYPE)
public class CourseService {
  //content remains the same
}
```

Run the application again; this time, you should see different instances of the `CourseService` component.

When Spring comes across the `@Autowire` annotation, it tries to find the component by type. In the preceding example, `courseDAO` is annotated with `@Autowire`. Spring tries to find a component of `CourseDAO` type; it finds an instance of `CourseDAO` and injects it. But what if there are multiple instances of the class in the context? In such a case, we can use the `@Qualifier` annotation to uniquely identify components. Let's now create the `ICourseDAO` interface, which will be implemented by two components, namely `CourseDAO` and `CourseDAO1`:

```
public interface ICourseDAO {
}
```

`CourseDAO` implements `ICourseDAO` and is uniquely qualified as `"courseDAO"`:

```
@Component
@Qualifier("courseDAO")
public class CourseDAO implements ICourseDAO {
}
```

`CourseDAO1` implements `ICourseDAO` and is uniquely qualified as `"courseDAO1"`:

```
@Component
@Qualifier("courseDAO1")
public class CourseDAO1 implements ICourseDAO {
}
```

In the `CourseService` class, we will use a qualifier to uniquely identify whether we want `CourseDAO` or `CourseDAO1` to be injected:

```
@Component
public class CourseService {

  @Autowired
  private @Qualifier("courseDAO1") ICourseDAO courseDAO;

  public ICourseDAO getCourseDAO() {
    return courseDAO;
  }
}
```

The qualifier can also be specified at method arguments, for example:

```
@Autowired
public void setCourseDAO (@Qualifier("courseDAO1") ICourseDAO
 courseDAO) {
   this.courseDAO = courseDAO;
}
```

Run the application now. You should see that an instance of `CourseDAO1` is printed in the console.

We have covered the basics of dependency injection in Spring. However, Spring offers a lot more options and features for dependency injection than we have covered here. We will see more DI features as and when required in this chapter.

 Visit `https://docs.spring.io/spring/docs/current/spring-framework-reference/core.html#beans-dependencies` for more information about dependency injection in Spring.

Installing Spring Tool Suite

Spring Tool Suite (**STS**) is a set of tools in Eclipse for creating Spring applications. It can be either installed as a plugin to an existing installation of Eclipse JEE or can be installed standalone. The standalone version of STS is also packaged with Eclipse EE, so all Eclipse features for Java EE development are available in STS too. You can download STS from `https://spring.io/tools`. Since we have already installed Eclipse EE, we will install STS as a plugin. The easiest way to install the STS plugin is from **Eclipse Marketplace**. Select the **Help | Eclipse Marketplace...** menu.

Type `Spring Tool Suite` in the **Find** box, and click the **Go** button:

Figure 8.1: Search fir STS in Eclipse Marketplace

Click **Install**. The next page shows the features of STS that will be installed. Click **Confirm** to install the selected features.

Creating a Spring MVC application

Spring MVC can be used for creating web applications. It provides an easy framework to map incoming web requests to a handler class (Controller) and create dynamic HTML output. It is an implementation of the MVC pattern. The Controller and Models are created as POJOs, and Views can be created using JSP, JSTL, XSLT, and even JSF. However, in this chapter, we will focus on creating Views using JSP and JSTL.

 You can find the Spring web documentation at `https://docs.spring.io/ spring/docs/current/spring-framework-reference/web.html`.

A web request is handled by four layers in Spring MVC:

- **Front controller**: This is a Spring servlet configured in `web.xml`. Based on the request URL pattern, it passes requests to the Controller.
- **Controller**: These are POJOs annotated with `@Controller`. For each Controller that you write, you need to specify a URL pattern that the Controller is expected to handle. Sub-URL patterns can be specified at the method level too. We will see examples of this later. Controller has access to Model and to HTTP request and response objects. Controller can delegate processing of a request to other business handler objects, get results, and populate the Model object, which is made available to View by Spring MVC.
- **Model**: These are data objects. The Controller and View layers can set and get data from Model objects.
- **View**: These are typically JSPs, but Spring MVC supports other types of Views too. See **View technologies** in the Spring documentation at `https://docs. spring.io/spring/docs/current/spring-framework-reference/web.html#mvc-view`.

We will learn Spring MVC in this chapter through examples, as we have been learning in some other chapters in this book. We will create a part of the same *Course Management* application using Spring MVC. The application will display a list of courses with options to add, remove, and modify them.

Creating a Spring project

First, make sure that you have installed STS in Eclipse EE. From the Eclipse menu, select **File** | **New** | **Other** and then select the **Spring** | **Spring Legacy Project** option. Enter the project name and select the **Spring MVC Project** template:

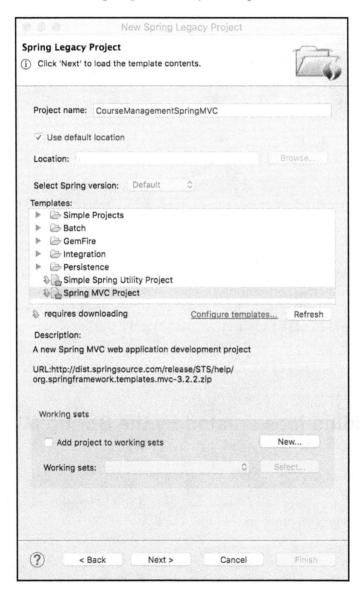

Figure 8.2: Select the Spring MVC Project template

Click on **Next**. The page will ask you to enter the top-level package name:

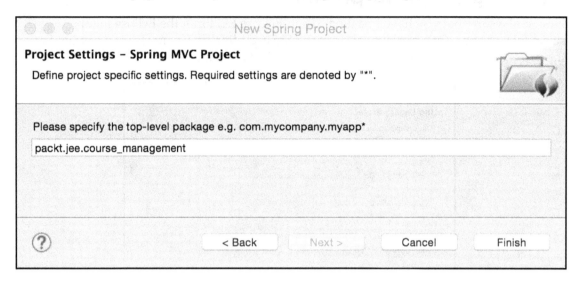

Whatever you enter as a top-level package, the wizard takes the third sub-package as the application name. When the application is deployed in a server, the application name becomes the context name. For example, if you enter the package name as `packt.jee.course_management`, then `course_management` becomes the application name, and the base URL of the application on the local machine would be `http://localhost:8080/course_management/`.

Click **Finish**. This creates a Maven project with the required libraries for Spring MVC.

Understanding files created by the Spring MVC project template

Let's examine some of the files created by the template:

- `src/main/webapp/WEB-INF/web.xml`: A front Controller servlet is declared here, along with other configurations:

```
<!-- Processes application requests -->
<servlet>
  <servlet-name>appServlet</servlet-name>
  <servlet-
```

```
class>org.springframework.web.servlet.DispatcherServlet</servlet-
class>
  <init-param>
    <param-name>contextConfigLocation</param-name>
    <param-value>/WEB-INF/spring/appServlet/servlet-
    context.xml</param-value>
  </init-param>
  <load-on-startup>1</load-on-startup>
</servlet>
```

`DispatcherServlet` is the front Controller servlet. It is passed the path of the context (XML) file for configuring Spring DI. Recall that in the standalone Spring application, we created `context.xml` to configure dependency injection. The `DispatcherServlet` servlet is mapped to handle requests to this web application.

- `src/main/webapp/WEB-INF/spring/appServlet/servlet-context.xml`: Context configuration for Spring DI. Some of the notable configuration parameters in this file are as follows:

```
<annotation-driven />
```

This enables annotations for configuring dependency injection at the class level:

```
<resources mapping="/resources/**" location="/resources/" />
```

Static files, such as CSS, JavaScript, and images, can be placed in the `resources` folder (`src/main/webapp/resources`):

```
<beans:bean
  class="org.springframework.web.servlet.view.InternalResourceViewResolver">
  <beans:property name="prefix" value="/WEB-INF/views/" />
  <beans:property name="suffix" value=".jsp" />
</beans:bean>
```

This tells Spring to use the `InternalResourceViewResolver` class to resolve Views. Properties of this bean tell the `InternalResourceViewResolver` class to look for the View files in the `/WEB-INF/views` folder. Furthermore, Views will be JSP files, as indicated by the suffix property. Our Views will be the JSP files in the `src/main/webapp/WEB-INF/views` folder:

```
<context:component-scan base-package="packt.jee.course_management" />
```

This tells Spring to scan the `packt.jee.course_management` package and its sub-packages to search for components (annotated by `@Component`).

The default template also creates one Controller and one View. The controller class is `HomeController` in the package that you specified in the Spring project wizard (in our example, it is `packt.jee.course_management`). Controller in Spring MVC is called by the dispatcher servlet. Controllers are annotated by `@Controller`. To map the request path to a Controller, you use the `@RequestMapping` annotation. Let's see the code generated by the template in the `HomeController` class:

```
@Controller
public class HomeController {

  private static final Logger logger =
   LoggerFactory.getLogger(HomeController.class);

  /**
    * Simply selects the home view to render by returning its name.
    */
  @RequestMapping(value = "/", method = RequestMethod.GET)
  public String home(Locale locale, Model model) {
     logger.info("Welcome home! The client locale is {}.", locale);

     Date date = new Date();
     DateFormat dateFormat =
  DateFormat.getDateTimeInstance(DateFormat.LONG, DateFormat.LONG, locale);

     String formattedDate = dateFormat.format(date);

     model.addAttribute("serverTime", formattedDate );

     return "home";
   }
}
```

The `home` method is annotated with `@RequestMapping`. The value of mapping is `/`, which tells the dispatcher servlet to send all requests coming its way to this method. The `method` attribute tells the dispatcher to call the `home` method only for HTTP requests of the `GET` type. The `home` method takes two arguments, namely `Locale` and `Model`; both are injected at runtime by Spring. The `@RequestMapping` annotation also tells Spring to insert any dependencies when calling the `home` method, and so `locale` and `model` are auto-injected.

The method itself does not do much; it gets the current date-time and sets it as an attribute in the Model. Any attributes set in the Model are available to the View (JSP). The method returns a string, `"home"`. This value is used by Spring MVC to resolve the View to be displayed. The `InternalResourceViewResolver` that we saw in `servlet-context.xml` previously resolves this as `home.jsp` in the `/WEB-INF/views` folder. `home.jsp` has the following code in the `<body>` tag:

```
<P>  The time on the server is ${serverTime}. </P>
```

The `serverTime` variable comes from the Model object set in the `home` method of `HomeController`.

To run this project, we need to configure a server in Eclipse and add this project to the server. Refer to the *Configuring Tomcat in Eclipse* and *Running JSP in Tomcat* sections in `Chapter 2`, *Creating a Simple JEE Web Application*.

Once you configure Tomcat and add the project to it, start the server. Then, right-click on the project and select **Run As** | **Run on Server**. You should see a **hello** message with the timestamp displayed in the internal Eclipse browser. The URL in the browser's address bar should be `http://localhost:8080/course_management/`, assuming that Tomcat is deployed on port `8080` and the context name (derived from the top-level package name) is `course_management`. If you want to change the default context name or remove the context, that is, deploy the application in the root context, then open the project properties (right-click on the project and select **Properties**) and go to **Web Project Settings**. You can change the context root name or remove it from this page:

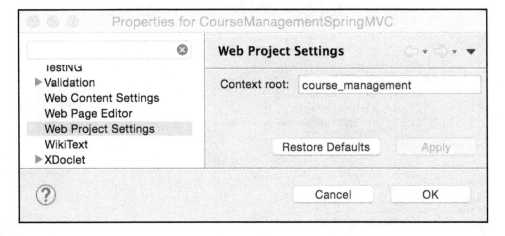

Figure 8.4: Context root setting

For our *Course Management* application, we are not going to need the `HomeController` class or `home.jsp`, so you can go ahead and delete these files.

Building the Spring MVC application using JDBC

In this section, we will build a part of the course management application using Spring MVC and JDBC. The application will display a list of courses and options for adding, deleting, and modifying courses. We will continue using the project that we created in the previous section. We will learn many of the features of Spring for data access using JDBC as we go along.

First, we will configure our datasource. We will use the same MySQL database that we created in the *Creating database schema* section of `Chapter 4`, *Creating JEE Database Applications*.

Configuring a datasource

In Spring, you can configure a JDBC datasource either in Java code or in the XML configuration (context) file. Before we see how to configure a datasource, we need to add some dependencies in Maven. In this chapter, we will use Apache's Commons DBCP component for connection pooling (recall that in `Chapter 4`, *Creating JEE Database Applications*, we selected the Hikari connection pool). Visit `https://commons.apache.org/proper/commons-dbcp/` for details on Apache DBCP. In addition to adding a dependency for Apache DBCP, we need to add dependencies for Spring JDBC and the MySQL JDBC driver. Add the following dependencies to the `pom.xml` of the project:

```
<!-- Spring JDBC -->
<dependency>
  <groupId>org.springframework</groupId>
  <artifactId>spring-jdbc</artifactId>
  <version>${org.springframework-version}</version>
</dependency>

<!-- Apache DBCP -->
<dependency>
  <groupId>commons-dbcp</groupId>
  <artifactId>commons-dbcp</artifactId>
  <version>1.4</version>
</dependency>

<!-- MySQL -->
```

```xml
<dependency>
  <groupId>mysql</groupId>
  <artifactId>mysql-connector-java</artifactId>
  <version>8.0.9-rc</version>
</dependency>
```

If you want to create a datasource in Java code, you can do so as follows:

```java
DriverManagerDataSource dataSource = new
 DriverManagerDataSource();
dataSource.setDriverClassName("com.mysql.jdbc.Driver");
dataSource.setUrl("jdbc:mysql://localhost:3306/course_management");
dataSource.setUsername("your_user_name");
dataSource.setPassword("your_password");
```

However, we will configure a datasource in an XML configuration file. Open `servlet-context.xml` (you will find it in the `src/main/webapp/WEB-INF/spring/appServlet` folder) and add the following bean:

```xml
<beans:bean id="dataSource"
  class="org.apache.commons.dbcp.BasicDataSource" destroy- method="close">
    <beans:property name="driverClassName"
 value="com.mysql.jdbc.Driver"/>  <beans:property name="url"
 value="jdbc:mysql://localhost:3306/course_management" />
  <beans:property name="username" value="your_user_name"/>
  <beans:property name="password" value="your_password"/>
</beans:bean>
```

If you are wondering what *bean* means, it is the same as the component that we created in the examples earlier in the chapter. We have so far created a component using annotations, but the component and the bean can be declared in an XML file too. In fact, this is how it used to be in earlier versions, till support for annotations was added in Spring. In a real-world application, you may want to encrypt database passwords before specifying them in a configuration file. One way to decrypt a password before sending it to the database is to create a wrapper class for the datasource (in the previous example, create a wrapper for `org.apache.commons.dbcp.BasicDataSource`) and override the `setPassword` method, where you can decrypt the password.

If you want to keep the database connection parameters separate from the Spring configuration, then you can use a `properties` file. Spring provides a consistent way to access resources such as a `properties` file. Just as you can access web URLs using the `http` protocol prefix or the file URL using the `file` protocol prefix, Spring allows you to access resources in the classpath using the `classpath` prefix. For example, if we create a `jdbc.properties` file and save it in one of the folders in the classpath, then we could access it as `classpath:jdbc.properties`.

Visit `https://docs.spring.io/spring/docs/current/spring-framework-reference/core.html#resources` for detailed information on accessing resources using Spring. The Spring resource URL formats can be used in configuration files or Spring APIs where the resource location is expected.

Spring also provides a convenient tag to load property files in context config XML. You can access the values of properties in a `property` file in the config XML using the `${property_name}` syntax.

We will move the database connection properties to a file in this example. Create `jdbc.properties` in the `src/main/resources` folder. Maven makes this folder available in the classpath, so we can access it using the Spring resource format in the XML configuration file:

```
jdbc.driverClassName=com.mysql.jdbc.Driver
jdbc.url=jdbc:mysql://localhost:3306/course_management
jdbc.username=your_user_name
jdbc.password=your_password
```

We will load this `properties` file from `servlet-context.xml` using the `property-placeholder` tag:

```
<context:property-placeholder location="classpath:jdbc.properties"/>
```

Notice that the location of the `property` file is specified using the Spring resource format. In this case, we ask Spring to look for the `jdbc.properties` file in the classpath. Further, because the `src/main/resources` folder is in the classpath (where we saved `jdbc.properties`), it should be loaded by Spring.

Let's now modify the `datasource` bean declaration in `servlet-context.xml` to use the property values:

```
<beans:bean id="dataSource"
  class="org.apache.commons.dbcp.BasicDataSource" destroy- method="close">
    <beans:property name="driverClassName"
 value="${jdbc.driverClassName}"/>
  <beans:property name="url" value="${jdbc.url}" />
  <beans:property name="username" value="${jdbc.username}"/>
  <beans:property name="password" value="${jdbc.password}"/>
</beans:bean>
```

Note that the order of the `property-placeholder` tag and where the properties are used does not matter. Spring loads the entire XML configuration file before replacing `property` references with their values.

Using the Spring JDBCTemplate class

Spring provides a utility class called `JDBCTemplate` that makes it easy to perform many operations using JDBC. It provides convenient methods to execute SQL statements, map results of a query to an object (using the `RowMapper` class), close a database connection at the end of database operations, and many others.

Visit `https://docs.spring.io/spring/docs/current/spring-framework-reference/data-access.html#jdbc` for more information on `JDBCTemplate`.

Before we write any data access code, we will create a **Data Transfer Object (DTO)**, `CourseDTO`, which will just contain members that describe one `Course` and setters and getters for them. Create `CourseDTO` in the `packt.jee.course_management.dto` package. Instances of this class will be used to transfer data between different tiers of our application:

```
public class CourseDTO {
    private int id;
    private int credits;
    private String name;

    //skipped setters and getters to save space
}
```

We will now create a simple DAO that will use the `JdbcTemplate` class to execute a query to get all courses. Create the `CourseDAO` class in the `packt.jee.course_management.dao` package. Annotate the `CourseDAO` class with `@Repository`. Similar to `@Component`, the `@Repository` annotation marks the class as a Spring DI container-managed class.

As per the Spring documentation (`https://docs.spring.io/spring/docs/current/spring-framework-reference/core.html#beans-stereotype-annotations`), `@Component` is a generic annotation to mark a class as Spring container-managed, and `@Repository` and `@Controller` are more specific ones. More specific annotations help to identify classes for specific treatments. It is recommended to use `@Repository` annotations for DAOs.

`CourseDAO` needs to have an instance of the `JdbcTemplate` class to execute queries and other SQL statements. `JdbcTemplate` needs a `DataSource` object before it can be used. We will have `DataSource` injected in a method in `CourseDAO`:

```
@Repository
public class CourseDAO {

  private JdbcTemplate jdbcTemplate;

  @Autowired
  public void setDatasource (DataSource dataSource) {
    jdbcTemplate = new JdbcTemplate(dataSource);
  }
}
```

The `datasource` that we have configured in `servlet-context.xml` will be injected by Spring when the `CourseDAO` object is created.

We will now write the method to get all courses. The `JdbcTemplate` class has a `query` method that allows you to specify `RowMapper`, where you can map each row in the query to a Java object:

```
public List<CourseDTO> getCourses () {
  List<CourseDTO> courses = jdbcTemplate.query ("select * from
  course",
    new CourseRowMapper());

  return courses;
}

public static final class CourseRowMapper implements
 RowMapper<CourseDTO> {
  @Override
  public CourseDTO mapRow (ResultSet rs, int rowNum) throws
   SQLException {
    CourseDTO course = new CourseDTO();
    course.setId(rs.getInt("id"));
    course.setName(rs.getString("name"));
    course.setCredits(rs.getInt("credits"));
    return course;
  }
}
```

In the `getCourses` method, we will execute a static query. Later, we will see how to execute parameterized queries too. The second argument to the `query` method of `JDBCTemplate` is an instance of the `RowMapper` interface. We have created the static inner class `CourseRowMapper` that implements the `RowMapper` interface. We override the `mapRow` method, which is called for each row in `ResultSet`, and then we create/map the `CourseDTO` object from the `ResultSet` passed in the arguments. The method returns a `CourseDTO` object. The result of `JdbcTemplate.query` is a list of `CourseDTO` objects. Note that the `query` method can also return other Java collection objects, such as `Map`.

Now, let's write a method to add a course to the table:

```
public void addCourse (final CourseDTO course) {
   KeyHolder keyHolder = new GeneratedKeyHolder();
   jdbcTemplate.update(new PreparedStatementCreator() {

     @Override
     public PreparedStatement createPreparedStatement(Connection
      con)
         throws SQLException {
       String sql = "insert into Course (name, credits) values
        (?,?)";        PreparedStatement stmt = con.prepareStatement(sql, new
        String[] {"id"});
       stmt.setString(1, course.getName());
       stmt.setInt(2, course.getCredits());
       return stmt;
     }
   }, keyHolder);

   course.setId(keyHolder.getKey().intValue());
}
```

When we add or insert a new course, we want to get the ID of the new record, which is autogenerated. Furthermore, we would like to use the prepared statement to execute SQL. Therefore, first we create `KeyHolder` for the auto-generated field. The `update` method of `JdbcTemplate` has many overloaded versions. We use the one that takes `PreparedStatementCreator` and `KeyHolder`. We create an instance of `PreparedStatementCreator` and override the `createPreparedStatement` method. In this method, we create a JDBC `PreparedStatement` and return it. Once the `update` method is successfully executed, we retrieve the auto-generated value by calling the `getKey` method of `KeyHolder`.

The methods to update or delete a course are similar:

```
public void updateCourse (final CourseDTO course) {
  jdbcTemplate.update(new PreparedStatementCreator() {
    @Override
    public PreparedStatement createPreparedStatement(Connection
     con)
        throws SQLException {
      String sql = "update Course set name = ?, credits = ? where
       id = ?";
      PreparedStatement stmt = con.prepareStatement(sql);
      stmt.setString(1, course.getName());
      stmt.setInt(2, course.getCredits());
      stmt.setInt(3, course.getId());
      return stmt;
    }
  });
}

public void deleteCourse(final int id) {
  jdbcTemplate.update(new PreparedStatementCreator() {
    @Override
    public PreparedStatement createPreparedStatement(Connection
     con)
        throws SQLException {
      String sql = "delete from Course where id = ?";
      PreparedStatement stmt = con.prepareStatement(sql);
      stmt.setInt(1, id);
      return stmt;
    }
  });
}
```

We need to add one more method to CourseDAO, to get the details of a course, given the ID:

```
public CourseDTO getCourse (int id) {
  String sql = "select * from course where id = ?";
  CourseDTO course = jdbcTemplate.queryForObject(sql, new
   CourseRowMapper(), id);
  return course;
}
```

`queryForObject` returns a single object for a given query. We use a parameterized query here, and the parameter is passed as the last argument to the `queryForObject` method. Further, we use `CourseRowMapper` to map the single row returned by this query to `CourseDTO`. Note that you can pass a variable number of parameters to the `queryForObject` method, although in this case, we pass a single value, that is, the ID.

We now have all the methods in the `CourseDAO` class to access data for `Course`.

> For a detailed discussion on data access using JDBC in Spring, refer to
> https://docs.spring.io/spring/docs/current/spring-framework-reference/data-access.html#jdbc.

Creating the Spring MVC Controller

We will now create the `Controller` class. In Spring MVC, the Controller is mapped to the request URL and handles requests matching the URL pattern. The request URL for matching an incoming request is specified at the method level in the controller. However, more generic request mapping can be specified at the `Controller` class level, and a specific URL, with respect to the URL at the class level, can be specified at the method level.

Create a class named `CourseController` in the `packt.jee.course_management.controller` package. Annotate it with `@Controller`. The `@Controller` annotation is of type `@Component`, and allows the Spring Framework to identify that class specifically as a controller. Add the method to get courses in `CourseController`:

```
@Controller
public class CourseController {
  @Autowired
  CourseDAO courseDAO;

  @RequestMapping("/courses")
  public String getCourses (Model model) {
    model.addAttribute("courses", courseDAO.getCourses());
    return "courses";
  }
}
```

The `CourseDAO` instance is autowired; that is, it will be injected by Spring. We have added the `getCourses` method, which takes a Spring Model object. Data can be shared between View and Controller using this Model object. Therefore, we add an attribute to Model, named `courses`, and assign the list of courses that we get by calling `courseDAO.getCourses`. This list could be used in the View JSP as the `courses` variable. We have annotated this method with `@RequestMapping`. This annotation maps the incoming request URL to a controller method. In this case, we are saying that any request (relative to the root) that starts with `/courses` should be handled by the `getCourses` method in this controller. We will add more methods to `CourseController` later and discuss some of the parameters that we can pass to the `@RequestMapping` annotation, but first let's create a View to display the list of courses.

Creating View

We have created data access objects for `Course` and a Controller. Let's see how we can call them from a View. Views in Spring are typically JSPs. Create a JSP (name it `courses.jsp`) in the `src/main/webapp/WEB-INF/views` folder. This is the folder that we configured in `servlet-context.xml` to hold the Spring View files.

Add the JSTL tag library in `courses.jsp`:

```
<%@ taglib prefix="c" uri="http://java.sun.com/jsp/jstl/core" %>
```

The markup code to display courses is very simple; we make use of the `courses` variable, which is made available in the Model from the `CourseController.getCourses` method and displays values using JSTL expressions:

```
<table>
  <tr>
    <th>Id</th>
    <th>Name</th>
    <th>Credits</th>
    <th></th>
  </tr>
  <c:forEach items="${courses}" var="course">
    <tr>
      <td>${course.id}</td>
      <td>${course.name}</td>
      <td>${course.credits}</td>
    </tr>
  </c:forEach>
</table>
```

Recall that `courses` is a list of objects of `CourseDTO` type. Members of `CourseDTO` are accessed in the `forEach` tag to display the actual values.

Unfortunately, we can't run this page from Eclipse the way we have so far in this book, that is, by right-clicking on the project or page and selecting **Run As** | **Run on Server**. If you try to run the project (right-click on the project and select the **Run** menu), then Eclipse will try to open the `http://localhost:8080/course_management/` URL, and because we do not have any start page (`index.html` or `index.jsp`), we will get an **HTTP 404 error**. The reason that we can't run the page by right-clicking and selecting the run option is that Eclipse tries to open `http://localhost:8080/course_management/WEB-INF/views/courses.jsp`, and this fails because files in `WEB-INF` are not accessible from outside the server. Another reason, or rather the primary reason, that this URL will not work is that in `web.xml`, we have mapped all requests to be handled by `DispatcherServlet` of the Spring Framework and it does not find a suitable mapping for the request URL. To run the application, open the URL `http://localhost:8080/course_management/courses` in the browser.

Mapping data using @ModelAttribute

In this section, we will implement the feature to insert a new course. In the process, we will learn more about mapping requests to methods and mapping request parameters to method arguments.

In the previous section, we implemented `CourseController` with one method, `getCourses`. We will now add methods to insert new courses. To add a course, we first need to display a View with a form that accepts the user input. When the user actually submits the form, the form data should be posted to a URL that handles insertion of the data to the database. Therefore, there are two requests involved here: the first is to display the *add course* form, and the second is to handle the data posted from the form. We will call the first request `addCourse` and the second request `doAddCourse`. Let's first create the user interface. Create a new JSP and name it `addCourse.jsp`. Add the following markup to the `body` of the page (JSTL and other header declarations are skipped to save space):

```
<h2>Add Course</h2>
<c:if test="${not empty error}">
  <span style="color:red;">
    ${error}<br>
  </span>
</c:if>

<c:set var="actionPath"
```

```
      value="${pageContext.request.contextPath}/doAddCourse"/>
  <form method="post" action="${actionPath}">
    <table>
      <tr>
        <td>Course Name:</td>
        <td><input type="text" name="name" value="${course.name}">
          </td>
      </tr>
      <tr>
        <td>Credits:</td>
        <td><input type="text" name="credits"
          value="${course.credits}"> </td>
      </tr>
      <tr>
        <td colspan="2">
        <button type="submit">Submit</button>
        </td>
      </tr>
    </table>
    <input type="hidden" name="id" value="${course.id}">
  </form>
```

The page expects a course variable to be made available by the controller. In the form body, it assigns the values of the course to appropriate input fields; for example, the `${course.name}` value is assigned to the text input for `Course Name`. The form posts the data to the `"${pageContext.request.contextPath}/doAddCourse"` URL. Note that since our application is not deployed in the root context, we need to include the context name in the URL.

Let's now add Controller methods to handle two requests for add: `addCourse` and `doAddCourse`. When the `addCourse` request is made, we want to serve the page that displays the input form. When the user clicks the **Submit** button, we want form data to be sent using the `doAddCourse` request. Open the `CourseController` class and add the following method:

```
@RequestMapping("/addCourse")
public String addCourse (@ModelAttribute("course") CourseDTO
  course, Model model) {
  if (course == null)
    course = new CourseDTO();
  model.addAttribute("course", course);
  return "addCourse";
}
```

The `addCourse` method is configured, using the `@RequestMapping` annotation, to handle request URLs starting (relative to context root) with `"/addCourse"`. If previously the `course` attribute was added to Model, then we want this object to be passed as an argument to this function. Using `@ModelAttribute`, we tell the Spring Framework to inject the Model attribute called `course` if it is present and assign it to the argument named `course`; else, `null` is passed. In the case of the first request, Model would not have a `course` attribute, so it would be `null`. In the subsequent requests, for example, when the user-entered data in the form (to add a course) is not valid and we want to redisplay the page, Model will have the `course` attribute.

We will now create a handler method for the `'/doAddCourse'` request. This is a POST request sent when the user submits the form in `addCourse.jsp` (refer to the form and its POST attribute discussed earlier):

```
@RequestMapping("/doAddCourse")
public String doAddCourse (@ModelAttribute("course") CourseDTO
  course,  Model model) {
    try {
      coursesDAO.addCourse(course);
    } catch (Throwable th) {
      model.addAttribute("error", th.getLocalizedMessage());
      return "addCourse";
    }
    return "redirect:courses";
}
```

The `doAddCourse` method also asks Spring to inject the Model attribute called `course` as the first argument. It then adds the course to the database using `CourseDAO`. In the case of an error, it returns the `addCourse` string, and Spring MVC displays `addCourse.jsp` again. If the course is successfully added, then the request is redirected to `courses`, which tells Spring to process and display `courses.jsp`. Recall that in `servlet-context.xml` (the Spring context configuration file in the `src/main/webapp/WEB-INF/spring/appServlet` folder), we configured a bean with the `org.springframework.web.servlet.view.InternalResourceViewResolver` class. This class is extended from `UrlBasedViewResolver`, which understands how to handle URLs with `redirect` and `forward` prefixes. So, in `doAddCourse` we save the data in the database, and if successful, we redirect the request to `courses`, which displays (after processing `courses.jsp`) the list of courses.

At this point, if you want to test the application, browse to
`http://localhost:8080/course_management/addCourse`. Enter the course name and
credits and click **Submit**. This should take you to the courses page and display the list of
courses.

Note that Spring MVC looks at the form field names and properties of the object in Model
(in this case, `CourseDTO`) when mapping form values to the object. For example, the form
field `name` is mapped to the `CourseDTO.name` property. So, make sure that the names of
the form fields and the property names in the class (objects of which are added to the
Model) are the same.

Using parameters in @RequestMapping

We have seen how to use the `@RequestMapping` annotation to map the incoming request
to a Controller method. So far, we have mapped static URL patterns in `@RequestMapping`.
However, it is possible to map parameterized URLs (like those used in REST; see
`https://spring.io/understanding/REST`) using `@RequestMapping`. The parameters are
specified inside `{}`.

Let's add the feature to update an existing course. Here, we will only discuss how to code
the Controller method for this feature. The complete code is available when you download
the samples for this chapter.

Let's add the following method in `CourseController`:

```
@RequestMapping("/course/update/{id}")
public String updateCourse (@PathVariable int id, Model model) {
   //TODO: Error handling
   CourseDTO course = coursesDAO.getCourse(id);
   model.addAttribute("course", course);
   model.addAttribute("title", "Update Course");
   return "updateCourse";
}
```

Here, we map the `updateCourse` method to handle requests with the following URL
pattern: `/course/update/{id}`, where `{id}` could be replaced with the ID (number) of
any existing course, or for that matter, any integer. To access the value of this parameter,
we used the `@PathVariable` annotation in the arguments.

Using Spring interceptors

Spring interceptors can be used to process any request before it reaches the controller. These could be used, for example, to implement security features (authentication and authorization). Like request mappers, interceptors can also be declared for specific URL patterns. Let's add the login page to our application, which should be displayed before any other page in the application if the user has not already logged in.

We will first create `UserDTO` in the `packt.jee.course_management.dto` package. This class contains the username, password, and any message to be displayed on the login page, for example, authentication errors:

```java
public class UserDTO {
    private String userName;
    private String password;
    private String message;

    public boolean messageExists() {
        return message != null && message.trim().length() > 0;
    }

    //skipped setters and getters follow
}
```

Now, let's create the `UserController` that will process the login request. Once the user is logged in successfully, we would like to keep this information in the session. The presence of this object in the session can be used to check whether the user is already logged in. Create the `UserController` class in the `packt.jee.course_management.controller` package:

```java
@Controller
public class UserController {
}
```

Add a handler method for the GET request for the login page:

```java
@RequestMapping (value="/login", method=RequestMethod.GET)
public String login (Model model) {
    UserDTO  user = new UserDTO();
    model.addAttribute("user", user);
    return "login";
}
```

Note that we have specified the method attribute in the `@RequestMapping` annotation. When the request URL is `/login` and the HTTP request type is `GET`, only then will the `login` method be called. This method would not be called if a `POST` request is sent from the client. In the `login` method, we create an instance of `UserDTO` and add it to the Model so that it is accessible to the View.

We will add a method to handle `POST` requests from the login page. We will keep the same URL, that is, `/login`:

```
@RequestMapping (value="/login", method=RequestMethod.POST)
public String doLogin (@ModelAttribute ("user") UserDTO user,
Model model) {

    //Hard-coded validation of user name and
//password to keep this example simple
    //But validation could be done against database or
//any other means here.
    if (user.getUserName().equals("admin") &&
        user.getPassword().equals("admin"))
      return "redirect:courses";

    user.setMessage("Invalid user name or password. Please try
     again");
    return "login";
}
```

We now have two methods in `UserController` handling the request URL `/login`. However, the login method handles `GET` requests and `doLogin` handles `POST` requests. If authentication is successful in the `doLogin` method, then we redirect to the courses (list) page. Else, we set the error message and return to the login page.

Let's save the user object created in the login method in the HTTP session. This can be done with the simple `@SessionAttributes` annotation. You can specify the list of attributes in Model that need to be saved in the session too. Furthermore, we want to save the `user` attribute of Model in the session. Therefore, we will add the following annotation to the `UserController` class:

```
@Controller
@SessionAttributes ("user")

public class UserController {
}
```

Now, let's create the login page. Create `login.jsp` in the `views` folder and add the following code in the HTML `<body>`:

```
<c:if test="${user.messageExists()}">
  <span style="color:red;">
    ${user.message}<br>
  </span>
</c:if>

<form id="loginForm" method="POST">
  User Id : <input type="text" name="userName" required="required"
   value="${user.userName}"><br>
  Password : <input type="password" name="password"><br>
  <button type="submit">Submit</button>
</form>
```

The page expects `user` (instance of `UserDTO`) to be available. It is made available by `UserController` through Model.

We now have the login page and `UserController` to handle the authentication, but how do we make sure this page is displayed for every request when the user is not logged in? This is where we can use Spring interceptors. We will configure an interceptor in the Spring context configuration file: `servlet-context.xml`. Add the following code to `servlet-context.xml`:

```
<interceptors>
  <interceptor>
    <mapping path="/**"/>
      <beans:bean
 class="packt.jee.course_management.interceptor.LoginInterceptor"/>
  </interceptor>
</interceptors>
```

In this configuration, we are telling Spring to call `LoginInterceptor` before executing any request (indicated by `mapping path = "/**"`).

Let's now implement `LoginInterceptor`. Interceptors must implement `HandlerInterceptor`. We will make `LoginInterceptor` extend `HandlerInterceptorAdapter`, which implements `HandlerInterceptor`.

Create `LoginInterceptor` in the `packt.jee.course_management.interceptor` package:

```
@Component
public class LoginInterceptor extends HandlerInterceptorAdapter {

    public boolean preHandle(HttpServletRequest request,
        HttpServletResponse response, Object handler)
            throws Exception {

        //get session from request
        HttpSession session = request.getSession();
        UserDTO user = (UserDTO) session.getAttribute("user");

        //Check if the current request is for /login. In that case
        //do nothing, else we will execute the request in loop
        //Intercept only if request is not /login
        String context = request.getContextPath();
        if (!request.getRequestURI().equals(context + "/login") &&
            (user == null || user.getUserName() == null)) {
            //User is not logged in. Redirect to /login
            response.sendRedirect(request.getContextPath() + "/login");
            //do not process this request further
            return false;
        }

        return true;
    }

}
```

The `preHandle` method of the interceptor is called before Spring executes any request. If we return `true` from the method, then the request is handled further; else, it is aborted. In `preHandle`, we first check whether the `user` object is present in the session. The presence of the `user` object means that the user is already logged in. In such a case, we don't do anything more in this interceptor and return `true`. If the user is not logged in, then we redirect to the login page and return `false` so that Spring does not process this request further.

Browse to `http://localhost:8080/course_management/courses` to test the login page. If you are not already logged in, the login page should be displayed.

Spring MVC application using JPA

In the previous section, we learned how to create a web application using Spring and JDBC. In this section, we will take a quick look at how to use Spring with **JPA (Java Persistence API)**. We have already learned how to use JPA in Chapter 4, *Creating JEE Database Applications*, and in Chapter 7, *Creating JEE Applications with EJB*, so we won't go into detail of how to set up the Eclipse project for JPA. However, we will discuss how to use JPA along with Spring in detail in this section.

We will create a separate project for this example. Create a Spring MVC project as described in the *Creating Spring project* section of this chapter. On the second page of the project wizard, where you are asked to enter a top-level package name, enter packt.jee.course_management_jpa. Recall that the last part of this package name is also used as the web application context.

Configuring JPA

We are going to use the EclipseLink JPA provider and the MySQL database driver in this project. So, add the Maven dependencies for them in the pom.xml file of the project:

```
<!-- JPA -->
<dependency>
    <groupId>org.eclipse.persistence</groupId>
    <artifactId>eclipselink</artifactId>
    <version>2.7.1</version>
</dependency>
<dependency>
  <groupId>mysql</groupId>
  <artifactId>mysql-connector-java</artifactId>
  <version>8.0.9-rc</version>
</dependency>
```

We will now configure the project for JPA. Right-click on the project and select **Configure** |
Convert to JPA Project. This opens the **Project Facets** page, with JPA selected as one of the
facets:

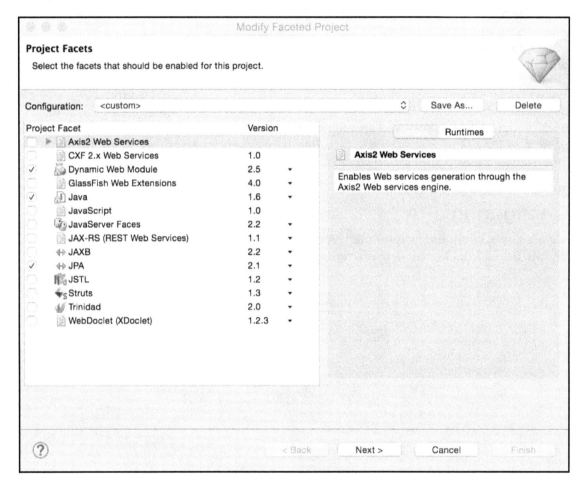

Figure 8.5: Project facets

Click the **Next** button to configure the JPA facet:

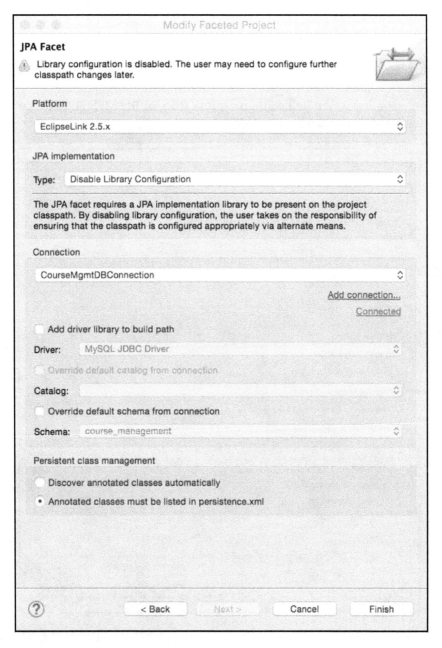

Figure 8.6: JPA facet

Select the **EclipseLink** platform in the preceding page. We will also disable the library configuration (select from the dropdown for the **Type** field). Configure the MySQL **Connection** (named **CourseMgmtDBConnection**), as described in the *Configuring JPA* section of `Chapter 7`, *Creating JEE Applications with EJB*.

Click **Finish**. `Persistence.xml` is created under the **JPA Content** group in **Project Explorer** (the actual location of this file is `src/main/resources/META-INF/persistence.xml`). We will configure properties for the MySQL JDBC connection in this. Open the file and click the **Connection** tab:

Figure 8.7: Configure connection in persistence.xml

Select **Transaction type** as `Resource Local`. Then, enter the JDBC driver details. Save the file.

Creating the Course entity

Let's now create the `Course` entity. Right-click on the project and select the **JPA Tools |
Generate Tables from Entities** menu:

Figure 8.8: Generate course entity

Make sure that `CourseMgmtDBConnection` is selected (refer to the *Configuring JPA* section of `Chapter 7`, *Creating JEE Applications with EJB*, for configuring a MySQL database connection in Eclipse) and that **List generated classes in persistence.xml** is selected. Click **Next** on this and the next page. On the **Customize Defaults** page, select **identity** as the **Key generator** and set the package name as `packt.jee.course_management_jpa.entity`:

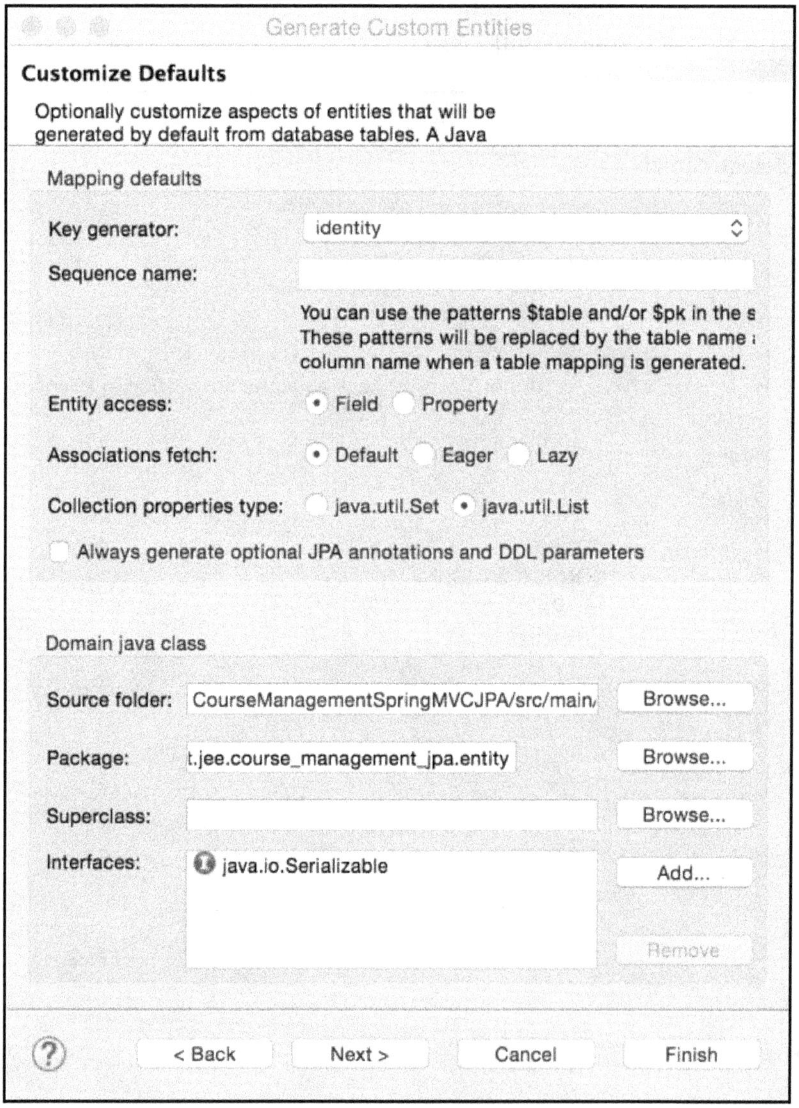

Figure 8.9: Customize JPA entity defaults

Click **Next**. Verify the entity class name and the other details:

Figure 8.10: Customize JPA entity details

Click **Finish**. The `Course` entity class will be created in the package selected:

```java
//skipped imports
@Entity
@Table(name="COURSE")
@NamedQuery(name="Course.findAll", query="SELECT c FROM Course c")
public class Course implements Serializable {
  private static final long serialVersionUID = 1L;

  @Id
  @GeneratedValue(strategy=GenerationType.IDENTITY)
  private int id;

  private int credits;

  private String name;

  @Column(name="teacher_id")
  private int teacherId;

  //skipped setter and getters
}
```

Note that the wizard has also created the named query to get all the courses from the table.

We now need to create `EntityManagerFactory` so that `EntityManager` can be created from it (refer to the *JPA concepts* section in `Chapter 4`, *Creating JEE Database Applications*). We will create a Spring bean/component to create and store `EntityManagerFactory`. Furthermore, we will inject (autowire) this component into the DAO class.

Create the `JPAEntityFactoryBean` class
in the `packt.jee.course_management_jpa.entity` package:

```java
//skipped imports

@Component
public class JPAEntityFactoryBean {

  EntityManagerFactory entityManagerFactory;

  @PostConstruct
  public void init() {
    entityManagerFactory =
Persistence.createEntityManagerFactory("CourseManagementSpringMVCJPA");
  }

  public EntityManagerFactory getEntityManagerFactory() {
```

```
        return entityManagerFactory;
    }
}
```

In the constructor of the class, we create `EntityManagerFactory`. The argument to `createEntityManagerFactory` is the name of the persistence unit, as specified in `persistence.xml`.

Creating CourseDAO and Controller

Let's now create the `CourseDAO` class. We will have an instance of `JPAEntityFactoryBean` injected (auto-wired) into this class.
Create the `packt.jee.course_management_jpa.dao` package and the `CourseDAO` class in it:

```
@Component
public class CourseDAO {

    @Autowired
    JPAEntityFactoryBean entityFactoryBean;

    public List<Course> getCourses() {
      //Get entity manager
      EntityManagerFactory emf =
       entityFactoryBean.getEntityManagerFactory();
      EntityManager em = emf.createEntityManager();

      //Execute Query
      TypedQuery<Course> courseQuery =
       em.createNamedQuery("Course.findAll", Course.class);
        List<Course> courses = courseQuery.getResultList();
        em.close();
        return courses;
    }
}
```

In the `getCourses` method, we first create `EntityManager` (from `JPAEntityFactoryBean`) and execute the named query. Once we get the results, we close `EntityManager`.

The `Controller` class for `Course` will have `CourseDAO` auto-injected (auto-wired). Create `CourseController` in the `packt.jee.course_management_jpa.controller` package:

```
//skipped imports
@Controller
public class CourseController {
  @Autowired
  CourseDAO courseDAO;

  @RequestMapping("/courses")
  public String getCourses(Model model) {
    model.addAttribute("courses", courseDAO.getCourses());
    return "courses";
  }
}
```

As we saw in the `CourseController` created for the JDBC application earlier, we get courses from the database and add the list of courses to the Model under the key name `courses`. This variable will be available to the View page that displays the list of courses.

Creating the course list view

We now have all the classes to get courses. Let's now create a JSP to display the list of courses. Create `courses.jsp` in the `src/main/webapp/WEB-INF/views` folder. Add the following content in the HTML `body` tag of the page:

```
<h2>Courses:</h2>

<table>
  <tr>
    <th>Id</th>
    <th>Name</th>
    <th>Credits</th>
    <th></th>
  </tr>
  <c:forEach items="${courses}" var="course">
    <tr>
      <td>${course.id}</td>
      <td>${course.name}</td>
      <td>${course.credits}</td>
    </tr>
  </c:forEach>
</table>
```

The View page makes use of JSTL tags to iterate over courses (using the variable that was made available in the Model by the Controller) and displays them.

We are not going to build the entire application here. The idea was to understand how to use JPA with Spring MVC, which we have learned in this section. Browse to `http://localhost:8080/course_management_jpa/courses` to run the application.

Summary

In this chapter, we learned how to use Spring MVC to create web applications. As the name indicates, Spring MVC implements the MVC design pattern, which enables clear separation of the user interface code and the business logic code.

Using the dependency injection feature of the Spring Framework, we can easily manage the dependencies of different objects in the application. We also learned how to use JDBC and JPA along with Spring MVC to create data-driven web applications.

In the next chapter, we will see how to create and consume web services in JEE applications. We will look at both SOAP-based and RESTful web services.

Creating Web Services

9

In the last chapter, we learned how to create web applications in Java using MVC frameworks. In this chapter, we will learn how to implement web services in Java.

We will cover the following topics:

- Java object binding and serialization using JAXB and JSON-B
- Implementing and consuming RESTful web services
- Implementing and consuming SOAP web services

What is a web service?

In Chapter 7, *Creating JEE Applications with EJB*, we learned that EJBs can be used to create distributed applications. EJBs can act as glue and help different JEE applications in the enterprise to communicate with each other. However, what if the enterprise wants to let its partners or customers make use of some of the application functionality? For example, an airline might want to let its partners make online reservations.

One option is for the partner to redirect its customers to the airline website, but this would not provide a unified experience to users. A better way to handle this would be for the airline to expose its reservation APIs to partners, who can integrate these APIs into their own applications, providing a unified user experience. This is an example of a distributed application, and EJBs can be used for this.

However, for EJBs to work in such scenarios, where API calls cross enterprise boundaries, the clients of the APIs also need to be implemented in Java. As we know, this is not practical. Some of the airline partners in this example may have their applications implemented using different programming platforms, such as .NET and PHP.

Web services are useful in situations such as the one mentioned here. Web services are self-contained APIs that are based on open standards and are platform independent. They are widely used for communication between disparate systems. There are mainly two types of web service implementations:

- Simple Object Access Protocol (SOAP)-based
- Representational State Transfer (RESTful) services

For many years, SOAP-based web services were quite popular, but recently, RESTful services have been gaining ground because of the simplicity in their implementation and consumption.

Web services provide a common integration platform and offer **service-oriented architecture (SOA)** in which certain components expose services for consumption by other components or applications. The consumer of such services can create an entire application by assembling a number of such loosely coupled services, possibly from different sources.

In this chapter, we will see how to develop and consume both SOAP and RESTful services by using JEE and Eclipse. However, first it would be useful to understand how to convert Java objects to XML and JSON, and vice versa, because both REST and SOAP web service implementations need to perform these operations. First, we will take a look at JAXB, Java XML binding, using which you can bind Java objects to both XML and JSON. Then we will take a look at JSON-B (a new specification added in JEE 8) for Java JSON binding.

JAXB

JAXB provides an easy way to convert XML or JSON representations of data into Java objects and vice versa. Using simple annotations, you can have a JAXB implementation create XML or JSON data from a Java object or create a Java object from XML or JSON.

 To understand how Java data types are mapped to XML schema types in JAXB, refer
to https://docs.oracle.com/javase/tutorial/jaxb/intro/bind.html.

The following are a few important JAXB annotations:

- `@XmlRootElement`: This annotation specifies the root element of the XML document and is typically used at the class level.
- `@XmlElement`: This annotation specifies an XML element that is not a root element. Java class members can be marked as `XMLElement` when the class is annotated with `@XmlRootElement`.
- `@XmlAttribute`: This annotation marks a member of the Java class as an attribute of the parent XML element.
- `@XmlAccessorType`: This annotation is specified at the class level. It lets you control how class fields are serialized to XML or JSON. Valid values are `XmlAccessType.FIELD` (every non-static and non-`@XmlTransient` field is serialized), `XmlAccessType.PROPERTY` (every pair of getter/setter that is not annotated with `@XmlTransient` is serialized), `XmlAccessType.NONE` (no fields are serialized, unless specific fields are annotated for serialization), and `XmlAccessType.PUBLIC_MEMBER` (all public getter/setter pairs are serialized, unless annotated with `@XmlTransient`).
- `@XMLTransient`: This annotation specifies a member or getter/setter pair that is not to be serialized.

For the complete list of JAXB annotations, refer to `https://jaxb.java.net/tutorial/section_6_1-JAXB-Annotations.html#JAXB`.

A JAXB example

Let's create a Maven project to try out JAXB APIs. Select the **File** | **Maven Project** menu:

Figure 9.1: Create a Maven project for a JAXB example

Make sure that the project is configured to use JRE 1.7 or later. Let's now create two classes, `Course` and `Teacher`. We want to serialize instances of these classes to XML and back. Create these classes in the `packt.jee.eclipse.jaxb.example` package. Here is the source code of the `Course` class:

```
package packt.jee.eclipse.jaxb.example;
//Skipped imports

@XmlRootElement
@XmlAccessorType(XmlAccessType.FIELD)
public class Course {
  @XmlAttribute
  private int id;
  @XmlElement(namespace="http://packt.jee.eclipse.jaxb.example")
  private String name;
  private int credits;
  @XmlElement(name="course_teacher")
  private Teacher teacher;

  public Course() {}

  public Course (int id, String name, int credits) {
    this.id = id;
    this.name = name;
    this.credits = credits;
  }

  //Getters and setters follow
}
```

When a `Course` is marshalled to an XML document, we want the `course` element to be the root. Therefore, the class is annotated with `@XmlRootElement`.

 Marshalling is the process of writing the data, typically an object, to a format link XML or JSON. Unmarshalling is the process of reading the data from a format and creating an object.

You can specify a different name for the root element (other than the class name) by specifying the `name` attribute, for example:

```
@XmlRootElement(name="school_course")
```

The id field is marked as an attribute of the root element. You don't have to mark fields specifically as elements if there are public getters/setters for them. However, if you want to set additional attributes, then you need to annotate them with @XmlElement. For example, we have specified a namespace for the name field. The credits field is not annotated, but it will still be marshalled as an XML element.

Here is the source code for the Teacher class:

```
package packt.jee.eclipse.jaxb.example;

public class Teacher {
    private int id;
    private String name;

    public Teacher() {}

    public Teacher (int id, String name) {
        this.id = id;
        this.name = name;
    }

    //Getters and setters follow
}
```

We are not annotating the Teacher class for JAXB because we are not going to marshal it directly. It will be marshalled by JAXB when an instance of Course is marshalled.

Let's create the JAXBExample class with the main method:

```
package packt.jee.eclipse.jaxb.example;

//Skipped imports

public class JAXBExample {

    public static void main(String[] args) throws Exception {
        doJAXBXml();

    }

    //Create XML from Java object and then vice versa
    public static void doJAXBXml() throws Exception {
        Course course = new Course(1,"Course-1", 5);
        course.setTeacher(new Teacher(1, "Teacher-1"));

        JAXBContext context = JAXBContext.newInstance(Course.class);
```

```
        //Marshall Java object to XML
        Marshaller marshaller = context.createMarshaller();
        //Set option to format generated XML
        marshaller.setProperty(Marshaller.JAXB_FORMATTED_OUTPUT,
          true);
        StringWriter stringWriter = new StringWriter();
        //Marshal Course object and write to the StringWriter
        marshaller.marshal(course, stringWriter);
        //Get String from the StringWriter
        String courseXml = stringWriter.getBuffer().toString();
        stringWriter.close();
        //Print course XML
        System.out.println(courseXml);

        //Now unmarshall courseXML to create Course object
        Unmarshaller unmarshaller = context.createUnmarshaller();
        //Create StringReader from courseXml
        StringReader stringReader = new StringReader(courseXml);
        //Create StreamSource which will be used by JAXB unmarshaller
        StreamSource streamSource = new StreamSource(stringReader);
        Course unmarshalledCourse =
          unmarshaller.unmarshal(streamSource, Course.class).getValue();
          System.out.println("-----------------nUnmarshalled course name - "
              + unmarshalledCourse.getName());
        stringReader.close();
    }
}
```

To marshal or unmarshal using JAXB, we first create `JAXBContext`, passing it a Java class that needs to be worked on. Then, we create the marshaller or unmarshaller, set the relevant properties, and perform the operation. The code is quite simple. We first marshal the `Course` instance to XML, and then use the same XML output to unmarshal it back to a `Course` instance. Right-click on the class and select **Run As | Java Application**. You should see the following output in the console:

```
<?xml version="1.0" encoding="UTF-8" standalone="yes"?>
<course id="1" xmlns:ns2="http://packt.jee.eclipse.jaxb.example">
    <ns2:name>Course-1</ns2:name>
    <credits>5</credits>
    <course_teacher>
        <id>1</id>
        <name>Teacher-1</name>
    </course_teacher>
</course>

-----------------
Unmarshalled course name - Course-1
```

Let's now see how to marshal a Java object to JSON and back. JSON support in JAXB is not available out of the box in JDK. We will have to use an external library that supports JAXB APIs with JSON. One such library is EclipseLink MOXy (`https://eclipse.org/eclipselink/#moxy`). We will use this library to marshal an instance of `Course` to JSON.

Open `pom.xml` and add the dependency on EclipseLink:

```
<dependencies>
  <dependency>
    <groupId>org.eclipse.persistence</groupId>
    <artifactId>eclipselink</artifactId>
    <version>2.6.1-RC1</version>
  </dependency>
</dependencies>
```

We also need to set the `javax.xml.bind.context.factory` property to make the JAXB implementation use EclipseLink's `JAXBContextFactory`. Create the `jaxb.properties` file in the same package as the classes whose instances are to be marshalled. In this case, create the file in the `packt.jee.eclipse.jaxb.example` package. Set the following property in this file:

```
javax.xml.bind.context.factory=org.eclipse.persistence.jaxb.JAXBContextFactory
```

This is very important. If you do not set this property, then the example won't work. Next, open `JAXBExample.java` and add the following method:

```
//Create JSON from Java object and then vice versa
public static void doJAXBJson() throws Exception {

    Course course = new Course(1,"Course-1", 5);
    course.setTeacher(new Teacher(1, "Teacher-1"));

    JAXBContext context = JAXBContext.newInstance(Course.class);

    //Marshal Java object to JSON
    Marshaller marshaller = context.createMarshaller();
    //Set option to format generated JSON
    marshaller.setProperty(Marshaller.JAXB_FORMATTED_OUTPUT,
      true);     marshaller.setProperty(MarshallerProperties.MEDIA_TYPE,
      "application/json");
marshaller.setProperty(MarshallerProperties.JSON_INCLUDE_ROOT,
    true);

    StringWriter stringWriter = new StringWriter();
```

```
    //Marshal Course object and write to the StringWriter
    marshaller.marshal(course, stringWriter);
    //Get String from the StringWriter
    String courseJson = stringWriter.getBuffer().toString();
    stringWriter.close();
    //Print course JSON
    System.out.println(courseJson);

    //Now, unmarshall courseJson to create Course object
    Unmarshaller unmarshler = context.createUnmarshaller();
    unmarshler.setProperty(MarshallerProperties.MEDIA_TYPE,
      "application/json");
unmarshler.setProperty(MarshallerProperties.JSON_INCLUDE_ROOT,
      true);

    //Create StringReader from courseJson
    StringReader stringReader = new StringReader(courseJson);
    //Create StreamSource which will be used by JAXB unmarshaller
    StreamSource streamSource = new StreamSource(stringReader);
    Course unmarshalledCourse = unmarshler.unmarshal(streamSource,
      Course.class).getValue();
    System.out.println("-----------------nUnmarshalled course name - " +
unmarshalledCourse.getName());
    stringReader.close();
  }
```

Much of the code is the same as in the doJAXBXml method. Specific changes are as follows:

- We set the marshaller property for generating the JSON output (application/json)
- We set another marshaller property to include the JSON root in the output
- We set the corresponding properties on unmarshaller

Modify the main method to call doJAXBJson, instead of doJAXBXml. When you run the application, you should see the following output:

```
{
  "course" : {
    "id" : 1,
    "name" : "Course-1",
    "credits" : 5,
    "course_teacher" : {
      "id" : 1,
      "name" : "Teacher-1"
    }
  }
}
```

```
}
-----------------
Unmarshalled course name - Course-1
```

 We have covered the basics of JAXB in this chapter. For a detailed tutorial on JAXB, refer to
https://docs.oracle.com/javase/tutorial/jaxb/intro/index.html.

JSON-B

JSON-B is a new specification included in JEE 8. Using a simple annotation you can convert Java objects to JSON and vice versa. JSON-B has one important annotation, `@JsonProperty`. Specifying this annotation for a class member marks it for serialization to or from JSON.

JSON-B provides the `JsonbBuilder` class, using which you can perform actual serialization. Let's learn how to use JSON-B with a simple application.

A JSON-B example

Let's create a Maven project, with **Group Id** as **JAXBExample** and **Artifact Id** as **JSONBExampleProject**. JSON-B is not a part of the JDK, so we will need to add Maven dependencies for libraries that provide JSON-B APIs and their implementation. In this example, we will use Eclipse's Yasson (https://projects.eclipse.org/projects/ee4j.yasson) implementation of JSON-B. We will add the following dependencies in pom.xml:

```xml
<dependency>
  <groupId>javax.json.bind</groupId>
  <artifactId>javax.json.bind-api</artifactId>
  <version>1.0</version>
</dependency>

<dependency>
  <groupId>org.eclipse</groupId>
  <artifactId>yasson</artifactId>
  <version>1.0.1</version>
</dependency>

<dependency>
  <groupId>org.glassfish</groupId>
  <artifactId>javax.json</artifactId>
```

```
    <version>1.1.2</version>
  </dependency>
</dependencies>
```

Dependency on `javax.json` from GlassFish is added because the `yasson` implementation depends on its JSON-P implementation.

Let's now create the `Course` and `Teacher` classes as we created them in the previous section for JAXB, but with JSON-B annotations. Create both classes in the `packt.jee.eclipse.jsonb.example` package. Here is the source code for the `Course` class:

```
package packt.jee.eclipse.jsonb.example;
import javax.json.bind.annotation.JsonbProperty;

public class Course {
  @JsonbProperty
  private int id;

  @JsonbProperty
  private String name;

  @JsonbProperty
  private int credits;

  @JsonbProperty("course_teacher")
  private Teacher teacher;

  //skipped constructors, getters and setters to save space
}
```

We have annotated members of the `Course` class with `@JsonbProperty`. If you want to change the name of the field in JSON then you can specify it as a parameter to `@JsonbProperty`; for example, in the previous code we are mapping the `teacher` field to the `course_teacher` name in JSON.

The `Teacher` class is the same as the one we created in the section for JAXB. Let's now create the main application class, called `JSONBExample`, in which we will convert an instance of `Course` to `String` and then from `String` back to an instance of the `Course` object:

```
package packt.jee.eclipse.jsonb.example;
import javax.json.bind.Jsonb;
import javax.json.bind.JsonbBuilder;
public class JSONBExample {
  public static void main(String[] args) throws Exception {
    Course course = new Course(1,"Course-1", 5);
    course.setTeacher(new Teacher(1, "Teacher-1"));

    // Serialize to JSON string
    Jsonb jsonb = JsonbBuilder.create();
    String courseJson = jsonb.toJson(course, Course.class);
    System.out.println(courseJson);

    // De-serialize fromd JSON string
    Course deserializedCourse = jsonb.fromJson(courseJson, Course.class);
    System.out.println(deserializedCourse.getName());
  }
}
```

To serialize an instance of the `Course` class, we are first creating an instance of `JsonBuilder` and then calling the `toJson` method on that. To de-serialize the JSON representation of the `Course` class from String, we are calling `fromJson` on the same instance of `JsonBuilder`. If you run the application, you should see a JSON string for the course object we created.

 For further details on JSON-B, refer to `http://json-b.net/index.html`.

RESTful web services

We will start learning web services with RESTful services because they are widely used and are easy to implement. REST is not necessarily a protocol but an architectural style, and is typically based on HTTP. RESTful web services act on resources on the server, and actions are based on HTTP methods (Get, Post, Put, and Delete). The state of resources is transferred over HTTP in either XML or JSON format, although JSON is more popular. Resources on the server are identified by URLs. For example, to get details of a course with ID 10, you can use the HTTP GET method with the following URL: http://<server_address>:<port>/course/10. Notice that the parameter is part of the base URL. To add a new Course or modify a Course, you can use either POST or PUT methods. Furthermore, the DELETE method can be used to delete a Course by using the same URL as that used for getting the course, that is, http://<server_address>:<port>/course/10.

Resource URLs in RESTful web services can be nested too; for example, to get all courses in a particular department (with, say, an ID of 20), the REST URL can be as follows: http://<server_address>:<port>/department/20/courses.

> Refer to
> https://en.wikipedia.org/wiki/Representational_state_transfer for more details on the properties of RESTful web services and HTTP methods used for acting on REST resources on the server.

The Java specification for working with RESTful web services is called JAX-RS, Java API for RESTful services (https://jax-rs-spec.java.net/). Project Jersey (https://jersey.java.net/) is the reference implementation of this specification. We will use this reference implementation this chapter.

Creating RESTful web services using Jersey

We will create a web service for the *Course Management* example that we have been developing in this book. The web service will have methods to get all courses and create a new course. To keep the example simple, we will not write the data access code (you can use the JDBC or JDO APIs that we learned in previous chapters), but will hardcode the data.

First, create a Maven web project. Select **File** | **New** | **Maven Project**. Select the **Create a Simple Project** checkbox on the first page of the wizard and click **Next**:

Figure 9.2: Create a Maven project for a RESTful web service

Enter the project configuration details and click **Finish**. Make sure that the packaging is war.

Since we are going to use the `Jersey` library for the JAX-RS implementation, we will add its Maven dependency into the project. Open `pom.xml` and add the following dependency:

```
<dependencies>
  <dependency>
    <groupId>org.glassfish.jersey.containers</groupId>
    <artifactId>jersey-container-servlet</artifactId>
    <version>2.26</version>
  </dependency>
</dependencies>
```

Using the JAX-RS `@Path` annotation, we can convert any Java class into a REST resource. The value passed to the `@Path` annotation is a relative URI of the resource. Methods in the implementation class, to be executed for different HTTP methods, are annotated with one of the following annotations: `@GET`, `@PUT`, `@POST`, or `@DELETE`. The `@Path` annotation can also be used at the method level for a sub-resource path (the main resource or the root resource path is at the class level, again using the `@Path` annotation). We can also specify the MIME type that previous methods produce/consume by using the `@Produces` or `@Consumes` annotations, respectively.

Before we create a web service implementation class, let's create some utility classes, more specifically in this case DTOs.

Create the `Course` and `Teacher` classes in the `packt.jee.eclipse.rest.ws.dto` package. We will also annotate them with the JAXB annotations. Here is the source code for the `Teacher` class:

```
package packt.jee.eclipse.rest.ws.dto;

import javax.xml.bind.annotation.XmlAccessType;
import javax.xml.bind.annotation.XmlAccessorType;
import javax.xml.bind.annotation.XmlAttribute;
import javax.xml.bind.annotation.XmlElement;
import javax.xml.bind.annotation.XmlRootElement;

@XmlRootElement
@XmlAccessorType(XmlAccessType.FIELD)
public class Teacher {

  @XmlAttribute
  private int id;

  @XmlElement(name="teacher_name")
  private String name;
```

```
  //constructors
  public Course() {}

  public Course (int id, String name, int credits, Teacher
   teacher) {
    this.id = id;
    this.name = name;
    this.credits = credits;
    this.teacher = teacher;
  }

  //Getters and setters follow
}
```

The following is the source code for the `Course` class, which we will use for marshalling to XML and JSON in the subsequent sections:

```
package packt.jee.eclipse.rest.ws.dto;

import javax.xml.bind.annotation.XmlAccessType;
import javax.xml.bind.annotation.XmlAccessorType;
import javax.xml.bind.annotation.XmlAttribute;
import javax.xml.bind.annotation.XmlElement;
import javax.xml.bind.annotation.XmlRootElement;

@XmlRootElement
@XmlAccessorType(XmlAccessType.FIELD)
public class Course {

  @XmlAttribute
  private int id;

  @XmlElement(name="course_name")
  private String name;

  private int credits;

  private Teacher teacher;

  //constructors
  public Teacher() {}

  public Teacher (int id, String name) {
    this.id = id;
    this.name = name;
  }
```

```
    //Getters and setters follow
}
```

We have annotated the id fields in both classes as @XMLAttribute. If objects of these classes are marshalled (converted from Java objects) to XML, Course id and Teacher id would be attributes (instead of elements) of the root element (Course and Teacher, respectively). If no field annotation is specified and if public getters/setters for an attribute are present, then it is considered an XML element with the same name.

We have specifically used the @XMLElement annotation for name fields because we want to rename them as course_name or teacher_name when marshalled to XML.

Implementing a REST GET request

Let's now implement the RESTful web service class. Create the CourseService class in the packt.jee.eclipse.rest.ws.services package:

```
package packt.jee.eclipse.rest.ws.services;

import javax.ws.rs.GET;
import javax.ws.rs.Path;
import javax.ws.rs.PathParam;
import javax.ws.rs.Produces;
import javax.ws.rs.core.MediaType;

import packt.jee.eclipse.rest.ws.dto.Course;
import packt.jee.eclipse.rest.ws.dto.Teacher;

@Path("/course")
public class CourseService {

    @GET
    @Produces (MediaType.APPLICATION_XML)
    @Path("get/{courseId}")
    public Course getCourse (@PathParam("courseId") int id) {

        //To keep the example simple, we will return
        //hardcoded values here. However, you could get
        //data from database using, for example, JDO or JDBC

        return new Course(id,"Course-" + id, 5, new Teacher(2,
          "Teacher1"));
    }
}
```

The `@Path` annotation specifies that resources made available by this class will be accessible by relative URI `"/course"`.

The `getCourse` method has many annotations. Let's discuss them one at a time.

The `@GET` annotation specifies that when the relative URI (as specified by `@Path` on `CourseService` class) `"/course"` is called using the HTTP `GET` method, then this method will be invoked.

`@Produces`(`MediaType.APPLICATION_JSON`) specifies that this method generates a JSON output. If the client specifies the accepted MIME types, then this annotation would be used to resolve the method to be called, if more than one method is annotated with `@GET` (or, for that matter, any of the other HTTP method annotations). For example, if we have a method called `getCourseJSON` annotated with `@GET` , but producing data with different MIME types (as specified by `@Produces`), then the appropriate method will be selected on the basis of the MIME type requested by the client. The MIME type in the `@Produces` annotation also tells the JAX-RS implementation MIME type of the response to be created, when marshalling the Java object that is returned from that method. For example, in the `getCourse` method we return an instance of `Course`, and the MIME type specified in `@Produces` tells Jersey to generate an XML representation of this instance.

The `@Path` annotation can also be used at the method level to specify sub-resources. The value specified in `@Path` at the method level is relative to the path value specified at the class level. The resource (in this case, `Course`) with ID `20` can be accessed as `/course/get/20`. The complete URL can be `http://<server-address>:<port>/<app-name>/course/get/10`. Parameter names in the path value are enclosed in `{ }` in annotations.

Path parameters need to be identified in method arguments by using the `@PathParam` annotation and the name of the parameter as its value. The JAX-RS implementation framework matches the path parameters with arguments matching `@PathParam` annotations and appropriately passes parameter values to the method.

To keep the example simple and to keep the focus on implementation of RESTful web services, we are not going to implement any business logic in this method. We could get data from the database by using, for example, JDO or JDBC APIs (and we have seen examples of how to use these APIs in earlier chapters), but we are just going to return some hardcoded data. The method returns an instance of the Course class. The JAX-RS implementation would convert this object into an XML representation by using JAXB when the data is finally returned to the client.

We need to tell the Jersey framework what packages it needs to scan to look for REST resources. There are two ways to do this:

- Configuring the Jersey servlet in web.xml (see
  https://jersey.java.net/nonav/documentation/latest/user-guide.html#dep
  loyment.servlet).
- For Servlet 3.x containers, we could create a subclass of
  javax.ws.rs.core.Application. Tomcat 8.0, which we have been using in
  this book, is a Servlet 3.x container.

We will use the second option to create a subclass of Application. However, instead of directly subclassing Application, we will subclass the ResourceConfig class of Jersey, which in turn extends Application.

Create the CourseMgmtRESTApplication class in the packt.jee.eclipse.rest.ws package:

```
package packt.jee.eclipse.rest.ws;

import javax.ws.rs.ApplicationPath;

import org.glassfish.jersey.server.ResourceConfig;

@ApplicationPath("services")
public class CourseMgmtRESTApplication extends ResourceConfig {

  public CourseMgmtRESTApplication () {
    packages("packt.jee.eclipse.rest.ws.services");
  }

}
```

We have used the @ApplicationPath annotation to specify URL mapping for REST services implemented using JAX-RS. All @Path URIs on resource implementation classes will be relative to this path. For example, the "/course" URI that we specified for the CourseService class would be relative to "services", specified in the @ApplicationPath annotation.

Before we deploy the application and test our service, we need to generate web.xml. Right-click on the project in **Project Explorer** and select **Java EE Tools** | **Generate Deployment Descriptor Stub**. This will create web.xml in the WEB-INF folder. We don't need to modify it for this example.

Configure Tomcat in Eclipse as described in the *Installing Tomcat* section of Chapter 1, *Introducing JEE and Eclipse*, and in the *Configuring Tomcat in Eclipse* section of Chapter 2, *Creating a Simple JEE Web Application*. To deploy the web application, right-click on the configured Tomcat server in the **Servers** view and select the **Add and Remove** option. Add the current project.

Start the Tomcat server by right-clicking on the configured server in the Servers view and selecting **Start**.

Testing the REST GET request in the browser

In this section, we will test the web service we created in the previous section in the browser. To test the web service, browse to
http://localhost:8080/CourseManagementREST/services/course/get/10.

You should see the following XML displayed in the browser:

```
<?xml version="1.0" encoding="UTF-8" standalone="yes"?>
<course id="10">
  <course_name>Course-10</course_name>
  <credits>5</credits>
  <teacher id="2">
    <teacher_name>Teacher1</teacher_name>
  </teacher>
</course>
```

Instead of generating an XML response, let's say we want to create a JSON response, because it would be much easier to consume a JSON response from JavaScript in a web page than an XML response. To create a JSON response, we need to change the value of the `@Produces` annotation in the `CourseService` class. Currently, it is set to `MediaType.APPLICATION_XML` and we want to set it to `MediaType.APPLICATION_JSON`:

```
public class CourseService {

  @GET
  @Produces (MediaType.APPLICATION_JSON)
  @Path("get/{courseId}")
  public Course getCourse (@PathParam("courseId") int id) {
...
  }
}
```

We also need to add libraries to create the JSON response. Open the `pom.xml` of the project and add the following dependency:

```
<dependency>
  <groupId>org.glassfish.jersey.media</groupId>
  <artifactId>jersey-media-json-jackson</artifactId>
  <version>2.18</version>
</dependency>
```

Restart the Tomcat server and browse to the `http://localhost:8080/CourseManagementREST/services/course/get/10` URL again. This time, you should see a JSON response:

```
{
    id: 10,
    credits: 5,
    teacher: {
        id: 2,
        teacher_name: "Teacher1"
    },
    course_name: "Course-10"
}
```

Let's create two versions of the `getCourse` method, one that produces XML and the other that produces JSON. Replace the `getCourse` function with the following code:

```
@GET
@Produces (MediaType.APPLICATION_JSON)
@Path("get/{courseId}")
public Course getCourseJSON (@PathParam("courseId") int id) {

    return createDummyCourse(id);

}

@GET
@Produces (MediaType.APPLICATION_XML)
@Path("get/{courseId}")
public Course getCourseXML (@PathParam("courseId") int id) {

    return createDummyCourse(id);

}

private Course createDummyCourse (int id) {
    //To keep the example simple, we will return
    //hardcoded value here. However, you could get
    //data from database using, for example, JDO or JDBC

    return new Course(id,"Course-" + id, 5, new Teacher(2,
      "Teacher1"));
}
```

We have added the `createDummyCourse` method, which has the same code that we had earlier in the `getCourse` method. We now have two versions of the `getCourse` method: `getCourseXML` and `getCourseJSON`, producing the XML and JSON responses, respectively.

Creating a Java client for the REST GET web service

Let's now create a Java client application that calls the previous web service. Create a simple Maven project and call it `CourseManagementRESTClient`:

Figure 9.3: Create a JAX-RS client project

Open `pom.xml` and add a dependency for the Jersey client module:

```xml
<dependencies>
  <dependency>
    <groupId>org.glassfish.jersey.core</groupId>
    <artifactId>jersey-client</artifactId>
    <version>2.18</version>
  </dependency>
</dependencies>
```

Create a Java class called `CourseManagementRESTClient`
in the `packt.jee.eclipse.rest.ws.client` package:

Figure 9.4: Create a REST client main class

You could invoke a RESTful web service using `java.net.HttpURLConnection` or other external HTTP client libraries. But JAX-RS client APIs make this task a lot easier, as you can see in the following code:

```java
package packt.jee.eclipse.rest.ws.client;

import javax.ws.rs.client.Client;
import javax.ws.rs.client.ClientBuilder;
import javax.ws.rs.client.WebTarget;
import javax.ws.rs.core.MediaType;
import javax.ws.rs.core.Response;

/**
 * This is a simple test class for invoking RESTful web service
 * using JAX-RS client APIs
 */
public class CourseManagementClient {

  public static void main(String[] args) {

testGetCoursesJSON();

  }

  //Test getCourse method (XML or JSON) of CourseService
  public static void testGetCoursesJSON() {
    //Create JAX-RS client
    Client client = ClientBuilder.newClient();
    //Get WebTarget for a URL
    WebTarget webTarget =
client.target("http://localhost:8080/CourseManagementREST/services/course")
;
    //Add paths to URL
    webTarget = webTarget.path("get").path("10");

    //We could also have create webTarget in one call with the full URL -
    //WebTarget webTarget =
client.target("http://localhost:8080/CourseManagementREST/services/course/g
et/10");

    //Execute HTTP get method
    Response response =
     webTarget.request(MediaType.APPLICATION_JSON).get();

    //Check response code. 200 is OK
    if (response.getStatus() != 200) {
```

```
    System.out.println("Error invoking REST web service - " +
      response.getStatusInfo().getReasonPhrase());
    return;
  }

  //REST call was successful. Print the response
  System.out.println(response.readEntity(String.class));
  }
}
```

For a detailed description of how to use the JAX-RS client APIs, refer to
`https://jersey.java.net/documentation/latest/client.html`.

Implementing a REST POST request

We saw an example of how to implement an HTTP GET request by using JAX-RS. Let's now implement a POST request. We will implement a method to add a course in the CourseService class, which is our web service implementation class in the CourseManagementREST project.

As in the case of the getCourse method, we won't actually access the database but will simply write a dummy method to save the data. Again, the idea is to keep the example simple and focus only on the JAX-RS APIs and implementation. Open CourseService.java and add the following methods:

```
@POST
@Consumes (MediaType.APPLICATION_JSON)
@Produces (MediaType.APPLICATION_JSON)
@Path("add")
public Course addCourse (Course course) {

  int courseId = dummyAddCourse(course.getName(),
    course.getCredits());

  course.setId(courseId);

  return course;
}

private int dummyAddCourse (String courseName, int credits) {

  //To keep the example simple, we will just print
```

```
    //parameters we received in this method to console and not
    //actually save data to database.
    System.out.println("Adding course " + courseName + ", credits
= " + credits);

    //TODO: Add course to database table

    //return hard-coded id
    return 10;
}
```

The `addCourse` method produces and consumes JSON data. It is invoked when the resource path (web service endpoint URL) has the following relative path: `"/course/add"`. Recall that the `CourseService` class is annotated with the following path: `"/course"`. So, the relative path for the `addCourse` method becomes the path specified at the class level and at the method level (which in this case is `"add"`). We are returning a new instance of `Course` from `addCourse`. Jersey creates the appropriate JSON representation of this class on the basis of JAXB annotations in the `Course` class. We have already added the dependency in the project on a Jersey module that handles JSON format (in `pom.xml`, we added a dependency on `jersey-media-json-jackson`).

Restart the Tomcat server for these changes to take effect.

Writing a Java client for the REST POST web service

We will now add a test method in the `CourseManagementClient` class, in the `CourseManagementRESTClient` project:

```
//Test addCourse method (JSON version) of CourseService
public static void testAddCourseJSON() {

    //Create JAX-RS client
    Client client = ClientBuilder.newClient();

    //Get WebTarget for a URL
    WebTarget webTarget =
client.target("http://localhost:8600/CourseManagementREST/services/course/a
dd");

    //Create JSON representation of Course,
    //with course_name and credits fields. Instead of creating
    //JSON manually, you could also use JAXB to create JSON from
```

```
//Java object.
String courseJSON = "{"course_name":"Course-4",
 "credits":5}";

//Execute HTTP post method
Response response = webTarget.request().
    post(Entity.entity(courseJSON,
      MediaType.APPLICATION_JSON_TYPE));

//Check response code. 200 is OK
if (response.getStatus() != 200) {
  //Print error message
  System.out.println("Error invoking REST Web Service - " +
    response.getStatusInfo().getReasonPhrase() +
      ", Error Code : " + response.getStatus());
  //Also dump content of response message
  System.out.println(response.readEntity(String.class));
  return;
}

//REST call was successful. Print the response
System.out.println(response.readEntity(String.class));
}
```

We need to send input data (`Course` information) in JSON format. Although we have hardcoded JSON in our example, you could use JAXB or any other library that converts a Java object into JSON.

Note that we are executing the request using the HTTP POST method `webTarget.request().post(...)`. We have also set the content type of the request to `"application/JSON"`, because our web service to add `Course` consumes the JSON format. We have done this by creating the entity and setting its content type to JSON:

```
//Execute HTTP post method
Response response =
 webTarget.request().post(Entity.entity(courseJSON,
      MediaType.APPLICATION_JSON_TYPE));
```

Now modify the `main` method of the `CourseManagementClient` class to call the `testAddCourseJSON` method. Right-click on the class and select **Run As | Java Application**. You should see `Course` information in JSON format printed in the console. Also, check the Tomcat console in Eclipse. There, you should see the console message that we printed in the `CourseService.dummyAddCourse` method.

Invoking a POST RESTful web service from JavaScript

Here is a simple example of how to invoke our RESTful web service to add a course from JavaScript:

```html
<!DOCTYPE html>
<html>
<head>
<meta charset="UTF-8">
<title>Add Course - JSON</title>

<script type="text/javascript">

  function testAddCourseJSON() {

    //Hardcoded course information to keep example simple.
    //This could be passed as arguments to this function
    //We could also use HTML form to get this information from
     users
    var courseName = "Course-4";
    var credits = 4;

    //Create XMLHttpRequest
    var req = new XMLHttpRequest();

    //Set callback function, because we will have XMLHttpRequest
    //make asynchronous call to our web service
    req.onreadystatechange = function () {
      if (req.readyState == 4 && req.status == 200) {
        //HTTP call was successful. Display response
        document.getElementById("responseSpan").innerHTML =
         req.responseText;
      }
    };

    //Open request to our REST service. Call is going to be asyc
    req.open("POST",
 "http://localhost:8080/CourseManagementREST/services/course/add",
 true);
    //Set request content type as JSON
    req.setRequestHeader("Content-type", "application/JSON");

    //Create Course object and then stringify it to create JSON
     string
    var course = {
```

```
      "course_name": courseName,
      "credits" : credits
    };

    //Send request.
    req.send(JSON.stringify(course));
  }
</script>

</head>
<body>
  <button type="submit" onclick="return testAddCourseJSON();">Add
   Course using JSON</button>
  <p/>
  <span id="responseSpan"></span>
</body>
</html>
```

If you want to test this code, create an HTML file, say addCourseJSON.html,
in the src/main/webapp folder of the CourseManagementREST project. Then, browse to
http://localhost:8080/CourseManagementREST/addCourseJSON.html.
Click the **Add Course using JSON** button. The response is displayed in the same page.

Creating a RESTful web service with form POST

We have created RESTful web services so far with HTTP GET and POST methods. The web
service using the POST method took input in the JSON format. We can also have the POST
method in the web service take input from HTML form elements. Let's create a method that
handles the data posted from a HTML form. Open CourseService.java
from the CourseManagementREST project. Add the following method:

```
@POST
@Consumes (MediaType.APPLICATION_FORM_URLENCODED)
@Path("add")
public Response addCourseFromForm (@FormParam("name") String courseName,
    @FormParam("credits") int credits) throws URISyntaxException {

  dummyAddCourse(courseName, credits);

  return Response.seeOther(new
 URI("../addCourseSuccess.html")).build();
}
```

The method is marked to handle form data by specifying the @Consume annotation with the following value: "application/x-www-form-urlencoded". Just as we mapped parameters in the path in the getCourse method with @PathParam, we map the form fields to method arguments using the @FormParam annotation. Finally, once we successfully save the course, we want the client to be redirected to addCourseSuccess.html. We do this by calling the Response.seeOther method. The addCourseFromForm method returns the Response object.

 Refer to https://jersey.java.net/documentation/latest/representations.html for more information on how to configure Response from the web service.

We need to create addCourseSuccess.html to complete this example. Create this file in the src/main/webapp folder of the CourseManagementREST project with the following content:

```
<h3>Course added successfully</h3>
```

Creating a Java client for a form-encoded RESTful web service

Let's now create a test method for calling the previous web service that consumes form-encoded data. Open CourseManagementClient.java from the CourseManagementRESTClient project and add the following method:

```
//Test addCourse method (Form-Encoded version) of CourseService
public static void testAddCourseForm() {

    //create JAX-RS client
    Client client = ClientBuilder.newClient();

    //Get WebTarget for a URL
    WebTarget webTarget =
client.target("http://localhost:8600/CourseManagementREST/services/course/add");

    //Create Form object and populate fields
    Form form = new Form();
    form.param("name", "Course-5");
    form.param("credits", "5");
```

```
    //Execute HTTP post method
    Response response = webTarget.request().
        post(Entity.entity(form,
        MediaType.APPLICATION_FORM_URLENCODED));

    //check response code. 200 is OK
    if (response.getStatus() != 200) {
      //Print error message
      System.out.println("Error invoking REST Web Service - " +
       response.getStatusInfo().getReasonPhrase() +
          ", Error Code : " + response.getStatus());
      //Also dump content of response message
      System.out.println(response.readEntity(String.class));
      return;
    }

    //REST call was successful. Print the response
    System.out.println(response.readEntity(String.class));
  }
```

Notice that the form data is created by creating an instance of the Form object and setting its parameters. The POST request is encoded with MediaType.APPLICATION_FORM_URLENCODED, which has the following value: "application/x-www-form-urlencoded".

Now, modify the main method to call testAddCourseForm. Then, run the application by right-clicking the class and selecting **Run As | Java Application**. You should see the success message (from addCourseSuccess.html) printed in the console.

A RESTful web service using JSON-B

In the previous section, we implemented the RESTful web service using JAXB. As mentioned earlier, JEE 8 has added a new specification for JSON binding, called JSON-B. In this section, we will learn how to modify our web service to use JSON-B.

There is really not much that we need to change in the code to switch from JAXB to JSON-B. We will need to use the @JsonbProperty annotation of JSON-B to specify field binding in the Course class, instead of the @XmlAttribute annotation of JAXB. Then, we will need to add Maven dependencies to include libraries that provide JSON-B APIs and its implementations. Replace the dependencies section in pom.xml with the following:

```
<dependencies>
 <dependency>
  <groupId>org.glassfish.jersey.containers</groupId>
```

```
    <artifactId>jersey-container-servlet</artifactId>
    <version>2.26</version>
  </dependency>
  <dependency>
    <groupId>org.glassfish.jersey.media</groupId>
    <artifactId>jersey-media-json-binding</artifactId>
    <version>2.26</version>
  </dependency>
  <dependency>
    <groupId>org.glassfish.jersey.inject</groupId>
    <artifactId>jersey-hk2</artifactId>
    <version>2.26</version>
  </dependency>
</dependencies>
```

Dependency on `jersey-container-servlet` has not changed. However, we have replaced dependency on `jersey-media-json-jackson` with `jersey-media-json-binding` and `jersey-hk2`. The Jersey framework automatically handles conversion of Java objects to JSON when the web service method is annotated with:

```
@Produces (MediaType.APPLICATION_JSON)
```

This is specified in the `CourseService` class.

A separate project for this section, named `CourseManagementREST-JSONB`, is made available in the accompanying source code for this chapter.

SOAP web services

Simple Object Access Protocol (SOAP) is a specification from **World Wide Web Consortium (W3C)** (`http://www.w3.org/TR/2007/REC-soap12-part0-20070427/`). Although we are referring to SOAP-based web services here, SOAP is one of the specifications used to implement XML-based web services. There are a few other specifications required to implement SOAP web services, which we will see later. One of the premises of SOAP web services is the dynamic discovery and invocation of services. For example, an application can look for a service from the central directory and invoke it dynamically. However, in practice, very few enterprises would be willing to invoke services dynamically without testing them, so this aspect of SOAP web services is less utilized.

W3C has defined many specifications for SOAP web services, for example, specifications for messages, auto discovery, security, and service orchestration. However, at a minimum, we need to understand the following specification before we develop SOAP web services.

SOAP

SOAP defines the format of a message exchange between the web service provider and the consumer:

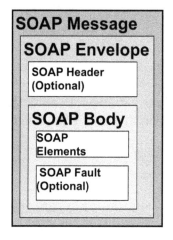

Figure 9.5: SOAP message structure

The top element in a **SOAP Message** is **SOAP Envelope**. It contains a **SOAP Header (Optional)** and a **SOAP Body**. The **SOAP Body** actually contains the message payload (for processing by the consumer) and optionally **SOAP Fault (Optional)**, if there is any error.

The SOAP header provides extensibility to the SOAP message. It can contain information such as user credentials, transaction management, and message routing.

WSDL

As the name suggests, **Web Service Description Language** (**WSDL**) describes web services; in particular, it describes data types used (schemas), input and output messages, operations (methods), and binding and service endpoints:

```
<definitions>
 <import>*
 <types>
  <schema></schema>*
 </types>
 <message>*
  <part></part>*
 </message>
 <PortType>
  <operation>*
   <input></input>
   <output></output>
   <fault></fault>
  </operation>
 </PortType>
 <binding>*
  <operation>*
   <input></input>
   <output></output>
  </operation>
 </binding>
 <service>*
  <port></port>*
 </service>
</definitions>
```

Figure 9.6: WSDL structure

Although you don't necessarily need to understand the details of WSDL when creating web services in Java, it is good to know the basic structure of WSDL. WSDLs are typically meant to be produced and processed by programs, and developers are not expected to hand-code them. Here are some of the elements in WSDL:

- definitions: This is the root element of WSDL.
- Import: This element allows you to import elements from an external file. This way, you can make the WSDL file modular.
- Types: This element defines the schema for different data types used in the WSDL.
- Messages: This element defines the format of input and output messages exchanged between the web service and the client.

- `PortType`: This defines methods or operations supported by the web service. Each operation in `PortType` can declare request and response messages. Operations in `PortType` refer to messages defined in a message element.

Although in *Figure 9.6*, the `binding` element looks the same as `PortType`, it actually specifies the transport protocol bound to operations and message type (**remote procedure call** or **document type**) and encoding (encoded or literal) for messages of each operation declared in `PortType`. The typical transport protocol is HTTP, but it could be other protocols such as JMS and SMTP. The difference between the RPC and document types is that the RPC message type contains the name of the remote method in the message, whereas the document type does not contain the method name. The name of the method to process the payload in a document type message is either derived from the endpoint URL or from information in the header. However, there is another type called **document wrapped**, which does contain the name of the method as the enclosing element for the actual message payload.

The `Service` element contains the actual location of each web service endpoint.

UDDI

Universal Description, Discovery and Integration (**UDDI**) is a directory of web services where you can publish your own web services or search for existing web services. The directory could be global or could be local to the enterprise. UDDI is also a web service with operations supported for publishing and searching contents.

 We will not be focusing on UDDI in this book, but you can visit `http://docs.oracle.com/cd/E14571_01/web.1111/e13734/uddi.htm#WSADV226` for more information.

Developing web services in Java

There are many frameworks around for developing web services in Java. New frameworks have evolved as specifications have changed. Some of the popular frameworks for developing web services in Java over the years are Apache Axis (`https://axis.apache.org/axis/`), Apache Axis2 (`http://axis.apache.org/axis2/java/core/`), Apache CFX (`http://cxf.apache.org/`), and GlassFish Metro (`https://metro.java.net/`).

Earlier implementations of web service frameworks were based on the **JAX-RPC (Java API for XML-based RPC)** specification (`http://www.oracle.com/technetwork/java/docs-142876.html`). JAX-RPC was replaced with **Java API for XML Web Services (JAX-WS)** in JEE 5. JAX-WS makes development of web services easier by supporting annotations. In this chapter, we will learn how to create and consume web services using JAX-WS. Continuing with the example (*Course Management*) that we have been following in this book, we will create web services to get all courses and add new courses.

First, let's create a Maven web project. Select **File | New | Maven Project**. Select the **Create a simple project** option:

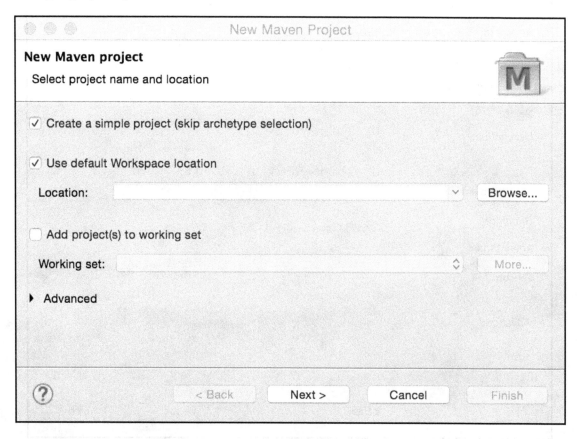

Figure 9.7: New Maven Project

Click **Next**. Enter **Group Id**, **Artifact id**, and **Version** in the next page. Select the `war` packaging:

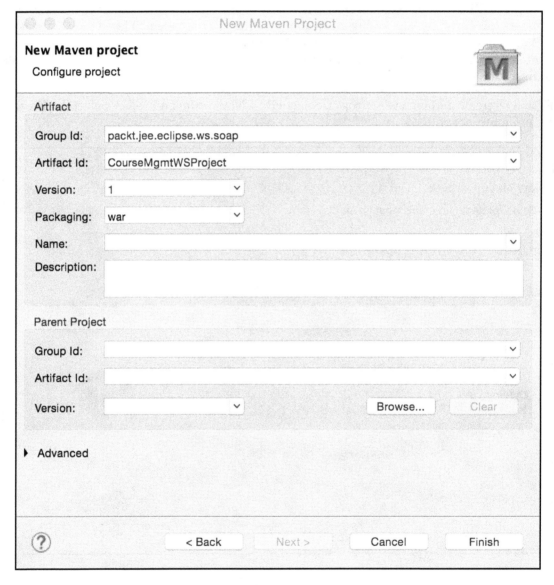

Figure 9.8: Enter artifact details

Click **Finish** to complete the wizard.

Creating a web service implementation class

JAX-WS annotations were added in Java EE 5.0. Using these annotations, we can turn any Java class (including POJOs) into a web service. Use the @Webservice annotation to make any Java class a web service. This annotation can be used either on an interface or on a Java class. If a Java class is annotated with @Webservice, then all public methods in the class are exposed in the web service. If a Java interface is annotated with @Webservice, then the implementation class still needs to be annotated with @Webservice and with the endpointInterface attribute and its value as the interface name.

Before we create the web service implementation class, let's create a few helper classes. The first one is the Course data transfer object. This is the same class that we created in previous chapters. Create the Course class in the packt.jee.eclipse.ws.soap package:

```
package packt.jee.eclipse.ws.soap;

public class Course {
   private int id;
   private String name;
   private int credits;

   //Setters and getters follow here
}
```

Let's now create the web service implementation class CourseManagementService in the packt.jee.eclipse.ws.soap package:

```
package packt.jee.eclipse.ws.soap;

import java.util.ArrayList;
import java.util.List;

import javax.jws.WebService;

@WebService
public class CourseManagementService {

   public List<Course> getCourses() {
     //Here courses could be fetched from database using,
     //for example, JDBC or JDO. However, to keep this example
     //simple, we will return hardcoded list of courses

     List<Course> courses = new ArrayList<Course>();

     courses.add(new Course(1, "Course-1", 4));
     courses.add(new Course(2, "Course-2", 3));
```

```
        return courses;
    }

    public Course getCourse(int courseId) {
        //Here again, we could get course details from database using
        //JDBC or JDO. However, to keep this example
        //simple, we will return hardcoded course

        return new Course(1,"Course-1",4);
    }
}
```

`CourseManagementService` has the following two methods: `getCourses` and `getCourse`. To keep the example simple, we have hardcoded the values, but you can very well fetch data from a database, for example, using the JDBC or JDO APIs that we have discussed earlier in this book. The class is annotated with `@WebService`, which tells the JAX-WS implementation to treat this class as a web service. All methods in this class will be exposed as web service operations. If you want a specific method to be exposed, you could use `@WebMethod`.

Using JAX-WS reference implementation (Glassfish Metro)

Annotating a class with `@WebService` is not enough to implement a web service. We need a library that implements JAX-WS specification. There are a number of JAX-WS frameworks available, for example, Axis2, Apache CFX, and Glassfish Metro. In this chapter, we will use the Glassfish Metro implementation, which is also a reference implementation (`https://jax-ws.java.net/`) of JAX-WS from Oracle.

Let's add Maven dependency for the JAX-WS framework. Open `pom.xml` and add the following dependency:

```
<dependencies>
  <dependency>
    <groupId>com.sun.xml.ws</groupId>
    <artifactId>jaxws-rt</artifactId>
    <version>2.2.10</version>
  </dependency>
</dependencies>
```

Replace the previous version number with the latest version of the framework. The Metro framework also requires you to declare web service endpoints in the configuration file called `sun-jaxws.xml`. Create the `sun-jaxws.xml` file in the `src/main/webapp/WEB-INF` folder and add the endpoint as follows:

```
<?xml version="1.0" encoding="UTF-8"?>
<endpoints xmlns="http://java.sun.com/xml/ns/jax-ws/ri/runtime"
 version="2.0">
  <endpoint name="CourseService"
implementation="packt.jee.eclipse.ws.soap.CourseManagementService"
        url-pattern="/courseService" />
</endpoints>
```

The endpoint implementation is the fully qualified name of our web service implementation class. `url-pattern` is just like servlet mapping that you specify in `web.xml`. In this case, any relative URL starting with `/courseService` would result in the invocation of our web service.

Inspecting WSDL

We are done with implementing our web service. As you can see, JAX-WS really makes it very easy to develop web services. Let's now inspect the WSDL of our web service. Configure Tomcat in Eclipse as described in *Installing Tomcat* section of Chapter 1, *Introducing JEE and Eclipse* and in the *Configuring Tomcat in Eclipse* section of Chapter 2, *Creating a Simple JEE Web Application*. To deploy the web application, right-click on the configured Tomcat server in **Servers** view and select the **Add and Remove** option:

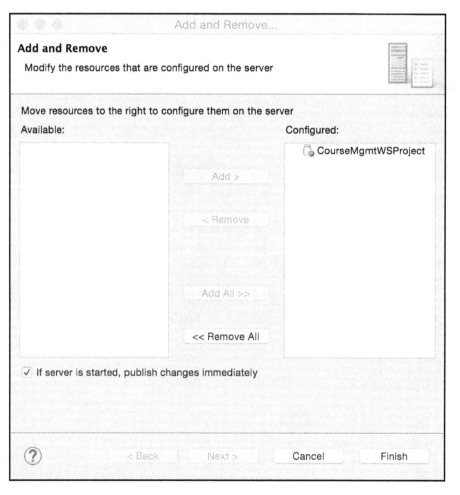

Figure 9.9: Add a project to Tomcat

Add the project and click **Finish**.

Start the Tomcat server by right-clicking on the configured server in the **Servers** view and selecting **Start**.

To inspect the WSDL of our web service, browse to `http://localhost:8080/CourseMgmtWSProject/courseService?wsdl` (assuming that Tomcat is running on port `8080`). The following WSDL should be generated (see the description following *Figure 9.6* in the *WSDL* section to understand the structure of the WSDL generated here):

```
<definitions
xmlns:wsu="http://docs.oasis-open.org/wss/2004/01/oasis-200401-wss-wssecuri
ty-utility-1.0.xsd"
  xmlns:wsp="http://www.w3.org/ns/ws-policy"
  xmlns:wsp1_2="http://schemas.xmlsoap.org/ws/2004/09/policy"
xmlns:wsam="http://www.w3.org/2007/05/addressing/metadata"
  xmlns:soap="http://schemas.xmlsoap.org/wsdl/soap/"
xmlns:tns="http://soap.ws.eclipse.jee.packt/"
  xmlns:xsd="http://www.w3.org/2001/XMLSchema"
xmlns="http://schemas.xmlsoap.org/wsdl/"
  targetNamespace="http://soap.ws.eclipse.jee.packt/"
  name="CourseManagementServiceService">
  <types>
    <xsd:schema>
      <xsd:import namespace="http://soap.ws.eclipse.jee.packt/"
schemaLocation="http://localhost:8080/CourseMgmtWSProject/courseService?xsd
=1" />
    </xsd:schema>
  </types>
  <message name="getCourses">
    <part name="parameters" element="tns:getCourses" />
  </message>
  <message name="getCoursesResponse">
    <part name="parameters" element="tns:getCoursesResponse" />
  </message>
  <message name="getCourse">
    <part name="parameters" element="tns:getCourse" />
  </message>
  <message name="getCourseResponse">
    <part name="parameters" element="tns:getCourseResponse" />
  </message>
  <portType name="CourseManagementService">
    <operation name="getCourses">
      <input
wsam:Action="http://soap.ws.eclipse.jee.packt/CourseManagementService/getCo
ursesRequest"
        message="tns:getCourses" />
      <output
```

```
wsam:Action="http://soap.ws.eclipse.jee.packt/CourseManagementService/getCo
ursesResponse"
        message="tns:getCoursesResponse" />
    </operation>
    <operation name="getCourse">
      <input
wsam:Action="http://soap.ws.eclipse.jee.packt/CourseManagementService/getCo
urseRequest"
        message="tns:getCourse" />
      <output
wsam:Action="http://soap.ws.eclipse.jee.packt/CourseManagementService/getCo
urseResponse"
        message="tns:getCourseResponse" />
    </operation>
  </portType>
  <binding name="CourseManagementServicePortBinding"
   type="tns:CourseManagementService">
    <soap:binding transport="http://schemas.xmlsoap.org/soap/http"
      style="document" />
    <operation name="getCourses">
      <soap:operation soapAction="" />
      <input>
        <soap:body use="literal" />
      </input>
      <output>
        <soap:body use="literal" />
      </output>
    </operation>
    <operation name="getCourse">
      <soap:operation soapAction="" />
      <input>
        <soap:body use="literal" />
      </input>
      <output>
        <soap:body use="literal" />
      </output>
    </operation>
  </binding>
  <service name="CourseManagementServiceService">
    <port name="CourseManagementServicePort"
     binding="tns:CourseManagementServicePortBinding">
      <soap:address
location="http://localhost:8080/CourseMgmtWSProject/courseService"
 />
    </port>
  </service>
</definitions>
```

Notice that the schema (see the definitions of the `/types/xsd:schemas` element) for this
web service is imported in the previous WSDL. You can see the schema generated at
`http://localhost:8080/CourseMgmtWSProject/courseService?xsd=1`:

```xml
<xs:schema xmlns:tns="http://soap.ws.eclipse.jee.packt/"
  xmlns:xs="http://www.w3.org/2001/XMLSchema" version="1.0"
  targetNamespace="http://soap.ws.eclipse.jee.packt/">

  <xs:element name="getCourse" type="tns:getCourse" />
  <xs:element name="getCourseResponse"
   type="tns:getCourseResponse" />
  <xs:element name="getCourses" type="tns:getCourses" />
  <xs:element name="getCoursesResponse"
 type="tns:getCoursesResponse" />

  <xs:complexType name="getCourses">
    <xs:sequence />
  </xs:complexType>
  <xs:complexType name="getCoursesResponse">
    <xs:sequence>
      <xs:element name="return" type="tns:course" minOccurs="0"
        maxOccurs="unbounded" />
    </xs:sequence>
  </xs:complexType>
  <xs:complexType name="course">
    <xs:sequence>
      <xs:element name="credits" type="xs:int" />
      <xs:element name="id" type="xs:int" />
      <xs:element name="name" type="xs:string" minOccurs="0" />
    </xs:sequence>
  </xs:complexType>
  <xs:complexType name="getCourse">
    <xs:sequence>
      <xs:element name="arg0" type="xs:int" />
    </xs:sequence>
  </xs:complexType>
  <xs:complexType name="getCourseResponse">
    <xs:sequence>
      <xs:element name="return" type="tns:course" minOccurs="0" />
    </xs:sequence>
  </xs:complexType>
</xs:schema>
```

The schema document defines data types for the `getCourse` and `getCourses` methods and their responses (`getCoursesResponse` and `getCourseResponse`), and also for the `Course` class. It also declares members of the `Course` data type (`id`, `credits`, and `name`). Notice that the `getCourse` data type has one child element (which is an argument to the call to the `getCourse` method in `CourseManagementService`) called `arg0`, which is actually the course ID of the `int` type. Further, notice the definition of `getCoursesResponse`. In our implementation class, `getCourses` returns `List<Course>`, which is translated in WSDL (or types in WSDL) as a sequence of course types.

The following four messages are defined in the previous WSDL: `getCourses`, `getCoursesResponse`, `getCourse`, and `getCourseResponse`. Each message contains a part element that refers to data types declared in types (or schema).

The `PortType` name is the same as the web service implementation class called `CourseManagementService` and operations of the port are the same as public methods of the class. The input and output of each operation refers to messages already defined in the WSDL.

The binding defines the network transport type, which in this case is HTTP, and the style of message in the SOAP body, which is of the document type. We have not defined any message type in our web service implementation, but the JAX-WS reference implementation (Glassfish Metro) has set a default message type to `document`. Binding also defines the message encoding type for the input and output messages of each operation.

Finally, the `Service` element specifies the location of the port, which is the URL that we access to invoke the web service.

Implementing a web service using an interface

All methods declared in our web service implementation class,
CourseManagementService, are exposed as web service operations. However, if you
want to expose only a limited set of methods from the web service implementation class,
then you can use the Java interface. For example, if we want to expose
only the getCourses method as a web service operation, then we can create an interface,
let's say ICourseManagementService:

```
package packt.jee.eclipse.ws.soap;

import java.util.List;

import javax.jws.WebService;

@WebService
public interface ICourseManagementService {
  public List<Course> getCourses();
}
```

The implementation class also needs to be annotated with @WebService,
with the endpointInterface attribute set to the interface name:

```
package packt.jee.eclipse.ws.soap;

import java.util.ArrayList;
import java.util.List;

import javax.jws.WebService;

@WebService
  (endpointInterface="packt.jee.eclipse.ws.soap.ICourseManagementService")
public class CourseManagementService implements ICourseManagementService {

  //getCourses and getCourse methods follow here
}
```

Now, restart Tomcat and inspect the WSDL. You will notice that only the getCourses
operation is defined in the WSDL.

Consuming a web service using JAX-WS

Let's now create a simple Java console app to consume the web service we created earlier. Select **File | New | Maven Project**. Select the **Create a simple project** option on the first page and click **Next**. Enter the following configuration details:

Figure 9.10: Create a Maven project for the web service client

Make sure that the **Packaging** type is jar. Click **Finish**.

We will now generate a stub and a supporting class on the client side for invoking the web service. We will use the **wsimport** tool to generate client classes. We will specify the package for the generated classes by using the -p option and the WSDL location to generate client classes. The wsimport tool is part of the JDK and should be available in the <JDK_HOME>/bin folder, if you are using JDK 1.7 or later.

Change the folder to <project_home>/src//main/java and run the following command:

```
wsimport -keep -p packt.jee.eclipse.ws.soap.client
http://localhost:8080/CourseMgmtWSProject/courseService?wsdl
```

The -keep flag instructs wsimport to keep the generated file and not delete it.

The -p option specifies the package name for the generated classes.

The last argument is the WSDL location for the web service. In **Package Explorer** or **Project Explorer** of Eclipse, refresh the client project to see the generated files. The files should be in the packt.jee.eclipse.ws.soap.client package.

wsimport generates a client-side class for each type defined in the schema (in the types element of WSDL). Therefore, you will find Course, GetCourse, GetCourseResponse, GetCourses, and GetCoursesResponse classes. Furthermore, it generates classes for the portType (CourseManagementService) and service (CourseManagementServiceService) elements of the WSDL. Additionally, it creates an ObjectFactory class that creates Java objects from XML using JAXB.

Let's now write the code to actually call the web service. Create the CourseMgmtWSClient class in the packt.jee.eclipse.ws.soap.client.test package:

```
package packt.jee.eclipse.ws.soap.client.test;

import packt.jee.eclipse.ws.soap.client.Course;
import packt.jee.eclipse.ws.soap.client.CourseManagementService;
import packt.jee.eclipse.ws.soap.client.CourseManagementServiceService;

public class CourseMgmtWSClient {

  public static void main(String[] args) {
    CourseManagementServiceService service = new
  CourseManagementServiceService();    CourseManagementService port =
      service.getCourseManagementServicePort();
```

```
    Course course = port.getCourse(1);
    System.out.println("Course name = " + course.getName());
  }

}
```

We first create the `Service` object and then get the port from it. The `port` object has operations defined for the web service. We then call the actual web service method on the `port` object. Right-click on the class and select **Run As | Java Application**. The output should be the name of the course that we hardcoded in the web service implementation, which is `Course-1`.

Specifying an argument name in a web service operation

As mentioned earlier, when WSDL was created for our `Course` web service, the argument for the `getCourse` operation name was created as `arg0`. You can verify this by browsing to `http://localhost:8080/CourseMgmtWSProject/courseService?xsd=1` and checking the `getCourse` type:

```
<xs:complexType name="getCourse">
    <xs:sequence>
        <xs:element name="arg0" type="xs:int"/>
    </xs:sequence>
</xs:complexType>
```

Thus, the client-side-generated code (by `wsimport`) in `CourseManagementService.getCourse` also names the argument as `arg0`. It would be nice to give a meaningful name to arguments. This could be done easily be adding the `@WSParam` annotation in our web service implementation class, `CourseManagementService`:

```
public Course getCourse(@WebParam(name="courseId") int courseId) {...}
```

Restart Tomcat after this change and browse to the WSDL schema URL
(`http://localhost:8080/CourseMgmtWSProject/courseService?xsd=1`) again. You
should now see a proper argument name in the `getCourse` type:

```
<xs:complexType name="getCourse">
    <xs:sequence>
        <xs:element name="courseId" type="xs:int"/>
    </xs:sequence>
</xs:complexType>
```

Generate the client-side code again by using `wsimport`, and you will see that argument
of the `getCourse` method is named `courseId`.

Inspecting SOAP messages

Although you don't necessarily need to understand the SOAP messages passed between
the web service and the client, sometimes inspecting SOAP messages exchanged between
the two could help debug some of the issues.

You can print request and response SOAP messages when running the client quite easily by
setting the following system property:

```
com.sun.xml.internal.ws.transport.http.client.HttpTransportPipe.dump=tr
ue
```

In Eclipse, right-click on the `CourseMgmtWSClient` class and select **Run As | Run Configurations**. Click on the **Arguments** tab and specify the following VM argument:

```
Dcom.sun.xml.internal.ws.transport.http.client.HttpTransportPipe.dump=true
```

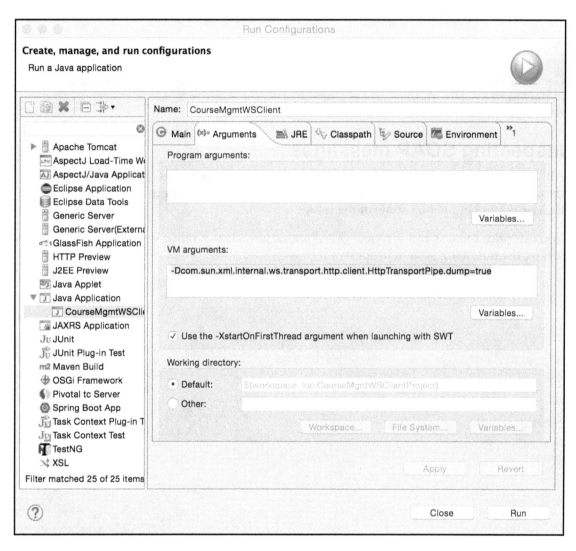

Figure 9.11: Set VM arguments

Click **Run**. You will see request and response SOAP messages printed in the **Console** window in Eclipse. After formatting the request message, this is what the request SOAP message looks like:

```
<?xml version="1.0" ?>
<S:Envelope xmlns:S="http://schemas.xmlsoap.org/soap/envelope/">
  <S:Body>
    <ns2:getCourse xmlns:ns2="http://soap.ws.eclipse.jee.packt/">
      <courseId>1</courseId>
    </ns2:getCourse>
  </S:Body>
</S:Envelope>
```

The response is as follows:

```
<?xml version='1.0' encoding='UTF-8'?>
<S:Envelope xmlns:S="http://schemas.xmlsoap.org/soap/envelope/">
  <S:Body>
    <ns2:getCourseResponse
     xmlns:ns2="http://soap.ws.eclipse.jee.packt/">
      <return>
        <credits>4</credits>
        <id>1</id>
        <name>Course-1</name>
      </return>
    </ns2:getCourseResponse>
  </S:Body>
</S:Envelope>
```

Handling interfaces in RPC-style web services

Recall that the message style for our web service implementation class is Document and the encoding is literal. Let's change the style to RPC. Open CourseManagementService.java and change the style of the SOAP binding from Style.DOCUMENT to Style.RPC:

```
@WebService
@SOAPBinding(style=Style.RPC, use=Use.LITERAL)
public class CourseManagementService {...}
```

Restart Tomcat. In the Tomcat console, you might see the following error:

```
Caused by: com.sun.xml.bind.v2.runtime.IllegalAnnotationsException: 1
counts of IllegalAnnotationExceptions
    java.util.List is an interface, and JAXB can't handle interfaces.
      this problem is related to the following location:
        at java.util.List
```

This problem is caused by the following method definition
in the `CourseManagementService` class:

```
public List<Course> getCourses() {...}
```

In RPC-style SOAP binding, JAX-WS uses JAXB, and JAXB cannot marshal interfaces very well. A blog entry at https://community.oracle.com/blogs/kohsuke/2006/06/06/jaxb-and-interfaces tries to explain the reason for this. The workaround is to create a wrapper for `List` and annotate it with `@XMLElement`. So, create a new class called `Courses` in the same package:

```java
package packt.jee.eclipse.ws.soap;

import java.util.List;

import javax.xml.bind.annotation.XmlAnyElement;
import javax.xml.bind.annotation.XmlRootElement;

@XmlRootElement
public class Courses {
  @XmlAnyElement
  public List<Course> courseList;

  public Courses() {

  }

  public Courses (List<Course> courseList) {
    this.courseList = courseList;
  }
}
```

Then, modify the `getCourses` method of `CourseManagementService` to return the `Courses` object instead of `List<Course>`:

```
public Courses getCourses() {
    //Here, courses could be fetched from database using,
    //for example, JDBC or JDO. However, to keep this example
    //simple, we will return hardcoded list of courses

    List<Course> courses = new ArrayList<Course>();

    courses.add(new Course(1, "Course-1", 4));
    courses.add(new Course(2, "Course-2", 3));

    return new Courses(courses);
}
```

Restart Tomcat. This time, the application should be deployed in Tomcat without any error. Re-generate the client classes by using `wsimport`, run the client application, and verify the results.

Handling exceptions

In JAX-WS, a Java exception thrown from a web service is mapped to SOAP fault when the XML payload is sent to the client. On the client side, JAX-WS maps SOAP fault to either `SOAPFaultException` or to the application-specific exception. The client code could wrap the web service call in a `try...catch` block to handle exceptions thrown from the web service.

For a good description of how SOAP exceptions are handled in JAX-WS, refer to
`https://docs.oracle.com/cd/E24329_01/web.1211/e24965/faults.htm#WSADV624`.

Summary

Web services are a very useful technology for enterprise application integration. They allow disparate systems to communicate with each other. Web service APIs are typically self-contained and lightweight.

There are broadly two types of web services: SOAP-based and RESTful. SOAP-based web services are XML-based and provide many features such as security, attachments, and transactions. RESTful web services can exchange data by using XML or JSON. RESTful JSON web services are quite popular because they can be easily consumed from JavaScript code.

In this chapter, we learned how to develop and consume RESTful and SOAP-based web services by using the latest Java specifications, JAX-RS and JAX-WS.

In the next chapter, we will take a look at another technology for application integration: asynchronous programming using **Java Messaging Service (JMS)**.

10
Asynchronous Programming with JMS

In the last chapter, we learned how to create web services in JEE. We learned to create both RESTful and SOAP-based web services. In this chapter, we will learn how to work with messaging systems in JEE. Thus far, we have seen examples of clients making requests to the JEE server and waiting till the server sends a response back. This is the synchronous model of programming. This model of programming may not be suitable when the server takes a long time to process requests. In such cases, a client might want to send a request to the server and return immediately without waiting for the response. The server would process the request and somehow make the result available to the client. Requests and responses in such scenarios are sent through messages. Furthermore, there is a message broker that makes sure that messages are sent to the appropriate recipients. This is also known as a **message-oriented architecture**. The following are some of the advantages of adopting a message-oriented architecture:

- It can greatly improve the scalability of the application. Requests are put in a queue at one end, and at the other end there could be many handlers listening to the queue and processing the requests. As the load increases, more handlers can be added, and when the load reduces, some of the handlers can be taken off.

- Messaging systems can act as glue between disparate software applications. An application developed using PHP can put a JSON or XML message in a messaging system, which can be processed by a JEE application.

- It can be used to implement an event-driven program. Events can be put as messages in a messaging system, and any number of listeners can process events at the other end.

- It can reduce the impact of system outages in your application because messages are persisted till they are processed.

There are many enterprise messaging systems, such as Apache ActiveMQ (`http://activemq.apache.org/`), RabbitMQ (`https://www.rabbitmq.com/`), and MSMQ (`https://msdn.microsoft.com/en-us/library/ms711472(v=vs.85).aspx`). The **Java Messaging Service** (**JMS**) specification provides a uniform interface for working with many different messaging systems. JMS is also a part of the overall Java EE specifications. Refer to `https://javaee.github.io/tutorial/jms-concepts.html#BNCDQ` for an overview of JMS APIs.

There are two types of message containers in any messaging system:

- **Queue**: This is used for point-to-point messaging. One message producer puts a message in a queue, and only one message consumer receives the message. There can be multiple listeners for a queue, but only one listener receives the message. However, the same listener doesn't necessarily get all the messages.
- **Topic**: This is used in the publish-subscribe type of scenario. One message producer puts a message in a topic, and many subscribers receive the message. Topics are useful for broadcasting messages.

We will cover the following topics:

- Sending and receiving messages to and from queues and topics using JMS APIs
- Creating JMS applications using JSP, JSF, and CDI beans
- Consuming messages using MDBs (message-driven beans)

We will see examples of how to use queues and topics in this chapter. We will use a GlassFish Server, which has a built-in JMS provider. We will use JMS APIs to implement a use case in the *Course Management* application, the same application that we have been building in the other chapters of this book.

Steps to send and receive messages using JMS

However, before we start using JMS APIs, let's take a look at the generic steps involved in using them. The following steps show how to send a message to a queue and receive it. Although the steps focus on queues, the steps for topics are similar, but with appropriate topic-related classes:

1. Look up `ConnectionFactory` using JNDI:

   ```
   InitialContext ctx = new InitialContext();
   QueueConnectionFactory connectionFactory =
   (QueueConnectionFactory)initCtx.lookup("jndi_name_of_connection_fac
   tory");
   ```

2. Create a JMS connection and start it:

   ```
   QueueConnection con = connectionFactory.createQueueConnection();
   con.start();
   ```

3. Create a JMS session:

   ```
   QueueSession session = con.createQueueSession(false,
   Session.AUTO_ACKNOWLEDGE);
   ```

4. Look up JMS `Queue`/`Topic`:

   ```
   Queue queue = (Queue)initCtx.lookup("jndi_queue_name");
   ```

5. For sending messages, perform the following steps:

   1. Create a sender:

      ```
      QueueSender sender = session.createSender(queue);
      ```

   2. Create the message. It can be of any of the following types: `TextMessage/ObjectMessage/MapMessage/BytesMessage/Stream Message`:

      ```
      TextMessage textMessage = session.createTextMessage("Test
      Message");
      ```

3. Send the message:

```
sender.send(textMessage);
```

4. Close the connection when no longer needed:

```
con.close();
```

6. For receiving messages, perform the following steps:

1. Create a receiver:

```
//create a new session before creating the receiver.
QueueReceiver receiver = session.createReceiver(queue);
```

2. Register a message listener or call the `receive` method:

```
receiver.setMessageListener(new MessageListener() {
    @Override
    public void onMessage(Message message) {
        try {
            String messageTxt =
                ((TextMessage)message).getText();
            //process message
        } catch (JMSException e) {
            //handle exception
        }
    }
});
```

3. Alternatively, you can use any variation of the receive method:

```
Message message = receiver.receive(); //this blocks the
thread till a message is received
```

4. Or you can use this:

```
Message message = receiver.receive(timeout); // with
timeout
```

5. Or you can use this:

```
Message message = receiver.receiveNoWait(); //returns null
if no message is available.
```

In a JEE application that uses EJB, it is recommended to use MDBs. We will see an example of MDBs later in this chapter.

7. When done, close the connection. This stops message listeners too:

```
con.close();
```

Some of the steps can be skipped when JMS annotations are used or when MDBs are used to receive messages. We will see examples later.

Now, let's create a working example of sending and receiving messages using JMS. Make sure that you have installed the GlassFish application server (refer to the *Installing the GlassFish Server* section in Chapter 1, *Introducing JEE and Eclipse*) and configured it in Eclipse JEE (refer to the *Configuring the GlassFish Server in Eclipse* section in Chapter 7, *Creating JEE Applications with EJB*). The use case that we will implement in this example is of adding a new course. Although this is not a strong use case for asynchronous processing, we will assume that this operation takes a long time and needs to be handled asynchronously.

Creating queues and topics in GlassFish

Let's create one queue and one topic in GlassFish. Make sure that the GlassFish Server is running. Open the GlassFish admin console. You can right-click the GlassFish Server instance configured in Eclipse (in the **Servers** view) and select **GlassFish** | **View Admin Console**. This opens the admin console in the built-in Eclipse browser. If you want to open it outside Eclipse, in a browser, then browse to http://localhost:4848/ (assuming the default GlassFish installation).

We will first create a JMS connection factory. In the admin console, go to the **Resources** | **JMS Resources** | **Connection Factories** page. Click the **New** button to create a new connection factory:

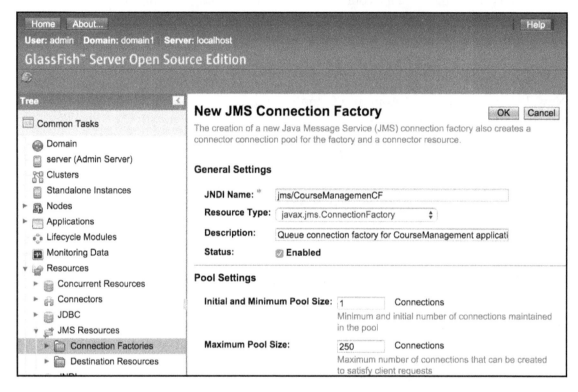

Figure 10.1: Create a JMS connection factory

Enter **JNDI Name** of the factory as `jms/CourseManagementCF` and select **javax.jms.ConnectionFactory** as the **Resource Type**. Leave the default values for **Pool Settings**. Click **OK**.

To create queues and topics, go to the **Resources** I **JMS Resources** I **Destination Resources** page. Click the **New** button:

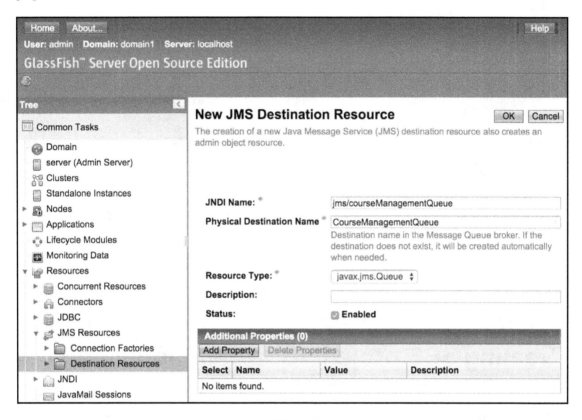

Figure 10.2: Create a JMS queue

Enter the **JNDI Name** of the queue as `jms/courseManagementQueue`, **Physical Destination Name** as `CourseManagementQueue`, and select **javax.jms.Queue** as the **Resource Type**. Click **OK** to create the queue.

Similarly, create the topic by entering the **JNDI Name** as `jms/courseManagementTopic`, **Physical Destination Name** as `CourseManagementTopic`, and select **javax.jms.Topic** as the **Resource Type**.

You should now have one queue and one topic configured in the **Destination Resources** page:

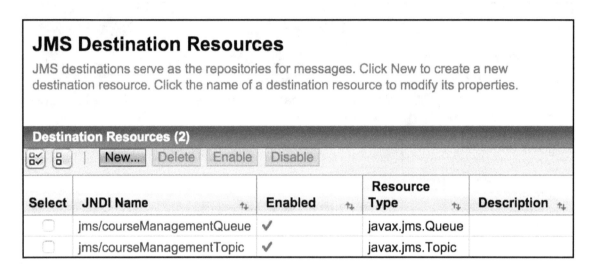

Figure 10.3: Queue and topic created in GlassFish

Creating JEE project for a JMS application

We will see examples of using JMS APIs in three different ways.

In the first example, we will create a simple `addCourse.jsp` page, one JSP bean, and one `Service` class that actually performs JMS tasks.

In the second example, we will use JSF and managed beans. We will use JMS APIs in the managed beans. We will also see how to use JMS annotations in JSF managed beans.

In the last example, we will use MDBs to consume JMS messages.

Let's start with the first example, which uses JSP, bean, and JMS APIs. Create a web project by selecting **File** | **New** | **Dynamic Web Project** or **File** | **New** | **Other** and then **Web** | **Dynamic Web Project**:

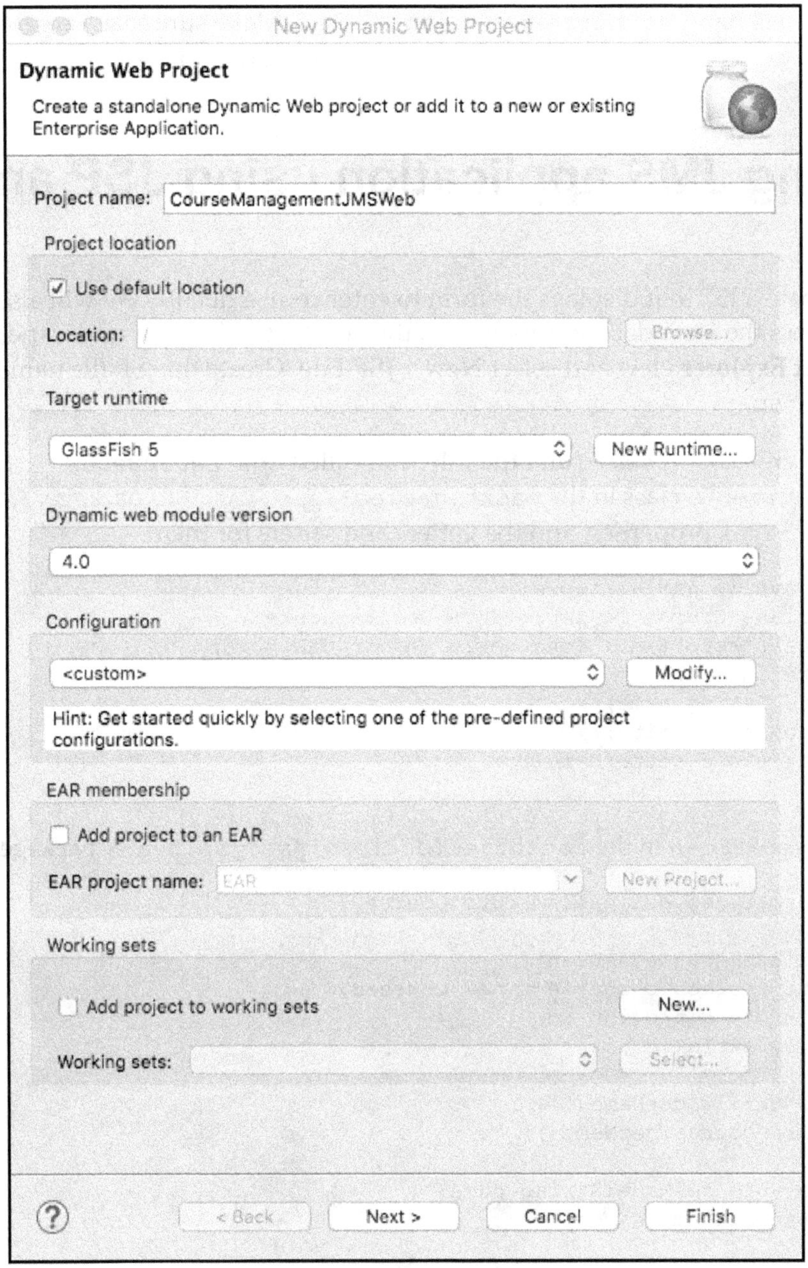

Figure 10.4: Create a dynamic web project for a JMS app

Enter the **Project name** as `CourseManagement JMSWeb`. Make sure that **Target runtime** is **GlassFish** . Click **Next**, and accept all the default options. Click **Finish** to create the project.

Creating JMS application using JSP and JSP bean

Let's first create a JSP that displays the form to enter course details. We will also create a JSP bean to process the form data. Right-click on the `WebContent` folder under the project in the **Project Explorer** view and select **New** | **JSP File**. Create the JSP file named `addCourse.jsp`.

We will now create `CourseDTO` and the JSP bean called `CourseJSPBean`. Create the `CourseDTO` class in the `packt.jee.eclipse.jms.dto` package. Add the `id`, `name`, and `credits` properties, and the getters and setters for them:

```
import java.io.Serializable;
public class CourseDTO implements Serializable {
  private static final long serialVersionUID = 1L;
  private int id;
  private String name;
  private int credits;
  //getters and setters follow
}
```

Create `CourseJSPBean` in the `packt.jee.eclipse.jms.jsp.beans` package:

```
import packt.jee.eclipse.jms.dto.CourseDTO;

public class CourseJSPBean {
  private CourseDTO course = new CourseDTO();
  public void setId(int id) {
    course.setId(id);
  }
  public String getName() {
    return course.getName();
  }
  public void setName(String name) {
    course.setName(name);
  }
  public int getCredits() {
    return course.getCredits();
  }
  public void setCredits(int credits) {
```

```
      course.setCredits(credits);
  }
  public void addCourse() {
    //TODO: send CourseDTO object to a JMS queue
  }
}
```

We will implement the code to send the `CourseDTO` object to the JMS queue later in the `addCourse` method. For now, add the following code to `addCourse.jsp`:

```
<%@ page language="java" contentType="text/html; charset=UTF-8"
    pageEncoding="UTF-8"%>
<%@ taglib uri="http://java.sun.com/jsp/jstl/core" prefix="c" %>
<!DOCTYPE html PUBLIC "-//W3C//DTD HTML 4.01 Transitional//EN"
 "http://www.w3.org/TR/html4/loose.dtd">
<html>
<head>
<meta http-equiv="Content-Type" content="text/html; charset=UTF-
 8">
<title>Add Course</title>
</head>
<body>
  <!-- Check if form is posted -->
  <c:if test="${"POST".equalsIgnoreCase(pageContext.request.method)
      && pageContext.request.getParameter("submit") != null}">

    <!-- Create CourseJSPBean -->
    <jsp:useBean id="courseService"
class="packt.jee.eclipse.jms.jsp_beans.CourseJSPBean"
 scope="page"></jsp:useBean>

    <!-- Set Bean properties with values from form submission -->
    <jsp:setProperty property="name" name="courseService"
    param="course_name"/>    <jsp:setProperty property="credits"
name="courseService"
    param="course_credits"/>

    <!-- Call addCourse method of the bean -->
    ${courseService.addCourse()}
    <b>Course detailed are sent to a JMS Queue. It will be
    processed later</b>
  </c:if>

  <h2>New Course:</h2>

  <!-- Course data input form -->
  <form method="post">
```

```
    <table>
      <tr>
        <td>Name:</td>
        <td>
          <input type="text" name="course_name">
        </td>
      </tr>
      <tr>
        <td>Credits:</td>
        <td>
          <input type="text" name="course_credits">
        </td>
      </tr>
      <tr>
        <td colspan="2">
          <button type="submit" name="submit">Add</button>
        </td>
      </tr>
    </table>
  </form>

</body>
</html>
```

At the top of the JSP file, we check whether the form is submitted. If yes, we then create an instance of `CourseJSPBean` and set its properties with values from the form submission. Then, we call the `addCourse` method of the bean.

Executing addCourse.jsp

We still haven't added any code to put the `Course` object in the JMS queue. However, if you want to test the JSP and bean, add the project to the GlassFish server configured in Eclipse. To do this, right-click on the configured server in the **Servers** view of Eclipse and select the **Add and Remove...** option. Select the web project that we created and click on **Finish**. Make sure that the server is started and the status is **[Started, Synchronized]**:

Figure 10.5: Status of GlassFish after adding web project

If the status is **Republish**, then right-click on the server and select the **Publish** option. If the status is **Restart**, right-click on the server and select the **Restart** option. You may not have to do this immediately after adding the project, but later when we make changes to the code, you may have to republish or restart the server, or both. So, keep an eye on the server status before you execute the code in Eclipse.

To execute `addCourse.jsp`, right-click on the file in either **Project Explorer** or the editor, and select the **Run As** | **Run on Server** option. This will open the built-in Eclipse browser and open JSP in it. You should see the form for adding the course details. If you click the **Submit** button, you should see the message that we added in JSP when the form is submitted.

Let's now add a class to send the course details to the JMS queue.

Implementing JMS queue sender class

Let's create the `CourseQueueSender` class in the `packt.jee.eclipse.jms` package with the following content:

```
package packt.jee.eclipse.jms;

//skipped imports

public class CourseQueueSender {
  private QueueConnection connection;
  private QueueSession session;
  private Queue queue;


  public CourseQueueSender() throws Exception {
    //Create JMS Connection, session, and queue objects
    InitialContext initCtx = new InitialContext();
    QueueConnectionFactory connectionFactory =
```

```
        (QueueConnectionFactory)initCtx.
             lookup("jms/CourseManagemenCF");
      connection = connectionFactory.createQueueConnection();
      connection.start();
      session = connection.createQueueSession(false,
        Session.AUTO_ACKNOWLEDGE);
      queue = (Queue)initCtx.lookup("jms/courseManagementQueue");
    }

   public void close() {
      if (connection != null) {
        try {
          connection.close();
        } catch (JMSException e) {
          e.printStackTrace();
        }
      }
   }
   @Override
   protected void finalize() throws Throwable {
      close(); //clean up
      super.finalize();
   }

   public void sendAddCourseMessage (CourseDTO course) throws
    Exception {
      //Send CourseDTO object to JMS Queue
      QueueSender sender = session.createSender(queue);
      ObjectMessage objMessage =
        session.createObjectMessage(course);
      sender.send(objMessage);
   }
  }
```

In the constructor, we look up the JMS connection factory and create the connection. We then create a JMS session and lookup queue with the JNDI name that we used for creating the queue in a previous section.

Note that we did not specify any configuration properties when constructing `InitialContext`. This is because the code is executed in the same instance of the GlassFish Server that hosts the JMS provider. If you are connecting to a JMS provider hosted in a different GlassFish Server, then you will have to specify the configuration properties, particularly for the remote host, for example:

```
Properties jndiProperties = new Properties();
jndiProperties.setProperty("org.omg.CORBA.ORBInitialHost",
 "<remote_host>");
```

```
//target ORB port. default is 3700 in GlassFish
jndiProperties.setProperty("org.omg.CORBA.ORBInitialPort",
  "3700");

InitialContext ctx = new InitialContext(jndiProperties);
```

The `CourseQueueSender.sendAddcourseMessage` method creates instances
of `QueueSender` and `ObjectMessage`. Because the producer and the consumer of the
message in this example are in Java, we use `ObjectMessage`. However, if you are to send a
message to a messaging system where the message is going to be consumed by a non-Java
consumer, then you could create JSON or XML from the Java object and send
`TextMessage`. We have already seen how to serialize Java objects to JSON and XML using
JAXB and JSON-B in `Chapter 9`, *Creating Web Services*.

Now, let's modify the `addCourse` method in `CourseJSPBean` to
use the `CourseQueueSender` class to send JMS messages. Note that we could create an
instance of `CourseQueueSender` in the bean class, `CouseJSPBean`, but the bean is created
every time the page is requested. So, `CourseQueueSender` will be created frequently and
the lookup for the JMS connection factory and the queue will also execute frequently, which
is not necessary. Therefore, we will create an instance of `CourseQueueSender` and save it
in the HTTP session. Then, we will modify the `addCourse` method to take
`HttpServletRequest` as a parameter. We will also get the `HttpSession` object from the
request:

```
public void addCourse(HttpServletRequest request) throws
  Exception {
  //get HTTP session
  HttpSession session = request.getSession(true);
  //look for instance of CourseQueueSender in Session
  CourseQueueSender courseQueueSender =
    (CourseQueueSender) session
                    getAttribute("CourseQueueSender");
  if (courseQueueSender == null) {
    //Create instance of CourseQueueSender and save in Session
    courseQueueSender = new CourseQueueSender();
    session.setAttribute("CourseQueueSender",
      courseQueueSender);
  }

  //TODO: perform input validation
  if (courseQueueSender != null) {
    try {
      courseQueueSender.sendAddCourseMessage(course);
    } catch (Exception e) {
      e.printStackTrace();
```

```
        //TODO: log exception
      }
    }
  }
```

If we don't find the `CourseQueueSender` object in the session, then we will create one and save it in the session.

We need to modify the call to the `addCourse` method from `addcourse.jsp`. Currently, we do not pass any argument to the method. However, with the preceding changes to the `addCourse` method, we need to pass the `HttpServletRequest` object to it. JSP has a built-in property called `pageContext` that provides access to the `HttpServletRequest` object. So, modify the code in `addCourse.jsp` where `courseService.addCourse` is called as follows:

```
<!-- Call addCourse method of the bean -->
${courseService.addCourse(pageContext.request)}
```

We can test our code at this point, but although messages are sent to the queue, we haven't implemented any consumer to receive them from the queue. So, let's implement a JMS queue consumer for our `Course` queue.

Implementing JMS queue receiver class

Let's create the `CourseQueueReceiver` class in the `packt.jee.eclipse.jms` package with the following content:

```
public class CourseQueueReceiver {

  private QueueConnection connection;
  private QueueSession session;
  private Queue queue;

  private String receiverName;

  public CourseQueueReceiver(String name) throws Exception{

    //save receiver name
    this.receiverName = name;

    //look up JMS connection factory
    InitialContext initCtx = new InitialContext();
    QueueConnectionFactory connectionFactory =
  (QueueConnectionFactory)initCtx.lookup("jms/CourseManagemenCF");
```

```java
//create JMS connection
connection = connectionFactory.createQueueConnection();
connection.start();

//create JMS session
session = connection.createQueueSession(false,
 Session.AUTO_ACKNOWLEDGE);
//look up queue
queue = (Queue)initCtx.lookup("jms/courseManagementQueue");

topicPublisher = new CourseTopicPublisher();

QueueReceiver receiver = session.createReceiver(queue);
//register message listener
receiver.setMessageListener(new MessageListener() {

  @Override
  public void onMessage(Message message) {
    //we expect ObjectMessage here; of type CourseDTO
    //skipping validation
    try {
      CourseDTO course = (CourseDTO)
      ((ObjectMessage)message).getObject();          //process
addCourse action. For example, save it in the
      database          System.out.println("Received addCourse message
for Course name - " +
            course.getName() + " in Receiver " + receiverName);
    } catch (Exception e) {
      e.printStackTrace();
      //TODO: handle and log exception
    }
  }
});
  }

  public void stop() {
    if (connection != null) {
      try {
        connection.close();
      } catch (JMSException e) {
        e.printStackTrace();
        //TODO: log exception
      }
    }
  }
}
```

Asynchronous Programming with JMS

The code to look up the connection factory and the queue is similar to that in
`CourseQueueSender`. Note that the constructor takes a `name` argument. We don't really
need to use the JMS API, but we will use it as an identifier for instances
of the `CourseQueueReceiver` class. We register a message listener in the constructor, and
in the `onMessage` method of the listener class we get the `CourseDTO` object from the
message and print the message to the console. This message will appear in the GlassFish
console in Eclipse when we execute the code. To keep the example simple, we have not
implemented the code to save the `Course` information to the database, but you can do so
using the JDBC or JDO APIs we learned about in `Chapter` `4`, *Creating JEE Database
Applications*.

We need to instantiate the `CourseQueueReceiver` class at application startup, so that it
will start listening for the messages. One way to implement this is in a servlet that loads on
startup.

Let's create the `JMSReceiverInitServlet` class
in the `packt.jee.eclipse.jms.servlet` package. We will mark this servlet to load at
startup using annotations and instantiate `CourseQueueReceiver` in the `init` method:

```
package packt.jee.eclipse.jms.servlet;

//skipped imports

@WebServlet(urlPatterns="/JMSReceiverInitServlet", loadOnStartup=1)
public class JMSReceiverInitServlet extends HttpServlet {
  private static final long serialVersionUID = 1L;

  private CourseQueueReceiver courseQueueReceiver = null;

    public JMSReceiverInitServlet() {
        super();
    }

    @Override
    public void init(ServletConfig config) throws ServletException
{
      super.init(config);
      try {
      courseQueueReceiver = new CourseQueueReceiver("Receiver1");
    } catch (Exception e) {
      log("Error creating CourseQueueReceiver", e);
    }
    }

    @Override
```

```
    public void destroy() {
      if (courseQueueReceiver != null)
        courseQueueReceiver.stop();
      super.destroy();
    }
}
```

Publish the project again in the server and execute `addCourse.jsp` (see the *Executing addCourse.jsp* section of this chapter). Switch to the **Console** view in Eclipse. You should see the message that we printed in the `onMessage` method in `CourseQueueReceiver`:

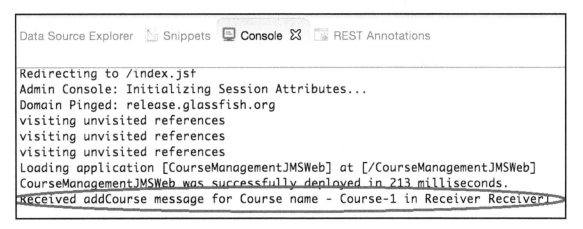

Figure 10.6: Example of a console message from the JMS receiver class

Adding multiple queue listeners

Queues are meant for point-to-point communication, but this does not mean that there can't be more than one listener for a queue. However, only one listener gets the message. Furthermore, it is not guaranteed that the same listener will get the message every time. If you want to test this, add one more instance of `CourseQueueReceiver` in `JMSReceiverInitServlet`. Let's add the second instance with a different name, say `Receiver2`:

```
@WebServlet(urlPatterns="/JMSReceiverInitServlet", loadOnStartup=1)
public class JMSReceiverInitServlet extends HttpServlet {
  private CourseQueueReceiver courseQueueReceiver = null;
  private CourseQueueReceiver courseQueueReceiver1 = null;
    @Override
    public void init(ServletConfig config) throws ServletException
  {
```

```
   super.init(config);
   try {
     //first instance of CourseQueueReceiver
   courseQueueReceiver = new CourseQueueReceiver("Receiver1");
     //create another instance of CourseQueueReceiver with a
      different name
   courseQueueReceiver1 = new CourseQueueReceiver("Receiver2");
   } catch (Exception e) {
     log("Error creating CourseQueueReceiver", e);
   }
   }

   @Override
   public void destroy() {
      if (courseQueueReceiver != null)
        courseQueueReceiver.stop();
      if (courseQueueReceiver1 != null)
        courseQueueReceiver1.stop();
      super.destroy();
   }

   //rest of the code remains the same
}
```

Republish the project, execute `addCourse.jsp`, and add a few courses. Check the **Console** messages. You may see that some of the messages were received by `Receiver1` and the others by `Receiver2`:

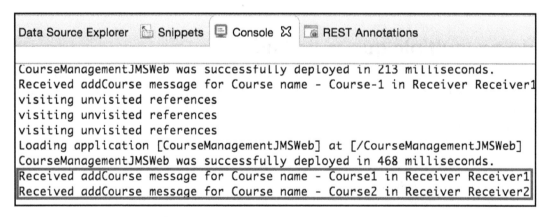

Figure 10.7: Console output showing multiple JMS receivers listening to a JMS queue

Implementing JMS topic publisher

Let's say that we want to inform a bunch of applications when a new course is added. Such use cases can be best implemented by a **JMS topic**. A topic can have many subscribers. When a message is added to the topic, all subscribers are sent the same message. This is unlike a queue, where only one queue listener gets a message.

Steps to publish messages to a topic and subscribe for messages are very similar to those for a queue, except for the different classes, and in some cases, different method names.

Let's implement a topic publisher, which we will use when the message for adding a course is successfully handled in the onMessage method of the listener class implemented in CourseQueueReceiver.

Create CourseTopicPublisher in the packt.jee.eclipse.jms package with the following content:

```
package packt.jee.eclipse.jms;

//skipped imports

public class CourseTopicPublisher {
  private TopicConnection connection;
  private TopicSession session;
  private Topic topic;

  public CourseTopicPublisher() throws Exception {
    InitialContext initCtx = new InitialContext();
    TopicConnectionFactory connectionFactory =
     (TopicConnectionFactory)initCtx.
        lookup("jms/CourseManagemenCF");
    connection = connectionFactory.createTopicConnection();
    connection.start();
    session = connection.createTopicSession(false,
     Session.AUTO_ACKNOWLEDGE);
    topic = (Topic)initCtx.lookup("jms/courseManagementTopic");
  }

  public void close() {
    if (connection != null) {
      try {
        connection.close();
      } catch (JMSException e) {
        e.printStackTrace();.
      }
    }
```

```
  }

  public void publishAddCourseMessage (CourseDTO course) throws
   Exception {
    TopicPublisher sender = session.createPublisher(topic);
    ObjectMessage objMessage =
      session.createObjectMessage(course);
    sender.send(objMessage);
  }
}
```

The code is quite simple and self-explanatory. Let's now modify the queue receiver class that we implemented, `CourseQueueReceiver`, to publish a message to the topic from the `onMessage` method, after the message from the queue is handled successfully:

```
public class CourseQueueReceiver {

  private CourseTopicPublisher topicPublisher;

  public CourseQueueReceiver(String name) throws Exception{

    //code to lookup connection factory, create session,
    //and look up queue remains unchanged. Skipping this code

    //create topic publisher
    topicPublisher = new CourseTopicPublisher();

    QueueReceiver receiver = session.createReceiver(queue);
    //register message listener
    receiver.setMessageListener(new MessageListener() {

      @Override
      public void onMessage(Message message) {
        //we expect ObjectMessage here; of type CourseDTO
        //Skipping validation
        try {
          //code to process message is unchanged. Skipping it

          //publish message to topic
          if (topicPublisher != null)
            topicPublisher.publishAddCourseMessage(course);

        } catch (Exception e) {
          e.printStackTrace();
          //TODO: handle and log exception
        }
      }
```

```
    });
  }

  //remaining code is unchanged. Skipping it
}
```

Implementing JMS topic subscriber

We will now implement a topic subscriber class to receive messages published to the topic we created earlier. Create a `CourseTopicSubscriber` class in the `packt.jee.eclipse.jms` package with the following content:

```
package packt.jee.eclipse.jms;
//skipping imports
public class CourseTopicSubscriber {

  private TopicConnection connection;
  private TopicSession session;
  private Topic topic;

  private String subscriberName;

  public CourseTopicSubscriber(String name) throws Exception{

    this.subscriberName = name;

    InitialContext initCtx = new InitialContext();
    TopicConnectionFactory connectionFactory =
(TopicConnectionFactory)initCtx.lookup("jms/CourseManagemenCF");
    connection = connectionFactory.createTopicConnection();
    connection.start();
    session = connection.createTopicSession(false,
      Session.AUTO_ACKNOWLEDGE);
    topic = (Topic)initCtx.lookup("jms/courseManagementTopic");

    TopicSubscriber subscriber = session.createSubscriber(topic);
    subscriber.setMessageListener(new MessageListener() {

      @Override
      public void onMessage(Message message) {
        //we expect ObjectMessage here; of type CourseDTO
        //skipping validation
        try {
          CourseDTO course = (CourseDTO)
            ((ObjectMessage)message).getObject();            //process
```

```
addCourse action. For example, save it in
          database               System.out.println("Received addCourse
notification for
          Course name - "                 + course.getName() + " in
Subscriber " +
               subscriberName);

        } catch (JMSException e) {
          e.printStackTrace();
          //TODO: handle and log exception
        }
      }
    });
  }

  public void stop() {
    if (connection != null) {
      try {
        connection.close();
      } catch (JMSException e) {
        e.printStackTrace();
        //TODO: log exception
      }
    }
  }
}
```

Again, the JMS APIs to subscribe to a topic are similar to those in `CourseQueueReceiver`, but with different class names and method names. We also identify subscribers with names so that we know which instance of the class receives the message.

In the preceding example, we created the topic subscriber by calling `TopicSession.createSubscriber`. In this case, the subscriber will receive messages from the topic as long as the subscriber is active. If the subscriber becomes inactive and then active again, it loses messages published by the topic during that period. If you want to make sure that the subscriber receives all the messages, you need to create a durable subscription using `TopicSession.createDurableSubscriber`. Along with the topic name, this method takes the subscriber name as the second argument. Refer to `https://javaee.github.io/javaee-spec/javadocs/javax/jms/TopicSession.html#createDurableSubscriber-javax.jms.Topic-java.lang.String-` for more information.

We will create two instances of the `CourseTopicSubscriber` class (so there will be two topic subscribers) in `JMSReceiverInitServlet`. These two instances will start listening for messages on application startup (the servlet is loaded on startup):

```
@WebServlet(urlPatterns="/JMSReceiverInitServlet", loadOnStartup=1)
public class JMSReceiverInitServlet extends HttpServlet {
  private CourseQueueReceiver courseQueueReceiver = null;
  private CourseTopicSubscriber courseTopicSubscriber = null;
  private CourseQueueReceiver courseQueueReceiver1 = null;
  private CourseTopicSubscriber courseTopicSubscriber1 = null;

    @Override
    public void init(ServletConfig config) throws ServletException
  {
      super.init(config);
      try {
      courseQueueReceiver = new CourseQueueReceiver("Receiver1");
      courseQueueReceiver1 = new CourseQueueReceiver("Receiver2");
      courseTopicSubscriber = new
        CourseTopicSubscriber("Subscriber1");        courseTopicSubscriber1 =
new
        CourseTopicSubscriber("Subscriber2");

    } catch (Exception e) {
      log("Error creating CourseQueueReceiver", e);
    }
    }

    //remaining code is unchanged. Skipping it
  }
```

We now have two queue listeners and two topic listeners ready when the application starts. Republish the project, execute `addCourse.jsp`, and add a course. Check the messages in the **Console** view of Eclipse. You will see that the message published in the topic is received by all subscribers, but the same message published in the queue is received by only one receiver:

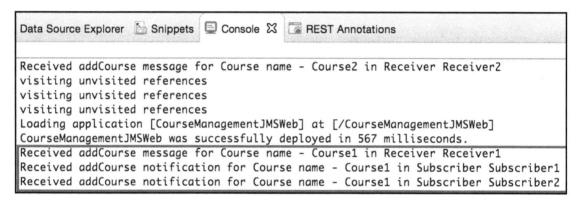

Data Source Explorer 📋 Snippets 🖥 Console ⌘ 🔳 REST Annotations

```
Received addCourse message for Course name - Course2 in Receiver Receiver2
visiting unvisited references
visiting unvisited references
visiting unvisited references
Loading application [CourseManagementJMSWeb] at [/CourseManagementJMSWeb]
CourseManagementJMSWeb was successfully deployed in 567 milliseconds.
Received addCourse message for Course name - Course1 in Receiver Receiver1
Received addCourse notification for Course name - Course1 in Subscriber Subscriber1
Received addCourse notification for Course name - Course1 in Subscriber Subscriber2
```

Figure 10.8: Console output showing multiple JMS receivers listening to JMS queue and topic

Creating JMS application using JSF and CDI beans

In this section, we will see how to create a JMS application using JSF and **Component Dependency Injection** (**CDI**) beans. With CDI beans, we can reduce the code that we wrote using JMS APIs, because we can use annotations to inject objects such as the JMS connection factory, queue, and topic. Once we obtain references to these objects, the steps to send or receive data are the same as those discussed in the previous section. Therefore, our examples in this section do not list the entire code. For the complete source code, download the source code for this chapter.

To prepare our project for using JSF, we need to create `web.xml` and add the JSF servlet definition and mapping in it. Right-click on the project and select the **Java EE Tools | Generate Deployment Descriptor Stub** option. This creates `web.xml` in the `WebContent/WEB-INF` folder. Add the following servlet definition and mapping (within the `web-app` tag) in `web.xml`:

```
<servlet>
  <servlet-name>JSFServelt</servlet-name>
```

```
    <servlet-class>javax.faces.webapp.FacesServlet</servlet-class>
    <load-on-startup>1</load-on-startup>
  </servlet>

  <servlet-mapping>
    <servlet-name>JSFServelt</servlet-name>
    <url-pattern>*.xhtml</url-pattern>
  </servlet-mapping>
```

For CDI beans to work, we need to create a `beans.xml` file in the `META-INF` folder. You will find the `META-INF` folder under the `WebContent` folder in the project in Eclipse. Let's create the `bean.xml` file in `META-INF` with the following content:

```
<beans xmlns="http://java.sun.com/xml/ns/javaee"
  xmlns:xsi="http://www.w3.org/2001/XMLSchema-instance"
  xsi:schemaLocation="
    http://java.sun.com/xml/ns/javaee
    http://java.sun.com/xml/ns/javaee/beans_1_0.xsd">
</beans>
```

We will now create two CDI beans for the JSF page. The first one is `CourseManagedMsgSenderBean`. The second one is `CourseJSFBean`, which will be referenced from the JSF page.

Create the `CourseManagedMsgSenderBean` class in the `packt.jee.eclipse.jms.jsf_bean` package with the following content:

```
package packt.jee.eclipse.jms.jsf_bean;

import javax.enterprise.context.SessionScoped;
import javax.inject.Named;
//skipped other imports

@Named("courseMessageSender")
@SessionScoped
public class CourseManagedMsgSenderBean implements Serializable {

  @Resource(name = "jms/CourseManagementCF")
  private QueueConnectionFactory connectionFactory;
  @Resource(lookup = "jms/courseManagementQueue")
  private Queue queue;
  QueueConnection connection;
  QueueSession session;
  Exception initException = null;
  @PostConstruct
  public void init() {
    try {
```

```
      connection = connectionFactory.createQueueConnection();
      connection.start();
      session = connection.createQueueSession(false,
Session.AUTO_ACKNOWLEDGE);
    } catch (Exception e) {
      initException = e;
    }
  }
  @PreDestroy
  public void cleanup() {
    if (connection != null) {
      try {
        connection.close();
      } catch (JMSException e) {
        e.printStackTrace();
        //TODO: log exception
      }
    }
  }
  public void addCourse(CourseDTO courseDTO) throws Exception {
    if (initException != null)
      throw initException;
    QueueSender sender = session.createSender(queue);
    ObjectMessage objMessage = session.createObjectMessage(courseDTO);
    sender.send(objMessage);
  }
}
```

Notice that the JMS connection factory and queue objects are injected using the `@Resource` annotation. We have used the `@PostConstruct` annotation to create a JMS a connection and a session and the `@PreDestroy` annotation for the clean-up operation. The `addCourse` method is similar to the code that we already implemented in the `CourseQueueSender` class in the previous section.

Let's now create the `CourseJSFBean` class in the `packt.jee.eclipse.jms.jsf_bean` package with the following content:

```java
package packt.jee.eclipse.jms.jsf_bean;

import javax.enterprise.context.RequestScoped;
import javax.inject.Inject;
import javax.inject.Named;

import packt.jee.eclipse.jms.dto.CourseDTO;;

@Named("course")
@RequestScoped
```

```
public class CourseJSFBean {
  private CourseDTO courseDTO = new CourseDTO();
  @Inject
  private CourseManagedMsgSenderBean courseMessageSender;

  public String getName() {
    return this.courseDTO.getName();
  }
  public void setName(String name) {
    this.courseDTO.setName(name);
  }
  public int getCredits() {
    return this.courseDTO.getCredits();
  }
  public void setCredits(int credits) {
    this.courseDTO.setCredits(credits);;
  }
  public void addCourse() throws Exception {
    //skipping validation
    //TODO: handle exception properly and show error message
    courseMessageSender.addCourse(courseDTO);
  }
}
```

An instance of `CourseManagedMsgSenderBean` is injected
into `CourseJSFBean` using the `@Inject` annotation. The `addCourse` method simply calls
the same named method in `CourseManagedMsgSenderBean`.

Finally, let's create `addCourse.xhtml` in the `WebContents` folder with the following
content:

```
<html xmlns="http://www.w3.org/1999/xhtml"
 xmlns:f="http://java.sun.com/jsf/core"
 xmlns:h="http://java.sun.com/jsf/html">

<head>
  <title>Add Course</title>
</head>

 <body>
  <h2>Course Details</h2>

  <h:form>
    <table>
      <tr>
        <td>Name:</td>
        <td>
```

```
        <h:inputText id="course_name" value="#{course.name}"/>
      </td>
    </tr>
    <tr>
      <td>Credits:</td>
      <td>
        <h:inputText id="course_credits"
         value="#{course.credits}"/>
      </td>
    </tr>
    <tr>
      <td colspan="2">
          <h:commandButton value="Submit"
           action="#{course.addCourse}"/>
      </td>
    </tr>
  </table>
  </h:form>

</body>

</html>
```

Form fields are bound to fields in `CourseJSFBean`. When the **Submit** button is clicked, the `addCourse` method of the same bean is called, which puts a message in the JMS queue.

Republish the project and execute `addCourse.xhtml` by right-clicking it and selecting **Run As** | **Run on Server**. Add a course and see the message printed in the GlassFish **Console** view of Eclipse.

Consuming JMS messages using MDBs

Message-driven beans (MDBs) make consuming JMS messages a lot easier. With just a couple of annotations and implementing the `onMessage` method, you can make any Java object a consumer of JMS messages. In this section, we will implement an MDB to consume messages from the `Course` queue. To implement MDBs, we need to create an EJB project. Select **File** | **New** | **EJB Project** from the main menu:

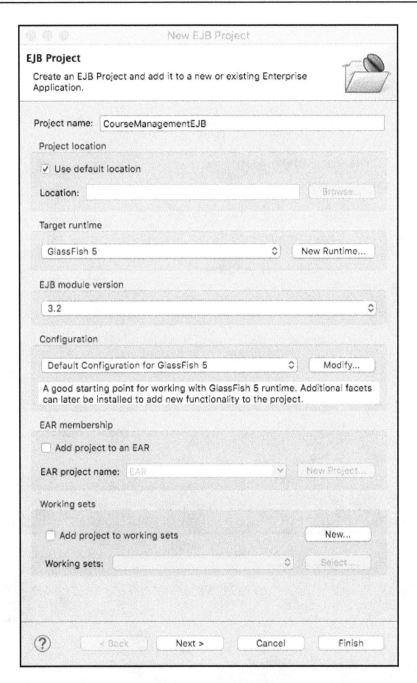

Figure 10.9: Create a EJB project to implement MDBs

Enter **Project name** as `CourseManagementEJB`. Click **Next**. Accept the default values on the subsequent pages and click **Finish** on the last page.

Right-click on the project and select the **New** | **Message-Driven Bean** option. This opens the MDB creation wizard:

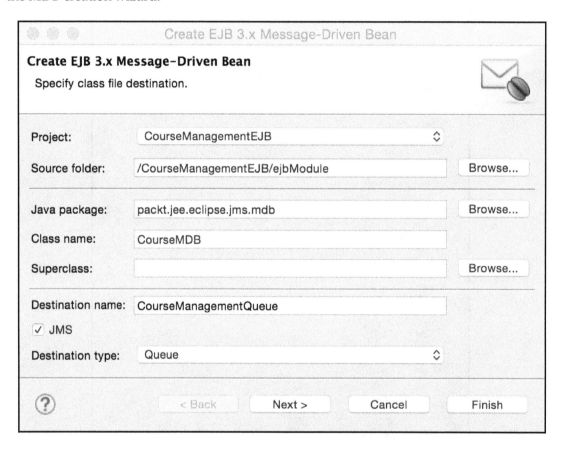

Figure 10.10: MDB creation wizard – class file information

Enter `packt.jee.eclipse.jms.mdb` as **Java package** and `CourseMDB` as **Class name**. Keep **Destination type** as **Queue**.

Destination name is the physical destination name that we specified when creating the queue and is not the JNDI name:

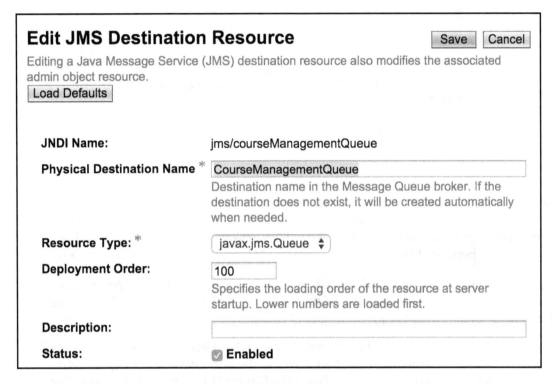

Figure 10.11: JMS queue physical destination name in the GlassFish admin console

Enter `CourseManagementQueue` as **Destination type**. Click **Next**. Accept the default values on the second page and click **Finish**. The wizard generates the following code:

```
@MessageDriven(
    activationConfig = {
        @ActivationConfigProperty(propertyName = "destinationType",
            propertyValue = "javax.jms.Queue"),
        @ActivationConfigProperty(propertyName = "destination",
            propertyValue = "CourseManagementQueue")
    },
    mappedName = "jms/courseManagementQueue")
public class CourseMDB implements MessageListener {

    /**
     * Default constructor.
     */
```

```
    public CourseMDB() {
        // TODO Auto-generated constructor stub
    }

/**
    * @see MessageListener#onMessage(Message)
    */
    public void onMessage(Message message) {
        System.out.println("addCourse message received in
          CourseMDB");

    }

}
```

The class is annotated with @MessageDriven with activationConfig and the JMS destination parameters specified in the wizard. It also creates the onMessage method. In this method, we just print the message that the MDB received for adding a course. To process ObjectMessage in this class, we will have to refactor the CourseDTO class to a shared .jar between EJB and the web project. This is left to the readers as an exercise.

The JEE container creates a pool of MDB objects for a single MDB class. An incoming message can be handled by any one of the instances of MDB in the pool. This can help in building a scalable message processing application.

If you want to test the MDB, add the project to the GlassFish Server configured in Eclipse. To do this, right-click on the configured server in the **Servers** view of Eclipse and select the **Add and Remove...** option. Select the **CourseManagementEJB** project that we created and click **Finish**. Make sure that the server is started and the status is **[Started, Synchronized]**. You also need to add the **CourseManagementJMSWeb** project to the server, because we have JSF and JSP pages to add a course in that project. Run addCourse.xhtml or addCourse.jsp from the **CourseManagementJMSWeb** project, add a course, and check the GlassFish console in Eclipse for messages printed from message receivers and the MDB we created in this section. However, note that either the MDB or one of the queue listeners we developed in **CourseManagementJMSWeb** will be receiving the message, and not all of the receivers.

Summary

A messaging system can be a powerful tool for integrating disparate applications. It provides an asynchronous model of programming. The client does not wait for the response from the server and the server does not necessarily process requests at the same time that the client sends them. A messaging system can also be useful for building scalable applications and batch processing. JMS provides uniform APIs to access different messaging systems.

In this chapter, we learned how to send and receive messages from queues and to publish and subscribe messages from topics. There are many different ways to use JMS APIs. We started with the basic JMS APIs and then learned how annotations can help reduce some of the code. We also learned how to use MDBs to consume messages.

In the next chapter, we will see some of the techniques and tools used for profiling CPU and memory usages in Java applications.

11
Java CPU Profiling and Memory Tracking

In the previous chapter, we learned how to use the JMS (Java Messaging Service) APIs to write asynchronous applications. In this chapter, we will learn about some of the techniques and tools used to profile Java applications. Enterprise applications tend to be quite complex and big. There could be situations where the application does not perform as per your requirements or expectations. For example, some of the operations performed in the application might be taking too long or consuming more memory than you expected. Furthermore, debugging performance and memory issues can sometimes become very difficult.

Fortunately, there are tools available, both in JDK and Eclipse, to help us debug these issues. JDK 6 (update 7) and above are bundled with the **jVisualVM** application that can connect to remote or local applications. You can find this tool in the `<JDK_HOME>/bin` folder. jVisualVM can help you profile memory and CPU usage. It can also be configured to launch from Eclipse when an application is run from Eclipse. We will learn how to use VisualVM to profile Java applications in this chapter. You can find detailed information about jVisualVM/VisualVM at `https://visualvm.github.io/`.

We will create a small standalone Java application to simulate performance and memory issues, and will see how to use VisualVM for troubleshooting. Although the real applications that you may want to troubleshoot will be a lot more complex, the techniques that we will learn in this chapter can be used for complex applications too.

In this chapter, we will cover the following topics:

- CPU and memory profiling using VisualVM
- Techniques to detect memory leaks and deadlocks
- Using the Eclipse Memory Analyzer to analyze heap dumps created from VisualVM

Creating a sample Java project for profiling

We will create a simple standalone Java application so that it is easy for you to learn how to profile using VisualVM. Although it will be a standalone application, we will create classes that are similar to those we created for the `CourseManagement` web application in some of the previous chapters, particularly `CourseDTO`, `CourseBean` (JSP bean), `CourseService` (service bean), and `CourseDAO` (for database access).

1. Create a standard Java project in Eclipse, named `CourseManagementStandalone`. Create the `CourseDTO` class in the `packt.jee.eclipse.profile.dto` package:

   ```
   package packt.jee.eclipse.profile.dto;

   public class CourseDTO {
     private int id;
     private String name;
     private int credits;

     //skipped Getters and Setters
   }
   ```

2. Create the `CourseDAO` class in the `packt.jee.eclopse.profile.dao` package:

   ```
   //skipped imports
   public class CourseDAO {

     public List<CourseDTO> getCourses() {
       //No real database access takes place here
       //We will just simulate a long-running database operation

       try {
         Thread.sleep(2000); //wait 2 seconds
       } catch (InterruptedException e) {
         e.printStackTrace();
       }

       //return dummy/empty list
       return new ArrayList<>();
     }
   }
   ```

   We have simulated a long-running database operation in the `getCourses` method by making the thread sleep for a few seconds.

3. Create the `CourseService` class in the
   `packt.jee.eclipse.profile.service` package:

```
//skipped imports
public class CourseService {

    private CourseDAO courseDAO = new CourseDAO();


    public List<CourseDTO> getCourses() {
        return courseDAO.getCourses();
    }
}
```

`CourseService.getCourses` delegates the call to `CourseDAO`.

4. Create the `CourseBean` class in the `packt.jee.eclipse.profile.bean`
   package:

```
//skipped imports
public class CourseBean {
    private CourseService courseService = new CourseService();
    public List<CourseDTO> getCourses() {
        return courseService.getCourses();
    }
}
```

`CourseBean.getcourses` delegates to `CourseService`.

5. Finally, create the `CourseManagement` class in
   the `packt.jee.eclipse.profile` package. This class contains the `main`
   method and starts the loop to call the `getCourses` method repeatedly after
   reading any character from the standard input:

```
//skipped imports
public class CourseManagement {

    public static void main(String[] args) throws IOException {

        CourseBean courseBean = new CourseBean();

        System.out.println("Type any character to get courses. Type q
          to quit.");

        int ch;
        while ((ch = System.in.read()) != -1) {
```

```
            if (ch != 10 && ch != 13) { //ignore new lines
              if (ch == 'q') //quit if user types q
                break;

            System.out.println("Getting courses");
            List<CourseDTO> courses = courseBean.getCourses();
            System.out.println("Got courses");

            System.out.println("Type any character to get courses.
              Type q to quit.");
          }
        }

        System.out.println("Quitting ...");
      }
    }
```

6. Run the application (right-click on the file and select **Run As | Java Application**). In the console window, type any character and press *Enter*. You should see the **Getting courses** and **Got courses** messages.

Profiling the Java application

1. Run jvisualvm from the `<JDK_HOME>/bin` folder:

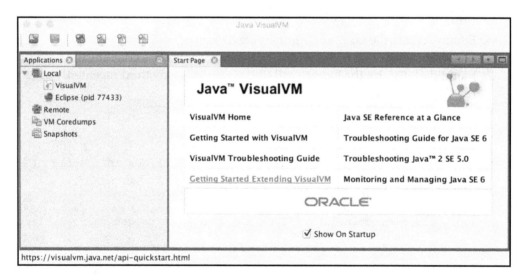

Figure 11.1: Java VisualVM profiler

VisualVM lists all the Java processes that can be profiled by it on the local machine under the **Local** node. You can see VisualVM itself listed along with Eclipse.

2. Once you run the `CourseManagement` application, the process should also show up under **Local**:

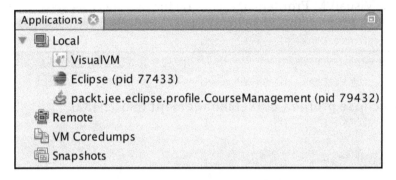

Figure 11.2: The CourseManagement application available for profiling

3. Double-click on the process (or right-click and select **Open**). Then, go to the **Profile** tab and click on the **CPU** button:

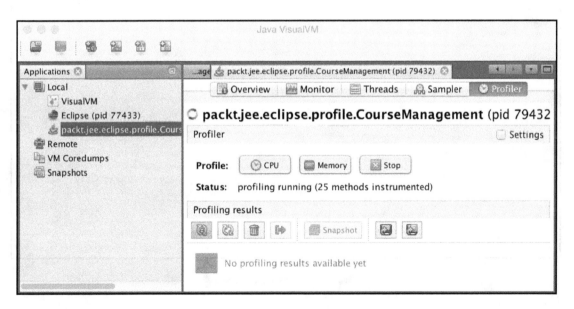

Figure 11.3: VisualVM Profiler tab

You should see the status set as **profiling running**.

4. After starting CPU profiling, if you get an error such as **Redefinition failed with error 62**, try running the application with the `-XVerify:none` parameter. In Eclipse, select the **Run | Run Configurations** menu and then select the **CourseManagement** application under the **Java Application** group. Go to the **Arguments** tab and add `-Xverify:none` to **VM arguments**. Run the application again.

5. In the VisualVM **Profiler** page, click on the **Settings** checkbox to see the packages included for profiling. Note that VisualVM selects these packages automatically:

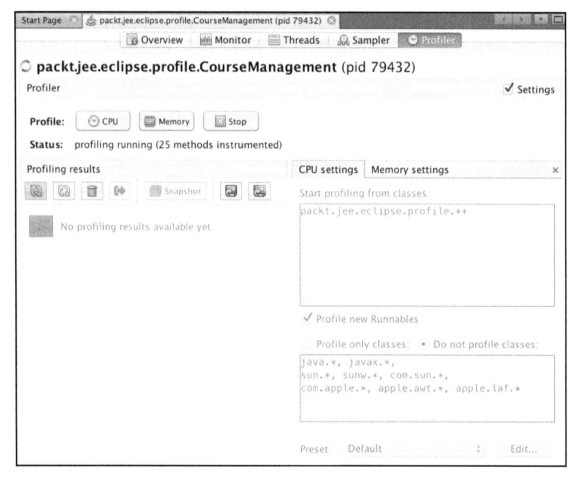

Figure 11.4: VisualVM Profiler settings

6. You must stop CPU profiling to edit the settings. However, we will retain the default settings. Uncheck the **Settings** box to hide the settings.

7. Click on the **Monitor** table for the overview of profiling activities:

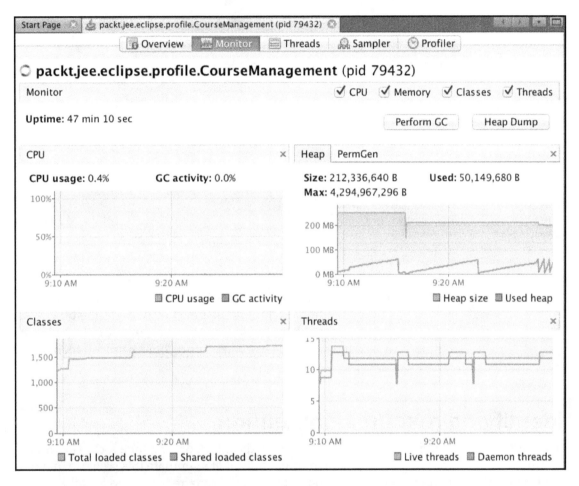

Figure 11.5: Overview of profiling activities

8. Now, let's execute the getCourse method in our application. Go to the console view of Eclipse in which our application is running, type a character (other than q), and hit *Enter*. Go to the **Profiler** tab of VisualVM to view the profiled data:

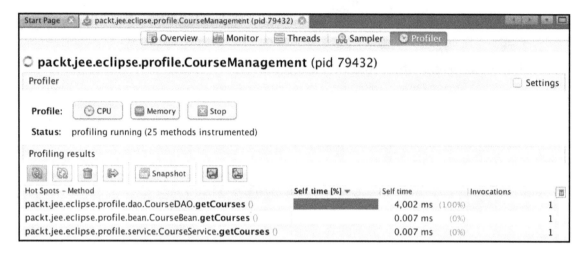

Figure 11.6: CPU profiling of CourseManagement

Observe the **Self time** column. This indicates the CPU time or the elapsed time to execute the corresponding method, excluding the time taken to execute other methods called from this method. In our case, CourseDAO.getCourses took the maximum time, so it is at the top of the list. This report could help you identify the bottlenecks in your application.

Identifying resource contention

In a multithreaded application, it is typical for threads to lock or wait for a lock. The thread dump can be used for identifying resource contentions. Let's simulate this scenario in our application by modifying the main method of the CourseManagement class to call courseBean.getCourses in separate threads:

```
public class CourseManagement {

    public static void main(String[] args) throws IOException {

        final CourseBean courseBean = new CourseBean();

        System.out.println("Type any character to get courses. Type q
        to quit.");
```

```
    int ch, threadIndex = 0;
    while ((ch = System.in.read()) != -1) {
      if (ch != 10 && ch != 13) { //ignore new lines
        if (ch == 'q') //quit if user types q
          break;

        threadIndex++; //used for naming the thread
        Thread getCourseThread = new Thread("getCourseThread" +
        threadIndex)
{

          @Override
          public void run() {
            System.out.println("Getting courses");
            courseBean.getCourses();
            System.out.println("Got courses");
          }
        };

        //Set this thread as Daemon so that the application can exit
        //immediately when user enters 'q'
        getCourseThread.setDaemon(true);

        getCourseThread.start();

        System.out.println("Type any character to get courses.
          Type q to quit.");
      }
    }

    System.out.println("Quitting ...");
  }
}
```

Note that we create a new `Thread` object in the `while` loop and call
`courseBean.getCourses` in the `run` method of the thread. The `while` loop does not wait
for `getCourses` to return results and can process the next user input immediately. This
will allow us to simulate resource contention.

To actually cause resource contention, let's synchronize `CourseService.getCourses`:

```
public class CourseService {

  private CourseDAO courseDAO = new CourseDAO();

  public synchronized List<CourseDTO> getCourses() {
    return courseDAO.getCourses();
  }
}
```

The synchronized `getCourses` method will result in only one thread executing this method in an instance of the `CourseService` class. We can now trigger multiple `getCourses` calls simultaneously by typing characters in the console without waiting for the previous calls to the `getCourse` method to return. To give us more time to get the thread dump, let's increase the thread sleep time in `CourseDAO.getCourses` to, say, 30 seconds:

```
public class CourseDAO {

    public List<CourseDTO> getCourses() {
      //No real database access takes place here.
      //We will just simulate a long-running database operation

      try {
        Thread.sleep(30000); //wait 30 seconds
      } catch (InterruptedException e) {
        e.printStackTrace();
      }

      //return dummy/empty list
      return new ArrayList<>();
    }
}
```

Run the application and let's start monitoring this process in VisualVM. In the console window where the application is running in Eclipse, type a character and press *Enter*. Repeat this one more time. Now, two calls to `getCourses` will be triggered. In VisualVM, go to the **Threads** tab and click on the **ThreadDump** button. A new thread dump will be saved under the process node and will be displayed in a new tab. Look for threads starting with the `getCourseThread` prefix. Here is a sample thread dump of two `getCourseThreads`:

```
"getCourseThread2" daemon prio=6 tid=0x000000001085b800 nid=0x34f8 waiting
for monitor entry [0x0000000013aef000]
```

```
    java.lang.Thread.State: BLOCKED (on object monitor)
    at
packt.jee.eclipse.profile.service.CourseService.getCourses(CourseService.ja
va:13)  - waiting to lock <0x00000007aaf57a80> (a
 packt.jee.eclipse.profile.service.CourseService)
    at
packt.jee.eclipse.profile.bean.CourseBean.getCourses(CourseBean.java:12)
    at
packt.jee.eclipse.profile.CourseManagement$1.run(CourseManagement.java:27)

    Locked ownable synchronizers:
    - None

"getCourseThread1" daemon prio=6 tid=0x000000001085a800 nid=0x2738 waiting
on condition [0x000000001398f000]
    java.lang.Thread.State: TIMED_WAITING (sleeping)
    at java.lang.Thread.sleep(Native Method)
    at packt.jee.eclipse.profile.dao.CourseDAO.getCourses(CourseDAO.java:15)
    at
packt.jee.eclipse.profile.service.CourseService.getCourses(CourseService.ja
va:13)
    - locked <0x00000007aaf57a80> (a
packt.jee.eclipse.profile.service.CourseService)
    at
packt.jee.eclipse.profile.bean.CourseBean.getCourses(CourseBean.java:12)
    at
packt.jee.eclipse.profile.CourseManagement$1.run(CourseManagement.java:27)

    Locked ownable synchronizers:
    - None
```

From the preceding thread dumps, it is clear that `getCourseThread2` is waiting (`to lock <0x00000007aaf57a80>`) and that `getCourseThread1` is holding lock on the same object (`locked <0x00000007aaf57a80>`).

Using the same technique (of inspecting locks), you can also detect deadlocks in the application. In fact, VisualVM can detect deadlocks and explicitly point to threads that are deadlocked. Let's modify the `main` method in the `CourseManagement` class to cause a deadlock. We will create two threads and make them lock two objects in the reverse order:

Warning

The following code will cause the application to hang. You will have to kill the process to exit.

```
public static void main(String[] args) throws IOException {

    System.out.println("Type any character and Enter to cause
     deadlock - ");
    System.in.read();

    final Object obj1 = new Object(), obj2 = new Object();

    Thread th1 = new Thread("MyThread1") {
      public void run() {
        synchronized (obj1) {
          try {
            sleep(2000);
          } catch (InterruptedException e) {
            e.printStackTrace();
          }

          synchronized (obj2) {
            //do nothing
          }
        }
      }
    };

    Thread th2 = new Thread("MyThread2") {
      public void run() {
        synchronized (obj2) {
          try {
            sleep(2000);
          } catch (InterruptedException e) {
            e.printStackTrace();
          }

          synchronized (obj1) {

          }
```

```
        }
      }
   };
```

```
   th1.start();
   th2.start();
```

`MyThread1` first locks `obj1` and then it tries to lock `obj2`, whereas `MyThread2` locks `obj2` first and then tries to lock `obj1`. When you monitor this application using VisualVM and switch to the **Threads** tab, you will see the **Deadlock detected!** message:

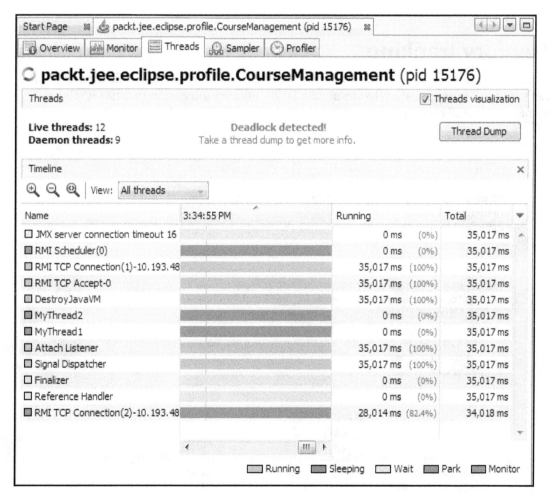

Figure 11.7: Detecting deadlock with VisualVM

If you take the thread dump, it will specifically show you where the deadlock is caused:

```
Found one Java-level deadlock:
=============================
"MyThread2":
  waiting to lock monitor 0x000000000f6f71a8 (object
0x00000007aaf56538, a java.lang.Object),
  which is held by "MyThread1"
"MyThread1":
  waiting to lock monitor 0x000000000f6f4a78 (object
0x00000007aaf56548, a java.lang.Object),
  which is held by "MyThread2"
```

Memory tracking

VisualVM can be used to monitor memory allocations and detect possible memory leaks. Let's modify our application to simulate a large memory allocation that has not been released. We will modify the `CourseService` class:

```
public class CourseService {

    private CourseDAO courseDAO = new CourseDAO();

    //Dummy cached data used only to simulate large
    //memory allocation
    private byte[] cachedData = null;

    public synchronized List<CourseDTO> getCourses() {

      //To simulate large memory allocation,
      //let's assume we are reading serialized cached data
      //and storing it in the cachedData member
      try {
        this.cachedData = generateDummyCachedData();
      } catch (IOException e) {
        //ignore
      }

      return courseDAO.getCourses();
    }

    private byte[] generateDummyCachedData() throws IOException {
      ByteArrayOutputStream byteStream = new ByteArrayOutputStream();
      byte[] dummyData = "Dummy cached data".getBytes();

      //write 100000 times
```

```
    for (int i = 0; i < 100000; i++)
      byteStream.write(dummyData);

    byte[] result = byteStream.toByteArray();
    byteStream.close();
    return result;
  }
}
```

In the `getCourses` method, we will create a large byte array and store it in a member variable. The memory allocated to the array will not be released until the instance of `CourseService` is not garbage collected. Now, let's see how this memory allocation shows up in VisualVM. Start monitoring the process and go to the **Profiler** tab. Click on the **Memory** button to start monitoring memory. Now, go back to the console window in Eclipse and enter a character to trigger the `getCourses` method. Go to VisualVM to inspect the memory profiling report:

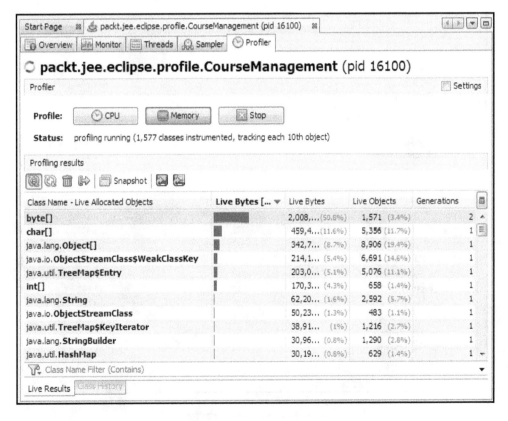

Figure 11.8: Memory monitoring with VisualVM

This report shows the live status of the memory consumed by different objects in the application. However, if you want to analyze and find where exactly the allocation is made, then take a heap dump. Go to the **Monitor** tab and click on the **Heap Dump** button. The heap dump report is saved under the process node. Click on the **Classes** button in the heap dump report, and then click on the **Size** column to sort objects in descending order of the amount of memory consumed:

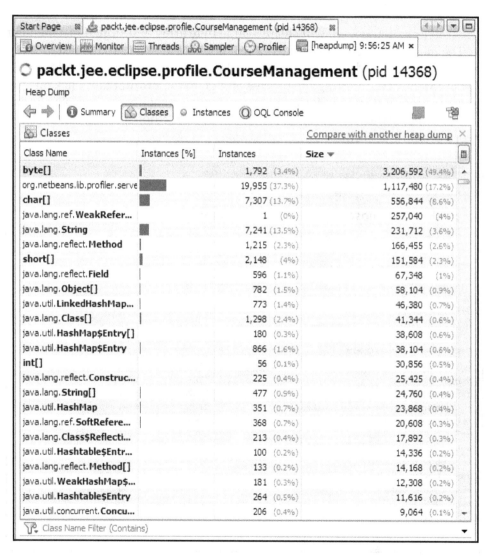

Figure 11.9: Classes in the heap dump report

According to the report, `byte[]` takes up the maximum memory in our application. To find where the memory is allocated, double-click on the row containing `byte[]`:

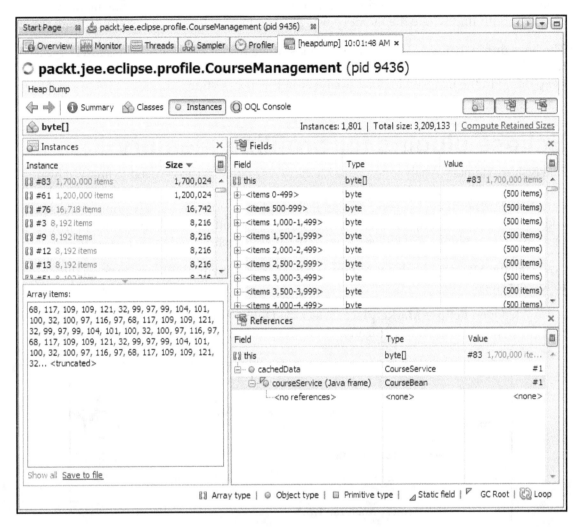

Figure 11.10: Object instance report in heap dump

The references window at the bottom-right shows objects holding a reference to the selected instance in the top-left window. As you can see, a reference to `byte[]` is held by the `cachedData` field of `CourseServe`. Furthermore, a reference to `CourseService` is held by `CourseBean`.

Large memory allocation does not necessarily mean a memory leak. You may want to keep a reference to a large object in your application. However, the heap dump can help you find where the memory was allocated and if that instance is intended to be in the memory. If not, you could find where the memory was allocated and release it at the appropriate place.

The heap dump that we have taken will be lost if we restart VisualVM. Therefore, save it to the disk; to do so, right-click on the **Heap Dump** node and select **Save As**. We will use this heap dump in the Eclipse Memory Analyzer in the next section.

Eclipse plugins for profiling memory

The Eclipse Memory Analyzer (`https://eclipse.org/mat/`) can be used to analyze heap dumps created by VisualVM. It provides additional features such as auto memory leak detection. Furthermore, by using it as an Eclipse plugin, you can quickly jump to the source code from the heap dump reports. You can use this tool either as a standalone application or as an Eclipse plugin. We will see how to use it as an Eclipse plugin in this section.

To install the Memory Analyzer plugin and analyze the memory dump, perform the following steps:

1. Open **Eclipse Marketplace** (select the **Help** | **Eclipse Marketplace** menu). Search for `Memory Analyzer` and install the plugin:

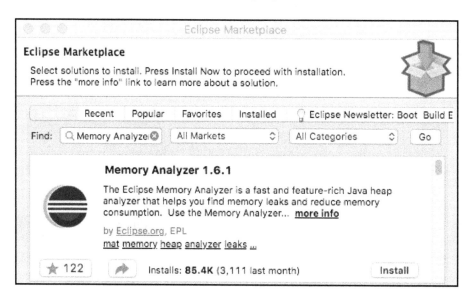

Figure 11.11: Searching for the Memory Analyzer plugin in Eclipse Marketplace

2. Open the heap dump that you saved in the previous section. Select the **File** |
   Open File menu and select the .hprof file that has been saved by VisualVM.
   Memory Analyzer will prompt you to select a report type:

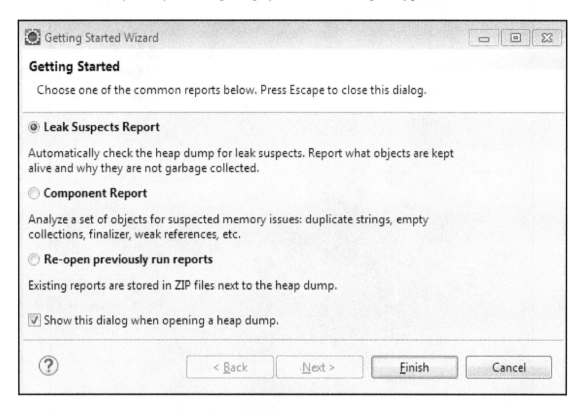

Figure 11.12: Eclipse Memory Analyzer: Getting Started Wizard

3. Select **Leak Suspects Report** and click on **Finish**. The Eclipse Memory Analyzer creates the **Leak Suspects** report with a couple of **Problem Suspects**:

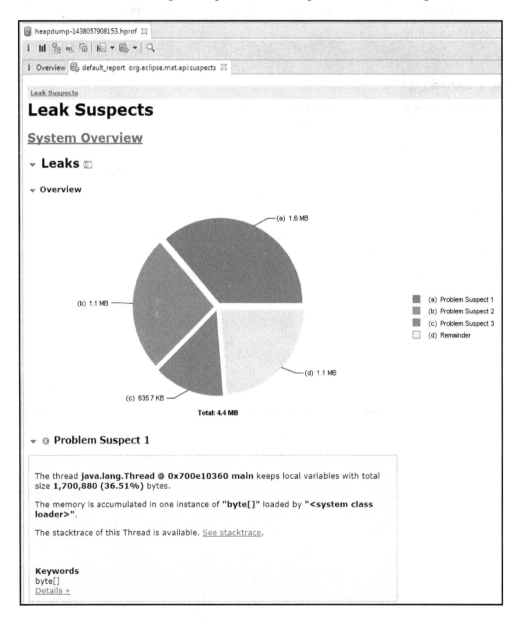

Figure 11.13: Eclipse Memory Analyzer: Leak Suspect report

4. Click on the **Details** link in the first **Problem Suspect**:

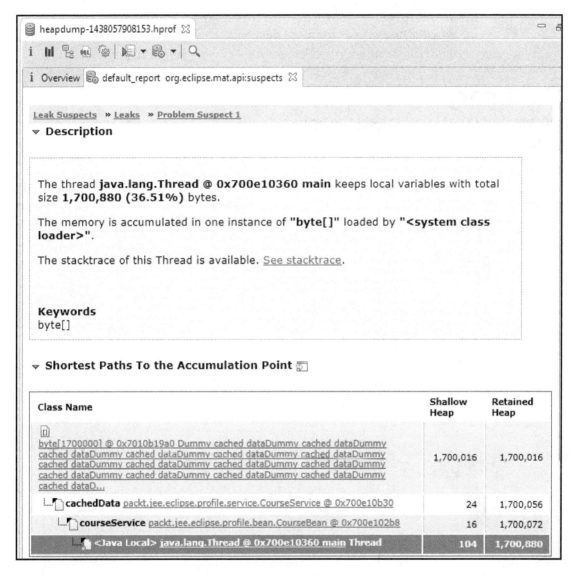

Figure 11.14: Eclipse Memory Analyzer: Details of Problem Suspect

The report clearly identifies cachedData in CourseService as a leak suspect. To open the source file, click on the node and select the **Open Source File** option.

Memory Analyzer also provides many other useful reports. Refer to
`http://help.eclipse.org/oxygen/index.jsp?topic=/org.eclipse.mat.`
`ui.help/welcome.html` for more details.

Summary

The VisualVM tool that is shipped with JDK 6 and above is useful for detecting performance bottlenecks and memory leaks.

In this chapter, we learned how to use this tool in a simple Java application. However, the technique can be used in large applications too. The Eclipse Memory Analyzer can be used to quickly detect memory leaks from a heap dump. In the next chapter we will learn how to develop Microservices in JEE.

12
Microservices

In the previous chapter, we learned how to profile Java applications in order to troubleshoot performance issues.

In this chapter, we will learn how to develop JEE microservices using Eclipse. We will also learn how to deploy microservices in Docker containers. We will develop simple microservices for our *Course Management* use case.

We will cover the following topics:

- Introduction to microservices and Eclipse MicroProfile
- Developing JEE microservices using the WildFly Swarm and Spring Boot frameworks
- Introduction to Docker and Docker Compose
- Deploying microservices in Docker containers

What is a microservice?

A microservice is a small application designed to perform a specific business task well. Microservices are typically implemented as RESTful web services. The following are some of the characteristics of a microservice:

- Smaller in size (compared to monolithic applications), and focuses on a single business task/module
- Has its own database, in contrast to a monolithic application that has one database for all business functionalities
- Is typically a standalone application, with a web container bundled into it

A large business application can be built by assembling smaller microservices. Compared to a large monolithic application, a microservice architecture provides the following benefits:

- They are easy to deploy. In a monolithic application, deployment can be quite cumbersome because of the complexity of the application. Microservices are small and can be easily deployed on servers.
- Microservices are loosely coupled, so changes in one can be isolated from other services in an application. Also, having a separate database for each service can further insulate the main application and other services from changes made in the schema of the database.

To understand the contrast between monolithic application architecture and microservice architecture, let's see an example. Throughout this book, we have been following the *Course Management* example. Let's say this module is part of a larger **University Management System**, which has many more modules. A monolithic architecture for this application can be viewed as follows:

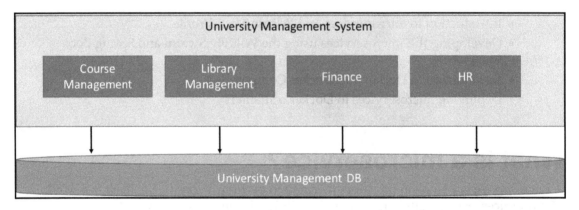

Figure 12.1: Monolithic application architecture

We have one large application, the **University Management System**, with multiple modules and a single database.

The same application can be architected using microservices as follows:

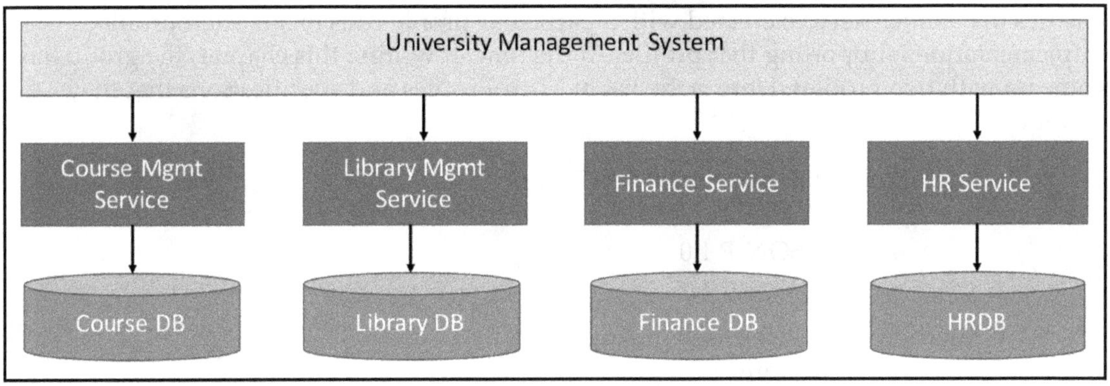

Figure 12.2: Microservice application architecture

In the microservice architecture, the **University Management System** is composed of many microservices, each with its own database.

Eclipse MicroProfile

Microservices can be built with the current JEE specification (JEE 8). However, there are certain specifications within JEE that are more important for developing microservices, such as JAX-RS (for RESTful Web Services) and JSON-P (for processing JSON data). So, a group of organizations has come together to create specifications for developing and running microservices, which are categorized as MicroProfile. Many of the specifications under MicroProfile are already part of the JEE specification (such as JAX-RS and JSON-P), but some are new specifications, such as for configuring and monitoring microservices.

The group has come up with two profiles so far. Each MicroProfile-compliant implementation is expected to implement each specification in the supported profile. This ensures that a microservice created with a particular profile runs on all Microprofile implementations supporting that profile. At the time of writing this chapter, the group has come up with two profiles. Here is the list of MicroProfiles and specifications that they include:

- MicroProfile 1.0 (released in Sep 2016):
    - CDI 1.2
    - JSON-P 1.0
    - JAX-RS 2.0
- MicroProfile 1.1 (released in August 2017):
    - Config 1.0
    - CDI 1.2
    - JSON-P 1.0
    - JAX-RS 2.0

MicroProfile 2.0 is expected to be released in June 2018, and it will include updates to some of the specifications as per JEE 8. Some of the implementations of MicroProfiles are WildFly Swarm (`http://wildfly-swarm.io/`), WebSphere Liberty (`https://developer.ibm.com/wasdev/websphere-liberty/`), Payara (`http://www.payara.fish/`), and Apache TomEE (`http://tomee.apache.org/`). Visit the official website for MicroProfiles at `https://microprofile.io/` for more information.

In the next section, we will see how to implement a microservice for our *Course Management* use case using two solutions:

- Using a MicroProfile implementation (WildFly Swarm)
- Using Spring Boot, which is not part of MicroProfile

Later, we will see how to deploy microservices in Docker containers.

 To follow the code examples in this chapter, you need to be familiar with JPA and REST APIs. Refer to `Chapter 4`, *Creating JEE Database Applications*, for JPA concepts and `Chapter 9`, *Creating Web Services*, for RESTful web services.

Setting up a database for a microservice project

We are going to implement a microservice to get a list of courses. We will use the same MySQL database, course_management, that we have been using in this book. Refer to *Installing MySQL* in Chapter 1, *Introducing JEE and Eclipse*, if you need information on how to install and set up MySQL. If you haven't already created the course_management schema, then refer to the *Creating database schema* section in Chapter 4, *Creating JEE Database Applications*. At this point, we will assume that the MySQL database is running and the course_management schema with the Course, Course_Student, Student, and Teacher tables exists.

We will use JPA to access this database. See the *Creating a database application using JPA* section in Chapter 4, *Creating JEE Database Applications*, if you are not familiar with JPA. We are going to use EclipseLink as the JPA provider.

Implementing microservices using WildFly Swarm

WildFly Swarm (http://wildfly-swarm.io/) is a MicroProfile implementation from Red Hat. It allows you to assemble an application container for running microservices with just the specifications you need.

Creating a WildFly Swarm project

Let's use WildFly Swarm Project Generator at http://wildfly-swarm.io/generator/ to select the specifications we want to include in our application and to create the starter project:

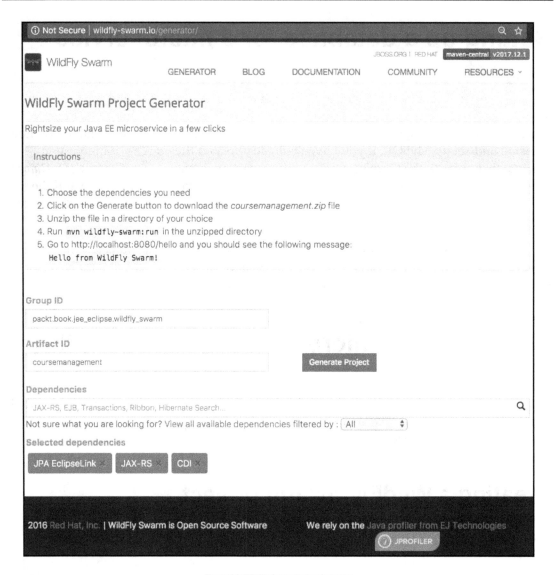

Figure 12.3: WildFly Swarm Project Generator

Enter **Group ID** and **Artifact ID** as shown in the previous screenshot. In the **Dependencies** textbox, start typing features such as **JPA** or **JAX-RS** and then select them from the auto-suggested options. Make sure **JPA EclipseLink** , **JAX-RS**, and **CDI** are selected as dependencies. If you want to see all available dependencies and select from that list, then click the **View all available dependencies** link.

Click the **Generate Project** button to create the project and download the ZIP file. This is a Maven project. Unzip the file in a folder and import the project as a Maven project in Eclipse (by selecting the menu option **File | Import** and then selecting **Existing Maven Projects** in the **Maven** category).

Right-click on the Eclipse **Project Explorer** and select **Run As | Maven Build**. In the configuration window, type `wildfly-swarm:run` in the **Goals** field:

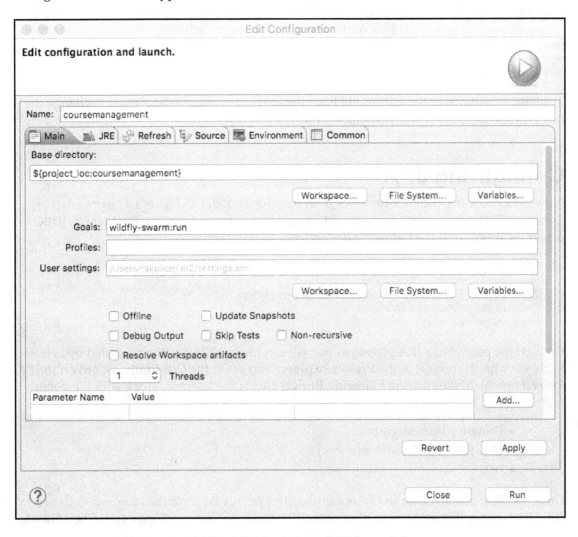

Figure 12.4: Maven Build Configuration to create a WildFly Swarm application

Click **Run**. Maven will download and install the dependencies and then run the application (you will see a **Wildfly Swarm is Ready** message in the console when the application is ready). Open `http://localhost:8080/hello` to test the default endpoint created by the application generator. You should see the `hello` message.

If you look into the target folder of the project, you will see `demo-swarm.jar` and `demo.war`. When we executed the **wildfly-swarm:run** goal, Maven starts a JBoss container and deploys the WAR file. The microservice can also be run by executing the single JAR file, `demo-swarm.jar`. This JAR contains all the packages, including the application server to run the microservice. Simply run this from the command line:

```
java -jar demo-swarm.jar
```

To change the name of the output file from demo to, say, `coursemanagement`, change the name in `pom.xml` in `<filename>` under the `<build>` tag.

Configuring JPA

Now, let's add a dependency for MySQL in the project. Refer to *Figure 4.11* in Chapter 4, *Creating JEE Database Applications*, for adding a Maven dependency for the MySQL JDBC driver, or simply add the following dependency to `pom.xml`:

```
<dependency>
    <groupId>mysql</groupId>
    <artifactId>mysql-connector-java</artifactId>
    <version>8.0.8-dmr</version>
</dependency>
```

Convert the project to a JPA project so that we can use the JPA tooling provided by Eclipse. Right-click on the project in the **Project Explorer** and select the **Configure** | **Convert to JPA Project** option. Make sure the following **Project Facets** are selected, along with the default facets:

- Dynamic Web Module
- JAX-RS (RESTful web services)
- JPA

Click the **Next** button (refer to *Figure 4.20 Add JPA facet to the project* of Chapter 4, *Creating JEE Database Applications*) and configure the JPA facet as shown in *Figure 4.21*. Click **Finish**.

Let's now configure the JDBC connection in `persistence.xml`. Follow steps 7 through 9 in the *Converting project into a JPA project* section in `Chapter 4`, *Creating JEE Database Applications*. Your `persistence.xml` should now have the following persistence unit:

```
<persistence-unit name="coursemanagement" transaction-
type="RESOURCE_LOCAL">
  <properties>
    <provider>org.eclipse.persistence.jpa.PersistenceProvider</provider>
<class>packt.book.jeeeclipse.wildflyswarm.coursemanagement.rest.Course</cla
ss>
    <property name="javax.persistence.jdbc.driver"
value="com.mysql.cj.jdbc.Driver"/>
    <property name="javax.persistence.jdbc.url"
value="jdbc:mysql://localhost/course_management"/>
    <property name="javax.persistence.jdbc.user"
value="<enter_your_user_name> "/>
    <property name="javax.persistence.jdbc.password"
value="<enter_your_password> "/>
  </properties>
</persistence-unit>
```

In the previous XML file, we are
specifying the `org.eclipse.persistence.jpa.PersistenceProvider` class as our JPA provider and then setting properties for connecting to the MySQL database.

Next, create folders named `resources/META-INF` under `src/main` and copy `persistence.xml` into the `src/main/resources` folder. If Eclipse displays errors in JPA configuration, right-click on the project name in **Project Explorer** and select **Maven | Update Project**. The reason for doing this is that Maven expects files that you want to copy to the `classes` folder to be in the `src/main/resources` folder. We need to have `META-INF/persistence.xml` in the `classes` folder so that the JPA provider can load it.

Creating a course entity bean and a JPA factory

If you are not familiar with JPA, refer to the *JPA concepts* section in `Chapter 4`, *Creating JEE Database Applications*.

We will now create `Course.java` in the
`packt.book.jeeeclipse.wildflyswarm.coursemanagement.rest` package:

```
package packt.book.jeeeclipse.wildflyswarm.coursemanagement.rest;

// skipping imports to save space

@Entity
@Table(name="\"Course\"")
@NamedQuery(name="Course.findAll", query="SELECT c FROM Course c")
public class Course implements Serializable {
  private static final long serialVersionUID = 2550281519279297343L;

  @Id
  @GeneratedValue(strategy=GenerationType.IDENTITY)
  @Column(name="id")
  private int id;

  @NotNull
  @Column(name="name")
  private String name;

  @Min(1)
  @Column(name="credits")
  private int credits;

  // skipping getter and setters to save space
}
```

This is a simple JPA entity class with appropriate annotations. We need to tell JPA that this
is a managed bean. To do this, open `persistence.xml` and in the **General** tab of the
editor, click the **Add** button in the **Managed Classes** section. Add the `Course` entity class to
the list.

Create a JPA `EntityManagerFactory` class called `CourseManagementJPAFactory`:

```
package packt.book.jeeeclipse.wildflyswarm.coursemanagement.rest;

// skipping imports to save space

@ApplicationScoped
public class CourseManagementJPAFactory {
  private EntityManager _entityManager;

  public EntityManager getEntityManager() {
    if (_entityManager != null) return _entityManager;
```

```
    EntityManagerFactory factory =
Persistence.createEntityManagerFactory("coursemanagement");

    _entityManager = factory.createEntityManager();

    return _entityManager;
  }
}
```

In this class, we are creating an instance of `EntityManager` from `EntityManagerFactory`. Note that name passed to the `Persistence.createEntityManagerFactory` method is the same as the name we specified in `persistence.xml`.

Finally, we will create the main class, called `CourseManagementEndpoint`, and also the REST endpoint function to handle the `/course_management/courses` URL path:

```
package packt.book.jeeeclipse.wildflyswarm.coursemanagement.rest;
// skipping imports to save space

@ApplicationScoped
@Path("/course_management")
public class CourseManagementEndpoint {
  @Inject
  private CourseManagementJPAFactory jpaFactory;

  @GET
  @Path("/courses")
  @Produces(MediaType.APPLICATION_JSON)
  public List<Course> doGet() {
    EntityManager entityManager = jpaFactory.getEntityManager();
    TypedQuery<Course> courseQuery =
entityManager.createNamedQuery("Course.findAll", Course.class);
    List<Course> courses = courseQuery.getResultList();
    return courses;
  }
}
```

If the application is not already running, right-click on the project in **Project Explorer** and select **Run As | Maven build**. Open `http://localhost:8080/course_managment/courses` in the browser and you should see a JSON list of courses in the database.

To change the default server port from `8080` to any other port number, say `8000`, set the `swarm.http.port=8000` environment variable. You can set this in the run configuration for the project (select **Run | Run Configurations** from the main menu and look for the configuration for your project in the **Maven Build** section):

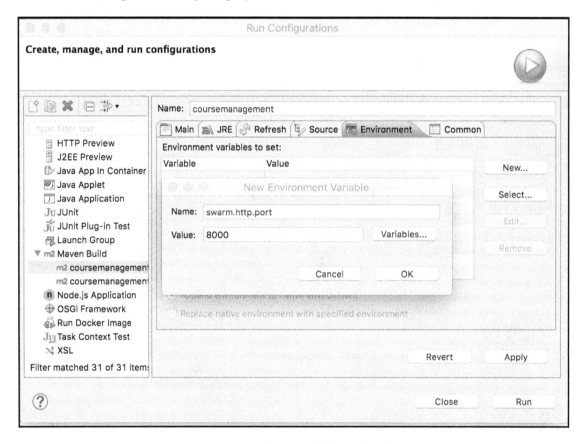

Figure 12.5: Set the environment variable in the run configuration

Click on the **Environment** tab and add the environment variable and its value.

Implementing microservices using Spring Boot

A microservice can be implemented in many ways; in the previous section, we saw one way to implement it, using WildFly Swarm, which is a MicroProfile implementation. In this section, we will see how to implement a microservice using Spring Boot, which is not a MicroProfile implementation but is a popular framework.

Spring Boot (`https://spring.io/projects/spring-boot/`) is a framework to create standalone Spring applications. Refer to `Chapter 8`, *Creating Web Applications with Spring MVC*, for more information on Spring and specific information on the Spring MVC framework. Similar to the WildFly Swarm Project Generator, Spring Boot also has a web page for creating a starter application for Spring Boot, where you can select the features/specifications of JEE that you want to be included in the application. Go to `https://start.spring.io/`:

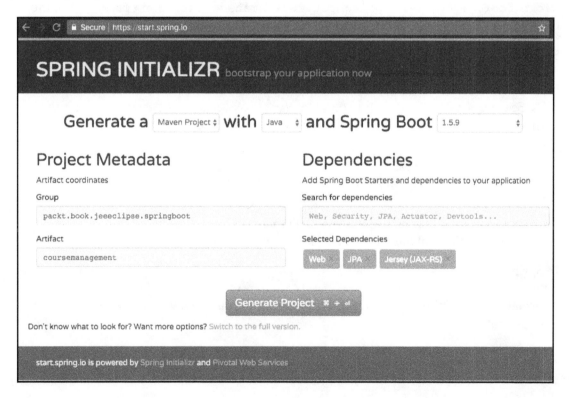

Figure 12.6: Spring Boot project generator

Select the **Web**, **JPA**, and **Jersey(JAX-RS)** dependencies. Download the starter project and unzip it in a folder. We won't be able to run the application yet. Since we have selected JPA as one of the dependencies of the application, Spring Boot expects us to configure database connection properties in the application.properties file, located in `src/main/resources`. Add the following properties to `application.properties`:

```
spring.datasource.url =
jdbc:mysql://localhost/course_management?autoReconnect=true&useSSL=false
spring.datasource.driver-class-name = com.mysql.cj.jdbc.Driver
spring.datasource.username=<your_user_name>
spring.datasource.password=<your_passwod>
spring.jpa.hibernate.naming.physical-
strategy=org.hibernate.boot.model.naming.PhysicalNamingStrategyStandardImpl
```

We can run the server now, but we haven't defined any REST endpoints yet. So, let's do that. We will use the `Course` entity bean that we created for the WildFly Swarm project in the previous section. So, copy the same file to this project, in the `packt.book.jeeeclipse.springboot.coursemanagementspring` package. See the *Create course entity bean and JPA factory* section for listings of the `Course` class.

Spring provides a utility interface named `CrudRepository` that tells the framework to create CRUD boilerplate code for the given entity/class. We will create a repository interface that extends `CrudRepository` and create a CRUD implementation for the `Course` class. See `https://docs.spring.io/spring-data/data-commons/docs/1.6.1.RELEASE/reference/html/repositories.html` for more information on `CrudRepository`:

```
package packt.book.jeeeclipse.springboot.coursemanagementspring;
import org.springframework.data.repository.CrudRepository;
public interface CourseRepository extends CrudRepository<Course, Long>{
}
```

This is just a marker interface to tell Spring Framework to create CRUD code for the `Course` class/entity that has the primary key of type `Long`.

In Spring, a REST endpoint is created by creating a controller, actually annotating the class with `@RestController`. See `https://spring.io/guides/gs/rest-service/` for information on creating RESTful web services using Spring. So, let's create the `CourseController` class:

```
package com.example.demo;
// skipping imports to save space

@RestController
public class CourseController {
```

```
    @Autowired
    private CourseRepository courseRepository;

    @RequestMapping(value = "/course_management/courses", method =
    RequestMethod.GET)
      public Iterable<Course> getCourses() {
        return courseRepository.findAll();
      }
    }
```

In this class, we are mapping the GET HTTP request to
the /course_management/courses URL to the getCourses method.

An instance of CourseRepository is auto injected into this class using the @Autowired
annotation.

We are now ready to run the application. Create a run configuration for this application by
right-clicking on the project in **Project Explorer** and selecting **Run As | Maven Build**. Then,
type spring-boot:run in the **Goals** field (see *Figure 12.4* for reference) and click the **Run**
button. Once the server is ready, browse to
http://localhost:8080/course_management/courses and you should see JSON
output (for Courses).

To change the default server port from 8080 to any other port number, say 8000, set the
environment variable server.port=8000. See *Figure 12.5* for reference.

See https://docs.spring.io/spring-boot/docs/current/reference/htmlsingle/ for a
complete reference to Spring Boot.

Deploying microservices in a Docker container

In this section, we will learn how to deploy a microservice in a Docker container, but let's
first understand what Docker is.

What is Docker?

Docker is container management software. In general, software containers allow you to package your application with all dependencies, including the OS, in one package. Your application runs in isolation in the container in which it is packaged. This reduces discrepancies in environments when developing, testing, and deploying. Since all the dependencies for your application are already resolved and packaged with it, you generally do not run into situations where your application ran fine in a dev/test environment, but failed in production—maybe because some of the dependencies were not met. For example, even if you have developed and tested in the same OS version, in production some of the dependencies may fail because of OS updates.

Docker is the most popular container management technology currently. Docker makes it easy to package and run your application in a container. It is often compared with virtual machines. The following diagram shows the difference between them:

App1	App2	App3	App1 Container1	App2 Container2	App3 Container3
Guest OS	Guest OS	Guest OS	Shared OS Kernel		
Hypervisor			Docker Engine		
Host OS (Windows/Mac/Linux)			Host OS (Windows/Max/Linux)		
Hardware			Hardware		
Virtual Machine technology			Docker container technology		

Figure 12.7: Difference between Virtual Machines Technology and Docker Container Technology

VMs are guest operating systems in *Figure 12.7*, running on top of hypervisor software (a hypervisor isolates the guest OS from the host OS and manages them). Docker containers run on top of Docker Engine and a shared OS kernel (for example, Linux or Windows). Docker containers are not full-fledged OSes; they are processes with isolated resources such as filesystems and networks.

Compared to VMs, Docker containers are easy to package and deploy, and they start much more quickly (because they are just processes and not complete OSes). Docker containers also take up a lot fewer resources than VMs. So, you can run more Docker containers in the same environment than VMs.

See this official Docker link, `https://www.docker.com/what-docker`, for more information.

How to get Docker

Download Docker for Mac from here: `https://docs.docker.com/docker-for-mac/install/`

Download Docker for Windows from here: `https://docs.docker.com/docker-for-windows/install/`

Download Docker for Linux: `https://docs.docker.com/engine/installation/`

How to use Docker

In this section, we will briefly see how to use Docker. To create a new container, you typically create a Dockerfile. In this file, you need to specify the base image to extend your container from, for example, the base image for Ubuntu or Debian. You can think of Docker images as templates, and containers as running instances of those templates. Docker Hub, `https://hub.docker.com/`, is a repository of Docker images.

Dockerfile

You create a Dockerfile to create an image for your own container. You can specify the base image for your container, commands to execute when setting up the container, ports to expose, files to copy to the container, and the entry point (the program to run when the container starts). Here are some of the frequently used instructions in a Dockerfile:

- `FROM`: Specify the base image for your Docker container, for example, `FROM Ubuntu`.
- `ADD`: Add file(s) from the host machine to the Docker container. For example, to copy the `setup.sh` file from the directory from where Docker commands are run to a container. For example, `ADD ./setup.sh /setup.sh`.
- `RUN`: Runs a command in the container. For example, to make the `setup.sh` file executable after copying to a container. Example, `RUN chmod +x /setup.sh`.

- `ENTRYPOINT`: Docker containers are meant to have one main application, and when it stops running, the container stops. That main program is specified using the `ENTRYPOINT` directive. For example, to run the Apache server after it is installed (possibly using the `RUN` command) `ENTRYPOINT apachectl start`.
- `CMD`: A command to execute. In the absence of `ENTRYPOINT`, `CMD` specifies the main application in the container. If specified along with `ENTRYPOINT`, then the value of `CMD` is passed as arguments to the application specified in `ENTRYPOINT`.
- `EXPOSE`: Tells Docker that the container listens on specified port(s) at runtime. For example, if the Apache server is listening on port `80` in a container, then you would specify `EXPOSE 80`.
- `ENV`: Sets environment variable(s) in a container. An example is `ENV PATH=/some/path:$PATH`.
- `VOLUME`: Creates a mountable point for a volume. A volume is just like a folder or virtual folder. From within the container, it can be accessed as any other folder. Volumes can be used to share folders across different running containers. One container can also import volumes from another container.

This is a list of commonly used Docker instructions in a Dockerfile. See the Dockerfile reference at `https://docs.docker.com/engine/reference/builder/` for all instructions.

Docker commands

Here is a short list of Docker commands for operations such as start, stop, and delete:

Operation	Command

Run a container from an image	The syntax is as follows:
	`docker run –name <container_name> <options> <base_image> <command_to_run>`
	For example, to run a container from an Ubuntu image, open a Terminal and execute the bash shell with the following command:
	`docker run –name my-ubuntu –it ubuntu bash`

Create an image from a Dockerfile	The syntax is as follows:
	`docker build <options> <folder_of_dockerfile>`
	For example, to create `my_image` from a Dockerfile in the current folder, run the following Docker command:
	`docker build -t image_name`

List currently running containers	`docker ps`
List all containers, including stopped containers	`docker ps -a`
Start (a stopped) container	The syntax is as follows: `docker start -i <container>` The `-i` option keeps `stdin` (standard input) open and allows you to run commands in the container. To identify the container, you can either use the container name or ID.
Remove a container	`docker rm <container>`

Execute command in running container	The syntax is as follows:
	`docker exec <options> <container> <command>`
	For example, to open a bash shell in a running container called `my_container`, execute the following command:
	`docker exec -it my_container bash`

Listing all images	`docker images`
Deleting images	Image IDs are space separated in this command: `docker rmi <image_ids>`
Get information about running container	`docker inspect <container>`

See `https://docs.docker.com/engine/reference/commandline/docker/` for the complete reference.

That was a short introduction to Docker. There are many more details of Docker that are out of the scope of this book. Please refer to the links provided and also the Docker website (`https://www.docker.com/`) for more information. We will now focus on Eclipse tooling for Docker and deploying microservices in Docker containers.

Setting up Docker Tooling in Eclipse

There is a Docker plugin for Eclipse, using which you can perform many of the mentioned Docker tasks from within Eclipse. To install the plugin in Eclipse, from the menu, select **Help | Eclipse Marketplace....** Search for `Eclipse Docker Tooling` and install it:

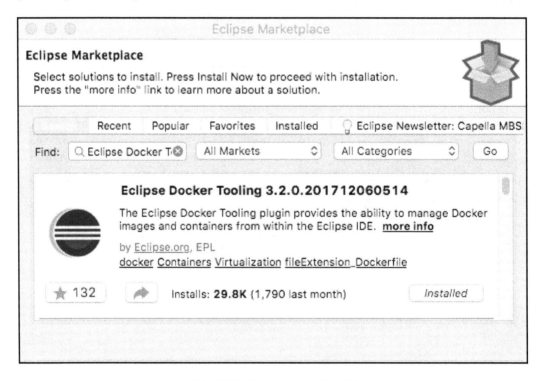

Figure 12.8: Install Eclipse Docker Tooling from Eclipse Marketplace

Switch to the **Docker Tooling** perspective (either click on the **Open Perspective** toolbar button at the top-right of the editor window, or select from the **Window | Perspective | Open Perspective | Other** menu).

We will now add a Docker connection in Eclipse (make sure the Docker daemon is running):

Figure 12.9: Add Docker connection

Click on the **Add Connection** toolbar button in **Docker Explorer** and create a connection, as shown in the following screenshot:

Figure 12.10: Add connection dialog box

On Windows, you need to select **TCP Connection** and specify the URI where Docker daemon is listening. You can find the URI in Docker settings, in **General** tab. Make sure **Expose daemon on...** option is selected. Copy the TCP URI from this option and paste it in **TCP Connection | URI** textbox in the dialog box shown in *Fig. 12.10*.

Once the connection is added successfully, you will see lists of existing containers and images, if any, on your local machine.

Creating a Docker network

We are going to deploy two servers in two separate Docker containers in the same machine: a MySQL DB server and an application server to run our microservice. The application server will need to know about the DB server to access it. The recommended way to allow two Docker containers to access each other is by deploying them in the same Docker network. A complete discussion of Docker networks is out of scope of this book, so readers are encouraged to read about Docker networks at `https://docs.docker.com/engine/userguide/networking`.

Knowing that the two containers we are going to create shortly need to run in the same Docker network, let's create a Docker network by running the following command:

```
docker network create --driver bridge coursemanagement
```

In this command, `coursemanagment` is the name of the network we are creating.

Creating MySQL container

We have been using a MySQL server installed on the host machine so far in this book. We will now see how to create a Docker container with MySQL. If you are running an instance of MySQL on your host OS (the OS in which Docker is running), then stop the instance or configure MySQL to run on a different port than `3306` in the Docker container (we will see how to do this shortly).

We will use the official MySQL Docker image; see `https://hub.docker.com/_/mysql/`. Run the following command:

```
docker run --name course-management-mysql -e
MYSQL_ROOT_PASSWORD=your_password -p 3306:3306 --network=coursemanagement -
d mysql
```

Replace `your_password` with the root password you want to set. This command will install the latest version of MySQL. The `-d` option runs the container in detached/background mode. Also note that the container is created in the `coursemanagement` network that we created in the previous section. If you want to use a specific version of MySQL, then tag that version; for example, to install MySQL Version 5.5.58, use the following command:

```
docker run --name course-management-mysql -e
MYSQL_ROOT_PASSWORD=your_password -d -p 3306:3306 --
network=coursemanagement mysql:5.5.58
```

`MySQL` will run on port `3306` in the container, and the container exposes the service at the same port on the host machine. To expose this service at a different port on the host machine, say port `3305`, use the `-p` or `--publish` option:

```
docker run --name course-management-mysql -e
MYSQL_ROOT_PASSWORD=your_password -p 3305:3306 --network=coursemanagement -d
mysql
```

The `-p` option in this command maps port `3306` in the Docker container to port `3305` on the host machine.

Once the command is executed successfully, you can verify that the container is running by executing the `docker ps` command. The container will also be visible in **Docker Explorer** in Eclipse. Switch to the **Docker Tooling** perspective in Eclipse and expand the **Containers** group under the **Local** connection:

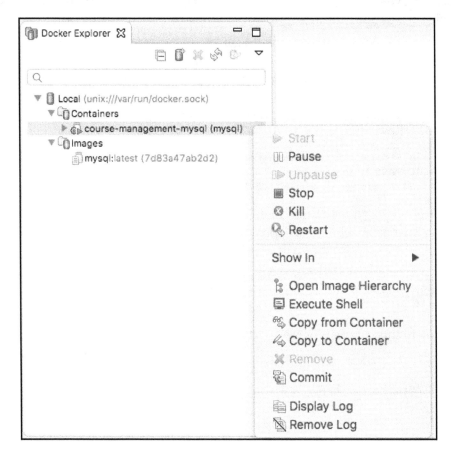

Figure 12.11: Docker Explorer listing containers and images

Right-click on the container name to show menu options for different actions on the container, such as **Start**, **Stop**, and **Restart**.

The **Execute Shell** option is very useful for opening a shell in the container and executing commands. For example, to execute MySQL commands from within the container, select the **Execute Shell** option and execute the `mysql -u root -p` command:

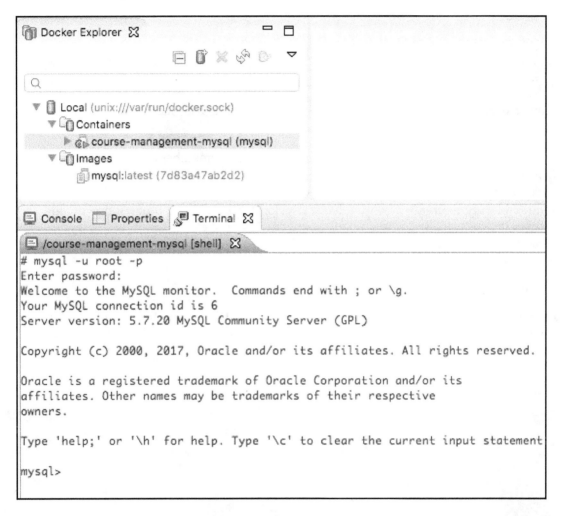

Figure 12.12: The Execute Shell in a Docker container

Assuming you have mapped port 3306 from the container to the same port on the host machine, you can connect to the instance of MySQL in the container from the host machine as follows:

```
mysql -h 127.0.0.1 -u root -p
```

Make sure you specify the -h or --host option, or it will try to connect using the local .sock file and that will fail. You can also connect to this MySQL instance from MySQL Workbench.

Next, create the course_management schema in the database. See the *Setting up Database* section of this chapter for details.

If you do not want to type long Docker commands and remember options, you can use Docker Explorer's user interface to create containers. We used the run command of Docker to run a MySQL container using the mysql image. The command first checks whether the required image is already downloaded on the local machine, and if not, it downloads it. Docker images can also be downloaded explicitly using the docker pull command. For example, we could have first downloaded the mysql image by executing the following command:

```
docker pull mysql
```

Once the image is downloaded, it will be displayed in **Docker Explorer**. Right-click the image and select **Run**:

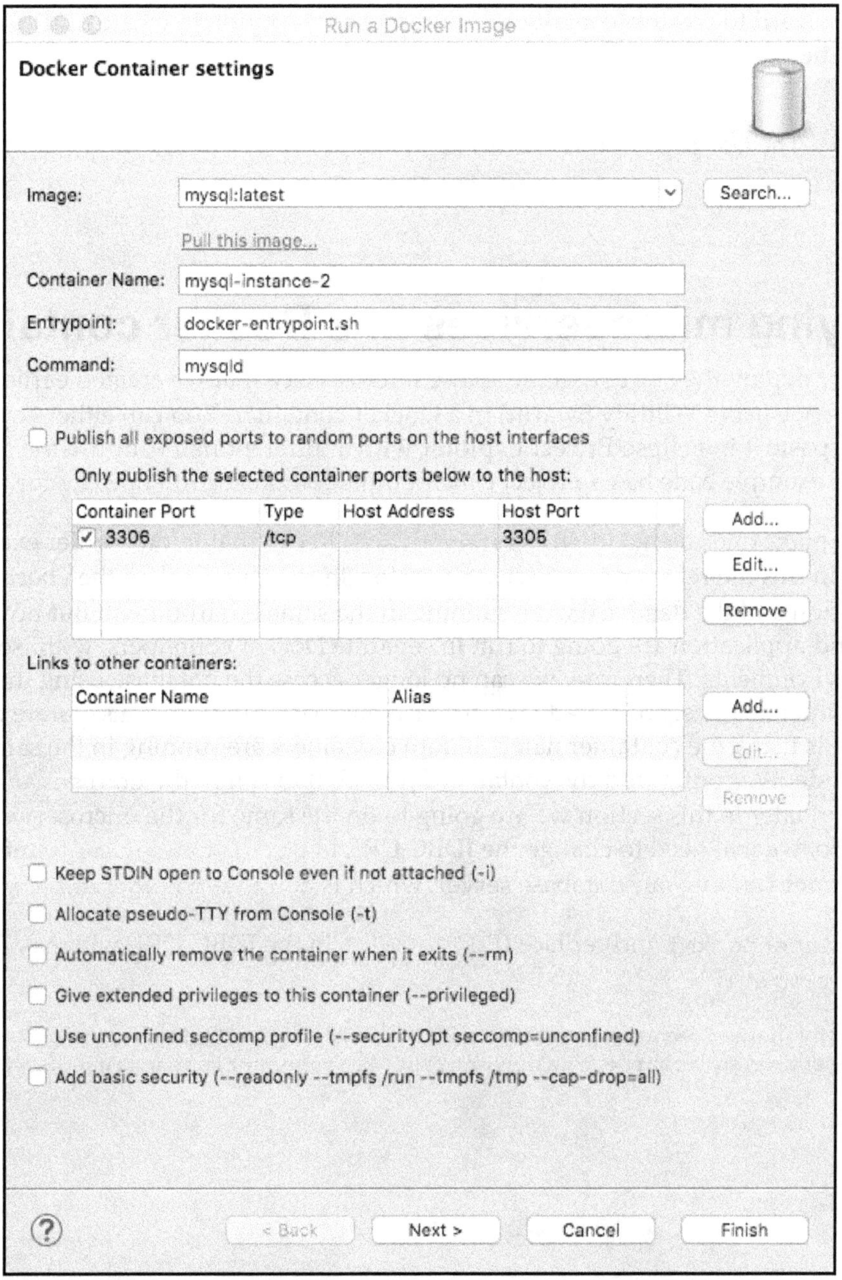

Figure 12.13: Create Docker container from image in Docker Explorer

Follow the wizard to create a container. You can use this option to create multiple instances from the same image, for example, to run multiple MySQL containers.

 The last page in this wizard lets you specify a network for the container.

Deploying microservices in a Docker container

We will now deploy the `CourseManagement` microservice that we created earlier in this chapter (the one using WildFly Swarm) in a Docker container. You can either copy the project and paste it in Eclipse Project Explorer with a different name, or use the same project. The example code has a project called `coursemanagement-docker` for this section.

We need to make one change in `persistence.xml`. Recall that in our earlier example, the JDBC URL in this file referred to `127.0.0.1` or localhost. This worked then because both the application and the database were running in the same environment. But now our database and application are going to run in separate Docker containers, with isolated runtime environments. Therefore, we can no longer access the database using the localhost URL in the microservice. So, how do we access a database running in a separate container? The answer is using the container name, if both containers are running in the same Docker network mode. We configured the container for the DB to run in the `coursemanagment` network, and later in this section we are going to do the same for the microservice container. So, we will need to change the JDBC URL in `persistence.xml` to refer to name of the container running our database server, which is `course-management-mysql`.

Open `persistence.xml` and replace IP `127.0.0.1` in the JDBC URL with `course-management-mysql`:

```
<property name="javax.persistence.jdbc.url" value="jdbc:mysql://course-
management-mysql/course_management?autoReconnect=true&amp;useSSL=false"/>
```

Next, create a file named Dockerfile in root of the project with the following content:

```
FROM openjdk:8
ENV swarm.http.port 8080
RUN mkdir microservices
COPY ./target/coursemanagement-swarm.jar ./microservices
EXPOSE 8080
ENTRYPOINT java -jar -Djava.net.preferIPv4Stack=true
./microservices/coursemanagement-swarm.jar
```

We will be using this Dockerfile to create the image for our microservice container. Let's understand each of the instructions in this file:

- `FROM openjdk:8`: The base image for this container is OpenJDK, Version 8.
- `ENV swarm.http.port 8080`: We are setting the `swarm.http.port` environment variable in the container. This is really not necessary for this example, because the WildFly Swarm server runs on port `8080` by default. Change the port number if you want to run the server on a different port.
- `RUN mkdir microservices`: We are creating a folder named `microservices` in the container.
- `COPY ./target/coursemanagement-swarm.jar ./microservices`: We are copying `coursemanagement-swarm.jar` from the target folder in our project to the `microservices` folder in the container.
- `EXPOSE 8080`: We ask Docker Engine to expose port `8080` from the container. Our application server listens for requests on port `8080` in the container.
- `ENTRYPOINT java -jar -Djava.net.preferIPv4Stack=true ./microservices/coursemanagement-swarm.jar`: Finally, we specify the main application to execute in the container, which is running the standalone microservice application.

We need to build the application to create a single JAR file that we will run in the Docker container. If you try to build the application by running the Maven goal `wildfly-swarm:run` (we did that to run the application earlier), it is going to fail because it will also try to run the application. This is not going to work because we modified the JDBC URL in `persistence.xml` with the name of the DB container. So, run the Maven goal to only package the application, without running tests. Right-click on the project in **Project Explorer** and select **Run As | Maven Build**:

Figure 12.14: Eclipse run configuration to package the Docker-microservice project

Enter `package` in the **Goals** field. Select the **Skip Tests** option and click **Run** to create the application JAR file in the target folder.

Let's now create the Docker image from the Dockerfile we created. Right-click on the file in **Project Explorer** and select the **Run As | Docker Image Build** menu option.

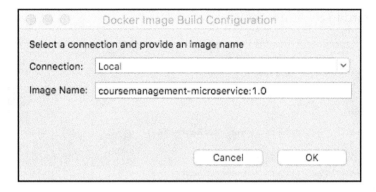

Figure 12.15: Building a Docker image from a Dockerfile

This will create a Docker image named **coursemanagement-microservice** and tag it as the **1.0** version. Switch to the **Docker Tooling** perspective in Eclipse and you should see this image listed.

We are going to create an instance of this image, that is, create a container from this image that will actually run our microservice. Right-click on the image and select **Run...**:

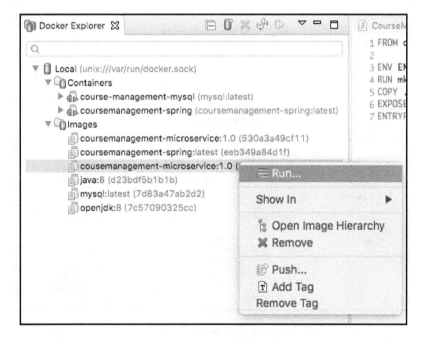

Figure 12.16: Creating a container from an image

This opens a wizard to configure the container:

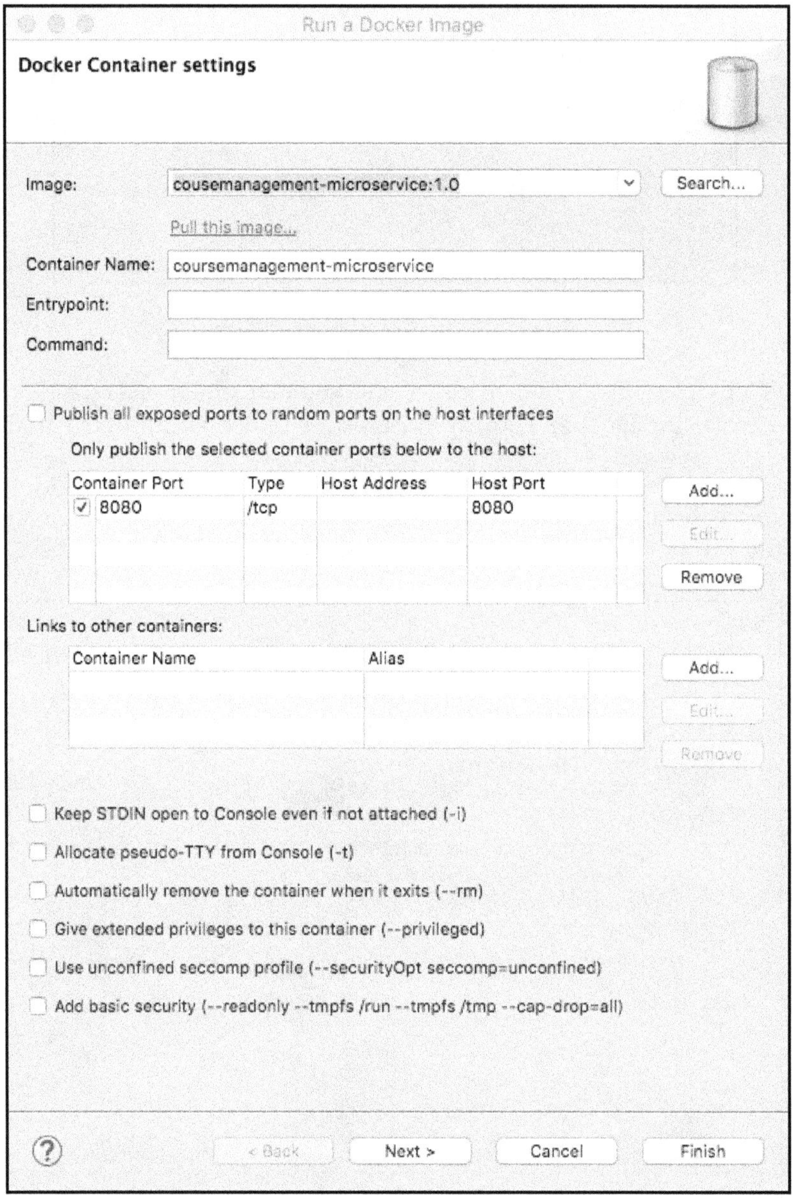

Figure 12.17: Configuring a Docker container

Specify a name for the container in the first page of the wizard. Leave **Endpoint** and **Command** empty; the image is already created with the ENTRYPOINT that we specified in the Dockerfile. You can override that in this page, but we are not going to do that. Make sure the **Publish all exposed ports to random ports on the host interfaces** option is unchecked. We want to publish port 8080 from the container as the same port number to the host. Click **Next**. Leave the default options on the second page and click **Next** again.

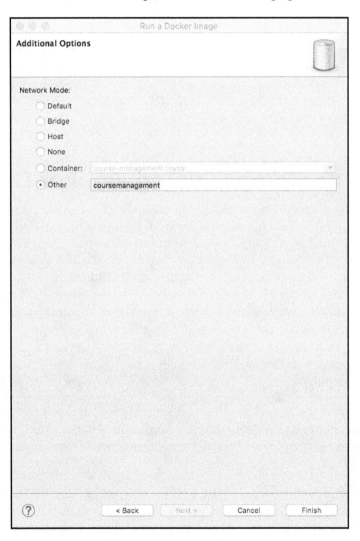

Figure 12.18: Setting network mode for a Docker container

The last page (see *Figure 12.18*) allows you to specify a network for the container. Here, we are going to specify the network we created earlier, `coursemanagement`. Recall that we also created a MySQL container with the same network, so that microservice container can access the MySQL container with the container name.

Once the application starts in the microservice container, browse to `http://localhost:8080/course_management/courses` and you should see list of courses in the database.

The process to deploy the microservice we created using Spring Boot earlier is also similar to the one we saw in this section. One main difference is that in the Spring Boot project, you need to update the JDBC URL in `application.properties`, instead of the `persistence.xml` that we modified in this section. For your reference, the sample code has a project named `coursemanagementspring-docker`.

Running containers using Docker Compose

We have seen in the preceding sections how to create Docker containers separately by running command-line Docker commands (or from Eclipse plugins). If you want to run multiple containers on a host machine, you should consider using Docker Compose. It allows you to configure multiple Docker containers in one file and also specify dependencies between them. A `docker-compose` command reads configuration/instructions from `docker-compose.yml`, and creates and runs containers. The `.yml` file requires the version number of `docker-compose` at the top, followed by a services section, which lists container definitions—specifying image or Dockerfile location, environment variables to be set in the container, ports to be exposed and mapped to the host OS, and many other configurations. See `https://docs.docker.com/compose/overview/` for more details.

In this section, we will use `docker-compose` to run MySQL and our webservice containers together. In the later chapter on deploying JEE applications in the cloud, we will use this configuration for deployment. First, install `docker-compose` from `https://docs.docker.com/compose/install/`.

Create a new **General** Eclipse project (**File** | **New** | **Project** and then **General** | **Project**) and name it `coursemanagement-docker-compose`. We don't need a JEE project for this section because we are going to take the single JAR file that we created in the last section for our microservice and deploy it in a Docker container. So, copy `coursemanagementspring-docker/coursemanagementspring-0.0.1-SNAPSHOT.jar` to the project folder.

We need to create and initialize a MySQL database in the container. We are going to use a SQL script with **data definition language** (**DDL** for example, CREATE) statements to create database schema and tables. The source code project for this section, coursemanagement-docker-compose, has a file, course-management-db.sql, containing DDL statements. This script creates empty tables with no data.

If you want also to export data from your existing database, then you can create the script from MySQL Workbench. From MySQL Workbench, select **Server** | **Data Export**. Select the schema to export, course_management. From the drop-down options, select **Dump Structure and Data**. In **Export Options**, select **Export to Self-Contained File** and specify the path of the file, for example, <your_project_path>/course-management-db.sql. Then, click the **Start Export** button.

Now, let's create two Dockerfiles in the project:

- course-management-db.dockerfile for the MySQL container
- course-management-service.dockerfile for the microservice container

Create course-management-db.dockerfile with the following content:

```
FROM mysql:5.7
COPY ./course-management-db.sql /docker-entrypoint-initdb.d
ENV MYSQL_ROOT_PASSWORD root
```

With the COPY statement in this file, we are copying course-management-db.sql from the project folder to the docker-entrypoint-initdb.d folder in the container. Any SQL script in this file will be executed by the base MySQL image to initialize the database. See the *Initializing a fresh instance* section at https://hub.docker.com/_/mysql/.

Create course-management-service.dockerfile with the following content:

```
FROM openjdk:8
RUN mkdir microservices
COPY ./coursemanagementspring-0.0.1-SNAPSHOT.jar ./microservices
EXPOSE 8080
ENTRYPOINT java -jar -Djava.net.preferIPv4Stack=true
./microservices/coursemanagementspring-0.0.1-SNAPSHOT.jar
```

In this Dockerfile, we are creating the container from the `openjdk:8` base image. Then, we are creating a folder, `microservices`, in the container and then copying `coursemanagementspring-0.0.1-SNAPSHOT.jar` from the project folder to the `microservices` folder in the container. We then set the `ENTRYPOINT` for the container with the command to execute the copied JAR file.

Lastly, create `docker-compose.yml` with the following content:

```
version: "3"
services:
  course-managemnt-db:
    build:
      context: .
      dockerfile: course-management-db.dockerfile
    container_name: course-management-mysql
    ports:
      - 3306:3306
  course-management-service:
    build:
      context: .
      dockerfile: course-management-service.dockerfile
    container_name: course-management-service
    ports:
      - 80:8080
    depends_on:
      - course-managemnt-db
```

We are creating two services in this file: `course-managemnt-db` for the DB container and `course-management-service` for the microservice container. Both are built from separate Dockerfiles. The context field specifies the path of the folder containing the Dockerfile; in this case it is the present folder (which is the project folder). Note that we have specified the dependency of `course-management-service` container on `course-managemnt-db`. This results in the DB container getting started before the microservice container.

We are mapping port `8080` from the microservice container to port `80` on the host. The reason is that we are going to deploy these services later in the cloud with the default web server on port `80`.

Warning
The deployment of JEE container in this chapter is meant for the purpose of development and testing only. It is not meant for production and does not follow best practices for a production environment. That falls under the realm of DevOps, which is not within the scope of this book.

Since both the services are in the same `docker-compose.yml`, `docker-compose` creates a network and adds both containers to the network. So, the `course-management-service` container can access the `course-management-mysql` container by its name. We do not need to create a separate network as we did in the previous section.

See the `docker-compose` file reference at `https://docs.docker.com/compose/compose-file/` for more configuration options.

To start all the containers configured in `docker-compose.yml` together, run the following command from the Command Prompt (make sure port `80` is not taken by another process, because we have mapped microservice container port `8080` to port `80` on the host):

```
docker-compose up
```

Once the containers have started successfully, browse to `http://localhost/course_management/courses` and you should see a list of courses, or an empty list if there are no courses in the database.

To run containers in detached/background mode, run the following command:

```
docker-compose up -d
```

To stop containers started with `docker-compose`, run the following command:

```
docker-compose down
```

If you make any changes to Dockerfiles or to `docker-compose.yml`, then you need to rebuild the images. Run the following command to do so:

```
docker-compose build
```

 Refer to `https://docs.docker.com/compose/reference/overview/` for details on `docker-compose` command-line options.

Summary

A microservice is a small application serving a single use case. Microservices are typically REST services and can be deployed quickly. Docker containers are ideally suited to deploying microservices because they allow applications to run in isolation, with little or no difference in development, testing, and production environments. Docker containers can also be deployed very quickly and can scale well.

In this chapter, we saw how to develop microservices using WildFly Swarm and Spring Boot. We created a simple microservice to list courses for our *Course Management* application. The concepts we learned can be extended to create microservices using other frameworks. We also learned how to deploy these services in Docker containers using the Eclipse plugin for **Docker Tooling**.

In the next chapter, we will learn how to deploy a JEE application in the cloud.

13
Deploying JEE Applications in the Cloud

In the last chapter, we learned how to develop JEE microservices and deploy them in Docker containers.

In this chapter, we will learn how to deploy JEE applications in the cloud, specifically in **Amazon Web Services** (**AWS**) cloud and Google Cloud Platform, using Eclipse tools. The focus is going to be more on using Eclipse tools to deploy JEE applications in the cloud, rather than learning about a specific cloud platform.

In this chapter, we will cover the following topics:

- Deploying the JEE application in an AWS EC2 instance
- Deploying the REST web service in AWS Beanstalk
- Deploying a Docker container in Google Compute Engine
- Deploying a RESTful web service in Google App Engine

Deploying in the cloud

There are many advantages to deploying applications in the cloud, such as scaling the application as per its load, and all the benefits of not having to maintain your own data center or physical machines. Other than hosting the application and flexibility, most cloud platforms also provide services like a database, file storage, messaging, and so on, which can be easily integrated into your applications.

Deployment services provided by cloud platforms can be broadly classified as follows:

- **Infrastructure as a service (IaaS)**: In this service, you get **virtual machines** (**VMs**) with complete control. You can install any software on them and set up load balancing, storage, network, and security. It is like having your own data center in the cloud. Examples of IaaS are Amazon **Elastic Compute Cloud** (**EC2**) and Google Compute Engine.
- **Platform as a service (PaaS)**: In this service, you get VMs with OS and server software installed. Services like load balancing, security, network, and so on are also pre-configured for you (or made very easy to configure). Therefore, you can focus on just application deployment. You can take, for example, a WAR file and deploy it directly in a PaaS. Examples of PaaS are Amazon Elastic Beanstalk and Google App Engine.

Though an IaaS offers more flexibility, it is more difficult to configure than a PaaS.

In the following sections, we will see how to deploy JEE applications in the aforementioned types of services in AWS and Google Cloud.

Note

This book, and this chapter in particular, explains deployment for development and testing, and not production. Deployment for production is a vast and complex topic and requires many considerations like security, scaling, and so on, which are not in the scope of this book.

You need to have accounts with cloud service providers you want to use in order to use the services. Depending on the services you use and the load on your servers, deployment to the cloud could cost you a lot of money. However, almost all cloud providers offer their services for free so that you can try them out for a limited period of time. To follow examples in this chapter, make sure you have accounts with AWS Cloud (`https://aws.amazon.com/`) and Google Cloud Platform (`https://cloud.google.com`).

Deploying in AWS Cloud

We will first create a user group and a user within it in AWS. When you set permissions on a user group, all users in that group also get the same permissions.

Creating the user group and user

We will perform the following steps to create a user group:

1. Go to the AWS Management Console (`https://console.aws.amazon.com/`) and log in.
2. Select **Services | IAM (Identity & Access Management)** from the menu at the top.
3. Select **Groups** from the list on the left-hand side.
4. Click the **Create New Group** button.
5. Follow the wizard to specify the group's name and attach the access policy. Let's name the group `aws_eclipse_users`.
6. Select the **Administrator Access** policy for the group.

We will perform the following steps to create a user:

1. Select **Users** from the list on the left-hand side and click the **Add User** button.
2. Let's set the **User Name** as **aws_eclipse_user**.
3. In the **Access Type** options, select the **AWS Management Console** access option. The **Require password reset** option can be turned off if you so desire.
4. Click the **Next: Permission** button and then select the group we created previously, which is **aws_eclipse_users**.
5. Follow the steps on the page to complete the workflow, which ultimately leads to you creating the user.

Now, you should have the **aws_eclipse_users** group with **Administrator Access** and the **aws_eclipse_user user** in that group.

The next step is to create an access key for the user. Go to the page that lists all users (click **Users** from the list on the left-hand side of the page) and click on the user **aws_eclipse_user**. Click on the **Security credentials** tab and then click the **Create access key** button. It creates an access key and displays **Access key ID** and **Secret access key**. Save this information for future use. AWS gives you the option to download the CSV file containing this information.

Note

Both **Access Key ID** and **Secret Access Key** are required to access AWS services from Eclipse. This is the only place AWS shows the **Secret Access Key**. If you lose this information, it is not possible to get it back later, so make sure that you save this information.

Next, we will add a security group and specify inbound traffic rules for the same. In the AWS Management Console, go to **Services** | **EC2** | **Network & Security** | **Security Groups** page. Click **Create Security Group** button. Enter **Security group name** as `eclipse-dev`. Enter any description (this is a mandatory field). Then create following inbound rules:

Type	Protocol	Port Range	Source
SSH	TCP	22	Anywhere *(see the note following this table)*
Custom TCP	TCP	8080	Anywhere

Note

SSH inbound rule above will give access to your EC2 instance from any IP. If you want to limit access, do not select source as **Anywhere**, but set specific IPs, selecting **Custom**.

Because this chapter explains how to deploy JEE applications in xloud for development and testing, **Source** is selected as **Anywhere** (any IP).

The preceding security group will provide SSH access to any external IP on port 22 and TCP access on port 8080.

Installing the AWS Toolkit for Eclipse

In this section, we will learn how to install the **AWS Toolkit** plugin in Eclipse. Go to the Eclipse menu's **Help | Eclipse Marketplace....** Search for the `AWS Toolkit`:

Figure 13.1: Installing the AWS Toolkit for Eclipse

Install the plugin. We will see many features of this plugin later in this chapter. Visit `http:/ /docs.aws.amazon.com/toolkit-for-eclipse/v1/user-guide/welcome.html` for the complete documentation.

We need to configure the plugin with the **Access Key ID** and **Secret Access Key** we created in the previous section. Open Eclipse **Preferences** and go to **AWS Toolkit** preferences:

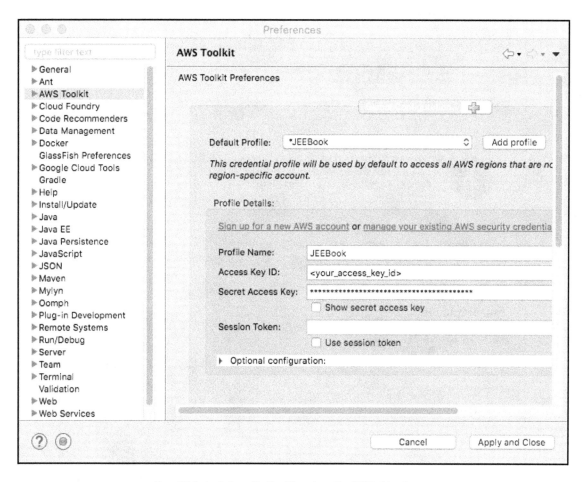

Figure 13.2: Setting the Access Key ID and Secret Access Key AWS Toolkit preferences

You can use the default profile or create a new profile. Enter the **Access Key ID** and **Secret Access Key** and click the **Apply and Close** button. This information will be used by the Eclipse plugin to access information about your configuration in AWS.

Once the authentication is successful, you can access most of the information that you can on the AWS Console web page from within Eclipse. Switch to the **AWS Management** perspective (select **Window | Perspective | Open Perspective** or click the **Open Perspective** toolbar button in the upper-right corner):

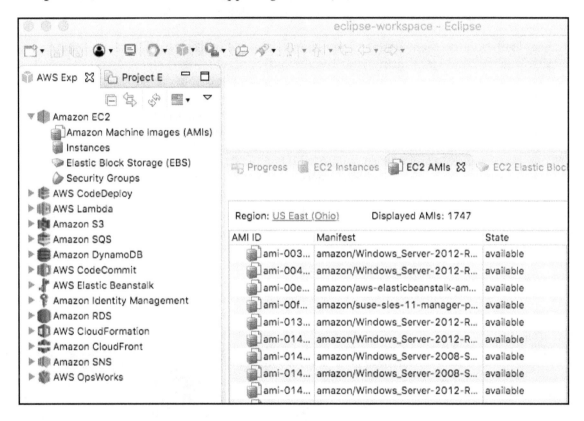

Figure 13.3: AWS Management perspective

Expand the **Amazon EC2** category in **AWS Explorer** and you will see options for viewing **EC2 AMIs**, **EC2 Instances**, and more. **Amazon Machine Image (AMI)** can be considered a template from which multiple VM instances can be created.

Launching the EC2 instance

Now, let's create an EC2 instance from an AMI. If the EC2 AMI view is not already open in the **AWS Management** perspective in Eclipse, right-click on the **AMIs** node in **AWS Explorer** (see *Figure 13.3*) and select the **Open EC2 AMIs** view. This view could take a long time to load, because there are many AMIs available. We will select a Linux AMI that is available in the Free Tier (during your trial period). Unfortunately, it is not easy to search for this AMI in the Eclipse view because the view does not display or allow you to search AMIs based on their description. This means that you can't search AMIs by typing `linux` into the search box. Surprisingly, the filter options for platforms in the view do not show the Linux option either, at least at the time of writing this book.

We are going to create an instance from AMI ID `ami-f63b1193` (you can see a better view of the list of AMIs when creating a new instance from the AWS Console web page). Type `ami-f63b1193` in the search box and you should see one result displayed in the view. Right-click on the AMI and select the **Launch** option:

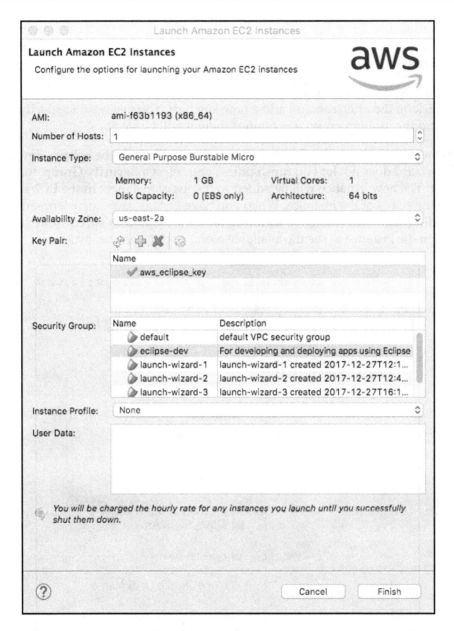

Figure 13.4: Launching an instance from AMI

Select the appropriate **Instance Type**. For this example, we will select the **General Purpose Burstable Micro** type.

Select an **Availability Zone**. See `https://docs.aws.amazon.com/AWSEC2/latest/` `UserGuide/using-regions-availability-zones.html#concepts-available-regions` for a list of availability zones.

Next, select a **Key Pair** to connect to the instance from your host machine. If no key pairs are listed, click on the plus icon and add a new key pair. You just need to specify the name of the key and the location on your machine where it will be saved.

Next, select a security group for the new instance. We will select the **eclipse-dev** security group (the wizard does not let you finish unless you select a **Security Group** and **Key Pair**). Click **Finish**. The new instance will be added to the list of instances in the **EC2 Instances** view. Note the status of the instance. When you have just created the instance, the status will be **Pending**. This will change to **Running** once the instance is successfully launched. Right-click on the instance to see the available menu options on the instance:

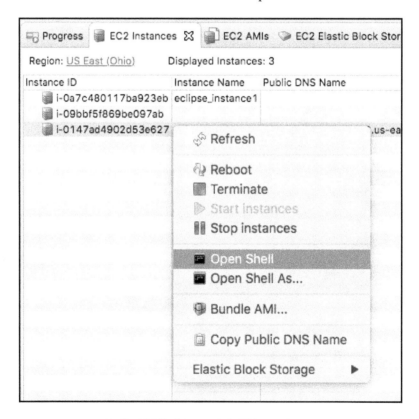

Figure 13.5: The Context menu in the EC2 Instances view

To open a shell to execute OS commands, select the **Open Shell** option from the pop-up menu:

```
ram$  /usr/bin/ssh -o CheckHostIP=no -o TCPKeepAlive=yes -o StrictHostKeyCheckin
g=no -o ServerAliveInterval=120 -o ServerAliveCountMax=100 -i /Users/rakulkar/.e
c2/aws_eclipse_key.pem ec2-user@ec2-18-218-173-243.us-east-2.compute.amazonaws.c
om
Warning: Permanently added 'ec2-18-218-173-243.us-east-2.compute.amazonaws.com'
(ECDSA) to the list of known hosts.

       __|  __|_  )
       _|  (     /    Amazon Linux AMI
      ___|\___|___|

https://aws.amazon.com/amazon-linux-ami/2017.09-release-notes/
1 package(s) needed for security, out of 1 available
Run "sudo yum update" to apply all updates.
-bash: warning: setlocale: LC_CTYPE: cannot change locale (UTF-8): No such file
or directory
[ec2-user@ip-172-31-1-125 ~]$ pwd
/home/ec2-user
[ec2-user@ip-172-31-1-125 ~]$ 
```

Figure 13.6: An opened shell in an AWS instance

We are going to use this option (**Open Shell**) to execute commands in our instance.

Installing the CourseManagement EJB application in the EC2 instance

In Chapter 7, *Creating JEE Applications with EJB*, we developed an EJB application for CourseManagement. We will see how to deploy this application in the EC2 instance that we created in the previous section. We will need to install GlassFish 5 and MySQL server in the instance. Although you can install these servers on separate instances (which is recommended for a production setup), we are going to install both of them in the same instance so that we can reduce the number of steps for creating a new instance. Let's start by installing the GlassFish 5 Server.

Installing the GlassFish 5 Server

At the time of writing this chapter, the Linux instance that's been created by AWS is preinstalled with JDK 7. However, we have been using JDK 8 in this book. Therefore, we will start by uninstalling JDK 7 and installing JDK 8. Open a shell in the instance from Eclipse (see the previous sections for details) and run the following commands:

Commands	Description
`sudo yum remove java-1.7.0-openjdk -y`	Removes JDK 7 from the instance.
`sudo yum install java-1.8.0 -y`	Installs JDK 8.
`wget http://download.oracle.com/glassfish/5.0/release/glassfish-5.0.zip`	Downloads GlassFish 5.
`unzip glassfish-5.0.zip`	Unzips the downloaded GlassFish 5 ZIP file.
`glassfish5/glassfish/bin/asadmin --host localhost --port 4848 change-admin-password`	Changes the password of the server. Default installation comes with an admin user and no password set. We need to set a password for the remote admin of the server to work. Note that the user ID is admin and that the old password is empty (no password). Set a new password, for example, `admin`.
`glassfish5/glassfish/bin/startserv > /dev/null 2>&1 &`	Starts the server.
`curl localhost:8080`	Checks if the server is up.

`glassfish5/glassfish/bin/asadmin --host localhost --port 4848 enable-secure-admin`	Enables the remote admin of the GlassFish 5 Server. See the note following this table.

`sudo glassfish5/glassfish/bin/asadmin`
 	
`  asadmin> create-service`
	Creates a service so that it is started when the VM instance starts. After you run the `asadmin` command, run the `create-service` command at `asadmin>` prompt.

`glassfish5/glassfish/bin/stopserv`
 	
`glassfish5/glassfish/bin/startserv > /dev/null 2>&1 &`
	Stops and starts the server so that the preceding changes take effect.

Note

Between writing this chapter and publishing of the book, the functionality to enable secure admin broke in GlassFish 5 if used with JDK version above 1.8.0.151. Remote access to GlassFish 5 administration console fails with the following error (logged on `glassfish/domains/domain1logs/server.log`):

`java.lang.NoClassDefFoundError:`
`sun/security/ssl/SupportedEllipticPointFormatsExtension`

You can refer to the GlassFish 5 bug at `https://github.com/javaee/glassfish/issues/22407`.

Now, we need to instruct AWS to allow TCP requests at port 4848 (for admin), 8080 (for access web applications), and 3306 (for remote connection to MySQL server) on this instance. We will do this by setting inbound rules on the security group on the instance. Recall that in the previous section we had selected the **eclipse-dev** security group. We need to set inbound rules on this group. Unfortunately, we can't do this from the Eclipse plugin (at the time of writing this book). Login to AWS Console on the web and go to **Services | EC2** and then to **NETWORK & SECURITY | Security Groups**. Right-click on the security group **eclipse-user** and select the **Edit inbound rules** option. Add rules to allow TCP traffic from the IP of your machine (from where you will remotely access the instance; you can use sites like https://www.whatismyip.com/what-is-my-public-ip-address/ to find the real IP address of your machine):

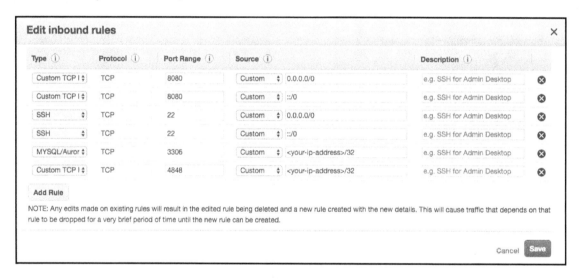

Figure 13.7: Setting inbound rules on the security group

Note that if your machine receives a dynamic IP, then you will have to update it on the preceding page.

You can now browse to the admin site of GlassFish 5 on your instance—go to https://<your-instance-public-address>:4848. You can find the public address from Eclipse view EC2 Instances, or from the AWS Console online.

Installing the MySQL server

As mentioned previously, we will install the MySQL server in the same EC2 instance. You can also use an RDS instance from AWS, which is what Amazon recommends for MySQL databases. RDS has many advantages, but to keep things short, we will install MySQL in the same VM instance. Make sure that a shell is open on the instance, as explained earlier, and execute the following commands:

Commands	Description
`sudo yum install mysql-server -y`	Installs MySQL
`sudo chkconfig mysqld on`	Activates the MySQL service
`sudo service mysqld start`	Starts the MySQL service
`mysqladmin -u root password [your_new_pwd]`	Sets the password
`mysqladmin -u root -p create course_management`	Creates `course_management` database
`create user 'eclipse-user'@'%' identified by 'enter_password_for_new_user'`	Creates a new user
`mysql -u root -p`	Logs in to MySQL from the command line
`create user 'eclipse-user'@'%' identified by 'password_for_eclipse_user';`	Execute this at `mysql>` prompt to create a new user called `eclipse-user`
`grant all privileges on *.* to 'eclipse-user'@'%' with grant option;`	Grants privileges to the new user
`exit`	Exits the MySQL console

You can now connect to this instance of the MySQL server from your host machine. But before you try to connect to the server, make sure that you have set an inbound rule on the EC2 instance to allow a connection from your machine (IP) on port 3306 (see *Figure 13.7*). You can then either connect from the Terminal (command line) or use MySQL Workbench (see `Chapter 1`, *Introducing JEE and Eclipse,* for more information on installing MySQL Workbench). Use the public DNS name of the instance to connect.

Create tables in this database as described in `Chapter 4`, *Creating JEE Database Applications.* Alternatively, use `course_management.sql`, which is in the `CourseManagementEAR` folder in the source code for this chapter, to import the tables. In MySQL Workbench, select the **Server | Data Import** menu. Select **Import from Self-Contained File** and enter the path to `course_management.sql`. Select **course_management** as the **Default Target Schema**. Select **Dump Structure and Data**. Then, click the **Start Import** button.

Configuring the datasource in the GlassFish 5 Server

To configure our data source in the GlassFish 5 Server, we first need to download the MySQL JDBC driver. You can find a link to download the driver at `https://dev.mysql.com/downloads/connector/j/`. Execute the following commands in the shell that is open for our EC2 instance:

Commands	Description
`wget` `https://dev.mysql.com/get/Downloads/Connector-J/mysql-connector-java-5.1.45.zip`	Downloads the driver
`unzip mysql-connector-java-5.1.45.zip`	Unzips the file
`cp mysql-connector-java-5.1.45/mysql-connector-java-5.1.45-bin.jar` `glassfish5/glassfish//domains/domain1//lib/ext/`	Copies the driver JAR file to a folder in the GlassFish Server classpath

Restart the EC2 instance (this is necessary so that GlassFish 5 can load the MySQL JAR file). Then, follow the instructions in the *Configuring the datasource in Glassfish* section in Chapter 7, *Creating JEE Applications with EJB*. Make sure that you use the domain name of your EC2 instance instead of localhost (specifically in **Additional Properties** when setting up the JDBC Connection Pool) when configuring the datasource. You can access the Admin console of GlassFish 5 by browsing to `https://<enter_domain_name_of_ec2_instance>:4848`.

Once you configure the connection pool and JDBC datasource in the GlassFish Admin console, deploy `CourseManagementMavenEAR-1.ear`. This is the same EAR file we created in Chapter 7, *Creating JEE Applications with EJB*, in the `CourseManagementMavenEAR` project (and dependent projects). For your convenience, the same EAR file is made available in the `CourseManagementEAR` folder in the source code for this chapter. In the Admin console, click **Applications** from the left-hand menu bar. Then, click the **Deploy** button. Select `CourseManagementMavenEAR-1.ear` from the `CourseManagementEAR` folder and deploy the application.

Once the application is deployed successfully, you should be able to browse to `http://<ec2_instance_domain_name>:8080/CourseManagementMavenWebApp/course.xhtml` and see a list of Courses (or an empty list if there is no data).

You can save the preceding setup as a template by creating an AMI and creating future instances based on that AMI. To create an AMI from a running instance, browse to the AWS Console and select the **Services | EC2** option. Then, go to the running instances list. Right-click on the instance you want to create an image from and select **Create Image**.

Installing the CourseManagmenet REST service using Elastic Beanstalk

Elastic Beanstalk (EBS) is a PaaS (Platform as a Service) offering from AWS (`https://aws.amazon.com/elasticbeanstalk/`). The idea is that you focus mostly on developing your application and leave configuration of servers (including installation of required software), load balancing, log file management, and so on to the PaaS provider. However, you do not have as much control over the servers in Elastic Beanstalk as you would when provisioning your own EC2 instances.

EBS provides preconfigured hosting solutions for different platforms, including one for Java. It provides servers with Tomcat preconfigured. You simply upload your WAR file and the application is deployed. In this section, we will learn how to deploy a RESTful web service in EBS.

Recall that we developed the `CourseManagmenetREST` service in `Chapter 9`, *Creating Web Services*. We will deploy the same service using EBS in a Tomcat EBS platform. Make sure that you have created the WAR file for the `CourseManagmenetREST` project—import the project in Eclipse, if you haven't already done so, right-click on the project in **Project Explorer**, and select **Run As | Maven Install**. This will create the `CourseManagementREST-1.war` file in the `target` folder. We will deploy this WAR file using EBS in a Tomcat server.

Creating Elastic Beanstalk application from Eclipse

We will first create a server for the EBS Tomcat platform in Eclipse. Go to the **Servers** view in Eclipse. In the default **JEE** perspective, this view is located in one of the tabs at the bottom, below editors. Right-click it and select **New | Server**:

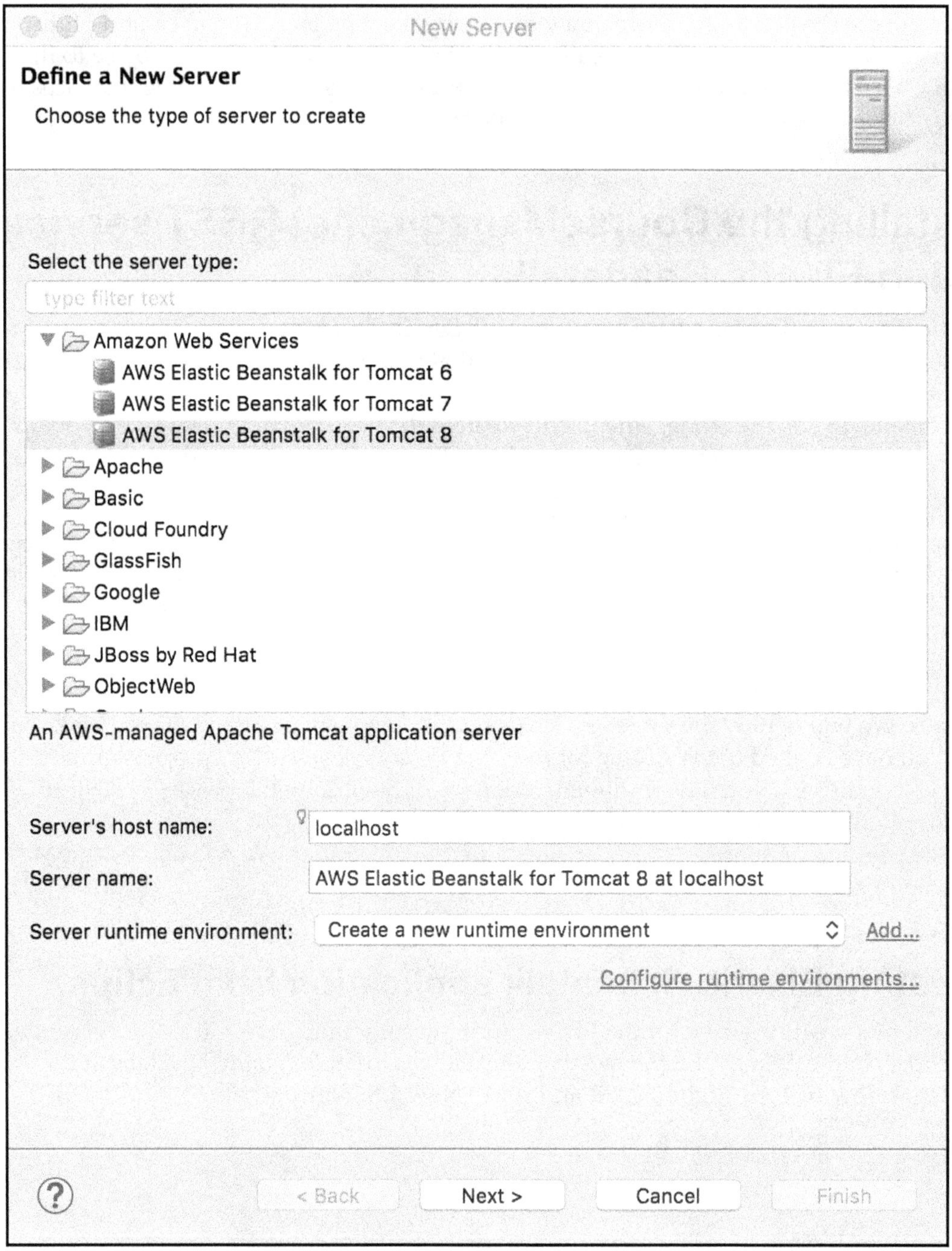

Figure 13.8: Adding the Elastic Beanstalk server in Eclipse

From the **Amazon Web Services** group, select **AWS Elastic Beanstalk for Tomcat 8**, or whichever is the latest Tomcat configuration that's available. Keep the other default options. Click **Next**:

Figure 13.9: Configuring the EBS application and environment

Select the option to **Create a new application**. Let's name this application
`CourseManagementREST` and the environment `CourseManagementREST-env`. Since we
are deploying a web application, either select **Single Instance Web Server Environment** or
Load Balanced Web Server Environment from the **Type** drop-down box. The third type,
Worker Environment, is normally used for long-running batch applications. Click **Next**. At
this point, the plugin may warn you that the **IAM operation is not allowed**. Click **OK** to
proceed:

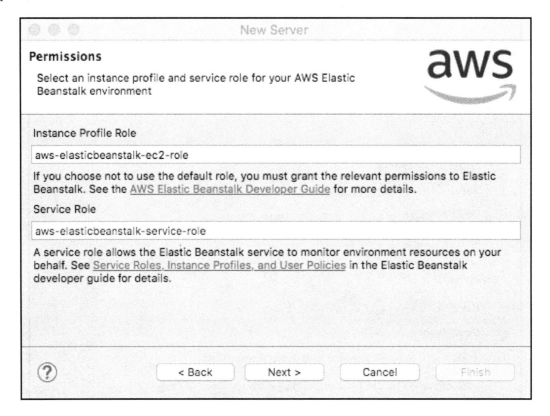

Figure 13.10: Selecting the instance profile and service role for the EBS application

Keep the default values on the **Permissions** page and click **Next**:

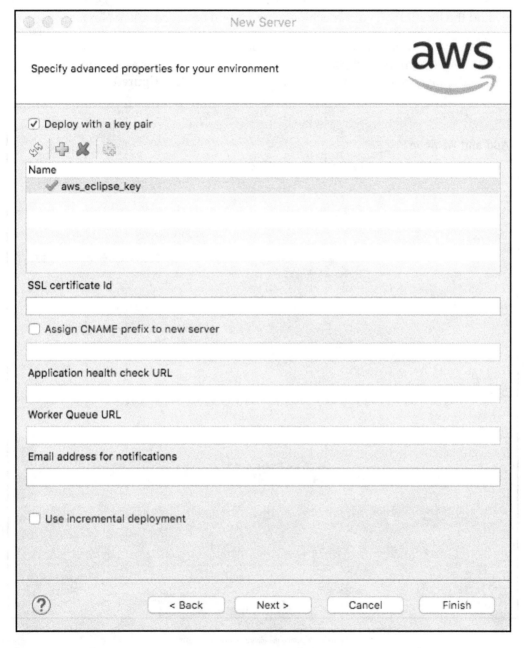

Figure 13.11: Selecting the key pair for EBS deployment

Check the **Deploy with a key pair** option and select a key from the list. If no key pairs are listed, click on the plus icon and add a new key pair. You just need to specify the name of the key and the location on your machine where it will be saved. Click **Next**.

If you have already imported the `CourseManagementREST` project from `Chapter 9,` *Creating Web Services*, in the Eclipse workspace, then it will appear as an application that is available to deploy. Click the **Add** button to move it to the **Configured** list:

Figure 13.12: Adding the application to deploy in EBS

Click **Finish**. The EBS server we just added should appear in the **Servers** view:

Figure 13.13: Servers view with the EBS server added

Click the **Start** button (or right-click on the server and select the **Start** option). Eclipse asks for the version label for your deployment:

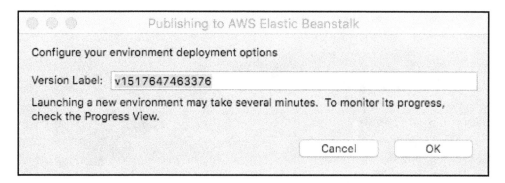

Figure 13.14: Setting the version label for EBS deployment

Set the label (or keep the default one) and click **OK**. Once the server is started (you can check the status in the **Servers** view—make sure that the status is **Started**), browse to `http://<your-ebs-app-domain>/services/course/get/1`. You should see the XML output with details of course ID 1.

To find the domain name of your EBS server, double-click on the server in the **Servers** view. This will display server properties in the editor:

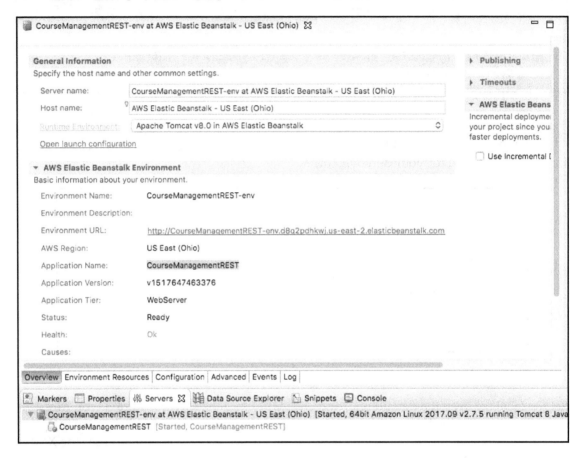

Figure 13.15: EBS server properties

You can find the domain name in the **Environment URL** link. Click on the other tabs to see more information about the configuration of your server. Clicking on the **Log** tab shows your server log, which will be useful for troubleshooting problems.

If you want to see EC2 instances created by AWS for your Beanstalk application, click on the **Environment Resources** tab:

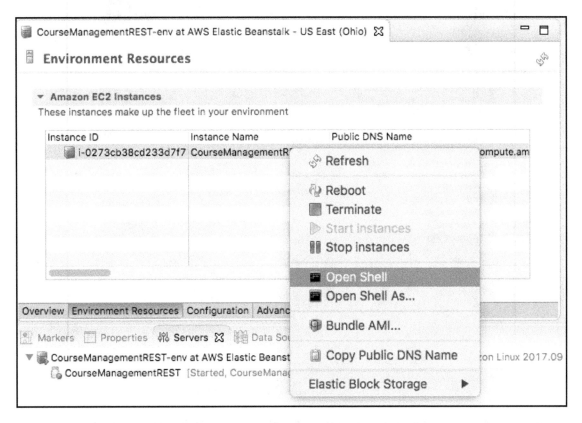

Figure 13.16: EC2 instances in EBS

Right-click on the instance row and select **Open Shell**. This can also be useful for troubleshooting the application. Note that any changes (like installing software) you make to the EC2 instance in EBS will be lost when a new version of the app is deployed.

You can see EBS applications and environments in **AWS Explorer** in Eclipse:

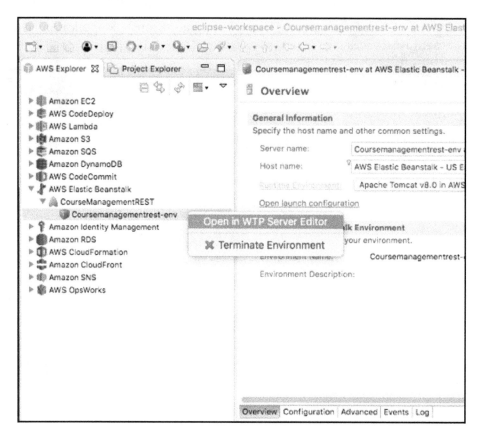

Figure 13.17: Browsing EBS applications and environments in AWS Explorer

Login to the AWS Console and go to **Services | Elastic Beanstalk** to see all your applications and environments, including ones created from Eclipse:

Figure 13.18: EBS dashboard

If you have a WAR file to deploy/update, click the **Upload and Deploy** button and select the WAR file you want to deploy.

You can modify the configuration of your environment by clicking the **Configuration** link, which is just below the **Dashboard**. Options in the configuration page allow you to modify settings for instances, capacity, the load balancer, security settings, and more. If your application uses a database, then you can configure that too.

You can browse the application, `CourseManagementREST,` by opening `<environment url in fig 13.15>/services/course/get/1.`

For some reason if the application does not get deployed properly from Eclipse then redeploy the application from AWS Console by click on **Upload and Deploy** button in *Fig 13.18* and browse to the WAR file created in the `target` folder of the project (if the WAR file was not created, then right-click on the project and select **Run As | Maven Install**).

Elastic Beanstalk can significantly save time in deploying applications to the cloud. It requires a lot less setup and configuration.

Deploying in Google Cloud

In this section, we will see how to deploy JEE applications in Google Compute Engine (IaaS offering) and Google App Engine (PaaS offering). Compute Engine (`https://cloud.google.com/compute/`) can be considered an AWS EC2 counterpart, and App Engine (`https://cloud.google.com/appengine`) an Elastic Beanstalk counterpart. You need to have a Google account to login to Cloud Console at `https://console.cloud.google.com.` You need to have at least one project created in Google Cloud to deploy applications. When you login to the Cloud Console, it will prompt you to create a project if there are no projects already available:

Figure 13.19: Creating a Google Cloud project from the Dashboard

All you need to enter in the **Create Project** page is the name of the project. The **Project ID** will be automatically selected for you. You should keep this Project ID handy, because many SDK commands need a Project ID as one of their parameters.

If you already have projects, but want to create a new project for this book, open the Google Cloud Console web page and go to the **IAM & admin** | **Manage resources** page. Click the **Create Project** link on the page.

Setting up Google Cloud Tools

Setting up Google Cloud Tools requires multiple steps. Let's start with installing the SDK.

Installing the Google Cloud SDK

Download the SDK from `https://cloud.google.com/sdk/`. Unzip it and run the following command from the `bin` folder:

```
gcloud init
```

See `https://cloud.google.com/sdk/docs/initializing` for more options regarding initializing the SDK.

Installing Java extensions for the App Engine SDK

Run the following command (make sure that the Cloud SDK is installed and configured):

```
gcloud components install app-engine-java
```

See `https://cloud.google.com/sdk/docs/managing-components` for details on managing Google Cloud components.

Next, set the default project name for `gcloud` commands:

```
gcloud config set project <your-project-name-here>
```

Installing Google Cloud Tools for Eclipse

To install the plugin for Google Cloud in Eclipse, open **Eclipse Marketplace** (select the
menu **Help | Eclipse Marketplace...**). Search for **Google Cloud Tools**:

Figure 13.20: Installing the Google Cloud Tools plugin from the Marketplace

Setting Eclipse Preferences for Google Cloud Tools

Open Eclipse **Preferences** and go to the **Google Cloud Tools** preferences:

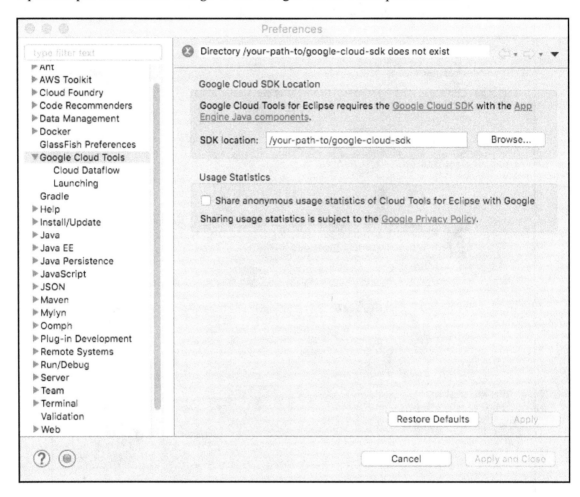

Figure 13.21: Setting the SDK path in Google Cloud Tools preferences

Enter the path to the folder where you unzipped the SDK in the **SDK location** field.

Deploying the application in Google Compute Engine

In this section, we will create an instance of a VM in Google Compute Engine and deploy a JEE application in it. Once we create a VM, we can follow the same steps we did to install the GlassFish Server and the *Course Management* application in the EC2 instance in the preceding *Installing the CourseManagement EJB application in an EC2 instance* section. But let's deploy a different application in the Compute Engine. In the last chapter, we saw how to deploy JEE applications in Docker containers. So, let's install Docker in a VM in Compute Engine and deploy the `CourseManagement` service in it. But first, let's create a VM. Unfortunately, at the time of writing this book, **Google Cloud Tools** for Eclipse does not provide much support for working with Compute Engine. Therefore, we will be using either the Google Cloud Console web page or Terminal on the host machine.

Creating a VM instance in Google Compute Engine

Login to the Google Cloud Console (`https://console.cloud.google.com`) and go to the **Compute Engine** | **VM Instances** page. Click the **Create Instance** link. Create an instance using **Debian GNU/Linux boot disk**. Make sure to select the **Allow HTTP traffic** and **Allow HTTPS traffic** options.

Installing Docker in a VM instance

In the VM instances page, select the instance you want to use and drop down the **SSH** options (in the **Connect** column in the table):

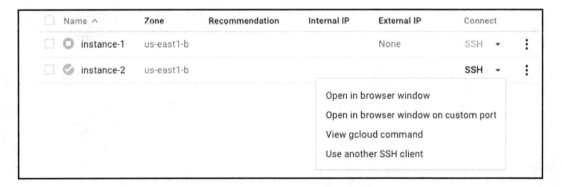

Figure 13.22: Opening an SSH connection to a VM instance

Select **Open in browser window**. This option opens a browser window and opens a SSH shell in the VM instance. Run the following commands in the shell to install Docker:

Command	Description
`sudo apt-get update`	Gets the latest version of packages and dependencies
`curl -fsSL get.docker.com -o get-docker.sh`	Downloads the Docker installer script
`sudo sh get-docker.sh`	Runs the installer script

 See `https://docs.docker.com/install/linux/docker-ce/debian/` for more information on installing Docker on a Debian distribution.

Once Docker is installed, we need to execute a few commands so that the Docker command can be called without using `sudo` (Docker runs as the root):

Command	Description
`sudo groupadd docker`	Creates a Docker user group. It probably already exists.
`sudo usermod -aG docker $USER`	Adds a current user to the Docker group.

See `https://docs.docker.com/install/linux/linux-postinstall/#manage-docker-as-a-non-root-user` for more details.

Log out of the shell and log back in (close the shell window and open a new shell window). If all of the preceding commands have been executed successfully, then you should be able to run the `docker ps` command without `sudo`.

Next, we will install `docker-compose` in the instance (see `https://docs.docker.com/compose/install/`). Execute the following commands (the version number might be different in the command to install `docker-compose`):

Command	Description
`sudo curl -L https://github.com/docker/compose/releases/download/1.18.0/docker-compose-`uname -s`-`uname -m` -o /usr/local/bin/docker-compose`	Downloads docker-compose
`sudo chmod +x /usr/local/bin/docker-compose`	Makes docker-compose executable

We created `docker-compose` deployment configuration in `Chapter 12`, *Microservices*. We will deploy the same in the VM instance we have created in this section. The source code for this chapter includes a folder named `coursemanagement-docker-compose`. Upload all files in that folder to the VM instance. You can either upload from the browser shell window or use the `gcloud` command from your host machine. In the browser shell, click on the Settings icon in the upper-right corner and select the **Upload File** option. Upload all of the files that are in the `coursemanagement-docker-compose` folder. To upload from Terminal, execute the following `gcloud` command after changing the folder to `coursemanagement-docker-compose`:

```
gcloud compute scp * <your-instance-name-here>:~/
```

This command copies all of the files in the current folder (which in our case is `coursemanagement-docker-compose`) to the user's home folder in the instance.

Whichever method you use to upload the files, make sure that you have the following files in the VM instance:

- `course-management-db.dockerfile`
- `course-management-service.dockerfile`
- `docker-compose.yml`
- `course-management-db.sql`
- `coursemanagementspring-0.0.1-SNAPSHOT.jar`

In the browser shell for the VM instance, execute the following command to set up the database and REST service in Docker containers:

```
docker-compose up -d
```

See `Chapter 12`, *Microservices*, for more details on the preceding files and the command. Once the command is executed successfully, browse to `http://<instance_external_ip>/course_management/courses`. You will just see an empty JSON array, because there is no data in the database. You can find the external IP of your instance from the **Compute Engine** | **VM Instances** page.

Run the `docker-compose down` command to shut down the containers.

Deploying the application in Google App Engine

App Engine is Google's **Platform as a Service (PaaS)** offering, similar to Elastic Beanstalk from Amazon. In the section *Creating Elastic Beanstalk application from Eclipse*, we deployed the `CourseManagementREST` service using Elastic Beanstalk. In this section, we will learn how to deploy the same service using Google App Engine.

Let's make a copy of the `CourseManagementREST` project. Right-click on the project in Eclipse **Project Explorer** and select **Copy**. Right-click anywhere in **Project Explorer** and select **Paste**. Eclipse will prompt you to name the project. Let's name it `CourseManagementREST-GAE`. We will deploy this project using Google App Engine.

Let's configure our project as an App Engine project. Right-click on the **CourseManagementREST-GAE** project in **Project Explorer** and select **Configure | Convert to App Engine Standard Project**.

> If you are creating a new project for deployment to Google App Engine, then go to the **File | New | Google App Engine Standard Java Project** menu. Or, go to the drop-down menu from the **Google Cloud Platform** icon in the toolbar and select **Create New Project | Google App Engine Standard Java Project**.

Before we deploy the project, remove `web.xml` from the `src/main/webapp/WEB-INF` folder. Google App Engine's Java platform uses the Jetty server and it does not need `web.xml` for this deployment.

> You may see an error stating `web.xml is missing` and `<failOnMissingWebXml>` is set to true `pom.xml` after deleting `web.xml`. To suppress this error, add the following property in `pom.xml`:
>
> ```
> <properties>
>     <failOnMissingWebXml>false</failOnMissingWebXml>
> </properties>
> ```

To test this application locally, go to the **Servers** view, right-click on it, and select **New |
Server**. Then, expand the **Google** group and select **App Engine Standard**:

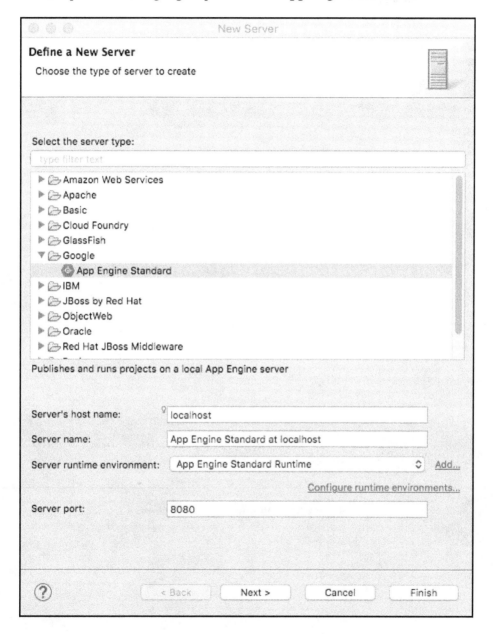

Figure 13.23: Creating a local App Engine server

Click **Next** and add the **CourseManagementREST-GAE** project for deployment:

Figure 13.24: Adding the CourseManagementREST-GAE project for deployment

Click **Finish** and start the server from the **Server** view. Then, browse to
`http://localhost:8080/services/course/get/1` to verify that the application has
been deployed properly.

If you get errors regarding the JDK version in `pom.xml`, add the following
section in `pom.xml`, above the dependencies section:

```
<properties>
    <maven.compiler.source>1.8</maven.compiler.source>
    <maven.compiler.target>1.8</maven.compiler.target>
</properties>
```

Before you deploy this project to Google App Engine, you should make sure that an
application has been created in Google App Engine. Browse to `https://console.cloud.`
`google.com/appengine` and check if any application exists. If not, you can create an
application from that page. Alternately, you can run the following command in Terminal:

```
gcloud app create
```

To deploy this project to Google App Engine, select the project in **Project Explorer** and the
drop-down menu from the **Google Cloud Platform** toolbar button:

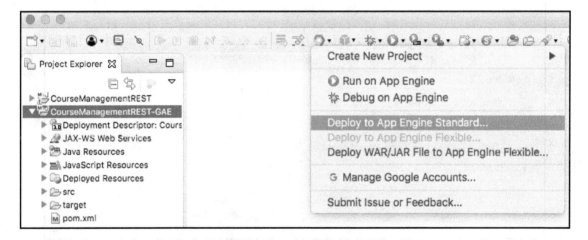

Figure 13.25: Deploying the project to Google App Engine

Select the **Deploy to App Engine Standard...** menu:

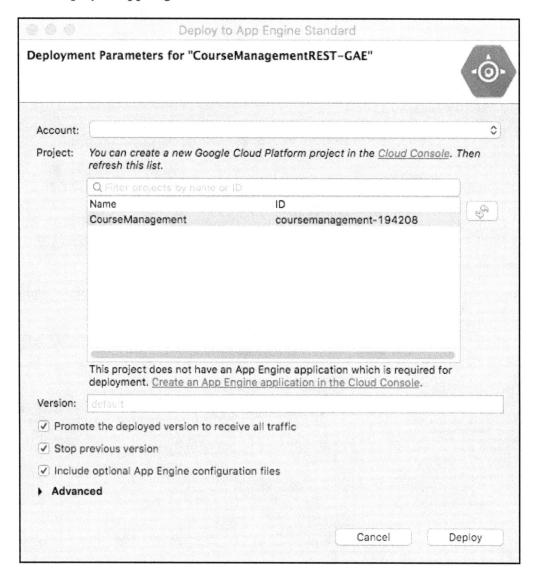

Figure 13.26: Setting deployment parameters for Google App Engine

Select your Google account from the drop-down menu, if not already selected, and then select the Google Cloud project you want the application deployed to.

Once the project is deployed, browse to
`https://<your_project_id>.appsport.com/services/course/get/1` to verify it.

To stop the application, you need to disable the application—open `https://console.cloud.google.com` and go to **App Engine** | **Settings** and click the **Disable Application** button.

Summary

In this chapter, we learned about two types of cloud deployment services provided by Amazon and Google. One is IaaS and the other is PaaS. PaaS lets you deploy your application in a pre-configured environment, while IaaS gives you complete control over deployment configuration. The IaaS offering from Amazon is called EC2 and the one from Google is called Compute Engine. The PaaS offering from Amazon is called Elastic Beanstalk and the one from Google is called App Engine.

We deployed the `CourseManagement` EJB application in the GlassFish Server in an instance of Amazon EC2. We then deployed the `CourseManagementREST` service in Elastic Beanstalk.

Then, we deployed a Docker container with the `CourseManagement` service in an instance of Google Compute Engine. Lastly, we deployed the `CourseManagementREST` service in Google App Engine.

In the next chapter, we will learn how to secure JEE applications.

Securing JEE Applications

14

In the previous chapter, we learned how to deploy JEE applications in the cloud. In this chapter, we will learn how to secure JEE applications—specifically, how to perform authentication and authorization.

We will cover the following topics:

- Securing JEE web applications using deployment descriptors
- Securing JEE web applications using annotations
- Securing web services
- Security enhancements in JEE 8

Authentication and authorization in JEE

Authentication is the process of verifying that the user is who he or she is claiming to be. This is typically done by asking the user to provide a username and password. Another way to verify the client identity is by asking for client certificates. In this chapter, we will look at password authentication only.

Authorization is the process of determining whether a user is allowed to perform certain actions in the application. The JEE specification allows role-based authorization. In the application, you specify roles that can perform an action, or access a resource, and then add users to these roles.

Unfortunately, securing JEE applications, as per JEE specifications, is not completely server-independent. There are parts of the configuration that are common across servers, and there are parts that are specific to server vendors. Common configurations are mostly done in web.xml or by using annotations. But, server-specific configurations vary from vendor to vendor. In this chapter, we will learn how to secure JEE applications in GlassFish and Tomcat servers.

But, before we learn details about securing applications, we need to understand certain terms commonly used in configurations, in the context of security:

- **User**: A client requesting access to a protected resource in an application
- **Group**: A set of users with similar characteristics
- **Role**: Determines what resources can be accessed in an application, by a user or group, with that particular role
- **Realm**: Can be considered a security domain, with its own users, groups, and storage method

Modifying a database to save authentication information

In this chapter, we will use a database to authenticate users. Other methods used to store security information include files and LDAP. We will need to update our course_management database with tables to store information about users and groups. Let's create three tables—User, Groups, and User_Group:

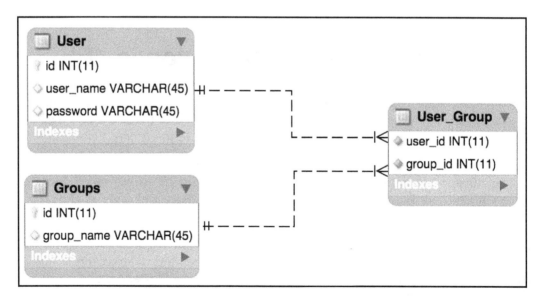

Figure 14.1: New tables for authentication

The `User` table stores the username and password. The `Groups` table stores the group names. We will group names directly into roles later. The `User_Group` table is a joint table, joining the `User` and `Groups` tables. One user can be in many groups, and one group can have many users.

To simplify mapping information from the preceding tables when configuring realms in JEE servers, we will create a view, named `user_group_view`, that makes information from all the preceding tables available in one view. The DDL script for the view is as follows:

```
CREATE
VIEW `user_group_view` AS
    SELECT
        `user`.`user_name` AS `user_name`,
        `groups`.`group_name` AS `group_name`,
        `user`.`password` AS `password`
    FROM
        ((`user`
        JOIN `groups`)
        JOIN `user_group`)
    WHERE
        ((`user`.`id` = `user_group`.`user_id`)
            AND (`groups`.`id` = `user_group`.`group_id`))
```

If you already have the `course_management` schema from earlier chapters, then run the script in the `add_auth_tables.sql` file (the file is in the source code folder for this chapter). If you are using `MySQLWorkbench`, you can run the script as follows:

1. Make sure `course_management` is the default schema; right-click on the schema and select the **Set as Default Schema** option.
2. Select the **File** | **Open SQL Script** menu, and then select the `add_auth_tables.sql` file. The file will open in a new tab.
3. Click on the **Execute** icon in the toolbar to execute this script.
4. Right-click on the **course_management** schema and select the **Refresh All** option. Make sure the new tables and the view are created in the schema.

For testing purpose, let's insert the following data in the `user` table:

ID	user_name	password
1	user1	user1_pass
2	user2	user2_pass

Groups:

ID	group_name
1	admin

User_Group:

user_ID	group_ID
1	1

As per the preceding data, `user1` is in the admin group, and `user2` is not in any group.

Securing applications in GlassFish

We will use the *Course Management* application that we developed in Chapter 7, *Creating JEE Applications with EJB,* to add security features. Follow these steps to import projects:

1. Create a new Eclipse workspace for this chapter.
2. Copy all the projects in the source code folder for Chapter 7, *Creating JEE Applications with EJB,* inside the `with-maven` folder, to the current workspace.
3. Import all the projects into the new workspace (open the **File** | **Import** menu and then select **Maven** | **Existing Maven Projects**).

You should now have the following projects in your Eclipse workspace: `CourseManagementMavenEAR`, `CourseManagementMavenEJBClient`, `CourseManagementMavenEJBs`, and `CourseManagementMavenWebApp`. Let's now learn how to protect access to JSPs in a folder.

Protecting access to folders in web applications

To protect any resources in a web folder, you need to declare security constraints in `web.xml`. In the security constraints, you can declare URLs that are to be protected, and which roles can access the protected URLs. Open `web.xml` in the `CourseManagementMavenWebApp` project and add the following declarations within the `<web-app>` tag:

```
<security-constraint>
    <display-name>Admin resources</display-name>
    <web-resource-collection>
```

```
        <web-resource-name>admins</web-resource-name>
        <url-pattern>/admin/*</url-pattern>
    </web-resource-collection>
    <auth-constraint>
        <role-name>admin </role-name>
    </auth-constraint>
    <!--
    <user-data-constraint>
        <transport-guarantee>CONFIDENTIAL</transport-guarantee>
    </user-data-constraint>
    -->
</security-constraint>
<security-role>
    <description>Admins</description>
    <role-name>admin</role-name>
</security-role>
```

Here, we are declaring all the resources accessed with the `/admin/*` URL to be protected, and also that only users in the `admin` role can access these resources. We are also declaring the `admin` role using the `<security-role>` tag. If you want the URL resources to be accessed only over SSL (using HTTPS), then set `<transport-guarantee>` to `CONFIDENTIAL`. However, you will need to obtain (buy) an SSL certificate from certificate authorities, such as Verisign, and install it on the server.

See `https://www.verisign.com/en_US/website-presence/website-optimization/ssl-certificates/index.xhtml` for details about SSL certificates.

Each server has a different process for installing the certificates. However, we will not discuss how to install an SSL certificate in this book. Therefore, the `<user-data-constraint>` configuration is described in the preceding code.

See `https://javaee.github.io/tutorial/security-webtier002.html#specifying-security-constraints` for more details on security constraints.

At this point, let's see how the application works. Before deploying the application in GlassFish, let's create a protected resource. Since we have protected all the accessed resources using the `/admin/*` URL, create a folder named `admin` in the `src/main/webapp` folder. Inside this folder, create `admin.jsp` using the following content:

```
<!DOCTYPE HTML>
<html>
<head>
<title>Course Management Admin</title>
</head>
<body>
      Welcome to Course Management Admin<br>
</body>
</html>
```

 Refer to the *Configuring GlassFish server in Eclipse* section in `Chapter 7`, *Creating JEE Applications with EJB*, for information on adding the GlassFish 5 Server to your Eclipse workspace.

We need to build two applications: `CourseManagementMavenWebApp` and `CourseManagementMavenEAR`. The EAR project is just a container project; the real content is served from `CourseManagementMavenWebApp`. So, we need to build both projects. Right-click on `CourseManagementMavenWebApp` in Eclipse **Project Explorer**, and select **Run As | Maven Install**. Do the same for the `CourseManagementMavenEAR` project. Then, deploy `CourseManagementMavenEAR-1.ear` from the target folder in GlassFish 5.

 To deploy the application in GlassFish 5, browse to `http://localhost:4848` and configure the datasource, as described in the *Configuring Datasource in GlassFish* section in `Chapter 7`, *Creating JEE Applications with EJB*. Then, click on the **Application** node and deploy `CourseManagementMavenEAR-1.ear`.

Once the application is deployed, browse to
`http://localhost:8080/CourseManagementMavenWebApp/course.xhtml` and make
sure the page can be accessed without any authentication required, because this is an
unprotected resource/page. Now, try to browse to
`http://localhost:8080/CourseManagementMavenWebApp/admin/admin.jsp`. Since
we have marked the `/admin/*` URL pattern as a protected resource, the browser pops up
this authentication dialog box:

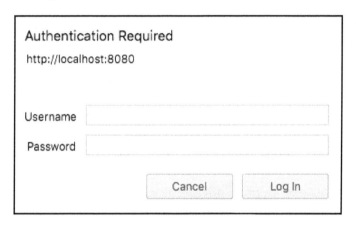

Figure 14.2: Browser authentication dialog box

We have not configured our application to authenticate the user. So, authentication will fail
in the preceding dialog box, no matter what you enter as the username and password. Let's
fix this by configuring the database to authenticate users in GlassFish.

Configuring a JDBC realm in GlassFish

GlassFish supports different realms for JEE authentication; for example, file, LDAP, and
JDBC realms. We are going to create a JDBC realm, which will use the information stored in
the `User`, `Groups`, and `User_Groups` tables (exposed by `user_group_view`).

To create a new JDBC realm in GlassFish, browse to the GlassFish admin page (`http://localhost:4848`), and in the navigation menu on the left-hand side, go to **Configurations** | **server-config** | **Security** | **Realms**. On the **Realms** page, click on the **New** button.

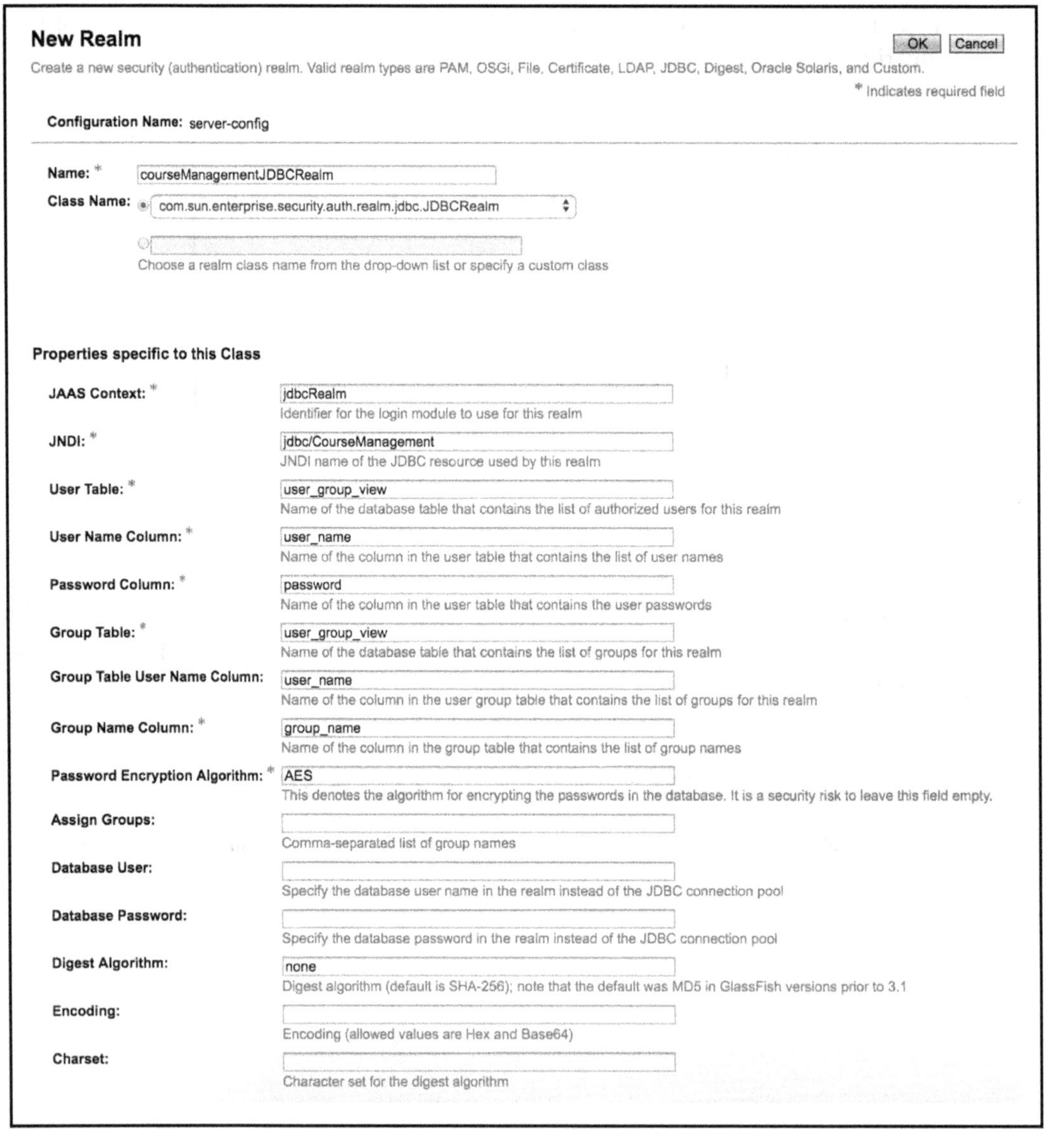

Figure 14.3: Creating a JDBC realm on the GlassFish admin page

Enter the following information into the form:

Class name

Field name	Value	Notes
Name	courseManagementJDBCRealm	
	com.sun.enterprise.security.auth.realm.jdbc.JDBCRealm	Select from the drop-down menu.
JAAS Context	jdbcRealm	
JNDI	jdbc/CourseManagement	The JDBC data source we have created. See Chapter 7, *Creating JEE Applications with EJB*, for more details.
User Table	user_group_view	The table containing the user information. We specify the view that we created earlier.
Username Column	user_name	The username column in our user_group_view.
Password Column	password	The password column in our user_group_view.
Group Table	user_group_view	The group data is also exposed through our user_group_view.
Group Table Username Column	user_name	In user_group_view.
Group Name Column	group_name	In user_group_view.
Password Encryption Algorithm	AES	The algorithm to encrypt passwords in the database. We are pre-populated passwords outside the application. So, this does not have much impact on our example.
Digest Algorithm	none	The passwords we entered in the table are not hashed, so enter none here.

Click on the **OK** button to create the realm.

We need to tell our application to use the JDBC realm created earlier. This is configured in the web.xml of the application, in the <login-config> tag. Two authentication methods are supported in <long-config>: basic and form-based.

In basic authentication, the browser displays the login form, just as in *Figure 14.2*. In fact, this is the default authentication method, so in the absence of the <login-config> tag in our web.xml previously, the server defaults to basic authentication.

In form-based authentication, you can specify the login page. This gives you a chance to customize the login experience.

Let's first configure the realm using basic authentication.

Basic authentication with the JDBC realm in GlassFish

We will make some changes to the tags we added to configure security in the *Protecting access to folders in web applications* section. Here are the changes:

1. Rename `role-name` from `admin` to `admin-role`
2. Remove the `<security-role>` tag
3. Add the `<login-config>` tag

Here is what the changed declaration should look like:

```
<security-constraint>
    <display-name>Admin resources</display-name>
    <web-resource-collection>
        <web-resource-name>admins</web-resource-name>
        <url-pattern>/admin/*</url-pattern>
    </web-resource-collection>
    <auth-constraint>
        <role-name>admin-role</role-name>
    </auth-constraint>
</security-constraint>
<login-config>
    <auth-method>BASIC</auth-method>
    <realm-name>courseManagementJDBCRealm</realm-name>
</login-config>
```

Note that we specified the name of the realm we configured (on the GlassFish admin page) in the `<login-config>` tag. We removed `<security-role>` because roles are now saved in the database, in the **Groups** table. However, we need to map the roles declared in `web.xml` to groups in the database. This mapping is done in `glassfish-web.xml`. Create `glassfish-web.xml` in the same folder as that of `web.xml`, that is, `src/main/webapp/WEB-INF`, in the `CourseManagementMavenWebApp` project. Add the following content to it:

```
<?xml version="1.0" encoding="UTF-8"?>
<!DOCTYPE glassfish-web-app PUBLIC "-//GlassFish.org//DTD GlassFish
```

```
Application Server 3.1 Servlet 3.0//EN"
"http://glassfish.org/dtds/glassfish-web-app_3_0-1.dtd">
<glassfish-web-app error-url="">
    <security-role-mapping>
        <role-name>admin-role</role-name>
        <group-name>admin</group-name>
    </security-role-mapping>
</glassfish-web-app>
```

Here, we are mapping **admin-role**, which we declared in web.xml, with the **admin** group in the **Groups** table in the database.

Now, build the CourseManagementMavenWebApp and CourseManagementMavenEAR projects (in the same order) by right-clicking on the projects and selecting **Run As | Maven Install**, and then deploy the application in GlassFish as described in the *Protecting access to folders in web applications* section.

Browse to http://localhost:8080/CourseManagementMavenWebApp/admin/admin.jsp. This time, the browser should display the contents of admin.jsp, once you enter the valid admin credentials; that is, the username as user1, and the password as user1_pass.

Form-based authentication with a JDBC realm in GlassFish

Let's change basic authentication to form-based authentication, so that we can customize the login page. We need to update <login-config> in web.xml. Replace the previous <login-config> block with the following:

```
<login-config>
    <auth-method>FORM</auth-method>
    <realm-name>courseManagementJDBCRealm</realm-name>
    <form-login-config>
        <form-login-page>/login.jsp</form-login-page>
        <form-error-page>/login-error.jsp</form-error-page>
    </form-login-config>
</login-config>
```

We have replaced <auth-method> from **BASIC** to **FORM**. For form-based authentication, we need to specify **form-login-page**, which we have specified as login.jsp. **form-error-page** is optional, but we have set that to login-error.jsp.

The next step is to create `login.jsp` and `login-error.jsp`. Create both the files in the `src/main/webapp` folder with the following contents.

Here is the source code of `login.jsp`. We have configured it as the login page in `<form-login-page>`, as shown in the preceding code block:

```
<!DOCTYPE HTML>
<html>
<head>
<title>Admin Login</title>
</head>
<body>
    <form method=post action="j_security_check">
        <table>
            <tr>
                <td>User Name: </td>
                <td><input type="text" name="j_username"></td>
            </tr>
            <tr>
                <td>Password: </td>
                <td><input type="password" name="j_password"></td>
            </tr>
            <tr>
                <td colspan="2"><input type="submit" value="Login"></td>
            </tr>
        </table>
    </form>
</body>
</html>
```

For form-based authentication to work, there are certain requirements:

1. The form action must be set to `j_security_check`
2. The username input field must be named `j_username`
3. The password input field must be named `j_password`

Here is the source code of `login-error.jsp`. We have configured it as the error page in `<form-error-page>`, as shown in the previous code block:

```
<!DOCTYPE HTML>
<html>
<head>
<title>Login Failed</title>
</head>
<body>
        Invalid user name or password<br>
```

```
        <a href="<%=request.getContextPath()%>/admin/admin.jsp">Try
Again</a>
</body>
</html>
```

The error page shows the error message and displays the link to try again. Even though the link **Try Again** points to admin.jsp, because it is a protected resource, the user will be redirected to login.jsp. If the login is successful, then redirection to admin.jsp will happen.

It would be nice to provide an option to log out after the user has successfully logged in. This option can be added to admin.jsp. Add a link to log out in admin.jsp as follows:

```
<!DOCTYPE HTML>
<html>
<head>
<title>Course Management Admin</title>
</head>
<body>
        Welcome to Course Management Admin<br>
        <a href="../logout.jsp">Logout</a>
</body>
</html>
```

Create logout.jsp in the same folder as login.jsp with the following content:

```
<%@ page session="true"%>
Logged out <%=request.getRemoteUser()%>
<% session.invalidate(); %>
```

The logout page simply calls session.invalidate() to log the user out.

To see form-based authentication in action, build the CourseManagementMavenWebApp and CourseManagementMavenEAR projects (in the same order) by right-clicking on the projects and selecting **Run As | Maven Install**, and then deploy the application in GlassFish, as described in the *Protecting access to folders in web applications* section.

Browse to http://localhost:8080/CourseManagementMavenWebApp/admin/admin.jsp. This time, the browser should display login.jsp, with the login form, instead of its own pop-up window for authentication.

Securing applications in Tomcat

In this section, we will learn how to protect resources in the Tomcat server. To keep the example consistent with the one we learned in the previous section for GlassFish, we will protect all pages in the admin folder. We will use the CourseManagementJDBC project we created in Chapter 4, *Creating JEE Database Applications,* to get started. Recall that in Chapter 4, *Creating JEE Database Applications,* we deployed this project in the Tomcat server. Perform the following steps to import a project into the new workspace for this chapter and configure Tomcat:

1. Copy the CourseManagementJDBC project from the Chapter 7, *Creating JEE Applications with EJB,* project folder to the current workspace. Import the project into the new workspace (open the **File** | **Import** menu and then select **Maven** | **Existing Maven Projects**).
2. Configure Tomcat, as described in the *Configuring Tomcat in Eclipse* section in Chapter 1, *Introducing JEE and Eclipse.*
3. Make sure the application is added to the server and runs as expected. See the *Running JSP in Tomcat* section in Chapter 2, *Creating a Simple JEE Web Application.*
4. Copy the admin folder from CourseManagementMavenWebApp (see the previous section in this chapter) to src/main/webapp in the CourseManagementJDBC project. So, the code to protect the admin folder is the same for projects in GlassFish and Tomcat.

So, now you should have the CourseManagementJDBC project and Tomcat configured in Eclipse.

We will now modify web.xml to add security constraints, as we did in the previous section for GlassFish:

```
<security-constraint>
    <display-name>Admin resources</display-name>
    <web-resource-collection>
        <web-resource-name>admins</web-resource-name>
        <url-pattern>/admin/*</url-pattern>
    </web-resource-collection>
    <auth-constraint>
        <role-name>admin</role-name>
    </auth-constraint>
</security-constraint>
<login-config>
    <auth-method>FORM</auth-method>
    <form-login-config>
        <form-login-page>/login.jsp</form-login-page>
```

```
        <form-error-page>/login-error.jsp</form-error-page>
    </form-login-config>
</login-config>
```

There are two differences in the preceding configuration compared with the same for GlassFish:

- There is no need to map `role-name` to group names as we did in GlassFish. Therefore, the role name is changed from `admin-role` to just `admin` in `<auth-constraint>`.
- There is no need for the `<realm-name>` tag in `<login-config>`.

Let's now configure the JDBC realm in Tomcat by adding the `<realm>` tag in `server.xml`. If you are using Tomcat configured in Eclipse to run the application, then you can access `server.xml` by expanding the **Servers** node in **Project Explorer**:

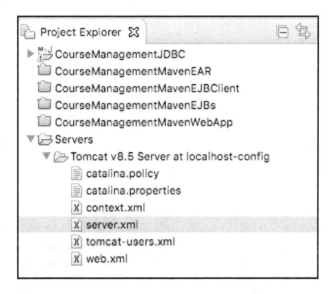

Figure 14.4: Access of server.xml in the Tomcat server configured in Eclipse

If you are running Tomcat outside Eclipse, then you will find `server.xml` at `$CATALINA_BASE/conf/server.xml`.

Add the following realm tag in `server.xml`, inside the `<Engine defaultHost="localhost" name="Catalina">` node:

```
<Realm  className="org.apache.catalina.realm.JDBCRealm"
    driverName="com.mysql.jdbc.Driver"
    connectionURL="jdbc:mysql://localhost:3306/course_management"
    connectionName="<your-db-username>"
    connectionPassword="<your-db-password>"
    userTable="user_group_view"
    userNameCol="user_name"
    userCredCol="password"
    userRoleTable="user_group_view"
    roleNameCol="group_name" />
```

The Tomcat admin module needs to access our MySQL database, so we need to make the MySQL JDBC driver available to the admin module. Copy the MySQL JDBC driver in `<tomcat-install-dir>/lib`. You can download the driver from `https://dev.mysql.com/downloads/connector/j/`, if you haven't already done so.

That is all that is required to protect folders in Tomcat. Restart the server and browse to `http://localhost:8080/CourseManagementJDBC/admin/admin.jsp`. You should see the login page.

Securing servlets using annotations

So far, we have seen declarative syntax for specifying security constraints; that is, by specifying `<security-constraint>` in `web.xml`. However, security constraints can also be specified using Java annotations, specifically for servlets. In this section, we will create `AdminServlet` and secure it with annotations. Follow the steps in the previous section to import the `CourseManagementJDBC` project from `Chapter09`, but rename it `CourseManagementJDBC-SecureAnnotations`, and import it into the workspace. Then, add only `<login-config>` in `web.xml`, but do not specify `<security-constraint>`:

```
<login-config>
  <auth-method>FORM</auth-method>
  <form-login-config>
    <form-login-page>/login.jsp</form-login-page>
    <form-error-page>/login-error.jsp</form-error-page>
  </form-login-config>
</login-config>
```

Make sure you have copied `login.jsp` and `login-error.jsp`, as described in the previous section.

Now create a servlet named `AdminServlet` in the `packt.book.jee.eclipse.ch4.servlet` package, with the following content:

```
package packt.book.jee.eclipse.ch4.servlet;
// skipping imports to save space
@WebServlet("/AdminServlet")
@ServletSecurity(@HttpConstraint(rolesAllowed = "admin"))
public class AdminServlet extends HttpServlet {
    private static final long serialVersionUID = 1L;
    public AdminServlet() {
        super();
    }

    protected void doGet(HttpServletRequest request, HttpServletResponse
response)
        throws ServletException, IOException {
        try {
            request.authenticate(response);
            response.getWriter()
                    .append("Served at:
").append(request.getContextPath());
        } finally {
            response.getWriter().close();
        }
    }

    protected void doPost(HttpServletRequest request,
        HttpServletResponse response) throws ServletException, IOException
{
        doGet(request, response);
    }
}
```

`@ServletSecurity(@HttpConstraint(rolesAllowed = "admin"))` specifies the security constraint for the servlet. With this annotation, we are allowing only users in the admin role to access the servlet. If you browse to `http://localhost:8080/CourseManagementJDBC-SecurityAnnotations/AdminServlet`, you should see the login page.

Securing web services

The process of securing web services is similar to that of protecting a web URL, and we have seen two examples of that in previous sections. We specify `<security-constraint>` and `<login-config>` in `web.xml`. Let's see how to protect the REST web service we developed in Chapter 9, *Creating Web Services:*

1. Copy and import the `CourseManagementREST` and `CourseManagementRESTClient` projects from Chapter09 into the workspace for this chapter. As the names suggests, the first project is the REST service, and the second project is a standalone client application that calls the web service.
2. Deploy the `CourseManagementREST` project in Tomcat (see the previous section for details on how to do this).
3. Make sure the `testGetCoursesJSON` method is called from the `main` method in `CourseManagementClient.java` from the *CourseManagementRESTClient* project.
4. Run the application (right-click on the file in **Project Explorer** and select **Run As | Java Application**), and verify that the service is working fine.

To secure the web service using basic authentication, add the following configuration in `web.xml`:

```
:<security-constraint>
    <display-name>Admin resources</display-name>
    <web-resource-collection>
        <web-resource-name>admins</web-resource-name>
            <url-pattern>/services/*</url-pattern>
        </web-resource-collection>
        <auth-constraint>
            <role-name>admin</role-name>
        </auth-constraint>
 </security-constraint>
<login-config>
    <auth-method>BASIC</auth-method>
</login-config>
```

With the above configuration, we are protecting any URL containing `/services/`. We have also specified that only the **admin** role can access this URL and the method of authentication is **BASIC**.

Now, add the `<Realm>` configuration in `server.xml` of Tomcat, as described in the previous section. If you run `CourseManagementClient.java` at this point, you will get an **Unauthorized** error. This is because the client application is not sending the authentication information—that is, the username and password—along with the `GET` request. For the basic authentication method, this information should be passed in the `authorization` header. The value of this header parameter should be set as `Basic`, followed by the base64-encoded `username:password` string; for example, `authorization: Basic dXNlcjE6dXNlcjFfcGFzcw==`.

In the preceding header, `dXNlcjE6dXNlcjFfcGFzcw==` is the base64-encoded format of the `user1:user1_pass` string.

Let's now modify the `testGetCoursesJSON` method in `CourseManagementClient.java` to pass the preceding header information. Here is the code you need to add just before checking the response status:

```
String userName = "user1";
String password = "user1_pass";
String authString = userName + ":" + password;
String encodedAuthStr =
Base64.getEncoder().encodeToString(authString.getBytes());
//Execute HTTP get method
Response response =
webTarget.request(MediaType.APPLICATION_JSON).header(HttpHeaders.AUTHORIZAT
ION, "Basic " + encodedAuthStr).get();
```

Note that `java.util.Base64` is available in JDK 1.8 onward. If you are using a version lower than 1.8, you can use `org.apache.commons.codec.binary.Base64` from Apache `commons-codec`. Add the following dependency in `pom.xml`:

```
<dependency>
    <groupId>commons-codec</groupId>
    <artifactId>commons-codec</artifactId>
    <version>1.11</version>
</dependency>
```

Right-click on the project and select **Run As | Maven Install**. Then, encode `String` by calling:

```
encodedAuthStr =   new
String(org.apache.commons.codec.binary.Base64.encodeBase64(authString.getBy
tes()));
```

When you run the application now, the web service should execute without any errors.

Security enhancements in JEE 8

JEE 8 has incorporated Java EE Security API 1.0 (JSR 375, `https://javaee.github.io/security-spec/`). Enhancements in these APIs are broadly classed into four categories:

- Support for the Servlet 4.0 authentication mechanism. You can specify the type of authentication in servlets using annotations. For example, `@BasicAuthenticationMechanismDefinition` for basic authentication, `@FormAuthenticationMechanismDefinition` for form-based authentication, and `@CustomFormAuthenticationMechanismDefinition` for custom authentication. For more information, refer to `https://javaee.github.io/security-spec/spec/jsr375-spec.html#authentication-mechanism`.

- Identity Store APIs. By implementing the Identity Store interface, you can specify how user, password, and group information is made available to JEE authentication and authorization APIs. You can make your security-related code portable across JEE 8 containers by implementing this interface. For more information, refer to `https://javaee.github.io/security-spec/spec/jsr375-spec.html#_introduction_2`.

- New `SecurityContext` APIs provide consistent APIs for acquiring information about users and roles. For more information, refer to `https://javaee.github.io/security-spec/spec/jsr375-spec.html#security-context`.

- The new `HttpAuthenticationMechanism` API gives you complete control over how you want to implement security in your application programmatically. For more information, refer to `https://javaee.github.io/security-api/apidocs/javax/security/enterprise/authentication/mechanism/http/HttpAuthenticationMechanism.html`.

We will not cover all the preceding enhancements in this chapter, but we will take a look at the first three APIs in some detail.

We have seen, in the previous sections of this chapter, how configuration of security is not uniform across containers. Specifically, the mapping of roles to groups is not uniform. This problem can be addressed by using new JEE 8 security APIs. Let's see how this can be done by developing an application. Refer to the `CourseManagementMavenWebApp-jee8` project in the source code for this chapter.

Implementing portable security in JEE 8

We will modify `CourseManagementMavenWebApp` from Chapter 7, *Creating JEE Applications with EJB*, in this section. This project was part of the EJB `CourseManagementMavenEAR` project, but in this section, we will work with `CourseManagementMavenWebApp` independently. Copy the `CourseManagementMavenWebApp` project from `Chapter07`, as `CourseManagementMavenWebApp-jee8` in the Eclipse workspace for this chapter.

We will modify this project to provide the following functionality:

- `AdminServlet` is a protected servlet requiring login. We will implement the basic authentication
- There are three possible user roles: **admin**, **manager**, and **user**
- Only users in the admin role can see the admin page, served by `AdminServlet`
- Only users in the manager role can see the management page, served by `ManagementServlet`

JEE 8 security APIs require **Contexts and Dependency Injection (CDI)** to be enabled in the application. We just need to create an empty `beans.xml` file in the `src/main/webapp/WEB-INF` folder to enable CDI.

Next, we need to add the following Maven dependency in `pom.xml` to make the JEE 8 APIs available in the application:

```
<dependency>
 <groupId>javax</groupId>
 <artifactId>javaee-api</artifactId>
 <version>8.0</version>
 <scope>provided</scope>
</dependency>
```

Let's create a class called `ApplicationConfig` (in the `packt.book.jee.eclipse.ch7.web.servlet` package) to declare all user roles allowed in the application. Here is the source code for the `ApplicationConfig` class:

```
package packt.book.jee.eclipse.ch7.web.servlet;
import javax.annotation.security.DeclareRoles;
import javax.enterprise.context.ApplicationScoped;
@DeclareRoles({"admin", "user", "manager"})
@ApplicationScoped
public class ApplicationConfig {}
```

Now, let's create two servlets, `AdminServlet` and `ManagementServlet`, in the `packt.book.jee.eclipse.ch7.web.servlet` package. If you create these classes using the Eclipse wizard, then it adds the servlet declarations and mappings in `web.xml`. If you are not using the Eclipse wizard, then either add the declarations and mappings manually, or add the `@WebServlet` annotation in the servlet classes. Here is the source code for `AdminServlet`:

```
package packt.book.jee.eclipse.ch7.web.servlet;

// skipped imports

@BasicAuthenticationMechanismDefinition()
@ServletSecurity(@HttpConstraint(rolesAllowed = {"admin", "manager"} ))
public class AdminServlet extends HttpServlet {

 private static final long serialVersionUID = 1L;

 @Inject
 private SecurityContext securityContext;

 public AdminServlet() {
 super();
 }

 protected void doGet(HttpServletRequest request, HttpServletResponse
response) throws ServletException, IOException {
 if (securityContext.isCallerInRole("manager")) {
 request.getRequestDispatcher("/ManagementServlet").forward(request,
response);
 } else {
 response.getWriter().append("Welcome to Admin Page!");
 }
 }

 protected void doPost(HttpServletRequest request, HttpServletResponse
response) throws ServletException, IOException {
 doGet(request, response);
 }
}
```

The servlet allows access to only the **admin** and **manager** roles, using the @ServletSecurity annotation. The servlet also specifies the basic authentication type using @BasicAuthenticationMechanismDefinition. We also ask the JEE container to inject an instance of SecurityContext, which is used in the doGet method to check the user's role. If the user is in the **manager** role, then the request is forwarded to ManagementServlet, otherwise, access is granted to the current servlet. Note the call to securityContext.isCallerInRole to check the user's role.

Here is the source code for ManagementServlet:

```
package packt.book.jee.eclipse.ch7.web.servlet;
// skipped imports
@BasicAuthenticationMechanismDefinition(realmName="basic")
@ServletSecurity(@HttpConstraint(rolesAllowed = {"manager"} ))
public class ManagementServlet extends HttpServlet {
 private static final long serialVersionUID = 1L;

 public ManagementServlet() {
    super();
 }

 protected void doGet(HttpServletRequest request, HttpServletResponse
response) throws ServletException, IOException {
 response.getWriter().append("Welcome to Management Page!");
 }

 protected void doPost(HttpServletRequest request, HttpServletResponse
response) throws ServletException, IOException {
 doGet(request, response);
 }
}
```

The preceding servlet also uses basic authentication, and allows access only to users in the **manager** role.

With the preceding annotations, no declarative configuration is required for web.xml or any custom container-specific file. But, how do we tell security APIs who are valid users and roles? We do that by implementing the IdentityStore interface. Create the SimpleMapIdentityStore class in the packt.book.jee.eclipse.ch7.web.servlet package. This class should implement the IdentityStore interface:

```
package packt.book.jee.eclipse.ch7.web.servlet;

// skipped imports
```

```
@ApplicationScoped
public class SimpleMapIdentityStore implements IdentityStore {
 class UserInfo {
    String userName;
    String password;
    String role;

    public UserInfo(String userName, String password, String role) {
      this.userName = userName;
      this.password = password;
      this.role = role;
    }
 }

 private HashMap<String, UserInfo> store = new HashMap<>();

 public SimpleMapIdentityStore() {
    UserInfo user1 = new UserInfo("user1", "user1_pass", "admin");
    UserInfo user2 = new UserInfo("user2", "user2_pass", "user");
    UserInfo user3 = new UserInfo("user3", "user3_pass", "manager");
    store.put(user1.userName, user1);
    store.put(user2.userName, user2);
    store.put(user3.userName, user3);
 }

 public CredentialValidationResult validate(UsernamePasswordCredential
usernamePasswordCredential) {
    String userName = usernamePasswordCredential.getCaller();
    String password = usernamePasswordCredential.getPasswordAsString();

    UserInfo userInfo = this.store.get(userName.toLowerCase());
    if (userInfo == null || !userInfo.password.equals(password)) {
      return INVALID_RESULT;
    }

    return new CredentialValidationResult(userInfo.userName, new
HashSet<>(asList(userInfo.role)));
 }
}
```

It is important that the preceding class is annotated with @ApplicationScoped, so that it is available throughout the application, and CDI can inject it. We have hardcoded users and roles in a HashMap in the preceding class, but you can write the code to get users and roles from any source, such as a database, LDAP, or a file. In the application, there can be more than one IdentityStore. The container would call the validate method of each one. In the validate method, we are first verifying that the username and password are valid, and then returning an instance of CredentialValidationResult, with the roles of the user attached to it.

Build the application (right-click on the project and select **Run As | Maven Install**), and deploy it in the GlassFish 5 Server, as described in previous sections. Make sure the context of the application is set to /CourseManagementMavenWebApp-jee8. You can verify this on the GlassFish admin page by editing the deployed application and verifying the value of the **Context Root** field. Then browse to http://localhost:8080/CourseManagementMavenWebApp-jee8/AdminServlet. If you log in with **user1** credentials, then the admin page will be displayed. If you log in as **user3**, then the management page will be displayed. Access to all other users is blocked. You would need to close the browser window to try to log in with different users, because once logged in, the user credentials are remembered till the session is invalidated. The application can be easily extended to add a logout option, as we did in previous sections.

In the previous example, we have created a custom identity store. You can implement any code in this to acquire user information, from either a database or LDAP. But, JEE security APIs provide built-in annotations for accessing a database and LDAP as identity stores; that is, @DatabaseIdentityStoreDefinition and @LdapIdentityStoreDefinition. For example, we could modify the ApplicationConfig class to declare a database identity store as follows:

```
package packt.book.jee.eclipse.ch7.web.servlet;

import javax.enterprise.context.ApplicationScoped;
import
javax.security.enterprise.identitystore.DatabaseIdentityStoreDefinition;
import javax.security.enterprise.identitystore.PasswordHash;

@DatabaseIdentityStoreDefinition (
  dataSourceLookup = "jdbc/CourseManagement",
  callerQuery = "select password from user_group_view where user_name = ?",
  groupsQuery = "select group_name from user_group_view where user_name =
?",
  hashAlgorithm = PasswordHash.class,
  priority = 10
)
```

```
@ApplicationScoped
public class ApplicationConfig {
}
```

We need to pass the JNDI lookup name for the JDBC resource, which
is `jdbc/CourseManagement`, and SQL queries to validate the username and password and
to get groups. These are similar to the SQL queries we configured when creating a
Realm on the GlassFish admin page, but with the new security APIs, making the
configuration more portable. See `https://javaee.github.io/security-spec/spec/`
`jsr375-spec.html#_annotations_and_built_in_identitystore_beans` for more details on
`IdentityStore` annotations.

In the preceding example, we have used the basic authentication type. But, you can use
form-based authentication using the `@FormAuthenticationMechanismDefinition`
annotation. For example, we could
replace `@BasicAuthenticationMechanismDefinition`
with `@FormAuthenticationMechanismDefinition`, as follows:

```java
package packt.book.jee.eclipse.ch7.web.servlet;
// ...
@FormAuthenticationMechanismDefinition(
 loginToContinue = @LoginToContinue(
 loginPage = "/loginServlet",
 errorPage = "/loginErrorServlet"
 )
)
@DeclareRoles({"admin"})
@ServletSecurity(@HttpConstraint(rolesAllowed = "admin"))
public class AdminServlet extends HttpServlet {
 ...
}
```

This configuration is similar to `<form-login-config>`, which we configured in `web.xml`
in earlier examples.

Note that the new security APIs work mostly on Java classes, such as servlets, EJBs, and
beans, but if you want to protect JSP pages, then you need to use the declarative
configuration we learned in previous sections.

> Security in JEE is a very large topic, which can't be covered in a book of
> generic nature. The scope of this chapter is limited to securing JEE
> resources with a username and password. For detailed information on
> security in JEE, refer to `https://javaee.github.io/tutorial/security-`
> `intro.html`.

Summary

In this chapter, we learned how to secure resources represented by URLs in JEE applications. The process to secure resources declaratively is not completely generic in JEE; part of it is common across all servers, specifically configurations in `web.xml`. Configuration of declarative security realms differs across servers. However, JEE 8 has added new Java EE Security APIs that make annotation-based configuration portable for Java classes.

We learned how to secure folders in GlassFish and Tomcat servers. We also learned how to secure RESTful web services and invoke them with security credentials in a client application.

Other Books You May Enjoy

If you enjoyed this book, you may be interested in these other books by Packt:

Java EE 8 Cookbook
Elder Moraes

ISBN: 978-1-78829-303-7

- Actionable information on the new features of Java EE 8
- Using the most important APIs with real and working code
- Building server side applications, web services, and web applications
- Deploying and managing your application using the most important Java EE servers
- Building and deploying microservices using Java EE 8
- Building Reactive application by joining Java EE APIs and core Java features
- Moving your application to the cloud using containers
- Practical ways to improve your projects and career through community involvement

Java EE 8 High Performance
Romain Manni-Bucau

ISBN: 978-1-78847-306-4

- Identify performance bottlenecks in an application
- Locate application hotspots using performance tools
- Understand the work done under the hood by EE containers and its impact on performance
- Identify common patterns to integrate with Java EE applications
- Implement transparent caching on your applications
- Extract more information from your applications using Java EE without modifying existing code
- Ensure constant performance and eliminate regression

Leave a review - let other readers know what you think

Please share your thoughts on this book with others by leaving a review on the site that you bought it from. If you purchased the book from Amazon, please leave us an honest review on this book's Amazon page. This is vital so that other potential readers can see and use your unbiased opinion to make purchasing decisions, we can understand what our customers think about our products, and our authors can see your feedback on the title that they have worked with Packt to create. It will only take a few minutes of your time, but is valuable to other potential customers, our authors, and Packt. Thank you!

Index

www.ingramcontent.com/pod-product-compliance
Lightning Source LLC
Chambersburg PA
CBHW060636060326
40690CB00020B/4415

* 9 7 8 1 7 8 8 8 3 3 7 7 6 *